www.brookscole.com

www.brookscole.com is the World Wide Web site for Brooks/Cole and is your direct source to dozens of online resources.

At *www.brookscole.com* you can find out about supplements, demonstration software, and student resources. You can also send email to many of our authors and preview new publications and exciting new technologies.

www.brookscole.com
Changing the way the world learns®

Career Counseling and Services

A Cognitive Information Processing Approach

James P. Sampson, Jr.
Florida State University

Robert C. Reardon
Florida State University

Gary W. Peterson
Florida State University

Janet G. Lenz
Florida State University

Australia • Canada • Mexico • Singapore • Spain
United Kingdom • United States

Executive Editor: Lisa Gebo
Acquisitions Editor: Julie Martinez
Assistant Editor: Shelley Gesicki
Editorial Assistant: Amy Y. Lam
Technology Project Manager: Barry Connolly
Marketing Manager: Caroline Concilla
Marketing Assistant: Mary Ho
Advertising Project Manager: Tami Strang
Project Manager, Editorial Production: Stephanie Zunich/Matt Ballantyne

Print/Media Buyer: Jessica Reed
Permissions Editor: Sarah Harkrader
Production Service: G&S Typesetters, Inc.
Copy Editor: Cynthia Lindlof
Cover Designer: Paula Goldstein, Blue Bungalow Design
Compositor: G&S Typesetters, Inc.
Text and Cover Printer: Webcom, Limited

Printed in Canada
1 2 3 4 5 6 7 07 06 05 04 03

For more information about our products, contact us at:
Thomson Learning Academic Resource Center
1-800-423-0563

For permission to use material from this text, contact us by:
Phone: 1-800-730-2214 **Fax:** 1-800-730-2215
Web: http://www.thomsonrights.com

Library of Congress Control Number: 2003103350

ISBN 0-534-61159-1

Brooks/Cole—Thomson Learning
10 Davis Drive
Belmont, CA 94002
USA

Asia
Thomson Learning
5 Shenton Way #01-01
UIC Building
Singapore 068808

Australia/New Zealand
Thomson Learning
102 Dodds Street
Southbank, Victoria 3006
Australia

Canada
Nelson
1120 Birchmount Road
Toronto, Ontario M1K 5G4
Canada

Europe/Middle East/Africa
Thomson Learning
High Holborn House
50/51 Bedford Row
London WC1R 4LR
United Kingdom

Latin America
Thomson Learning
Seneca, 53
Colonia Polanco
11560 Mexico D.F.
Mexico

Spain/Portugal
Paraninfo
Calle/Magallanes, 25
28015 Madrid, Spain

This book is dedicated to the practitioners and support staff who are working to make quality resources and services available to the many persons who are making career choices in an increasingly complex world.

About the Authors

JAMES P. SAMPSON, JR.

Jim Sampson is currently a professor in the Department of Educational Psychology and Learning Systems at Florida State University, where he has taught courses in career development and computer applications in counseling since 1982. Since 1986, he has served as codirector of the Center for the Study of Technology in Counseling and Career Development, a research center established at FSU to improve the design and use of computer applications in counseling and guidance. He writes and speaks on the appropriate use of computer technology in counseling and on the use of cognitive strategies in the improvement of career counseling and guidance services. He has presented or consulted in Australia, Canada, Costa Rica, Denmark, England, Finland, France, Germany, Hungary, Ireland, Japan, New Zealand, Romania, Scotland, Sweden, and Turkey, in addition to the United States. He is currently an Overseas Fellow of the National Institute for Careers Education and Counselling in England, as well as a Visiting Professor at the University of Derby in England and at the University of Jyväskylä in Finland.

Along with Gary Peterson and Robert Reardon, he is an author of the 1991 book *Career Development and Services: A Cognitive Approach.* As part of his efforts to translate theory into practice, he is an author of the Career Thoughts Inventory (CTI) along with Gary Peterson, Janet Lenz, Robert Reardon, and Denise Saunders. The CTI includes an instrument and an intervention workbook to measure and alter negative thoughts that impede career decision making. Along with Robert Reardon, Janet Lenz, and Gary Peterson, he is an author of the 2000 book *Career Development and Planning: A Cognitive Approach.*

In 1990, he received the National Career Development Association Merit Award, and in 1995, the National Occupational Information Coordinating Committee Recognition Award. Along with Robert Reardon, he received the 1996 American Counseling Association Ralph Berdie Memorial Research Award. In 1997, he received the Distinguished Service Award from the Association of Computer-Based Systems for Career Information, and in 1998, the President's Award from the National Career Development Association. Along with Robert Reardon, he received the 1999 American Counseling Association Extended Research Award. In 2001, he received the National Career Development Association Eminent Career Award.

Prior to joining the faculty at Florida State University, he was a senior counselor and the coordinator of the Career Planning Center at the Student Counseling and Career Planning Center, Georgia Institute of Technology. He is a National Certified Counselor, a National Certified Career Counselor, and a licensed Psychologist in Florida. He received his Ph.D. in counselor education from the University of Florida in 1977.

ROBERT C. REARDON

Robert Reardon is a native of the Texas Hill Country. He attended public schools in Mason, Texas, and received a B.S. in social studies from Texas Lutheran College in 1963. His graduate study at Florida State University in counseling and guidance and counselor education earned him M.S. and Ph.D. degrees in 1965 and 1968, respectively.

Dr. Reardon has held full-time counseling and teaching positions at FSU since 1966, when he was first employed as a counselor in the Counseling Center. As a faculty member in the Division of Student Affairs, his current position is director of instruction, research, and evaluation in the Career Center; professor in the Department of Educational Psychology and Learning Systems; and codirector of the Center for the Study of Technology in Counseling and Career Development. He is also the coordinator of the Career Specialization (www.career.fsu.edu/techcenter/student/prospective/programs.html) in the Psychological Studies in Education Program in the College of Education.

He has coauthored several books, including *Career Development and Planning: A Comprehensive Approach* (2000, with Janet Lenz, Jim Sampson, and Gary Peterson); *The Self-Directed Search and Related Holland Career Materials: A Practitioner's Guide* (1998, with Janet Lenz); *Career Development and Services: A Cognitive Approach* (1991, with Gary Peterson and Jim Sampson); *Career Development Interventions* (1984, with Harman Burck and others); *Facilitating Career Development* (1975, with Harman Burck and others); and *Counseling and Accountability* (1973, with Harman Burck and Harold Cottingham). He is a coauthor of the Career Thoughts Inventory (1996) and the author of the computer- and Internet-based "Interpretive and Professional Reports" for the Self-Directed Search interest inventory (1985, 1994, 1999; www.self-directed-search.com).

Dr. Reardon has published articles focusing on the research and development of innovative career interventions for college students and adults and featuring the use of educational and occupational information. The Curricular-Career Information Service (CCIS) program he developed at FSU in 1972 (now directed by Dr. Janet Lenz) logs 8,500 career services contacts annually, has been reported in more than 60 articles, and has served as a field training site for over 350 graduate students. Career services programs at FSU have attracted visitors from over 35 countries.

He received the Merit Award from the National Vocational Guidance Association in 1983 and the Certificate of Service from the Association of Computer-Based Systems for Career Information in 1986; he was corecipient with Dr. Jim Sampson of the Ralph Berdie Memorial Research Award and the Extended Research Award from the American Counseling Association in 1996 and 1999, respectively. He has made more than 100 professional presentations in 27 states and three countries. He has been a principal investigator or proposal coauthor on grant projects of over $1.2 million. The Career Advisor Scholarship Campaign he initiated in 1994 has led to the funding of four scholarships, with a total of over $235,000 in gifts and pledges.

Dr. Reardon's professional memberships include American Counseling Association, National Career Development Association, American Psychological Association, Association for Career and Technical Education, National Association of Colleges and Employers, Florida Counseling Association, Florida Career Development Association, and United Faculty of Florida. He is a National Certified Counselor and a National Certified Career Counselor.

GARY W. PETERSON

Gary Peterson has been a member of the Florida State University faculty since 1972. He presently is a professor in the College of Education and coordinator of the program Psychological Services in Education in the Department of Educational Psychology and Learning Systems. He is also the clinical training director of the Combined Doctoral Program in Counseling Psychology and School Psychology and a senior research associate in the Center for the Study of Technology in Counseling and Career Development. He is a Psychologist licensed in Florida. From 1972 through 1988, Dr. Peterson held the position of research associate in the Center for Educational Technology, and from 1988 through 1994, he served as associate dean of graduate studies in the College of Education. Prior to coming to Florida State University, he was a counselor in the counseling center at UNC-Charlotte from 1966 to 1968, and a senior counselor in the counseling center at Duke University from 1970 to 1972.

Dr. Peterson's educational history includes a B.A. in biology from Humboldt State University in California (1962), an M.A. in guidance from Duke University (1967), and a Ph.D. in counseling from Duke University (1970). He served in the Peace Corps in Nigeria as a science and math teacher from 1963 through 1965. He took a sabbatical leave in 1995 as a visiting scholar in the School of Education, Stanford University.

Within the Psychological Services in Education Program, he teaches courses in personality assessment, research methods, and consultation and organizational development, as well as conducts practica in the Career Center and supervises M.S./Ed.S.

interns. He has directed 25 doctoral dissertations. He also serves on a variety of college and university committees, including chair of the University Admission Committee.

During his career at Florida State University, he has published articles in areas of curriculum development, evaluation and accountability in education and human services, career problem solving and decision making, personality measurement and assessment, and career assessment. He has coauthored two books with colleagues Jim Sampson, Robert Reardon, and Janet Lenz, *Career Development and Services: A Cognitive Approach* and *Career Development and Planning: A Comprehensive Approach,* and has written 13 book chapters. He has also coauthored the development of the Family Role Behavior Inventory and the Career Thoughts Inventory. His present research interests include cognitive processes in career problem solving and decision making and the application of chaos theory to career development and services in an information society. He is an active member of American Psychological Association, American Educational Research Association, National Career Development Association, and the National Council on Measurement in Education and served as chair of the Career Development Special Interest Group of the American Educational Research Association, 1988–1992, and 2002–present.

JANET G. LENZ

Janet Lenz is currently the associate director for career advising, counseling, and programming in the Florida State University Career Center. Her responsibilities include training and development for graduate students pursuing careers in career services, providing direct services, and teaching an introduction to career development class. She also has a courtesy appointment as an assistant professor in the College of Education's Department of Educational Psychology and Learning Systems and serves as a senior research associate in the Center for the Study of Technology in Counseling and Career Development. Dr. Lenz has been a practicing professional in the career services area since 1976. She received her B.S. degree in sociology from Virginia Commonwealth University. She received her M.S. in student personnel administration in 1977 and her Ph.D. in counseling and human systems in 1990, both from Florida State University.

In addition to her experience at Florida State University, Dr. Lenz has worked as a placement coordinator and career counselor in the Career Center at the University of Texas at Austin, and as the assistant director in the Career Planning and Placement Center at the University of North Carolina at Greensboro. Dr. Lenz has made over 50 presentations on career counseling and development topics at regional and national meetings, including more than 30 presentations on using the Self-Directed Search and related Holland materials. She is the coauthor with Robert Reardon of *The Self-Directed Search and Related Holland Materials: A Practitioner's Guide* and is a chapter author in the book *The Self-Directed Search in Business and Industry.* With colleagues Robert Reardon, Jim Sampson, and Gary Peterson, she coauthored the textbook, student manual, and instructor's manual for *Career Development and Planning: A Comprehensive Approach.* She is also a coauthor of the Career Thoughts Inventory and the *Career Thoughts Inventory Workbook.*

She is a National Certified Counselor and a National Certified Career Counselor. She is also a certified instructor for the National Career Development Association's Career Development Facilitator curriculum. She is a member of the American Counseling Association, the National Career Development Association, and the American College Personnel Association. Since 2000, she has served on the board of the National Career Development Association as the Southern Region Trustee. She is currently President-Elect of the National Career Development Association.

Contents

SECTION 1: FOUNDATION FOR UNDERSTANDING THE CONTENT OF THIS BOOK

SECTION 5: DESIGN, MANAGEMENT, AND EVALUATION OF CAREER RESOURCES AND SERVICES

Preface

THE INTENT OF THIS BOOK

This book blends the study of *vocational behavior* (the factors that shape the choices that we make about work and life) with the study of *career assistance* (the career resources and career services we provide to help persons make informed career choices). This book is intended for counselors and other human service practitioners who are helping persons to more effectively cope with issues related to their work, as well as with the connection between work and various personal, social, and family issues.

We use the term *practitioner* in this book to refer to all persons (counselors and other human service workers) involved in helping clients solve problems and make decisions. After reading this book, all practitioners (irrespective of specialty) should know

- how to better integrate career issues into the counseling process,
- how to perform some basic career counseling functions,
- how to identify a competent career counselor in order to make an appropriate referral for their client.

This book is also intended for career practitioners who specialize in the design and delivery of career resources and career services. After reading this book, career practitioners should know

- how to translate the Cognitive Information Processing (CIP) approach into practice,

- how to integrate counseling theories and other career theories with the CIP approach in delivering career services,
- how to apply a cost-effective approach to delivering career services,
- how to use readiness assessment to improve the cost-effectiveness of service delivery,
- how to deliver self-help, brief staff-assisted, and individual case-managed career services,
- how to design career resource rooms to deliver career resources and services,
- how to design, manage, and evaluate career services.

Practitioners-in-training can use this book to add to their understanding of client needs and the resources and services available to meet those needs. Experienced practitioners can use this book to evaluate their current practice and add selected resources and strategies to improve their practice. Practitioners or practitioners-in-training seeking to apply the principles included in this book should seek appropriate supervision as they work with clients.

HOW THIS BOOK IS ORGANIZED

This book is organized into the following five sections and fifteen chapters:

Section 1: Foundation for Understanding the Content of This Book

Chapter 1 Introduction

Section 2: Theoretical Concepts for Guiding Practice

Chapter 2 Helping Persons Make Occupational, Educational, and Training Choices

Chapter 3 Helping Persons Make Employment Choices

Section 3: Strategies for Planning and Delivering Career Resources and Services

Chapter 4 Delivering Career Services

Chapter 5 Assessing Readiness for Career Choice and Selecting Appropriate Assistance

Chapter 6 Using the Career Thoughts Inventory to Measure Career Choice Readiness

Chapter 7 Planning and Delivering Career Resources

Section 4: Case Studies to Show How the CIP Approach Can Be Used in Practice

Chapter 8 Case Study for Individual Case-Managed Services

Chapter 9 Case Studies for Brief Staff-Assisted Services

Chapter 10 Case Study for Self-Help Career Resources and Services

Section 5: Design, Management, and Evaluation of Career Resources and Services

Chapter 11 Developing a Career Services Program

Chapter 12 Developing and Implementing a Career Services Program: A Personal Case History

Chapter 13 The Career Resource Library: Development and Management Issues

Chapter 14 Accountability and Evaluation in Career Services

Chapter 15 Strategic Planning for Career Services

There are two possible sequences for reading this book. The first strategy is to read the chapters in the order they are written, moving from the general to the specific. The second strategy is to begin by reading the case studies to get a sense of the process involved and then read the chapters in sequence to clarify the reasons for applying the procedures that were used in practice.

USING THIS BOOK WITH OTHER RESOURCES IN THE CIP APPROACH

As you will learn from the Background section in Chapter 1, the CIP approach includes a number of different theory-based resources. To get the most possible out of this book, you may also want to use the following CIP approach resources:

- Read Career Development and Planning: A Comprehensive Approach (Reardon, Lenz, Sampson, & Peterson, 2000a), and
- Read the Student Manual—Career Development and Planning: A Comprehensive Approach (Reardon et al., 2000b).

This comprehensive approach text and student manual provide a guide to career choice written directly for the person solving career problems and making career decisions.

- Complete the Career Thoughts Inventory (CTI) (Sampson, Peterson, Lenz, Reardon, & Saunders, 1996a),
- Complete the CTI Workbook (Sampson et al., 1996b), and then
- Read the CTI Professional Manual (Sampson et al., 1996c).

This readiness assessment measure and accompanying workbook and professional manual will help you better understand how readiness assessment can be used in the delivery of career services.

Additional details on the CIP approach can be obtained from the original source material cited in this book and from resources available on our Internet Web site at www.career.fsu.edu/techcenter/.

HOW TO USE THIS BOOK EFFECTIVELY

To get the most out of reading this book, use the following five steps: survey, question, read, recite, and review (SQ3R). This approach will help you to more effectively remember what you read.

1. *Survey.* Begin using this book by reflecting on what you already know about career resources and career services. Then, read the Preface to better understand who the intended readers are for this book, what may result from reading the book, and how the book is organized. Now, review the Table of Contents to more fully understand what is covered in the book. For each chapter, begin by briefly reviewing the chapter introduction, surveying the topic headings, and looking at the introduction for each section. Pay attention to any terms in boldface type and any tables or figures.
2. *Question.* Look at each topic heading in the chapter, and turn it into a question to better anticipate the information that will be covered. For example, if the heading reads, "How Persons Seek Career Assistance," then your question would be, "How do persons seek career assistance?" By turning each heading into a question, you are giving yourself a reason to read by anticipating the answers to the questions you have just posed.
3. *Read.* Now, read the chapter in chunks of about 8 to 10 pages, applying all SQ3R steps to each portion you read. Your goal is to divide the chapter into manageable portions to improve your comprehension.
4. *Recite.* As you complete each section within the chapter, stop and recite to yourself a short summary of what you just read. Check to make sure you understood each of the terms in boldface type. This is an important step in remembering what you read.
5. *Review.* When you finish your reading for a session, review what you have learned by writing a short summary or outline. Also, draw a diagram and label any figures in your reading. It can also be helpful to explain what you have learned to someone else. When you finish reading the chapter, review the chapter summary and consider completing one or more of the activities that are designed to help you get the most benefit from your reading.

ACKNOWLEDGMENTS

This book has been a collaborative effort of many persons. We have received helpful reviews from Darrin Carr, Susan Epstein, Jeff Garis, Lauren Hutto, Jill Lumsden, Elizabeth Reddoch, Corey Reed, Lauren Sampson, Sandy Sampson, and Stacie

Vernick. Darrin Carr, Jon Shy, and Beth Kegler provided valuable assistance in preparing the manuscript. We also received useful feedback from several external reviewers of the manuscript. Finally, we received consistent support and editorial guidance from Julie Martinez at Brooks/Cole Publishing throughout the development of this book. Andy Sieverman, Stephanie Zunich, and Matt Ballantyne provided very helpful management in producing the book; Cynthia Lindlof provided excellent copyediting; Vernon Boes managed the production of the cover and created the designs for the cover.

This book will always be a work in progress. The book continues to evolve as we integrate our previous work with our current research and development efforts. We are constantly learning from our clients, students, practitioners in our workshops, and colleagues. We look forward to your comments about this book and appreciate your patience with us as we continue to evolve as practitioners, theorists, researchers, teachers, and trainers.

REFERENCES

Reardon, R. C., Lenz, J. G., Sampson, J. P., Jr., & Peterson, G. W. (2000a). *Career development and planning: A comprehensive approach.* Pacific Grove, CA: Brooks/Cole.

Reardon, R. C., Lenz, J. G., Sampson, J. P., Jr., & Peterson, G. W. (2000b). *Student handbook for career development and planning: A comprehensive approach.* Pacific Grove, CA: Brooks/Cole.

Sampson, J. P., Jr., Peterson, G. W., Lenz, J. G., Reardon, R. C., & Saunders, D. E. (1996a). *Career Thoughts Inventory.* Odessa, FL: Psychological Assessment Resources.

Sampson, J. P., Jr., Peterson, G. W., Lenz, J. G., Reardon, R. C., & Saunders, D. E. (1996b). *Career Thoughts Inventory workbook.* Odessa, FL: Psychological Assessment Resources.

Sampson, J. P., Jr., Peterson, G. W., Lenz, J. G., Reardon, R. C., & Saunders, D. E. (1996c). *Career Thoughts Inventory: Professional manual.* Odessa, FL: Psychological Assessment Resources.

Career Counseling and Services

A Cognitive Information Processing Approach

Introduction

CHAPTER 1

This chapter introduces core constructs, aims, assumptions, and terminology associated with the Cognitive Information Processing approach to career problem solving and decision making (referred to in this book as the CIP approach). After reviewing this chapter, the reader should have a foundation for understanding and applying the theory-based practice strategies described in the remainder of the book. The chapter is organized as follows:

- Background of the CIP Approach
- Aims of the CIP Approach
- Assumptions of the CIP Approach
- Key Terms in the CIP Approach
- Potential Benefits Resulting from Effective Career Assistance
- Summary
- Getting the Most Benefit from Reading This Chapter

BACKGROUND OF THE CIP APPROACH

Beginning in 1971, an approach to delivering career services has evolved at Florida State University from the interaction among theory, practice, and research. This approach applies Cognitive Information Processing theory to the process individuals use to solve career problems and make career decisions (Peterson, Sampson, & Reardon, 1991; Peterson, Sampson, Reardon,

& Lenz, 1996; Sampson, Lenz, Reardon, & Peterson, 1999; Sampson, Peterson, Lenz, & Reardon, 1992; Sampson, Peterson, Reardon, & Lenz, 2000, 2002b). The CIP approach also builds on the self-directed career service delivery strategies developed at Florida State University (Reardon, 1996; Reardon & Minor, 1975).

The CIP approach is built on two core constructs: (a) The Pyramid of Information Processing Domains (the "content" of career problem solving and decision making involving self-knowledge, occupational knowledge, decision-making skills, and metacognitions); and (b) the CASVE cycle (the "process" of career problem solving and decision making involving the phases of Communication, Analysis, Synthesis, Valuing, and Execution). Chapter 2 presents figures showing practitioner and client versions of the pyramid and figures for practitioner and client versions of the CASVE cycle. These CIP constructs can be used by themselves or used to organize the application of other career theories and related resources, such as Holland's theory (1997) and the Self-Directed Search (Holland, 1994).

With the Pyramid of Information Processing Domains and CASVE cycle as a foundation, strategies have been developed for readiness assessment, intervention planning, career assessment, information use, counseling, and career resource room design. Resources to apply CIP theory to practice have also been developed that include a readiness assessment instrument for screening, needs assessment, and learning associated with negative career thoughts—the Career Thoughts Inventory (CTI) (Sampson, Peterson, Lenz, Reardon, & Saunders, 1996a, 1996b, 1996c, 1998), an assessment card sort (Peterson, 1998), and instruction for credit courses (Reardon, Lenz, Sampson, & Peterson, 2000a, 2000b). The CIP approach has also been applied to computer-assisted career guidance (CACG) (Sampson, Peterson, & Reardon, 1989), higher education (Reardon & Wright, 1999), community services (Lenz, 1998), and one-stop career service settings (Sampson & Reardon, 1998), as well as training career service providers (Saunders, Reardon, & Lenz, 1999). Updated citations of research and evaluation on the CIP approach may be found in Sampson, Peterson, Reardon, and Lenz (2002a) and in Reardon (2002) at www.career.fsu.edu/techcenter/designing_career_services/cip_bibliographies/. Updated versions of the above background information may also be found at this Web site.

AIMS OF THE CIP APPROACH

The aims of the CIP approach are to help persons make an appropriate current career choice and, while doing so, to learn improved problem-solving and decision-making skills that they will need for future choices. These aims reflect the wisdom of the oft-repeated adage, "Give people a fish and they eat for a day, but teach them how to fish and they eat for a lifetime." The dynamic nature of the job market in an information-based, global economy makes this adage even more relevant today.

ASSUMPTIONS OF THE CIP APPROACH

The CIP approach is based on the following assumptions (Peterson et al., 1996; Peterson, Sampson, Lenz, & Reardon, 2002; Sampson et al., 1996b):

1. Career problem solving and decision making involve our emotions (affect) as well as our thoughts (cognition). Although the term *cognitive* is used in the name of this approach, we view cognition and emotion as inseparable in career choice. As we "think through" our career problems and make decisions, our emotions can help motivate us to choose and follow through or cause us to act too slowly, too quickly, or too randomly to make an appropriate choice.
2. Effective career problem solving and decision making involve both knowledge and a process for thinking about the knowledge we have gained. *Knowledge* is the content of career choice (what we know), and *thinking* is the process we use (what we need to do) to make choices.
3. What we know about ourselves and the world we live in is constantly evolving and interacting. As we learn from experience in life, we organize what we know about ourselves and the world in more complex ways. We can use career resources and career services to help us think about and organize what we have learned, allowing us to sort through the vast amount of information available and use the most relevant information in making choices.
4. Career problem solving and decision making are skills. As with any other skill, we can improve our ability to make choices through learning and practice. We can use career resources and career services to help us learn about and practice the information processing skills needed to become more effective problem solvers and decision makers.

KEY TERMS IN THE CIP APPROACH

Various terms are used in this book that relate to helping people make career choices. Because authors differ in their use of terms in the career field, it is important to understand what we mean by the terms we use. Understanding the definitions of various terms will make it easier to read and understand the remainder of this book. After an overview of key terms presented in Table 1.1, this section begins with a review of terms associated with the nature of the career choice event and continues with who is served, how services are provided, who delivers career resources and services, and where career resources and services are provided.

Nature of the Career Choice Event

Almost all individuals in our society are engaged in some form of paid or unpaid work during their lifetimes. Whether an individual makes plans or responds to serendipitous events, a recurring sequence of career choices needs to be made about occupations, education, training, and employment. Providing assistance with career choice is concerned with helping persons to become more effective in solving career

Table 1.1 | Overview of Key Terms in the CIP Approach

Nature of the Career Choice Event

- Problem
- Career problem
- Problem solving
- Decision making
- Career development
- Lifestyle development
- Work
- Career
- Occupation
- Job
- Position
- Career decisions
  - Occupational decisions
  - Educational and training decisions
  - Employment decisions

How Persons Seek Career Assistance

- Career shoppers
- Individuals
- Clients
- Students/advisees
- Customers
- Patrons
- Employees

How Career Assistance Is Provided

- Career resources
  - Career assessment
    - Self-assessment
    - Practitioner-assisted assessment
  - Career information
    - Occupational information
    - Educational and training information
    - Employment information
  - Instruction
- Career services
  - Self-help services
  - Brief staff-assisted services
  - Individual case-managed services

Who Delivers Resources and Services

- Practitioners
  - Professionals
  - Paraprofessionals
- Support staff

Where Resources and Services Are Provided

- Career centers
- Counseling centers
- Internet Web sites providing distance guidance and cybercounseling

problems and making career decisions. But what is a career problem? What are the components of a career decision? It is important to understand the nature of career problem solving and decision making before we design resources and services to help people make appropriate career choices. This section includes definitions of a problem, career problem, problem solving, decision making, career development, lifestyle development, work, career, occupation, job, position, and career decision making.

Problem A *problem* is defined as a gap between an existing and a desired state of affairs. Or simply stated, a gap is the difference between where you are and where you want to be. Awareness of this gap helps you know that there is a problem that needs to be solved. Awareness of the gap provides a source of motivation to engage in problem solving (Peterson et al., 1996). A problem is not always something negative and is often positive—for example, choosing between two good employment offers, deciding how to invest a bonus, or considering leisure options as part of retirement planning.

Career Problem A *career problem* involves a gap between a person's current career situation and a future career situation that he or she desires. For example, you may be unhappy with your current job and want to have a job that is satisfying and provides enough income to meet your needs. The gap can also involve problems with the work itself, or the gap can be between work and various personal, social, and family factors. For example, your work may be very rewarding, but the amount of travel required may make it difficult to arrange child care.

Although career problems share many similarities with other problems we encounter in life, some important differences exist. Career problems are sometimes more complicated than other types of problems we face for the following reasons:

- Career problems involve self-knowledge that we remember from past events in our life. The difficulty is that these memories may change from day to day as a result of our current thoughts and feelings.
- We may have difficulty reconciling our opinion of what is best for us with the opinions of family, friends, and our cultural group about our best course of action.
- We are often overwhelmed with the amount of career information available to us in considering our options. Information is available from people we know, the media, the Internet, schools, employers, and organizations.
- An increasingly rapid rate of change in our society and our economy makes it more difficult to predict the outcomes of our decisions. What was true in the past may not necessarily be true today, much less tomorrow.
- Whereas some decisions have a clear pathway to reach a goal, other decisions have several paths available to reach the goal, with each path having specific advantages and disadvantages.
- A career choice often presents a subsequent set of problems that needs to be solved in order to make the initial decision effective.
- Given these reasons, it is easy to see why some persons may become overwhelmed, confused, and anxious about career choices. These powerful emotions can make it more difficult to concentrate and remember important facts during problem solving. More than ever, individuals need concrete and easy-to-understand career choice models to help them understand and manage the career choice process (Sampson et al., 1996b).

Problem Solving *Problem solving* involves a series of thought processes in which information about a problem is used to arrive at a plan of action necessary to remove the gap between an existing and a desired state of affairs. The outcome of problem solving is a choice that has a reasonable chance of closing the gap between where a person is and where he or she wants to be (Peterson et al., 1996; Peterson et al., 2002). For example, problem solving involves thinking about your job-satisfaction problem and selecting an employment option that has a good chance of providing more satisfaction.

Decision Making *Decision making* includes problem solving, along with the cognitive and affective processes needed to develop a plan for implementing the solution and taking the risks involved in following through to complete the plan. The outcome of decision making is personal behavior that is necessary to solve the problem (Peterson et al., 1996; Peterson et al., 2002). For example, now that you have made a choice of one or two new employment options (the problem-solving process described previously), you need to plan how you will make the transition.

Career Development *Career development* involves the implementation of a series of integrated career decisions over a person's life span (Peterson et al., 1996; Peterson et al., 2002). Career development is also defined as "the total constellation of economic, sociological, psychological, educational, physical, and chance factors that combine to shape one's career" (Sears, 1982, p. 139). For example, career development can involve the experiences and decisions that resulted in the development of a successful business and the subsequent interest in government action to promote private enterprise. Career development can also involve a high need for personal achievement, a family history of public service, and a time of extended economic prosperity.

Lifestyle Development *Lifestyle development* involves the integration of career, relationship, spiritual, and leisure decisions that contribute to a guiding purpose, meaning, and direction in one's life. Effective lifestyle development is dependent on effective career development, which, in turn, is dependent on effective decision making, which is further dependent on effective problem solving (Peterson et al., 1996; Peterson et al., 2002). For example, a couple may decide to start a business together that is consistent with their spiritual beliefs and provides adequate time for them to pursue the outdoor activities they enjoy. Figure 1.1 graphically depicts these relationships. Consider the following metaphor. Problem solving is the land where a building sits, decision making is the foundation for the building, career development represents the walls, and lifestyle development is the roof. For the roof to remain, the walls must be strong and sit on a stable foundation, which is dug into secure ground. The success of each element is dependent on the success of the element below. Ultimately then, success in life is at least partially dependent on successful career problem solving.

Work *Work* is defined as "an activity that produces something of value for oneself or others" (Reardon, Lenz, Sampson, & Peterson, 2000a, p. 7). Work can be a paid or an unpaid activity. For example, work can involve analyzing a person's income tax liability or donating time to help a public charity invest the profit earned from a recent fund-raising event.

Career *Career* is defined as "time extended working out of a purposeful life pattern through work undertaken by the person" (Reardon et al., 2000a, p. 6). For example, a person can have a career as a business entrepreneur, politician, and active community member in the community where his or her family has lived for several generations.

Figure 1.1 Interdependence of Problem Solving, Decision Making, Career Development, and Lifestyle Development

From *Career Development and Services: A Cognitive Approach* (p. 22), by G. W. Peterson, J. P. Sampson, Jr., and R. C. Reardon, 1991, Pacific Grove, CA: Brooks/Cole.

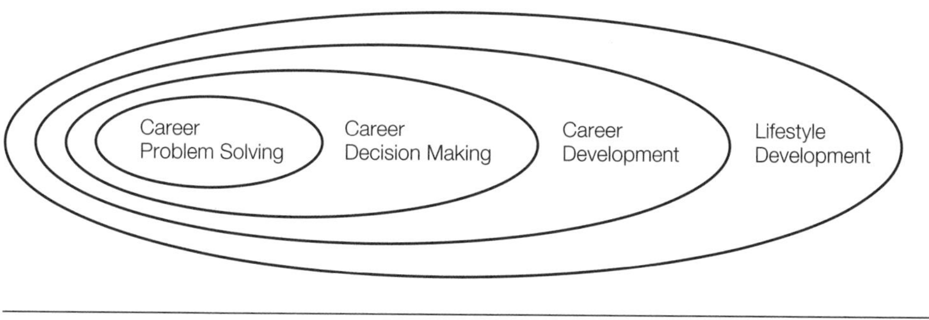

Occupation An *occupation* is defined as "a group of similar positions found in different industries or professions" (Reardon et al., 2000a, p. 8). For example, a person may major in accounting in college and then become credentialed as a certified public accountant.

Job A *job* is defined as "a paid position held by one or more persons requiring some similar attributes in a specific organization" (Reardon et al., 2000a, p. 8). For example, a person may have a job as an accountant in a large manufacturing company.

Position A *position* is defined as "a group of tasks performed by one person in an organization; a unit of work with a recurring or continuous set of tasks. A task is a unit of job behavior with a beginning point and an ending point performed in a matter of hours rather than days" (Reardon et al., 2000a, p. 8). For example, a position exists as the accounting supervisor in the purchasing department of a large manufacturing company.

Career Decisions *Career decisions* include choices individuals make about occupations, education, training, and employment. Although decisions about occupations, education, training, and employment may be related over time, a specific career decision may involve only one or two of these elements. The sequence and number of these decisions will vary among individuals depending on their situation. ***Occupational decisions*** involve choosing one occupation or a small group of related occupations as a focal point for making subsequent decisions about education, training, and employment. ***Educational and training decisions*** involve choosing a college major, program of study, or training opportunity that allows an individual to gain the general competencies (e.g., problem-solving skills, communication skills), specific competencies (e.g., work-related skills), knowledge base, and credentials necessary to obtain or maintain employment. ***Employment decisions*** involve choosing and applying for a position with an employer in an industry in a sector of the economy. An employment decision is both the ultimate outcome of career decision making and the starting point for ongoing choices about occupations, education, training, and employment. For example, a person may decide to become an accountant and major in accounting on the way to becoming a certified public accountant with a state government agency. Or a student may major in accounting and then consider various occupations and related employment opportunities close to the time of his or her graduation.

How Persons Seek Career Assistance

Persons assume different roles as they seek career assistance: individuals, clients, students/advisees, customers, patrons, and employees. The experience a person has receiving career assistance, including the amount and type of help he or she receives, is often influenced by the type of organization where the help is provided. Persons may begin the process of seeking assistance with career problems as "career shoppers" (Reardon, Sampson, & Lenz, 2000).

Career Shoppers *Career shoppers* are exploring and evaluating available options for obtaining career assistance. Each source of potential career assistance differs by cost and the nature of the help provided. Cost can be evaluated in terms of the financial resources required or the time and effort involved in receiving assistance. The nature of the help provided can range from anonymous over the Internet to personalized, individual counseling or range from brief involvement in a one-session workshop to intense involvement in a one-semester course. Persons may select the first source of career assistance they find, or they may comparison shop for some time before they select a source of assistance that provides the best chance of meeting their needs at an acceptable cost (Reardon et al., 2000).

Individuals *Individuals* receive career assistance by using self-help career resources available in books, magazines, CDs, videos, audiotapes, and Internet Web sites. Individuals can identify which resources meet their needs, locate the resources, sequence the appropriate order for using the resources they have obtained, and use the resource effectively. Individuals may also evaluate whether or not their needs have been met by resource use. If their needs have not been adequately met, they may select additional resources or seek assistance from a practitioner delivering career services.

Clients *Clients* use career assessment, information, and instructional resources within the context of a counseling relationship with a career counselor. Counselors and other service providers typically help clients select, locate, sequence, and use career resources. The counselor varies the pace of resource use to fit the career decision-making readiness of the client. The counselor may also monitor client progress and recommend other service providers that may be needed by the client. Career counseling can be provided in a variety of educational, agency, private, or organizational settings.

Students/Advisees *Students* use career assessment, information, and instructional resources within the context of a learning relationship with an instructor in an educational setting. The instructor is typically responsible for selecting, locating, sequencing, and using career resources for groups of students, as well as evaluating student outcomes. Students may voluntarily seek a career course in college to help them in solving a career problem, or they may involuntarily participate in a curricular intervention in school to meet their anticipated career development needs. ***Advisees*** may develop similar helping relationships with academic advisers, except that advisers may not be delivering instruction and evaluating class performance.

Customers *Customers* use career assessment, information, and instructional resources within the context of a helping relationship with a practitioner in an agency setting (such as a one-stop career center). Although the roles of the customer and the practitioner are similar to the roles of the client and counselor described previously, the use of the term *customer* represents an important philosophical shift in some career services delivery settings, particularly governmental agencies. Use of the term *customer* is meant to imply a greater emphasis on the person's ability to select the resources and services that the person perceives will best meet his or her needs. *Customer* also implies greater responsibility for the person to take an active part in the service delivery process (Sampson & Reardon, 1998).

Patrons *Patrons* use career information resources in a self-help context with support provided by a librarian, media, or information specialist in response to requests made by patrons in a library. On the basis of a reference information request, library staff members can assist patrons in locating information resources. With appropriate training, library staff may also help patrons select, sequence, and use resources, as well as make appropriate referrals to other resources or career service providers. In some libraries, self-assessment and instructional resources may also be available (Johnson & Sampson, 1985).

Employees *Employees* use career assessment, information, and instructional resources within the context of a helping relationship with a human resources practitioner affiliated with the employer. Similar to clients and customers, employees are responsible for using resources and their service providers (e.g., human resources practitioners) who assist employees in selecting, locating, sequencing, and using resources. Employees may also have the additional option of receiving assistance from human resources practitioners in negotiating internal training and employment opportunities not available to the general public.

How Career Assistance Is Provided

Career assistance involves providing career resources and career services to persons seeking help in making career choices. Almost all persons seeking assistance use some type of career resource. Some persons need and receive more personalized assistance through a particular career services setting.

Career Resources *Career resources* can include assessments, information sources, and instruction (Sampson, 1999). The intended outcome of career resource use is learning, but the learning that results is not an isolated event. What is learned from one resource can promote learning from previous and subsequent resources. For example, reading career information can cause persons to reconsider their prior responses to a values assessment in a computer-assisted career guidance system, leading to a more refined search for occupational alternatives.

Career Assessment ***Career assessment*** can be used to help persons clarify their self-knowledge. This enhanced self-knowledge often helps persons focus on the most relevant aspects of career information and evaluate the benefits and costs associated with various options. Some career assessments also generate occupational and educational options based on user responses to the construct being measured—for example, interests.

Career assessment can be categorized as self-assessment or practitioner assisted. ***Self-assessment*** resources, such as the Self-Directed Search (Holland, 1994), are designed to be used without the assistance of a practitioner to select, administer, score, profile, and interpret the measure, assuming the self-assessment has been validated for self-help use. Self-assessments include objective instruments and structured exercises and are available in paper-based, personal computer–based, and Internet-based versions. This type of assessment is appropriate for individuals with high decision-making readiness who are seeking independent use of career resources.

Practitioner-assisted assessment, such as the Revised NEO Personality Inventory (Costa & McCrae, 1992), is designed for use within the context of a helping relationship with a qualified practitioner. The person being served and the practitioner providing assistance collaboratively select an appropriate assessment, with the practitioner supervising or providing administration, scoring, profiling, and interpretation. Practitioner-assisted assessments include objective instruments, structured exercises, card sorts, and interviews (both structured and unstructured). Practitioner-assisted assessments are also available in paper-based, personal computer–based, and Internet-based versions. These types of assessments are appropriate for clients, students, customers, patrons, and employees with moderate to low decision-making readiness who are using career resources with assistance from a practitioner. Even though self-assessment measures can be used effectively in a practitioner-assisted environment, it is unethical to use counselor-assisted assessments in a self-help environment because these measures are not typically validated for this type of use.

Career Information ***Career information*** can be used to help persons clarify their knowledge of occupational, educational, training, and employment options. This enhanced knowledge of alternatives can provide a basis for narrowing occupational and educational options generated by career assessments, helping persons evaluate the benefits and costs associated with various alternatives, and providing a foundation for developing a plan of action for implementing a choice. Learning about occupations, educational institutions, training opportunities, and employment options can also help persons clarify their values, interests, skills, and employment preferences. Visualizing successful work behaviors (learned by using career information) can help to motivate the person to complete the education and training that is often necessary for employment. Career information is the most commonly available type of career resource.

Career information describes the characteristics of occupations, education, training, and employment that individuals use to clarify their knowledge of career options in problem solving and decision making. ***Occupational information*** describes the nature of work, the nature of employment, and the requirements for employment for individual occupations (e.g., accountant) and categories of occupations (e.g., Holland types). Occupational information is also used to choose and learn about job targets in employment decision making. ***Educational and training information*** describes the nature of education or training, the nature of the institution or training provider, and admissions for individual institutions (e.g., a particular university) or categories of institutions (e.g., community colleges), as well as admissions for individual training providers or categories of training providers. ***Employment information*** describes sectors, industries, employers, and positions in the job market.

Instruction ***Instruction*** is also used to help persons clarify their knowledge of self, of their options, and of the decision-making process. In this way, instruction is similar to career assessment and career information described previously, although several differences also exist. For example, instruction integrates several sources of data in a meaningful sequence designed to achieve a specific learning outcome. Instruction also includes some type of evaluation of how well persons have mastered the intended learning objectives. In comparison with career assessment and career information, instruction is a less commonly available type of career resource.

Career Services Some individuals need assistance from a practitioner to make effective use of career resources. ***Career services*** typically include a variety of practitioner interventions designed to provide persons with the type of assistance (e.g., counseling, career course, or workshop) and the amount of assistance (e.g., brief staff-assisted or individual case-managed services) they need to effectively solve career problems and make career decisions (Sampson, 1999). These are described more fully in the following sections.

Self-Help Services ***Self-help services*** involve self-guided use of self-assessment, information, and instructional resources in a library-like or Internet-based remote setting where resources have been designed for independent use by individuals with a high readiness for career decision making (Sampson et al., 2000). There is a difference between self-help resources and self-help services. Self-help resources are used independently by a person without help from a practitioner. Self-help services involve a person's self-guided use of resources in an actual setting (career center) or a virtual setting (Internet Web site) where it is possible to ask questions and receive support when needed.

Brief Staff-Assisted Services ***Brief staff-assisted services*** involve practitioner-guided use of assessment, information, and instructional resources in a library-like, classroom, or group setting for clients with moderate readiness for career decision making. Categories of brief staff-assisted services include (a) self-directed career decision making, (b) career courses with large group interaction, (c) short-term group counseling, and (d) workshops (Sampson et al., 2000).

Individual Case-Managed Services ***Individual case-managed services*** involve practitioner-guided use of assessment, information, and instructional resources in an individual office, classroom, or group setting for clients with low readiness for career decision making. This type of intervention provides the most substantial amount of assistance possible for persons with the greatest need for help. Categories of individual case-managed services include (a) individual counseling, (b) career courses with small-group interaction, and (c) long-term group counseling (Sampson et al., 2000).

Who Delivers Resources and Services

The delivery of career resources and services typically involves a team effort by practitioners and support staff. In large service delivery organizations, staff tend to be more specialized, whereas in small organizations, staff tend to be generalists performing a variety of functions.

Practitioners *Practitioners* include professionals and paraprofessionals from a variety of fields. ***Professionals*** include counselors, psychologists, vocational rehabilitation specialists, teachers/faculty/academic advisers, librarians and media specialists, human resources specialists, and social workers who are qualified to provide career services within the limits of their training and experience. ***Paraprofessionals*** include parent and community volunteers, career development facilitators, professionals-in-training, as well as student peer counselors who are qualified to provide career services within the limits of their training and experience.

Support Staff *Support staff* may include receptionists, secretaries, and clerks who interact with persons being served and provide various organizational functions that make the delivery of resources and services possible. Many support staff have considerable interaction with persons being served, answering questions and helping persons locate and use resources. It is important to make a distinction between professionals and professionalism. Many support staff exhibit considerable professionalism in their work even though their occupation does not have the credentialing or membership organizations typically associated with professions.

Where Resources and Services Are Provided

Career resources and career services are available in both actual physical settings and virtual settings. Actual physical settings include career and counseling centers in various organizations, and virtual settings include Internet Web sites.

Career Centers *Career centers* in educational and agency settings deliver resources and services to individuals seeking assistance with occupational, educational, training, and employment decision making (Sampson, 1999). These centers tend to emphasize the full range of career decisions that persons make, from exploring occupations through job placement. As stated previously, some career center functions are available to patrons in some libraries and to employees in some organizations.

Counseling Centers *Counseling centers* are most commonly found in institutions of higher education and in private-practice settings. These centers tend to emphasize occupational and educational decision making and the integration of personal, social, and family issues in career choice.

Internet Web Sites Providing Distance Guidance and Cybercounseling Internet Web sites are playing an increasingly important role in the distance delivery of resources and services by career centers and counseling centers. ***Distance guidance*** can be defined as "the delivery of self-assessment, information, and instruction in remote locations, with or without practitioner assistance, for the purpose of assisting individuals in making informed career, educational, training, and employment decisions. While distance guidance has been provided for some time using telephone-based technology, the Internet greatly expands resource and service options by adding the delivery of visual information" (Sampson, 1999, p. 244). ***Cybercounseling*** (Bloom & Walz, 2000) or ***Internet Counseling*** (National Board for Certified Counselors [NBCC] & the Center for Credentialing and Education [CCE], 2001) has the potential to improve clients' access to counseling. Internet Counseling "involves asynchronous and synchronous distance interaction among counselors and clients using e-mail, chat, and videoconferencing features of the Internet to communicate" (NBCC & CCE, 2001).

POTENTIAL BENEFITS RESULTING FROM EFFECTIVE CAREER ASSISTANCE

In addition to potentially benefiting persons with career problems, career assistance may have a positive impact on education and training providers, employers, and governments. Specifically, career assistance may benefit

- individuals by enabling them to cope with and gain optimal benefit from the complex range of available educational and vocational choices,
- education and training providers by increasing their effectiveness in helping learners affiliate with programs that meet their needs,
- employers by helping them identify employees whose skills and motivation are congruent with the employers' requirements,
- governments by making optimal economic use of society's human resources and relating this to chosen social and political goals.

Career assistance has the potential to foster efficiency in the allocation and use of human resources, as well as to foster social equity through the access persons have to educational and occupational opportunities (Watts, Dartois, & Plant, 1986).

SUMMARY

This chapter introduced the Cognitive Information Processing approach to providing career assistance to persons solving career problems and making career decisions. The development of the CIP approach at Florida State University was briefly described. The aims of the CIP approach in helping persons make current and future career choices were explained, and the four basic assumptions of the approach were then briefly described. Most of the remainder of the chapter explained our definition of key terms that are used throughout the book. Table 1.1 presented an overview of key terms showing how concepts are categorized. Figure 1.1 showed the connection between problem solving, decision making, career development, and lifestyle development. The chapter ended with a brief discussion of who may benefit from the availability of effective career assistance. The next chapter explores what people need to know and do in order to make appropriate choices about occupational, educational, and training options.

GETTING THE MOST BENEFIT FROM READING THIS CHAPTER

To effectively learn the material in this chapter, complete one or more of the following activities:

- In your own words, write the aims of the CIP approach, including the adage about fishing.
- Briefly paraphrase the four assumptions of the CIP approach, and state whether you agree or disagree with each assumption. If you disagree, how would you change the assumption?
- Write out the terms in Table 1.1, and show how the concepts are categorized.
- Draw and label Figure 1.1.
- Draw a picture of the house metaphor that was used to describe the relationships in Figure 1.1.
- Where possible, think of personal examples for the terms presented in this chapter.
- Think about your own experience with using career resources and career services. Have you benefited from using these resources and services? How could your experience have been improved?
- Talk with a friend about how the concepts you learned in this chapter apply to your life.

REFERENCES

Bloom, J., & Walz, G. (Eds.). (2000). *Cybercounseling and cyberlearning: Strategies and resources for the millennium.* Alexandria, VA: American Counseling Association.

Costa, P. T., Jr., & McCrae, R. R. (1992). *Revised NEO Personality Inventory.* Odessa, FL: Psychological Assessment Resources.

Holland, J. L. (1994). *Self-Directed Search* (4th ed.). Odessa, FL: Psychological Assessment Resources.

Holland, J. L. (1997). *Making vocational choices: A theory of vocational personalities and work environments* (3rd ed.). Odessa, FL: Psychological Assessment Resources.

Johnson, C. S., & Sampson, J. P., Jr. (1985). Training counselors to use computers. *Journal of Career Development, 12,* 118–128.

Lenz, J. G. (1998). A career center's community connection. *Australian Journal of Career Development, 7,* 3–4.

National Board for Certified Counselors & the Council for Credentialing and Education. (2001). *The practice of Internet counseling* [On-line]. Available: www.nbcc.org/ethics/webethics.htm.

Peterson, G. W. (1998). Using a vocational card sort as an assessment of occupational knowledge. *Journal of Career Assessment, 6,* 49–67.

Peterson, G. W., Sampson, J. P., Jr., Lenz, J. G., & Reardon, R. C. (2002). A Cognitive Information Processing approach to career problem solving and decision making. In D. Brown (Ed.), *Career choice and development* (4th ed.) (pp. 312–369). San Francisco: Jossey-Bass.

Peterson, G. W., Sampson, J. P., Jr., & Reardon, R. C. (1991). *Career development and services: A cognitive approach.* Pacific Grove, CA: Brooks/Cole.

Peterson, G. W., Sampson, J. P., Jr., Reardon, R. C., & Lenz, J. G. (1996). Becoming career problem solvers and decision makers: A cognitive information processing approach. In D. Brown & L. Brooks (Eds.), *Career choice and development* (3rd ed.) (pp. 423–475). San Francisco: Jossey-Bass.

Reardon, R. C. (1996). A program and cost analysis of a self-directed career decision-making program in a university career center. *Journal of Counseling and Development, 74,* 280–285.

Reardon, R. C. (2002). *Bibliographic references: Curricular-career information service* [On-line]. Available: www.career.fsu.edu/techcenter/designing_career_services/cip_bibliographies/.

Reardon, R. C., Lenz, J. G., Sampson, J. P., Jr., & Peterson, G. W. (2000a). *Career development and planning: A comprehensive approach.* Pacific Grove, CA: Brooks/Cole.

Reardon, R. C., Lenz, J. G., Sampson, J. P., Jr., & Peterson, G. W. (2000b). *Student manual for career development and planning: A comprehensive approach.* Pacific Grove, CA: Brooks/Cole.

Reardon, R. C., & Minor, C. (1975). Revitalizing the career information service. *The Personnel and Guidance Journal, 54,* 169–171.

Reardon, R. C., Sampson, J. P., Jr., & Lenz, J. G. (2000). Career assessment in a time of changing roles, relationships, and contexts. *Journal of Career Assessment, 8,* 351–359.

Reardon, R. C., & Wright, L. K. (1999). The case of Mandy: Applying Holland's theory and cognitive information processing theory. *The Career Development Quarterly, 47,* 195–203.

Sampson, J. P., Jr. (1999). Integrating Internet-based distance guidance with services provided in career centers. *The Career Development Quarterly, 47,* 243–254.

Sampson, J. P., Jr., Lenz, J. G., Reardon, R. C., & Peterson, G. W. (1999). A cognitive information processing approach to employment problem solving and decision making. *The Career Development Quarterly, 48,* 3–18.

Sampson, J. P., Jr., Peterson, G. W., Lenz, J. G., & Reardon, R. C. (1992). A cognitive approach to career services: Translating concepts into practice. *The Career Development Quarterly, 41,* 67–74.

Sampson, J. P., Jr., Peterson, G. W., Lenz, J. G., Reardon, R. C., & Saunders, D. E. (1996a). *Career Thoughts Inventory.* Odessa, FL: Psychological Assessment Resources.

Sampson, J. P., Jr., Peterson, G. W., Lenz, J. G., Reardon, R. C., & Saunders, D. E. (1996b). *Career Thoughts Inventory: Professional manual.* Odessa, FL: Psychological Assessment Resources.

Sampson, J. P., Jr., Peterson, G. W., Lenz, J. G., Reardon, R. C., & Saunders, D. E. (1996c). *Career Thoughts Inventory workbook.* Odessa, FL: Psychological Assessment Resources.

Sampson, J. P., Jr., Peterson, G. W., Lenz, J. G., Reardon, R. C., & Saunders, D. E. (1998). The design and use of a measure of dysfunctional career thoughts among adults, college students, and high school students: The Career Thoughts Inventory. *Journal of Career Assessment, 6,* 115–134.

Sampson, J. P., Jr., Peterson, G. W., & Reardon, R. C. (1989). Counselor intervention strategies for computer-assisted career guidance: An information processing approach. *Journal of Career Development, 16,* 139–154.

Sampson, J. P., Jr., Peterson, G. W., Reardon, R. C., & Lenz, J. G. (2000). Using readiness assessment to improve career services: A cognitive information processing approach. *The Career Development Quarterly, 49,* 146–174.

Sampson, J. P., Jr., Peterson, G. W., Reardon, R. C., & Lenz, J. G. (2002a). *Bibliography: A cognitive approach to career development and services* [On-line]. Available: www.career.fsu.edu/techcenter/designing_career_services/cip_bibliographies/.

Sampson, J. P., Jr., Peterson, G. W., Reardon, R. C., & Lenz, J. G. (2002b). *Key elements of the CIP approach to designing career services.* Unpublished manuscript, Florida State University, Center for the Study of Technology in Counseling and Career Development, Tallahassee [On-line]. Available: www.career.fsu.edu/techcenter/designing_career_services/.

Sampson, J. P., Jr., & Reardon, R. C. (1998). Maximizing staff resources in meeting the needs of job seekers in one-stop centers. *Journal of Employment Counseling, 35,* 50–68.

Saunders, D. E., Reardon, R. C., & Lenz, J. G. (1999). Specialty training for career counselors: Twenty-five years at Florida State University. *Career Planning & Adult Development Journal, 15,* 23–33.

Sears, S. (1982). A definition of career guidance terms: A National Vocational Guidance Association Perspective. *The Vocational Guidance Quarterly, 31,* 137–143.

Watts, A. G., Dartois, C., & Plant, P. (1986). *Educational and vocational guidance services for the 14–25 age group in the European Community.* Brussels, Belgium: Commission of the European Communities, Directorate-General for Employment, Social Affairs and Education.

Helping Persons Make Occupational, Educational, and Training Choices

CHAPTER **2**

This chapter explains how the two core constructs of the Cognitive Information Processing (CIP) approach can be used along with other career theories to help persons make decisions about occupations, education, and training. After reviewing this chapter, the reader should understand how practitioners and persons seeking career assistance could use the CIP approach. The chapter is organized as follows:

- Making Occupational, Educational, and Training Choices
- Using Theory to Improve Practice
- The Pyramid of Information Processing Domains
- The CASVE Cycle
- Using the CIP Approach with Other Career Theories
- Issues of Diversity and the CIP Approach
- Misconceptions About the CIP Approach
- Summary
- Getting the Most Benefit from Reading This Chapter

MAKING OCCUPATIONAL, EDUCATIONAL, AND TRAINING CHOICES

This chapter provides theoretical perspectives from the CIP approach for practitioners who are helping individuals and clients make occupational, educational, and training choices. As we stated in Chapter 1, *occupational decisions* involve choosing one occupation or a small group of related occupations as a focal point for making subsequent decisions about education, training, and employment. *Educational and training decisions* involve choosing a college major, program of study, or training opportunity that allows an individual to gain the general competencies (e.g., problem-solving skills or communication skills), specific competencies (e.g., work-related skills), a knowledge base, and credentials necessary to obtain or maintain employment. Chapter 3 applies CIP constructs to employment decisions. For updated information on the current status of the CIP approach, including evidence of the effectiveness of the application of the theory, see www.career.fsu .edu/techcenter/designing_career_services/.

USING THEORY TO IMPROVE PRACTICE

Solving career problems and making career decisions is often difficult. The individual making a career choice is confronted with a seemingly overwhelming number of things to know and do. Individuals need to clarify what they know about themselves, learn about the options available to them, and then use this information to identify and evaluate their options. What is needed is a set of easy-to-understand concepts that practitioners and individuals can use to guide career choice (Sampson, Peterson, Lenz, & Reardon, 1992). Practitioners need to understand problem solving and decision making in relation to their own careers, as well as know how to help individuals make appropriate career choices. Individuals need easy-to-understand concepts that they can readily apply to their own circumstances. This section continues with a brief discussion of the potential benefits of using theory for practitioners and persons seeking career assistance and concludes with an identification of learning strategies for practitioners using career theory.

Potential Benefits of Using Theory for Practitioners

There are several potential benefits of practitioners' use of career theory. First, career theory helps practitioners understand their own career choices. Before practitioners can successfully use theory to help other people with a career choice, they need to understand both how career theory explains their own vocational behavior and how career theory was (or could have been) used to help them make appropriate choices. This type of self-reflection and self-awareness is essential if practitioners are to engage in appropriate self-disclosure in career counseling. Second, career theory helps practitioners better understand the vocational behavior of their clients. This is particularly useful when clients ask questions such as "I have real difficulty in making career choices. How did I get in this mess?" Third, career theory helps practitioners understand the content and process of career problem solving and decision making, helping them recommend specific strategies to help the individual progress with career choice—that is, know what to do when in the counseling process. A thorough understanding and application of career theory helps practitioners have greater confidence that they understand their client and can be helpful. This practitioner

Table 2.1 Translating Core Theoretical Concepts for Use by Persons Seeking Career Assistance

Construct	Pyramid of Information Processing Domains	CASVE Cycle
Translation	What's involved in career choice	A guide to good decision making
	The *content* of career choice	The *process* of career choice
	What you need to *know*	What you need to *do*

confidence is communicated to the client, who, in turn, is more likely to perceive that counseling can be successful.

Potential Benefits of Using Theory for Persons Seeking Career Assistance

Theoretical concepts in the CIP approach are intended to be used by both practitioners and individuals seeking career services. In order for individuals to use theory effectively, theoretical constructs need to be translated into terminology that individuals can readily understand. The language of the Pyramid of Information Processing Domains and the CASVE cycle developed by Peterson, Sampson, and Reardon (1991) was translated by Sampson et al. (1992) and Sampson, Peterson, Lenz, Reardon, and Saunders (1996b) to avoid professional jargon and improve readability. These translated constructs, identified in Tables 2.1 and 2.2, are presented to individuals on handouts as part of service delivery to help individuals understand and manage career decision making. These translated concepts, supported by several metaphors, are also used in an instructional workbook designed to reframe negative cognitions and to enhance career decision-making knowledge and skills (Sampson et al., 1996b).

There are several potential benefits of individuals' use of career theory. First, by concentrating on a limited number of key constructs, individuals are better able to focus on what they need to know and do in order to make an appropriate career choice. Focusing on key constructs helps individuals avoid being overwhelmed with information. Second, by having client versions of key theoretical constructs, both verbally in text and visually in figures, clients and counselors have a common language for talking about career choice. Third, by including both the *content* and the *process* of career decision making, clients have clear criteria for self-monitoring their progress in decision making (Sampson et al., 1992).

The content (knowing) and process (doing) aspects of career problem solving and decision making can be communicated in a metaphor about using a recipe in cooking (Sampson et al., 1996b). The content of career choice can be represented by the list of ingredients, and the process of career choice can be represented by the instructions for combining and preparing the ingredients.

Table 2.2 Translating the Pyramid and the CASVE Cycle for Use by Persons Seeking Career Assistance

The Pyramid of Information Processing Domains

Practitioner Terminology	Client Terminology
Self-knowledge domain	Knowing about myself
Occupational knowledge domain	Knowing about my options
Decision-making skills domain	Knowing how I make decisions
Executive processing domain	Thinking about my decision making

The CASVE Cycle

Practitioner Terminology	Client Terminology
Communication	Knowing I need to make a choice
Analysis	Understanding myself and my options
Synthesis	Expanding and narrowing my list of options
Valuing	Choosing an occupation, program of study, or job
Execution	Implementing my choice
Communication	Knowing I made a good choice

Learning How Theory Can Be Applied to Practice

Practitioners need to be effective learners if they are to attain the potential benefits of using theory identified in the previous section. The following steps can help you in learning and using theory in practice:

1. Read about existing theories;
2. Select a theory (or combination of theories) that makes sense to you and has adequate evidence of effectiveness;
3. Visualize concepts in the theory contained in any figures, and then draw the figures from memory;
4. Visualize concepts in the theory contained in any metaphors, and explain these concepts to a friend;
5. Use the theory to explain your own career choices by writing an outline that integrates key life events with key theoretical concepts;
6. Explain to a friend how you would use the theory with two different types of clients;
7. Use the theory with a client, reflect on your experience, and then review your work with your supervisor;
8. Continue using the theory, or select a new theory, repeating the steps above.

Figure 2.1 | Pyramid of Information Processing Domains

From *Career Development and Services: A Cognitive Approach* (p. 28), by G. W. Peterson, J. P. Sampson, Jr., and R. C. Reardon, 1991, Pacific Grove, CA: Brooks/Cole.

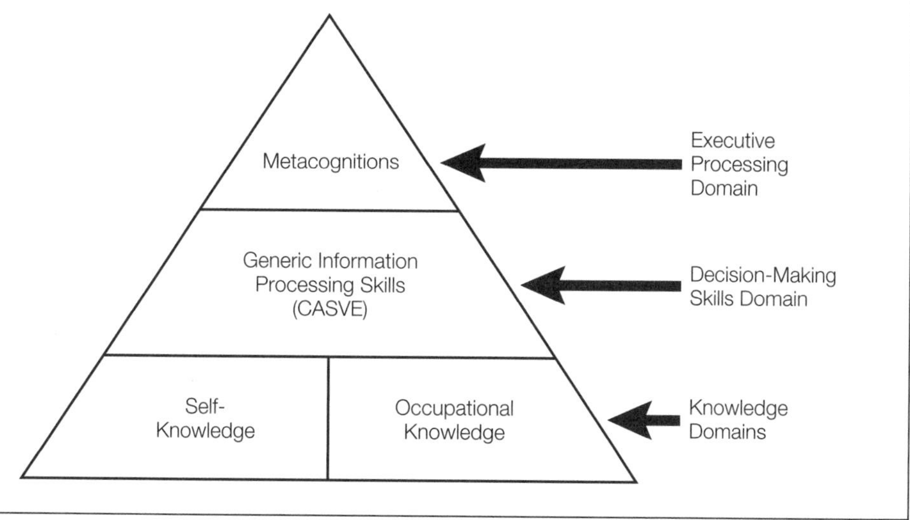

To make it easier for a practitioner to learn and apply the theory included in this book, the text presents theoretical constructs that are often supported by drawings presented in figures, metaphors, and case studies.

THE PYRAMID OF INFORMATION PROCESSING DOMAINS

The information processing domains related to career problem solving and decision making can be conceptualized as a pyramid with three levels or domains, as shown in Figure 2.1 (Peterson et al., 1991; Peterson, Sampson, Lenz, & Reardon, 2002; Peterson, Sampson, Reardon, & Lenz, 1996). The three domains are the knowledge domain, the decision-making skills domain, and the executive processing domain. The pyramid is intended to increase practitioner and client awareness of key aspects of career problem solving and decision making. By being better focused, practitioners and clients can make better use of the time available for receiving services. Figure 2.2 presents the client version of the Pyramid of Information Processing Domains.

Knowledge Domains

The base of the pyramid includes the knowledge domains of self-knowledge and occupational knowledge. As in a real pyramid, these domains provide a foundation for the domains above. Self-knowledge and occupational knowledge consist of networks

Figure 2.2 Client Version of the Pyramid of Information Processing Domains: "What's Involved in Career Choice"

From "A Cognitive Approach to Career Development and Services: Translating Concepts into Practice," by J. P. Sampson, Jr., G. W. Peterson, J. G. Lenz, and R. C. Reardon, 1992, *The Career Development Quarterly, 41,* p. 70.

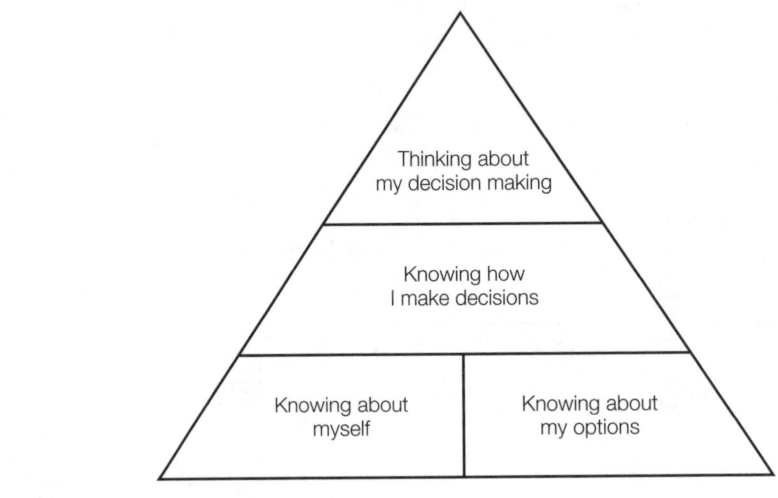

of memory structures called *schemata* (singular, *schema*) that develop over the life of the individual (Peterson et al., 2002).

Self-Knowledge or "Knowing About Myself" *Self-knowledge* includes individuals' perceptions of such things as their values, interests, skills, and employment preferences. Although there are a wide variety of self-knowledge characteristics that might be included under this aspect of the pyramid, for purposes of parsimony and clarity for the reader, the authors have chosen to focus on values, interests, skills, and employment preferences as key components of self-knowledge. ***Values*** are defined as motivators for work. ***Interests*** are defined as activities (behaviors) that people enjoy. ***Skills*** are defined as activities (behaviors) that people perform well. We use the terms *skills* and *abilities* as synonyms, although we prefer the term *skills,* as we judge this to be a less threatening concept for adolescents and adults. ***Employment preferences*** are defined as factors people seek in their job (such as opportunities for travel) or seek to avoid (such as lifting heavy objects). Individuals' values, interests, skills, and employment preferences are typically influenced by individuals' characteristics and life experiences. Values, interests, skills, and employment preferences may be further influenced by individuals' religious or spiritual beliefs. Values, interests, skills, and employment preferences are learned as individuals mature and gain life experience.

Individuals clarify their self-knowledge by reflecting on what they have learned about themselves and by engaging in additional life experiences, such as volunteer work. Individuals can also clarify their self-knowledge by interacting with a practitioner who helps clients make sense of data from career assessments or recommends intentional life experiences, such as academic course work.

Self-knowledge is stored in episodic memory (Tulving, 1972, 1984). Episodic memory is structured as a series of episodes over time and consists of perceptions rather than verifiable facts. Episodic memory is influenced by an individual's interpretation of past events. For example, individuals who have had an embarrassing failure experience at a prior job may then remember only the negative aspects of their skills in that employment. Episodic memory is also influenced by present emotions. For example, individuals who are depressed may selectively remember only failure experiences at previous jobs and thus generalize that they have limited interests and skills as they prepare for a job interview. For this reason, it may not be advisable to use interest inventories without first assessing the readiness of an individual for career problem solving and decision making. By readiness, we mean the capability of an individual to make appropriate career choices taking into account the capability of the individual and the complexity of family, social, economic, and organizational factors that influence an individual's career development.

Occupational Knowledge or "Knowing About My Options" *Occupational knowledge* includes knowledge of individual occupations and possession of a schema for how the world of work is organized. Increasingly, we are using the term *options knowledge* as a synonym for occupational knowledge to recognize that knowledge of education, training, and employment options is as important as occupational knowledge in career problem solving and decision making. Knowledge of individual occupational, educational, training, and employment options occurs as a result of direct experience or observation of the experience of others in real life or through the media. Therefore, knowledge of individual career options increases over time with experience. A schema for the world of work helps people organize what they know about individual occupations. A good world-of-work schema reduces complexity enough that individuals do not feel overwhelmed with information yet provides enough valid links to occupations to facilitate exploration. Brown and Brooks (1991) noted that in order for clients to make effective use of information, they need a schema to organize the information they obtain. Law (1996) noted that individuals need to develop constructs to organize information in order to avoid being overwhelmed by what they learn. The Holland Hexagon (Holland, 1997) is an example of a world-of-work schema that is simple, easy to use for exploration, and valid.

Occupational (or options) knowledge is stored in semantic memory. Semantic memory is structured as a series of verifiable facts rather than personal perceptions. Semantic memory is not overly influenced by the interpretation of past events nor is it overly influenced by present emotions. For example, individuals who had previously learned the work activities of an accountant and an auditor would likely be able to distinguish the work activities of the two occupations even when they are moderately depressed or anxious.

Decision-Making Skills Domain or "Knowing How I Make Decisions"

Above the knowledge domains is the decision-making skills domain, which includes the generic information processing skills that individuals use to solve problems and make decisions. The *CASVE cycle* (described later in this chapter) is one example of a specific approach to problem solving and decision making. Other theoretical perspectives on decision-making processes (e.g., Gati & Asher, 2001; Gelatt, 1962, 1989; Harris-Bowlsbey & Lisansky, 1998; Katz, 1966; Kinnier & Krumboltz, 1986; Tiedeman & O'Hara, 1963; Yost & Corbishley, 1987) and decision-making styles (e.g., Johnson, 1978) can also be used to enhance one's knowledge about career decision making.

Executive Processing Domain or "Thinking About My Decision Making"

At the top of the pyramid is the executive processing domain, which includes metacognitions. ***Metacognitions*** control the selection and sequencing of cognitive strategies used to solve a career problem through self-talk, self-awareness, and monitoring and control.

Self-Talk *Self-talk* is the quick, silent conversation people have with themselves about how well they are completing a given task, such as career problem solving and decision making. Positive self-talk helps individuals make career choices by helping to keep them motivated to engage in various career problem-solving and decision-making tasks. An example of positive self-talk would be "I can make a good choice; I just need to get the information I need and then think through my options." Self-talk can also be negative, which inhibits the process of career problem solving and decision making. An example of negative self-talk would be "I am no good at making decisions, so I might as well give up."

Self-Awareness *Self-awareness* is the extent to which people are aware of themselves as they progress through the problem-solving and decision-making process (including an awareness of the nature and impact of self-talk on their behavior). An example of self-awareness would be recognizing when old patterns of negative self-talk are causing an individual to lose motivation for solving his or her career problem ("What's the point of continuing to job search? No one is going to hire me with my background").

Monitoring and Control *Monitoring and control* refer to the extent to which people are able to monitor where they are in the problem-solving process and control the amount of attention and information required for problem solving (including monitoring when their self-talk is dysfunctional and subsequently controlling or altering their thoughts to be more appropriate). An example of monitoring and control would be knowing when enough information has been obtained at a given phase of the CASVE cycle and moving on to the next phase.

Interrelated and Interdependent Nature of Domains in the Pyramid

The domains of the pyramid are strongly interrelated from the top down. The executive processing domain influences the content and functioning of all other domains. Decision-making skills influence the content and functioning of the knowledge domains. For example, assume that a client is engaging in negative self-talk such as "I'm not very good at making big decisions. I can't make a decision until all of my family agrees that my choice is the right choice for me. Then I will know what to do." The client may be less likely to take responsibility for choosing and attempt a systematic decision-making strategy, given the perception of being a poor decision maker. In this situation, dependency might then be used to cope with the anxiety accompanying the choice process. Negative self-talk and the accompanying anxiety will influence the interpretation of past events, likely resulting in negative self-perceptions of interests and skills. Given the perception of not being a good decision maker, the client in this example is also not likely to engage in the exploratory behaviors necessary to obtain accurate occupational knowledge. Negative self-talk can have an unfavorable influence on all aspects of career choice. However, through self-awareness and monitoring and control of negative self-talk, individuals can learn to reframe negative self-talk into positive self-talk, which allows them to apply their own effective problem-solving and decision-making skills, enhancing self-knowledge and occupational knowledge in the process. Individuals with positive self-talk are more capable of independent and effective career problem solving and, hence, are less likely to need practitioner help in making career choices (Sampson, Peterson, Lenz, Reardon, & Saunders, 1996a).

It is important to acknowledge the existence of models that are similar to the Pyramid of Information Processing Domains, such as knowledge of self, knowledge of occupations, and true reasoning (Parsons, 1909), and the DOTS model, which includes self-awareness, opportunity awareness, decision learning, and transition learning (Law, 1999; Law & Watts, 1977). The similarity of these models over time indicates that these theoretical models provide a useful framework for making career choices.

THE CASVE CYCLE

The process involved with problem solving and decision making can be conceptualized in terms of the CASVE cycle presented in Figure 2.3 (Peterson et al., 1991; Peterson et al.,1996; Peterson et al., 2002). The CASVE cycle is intended to increase client and practitioner awareness of the key phases in the career problem-solving and decision-making process. By improving their decision-making skills, clients can increase the likelihood of making effective career choices. Figure 2.4 presents the client version of the CASVE cycle. The CASVE cycle includes the sequential phases

Figure 2.3 | The CASVE Cycle

From *Career Development and Services: A Cognitive Approach* (p. 33), by G. W. Peterson, J. P. Sampson, Jr., and R. C. Reardon, 1991, Pacific Grove, CA: Brooks/Cole.

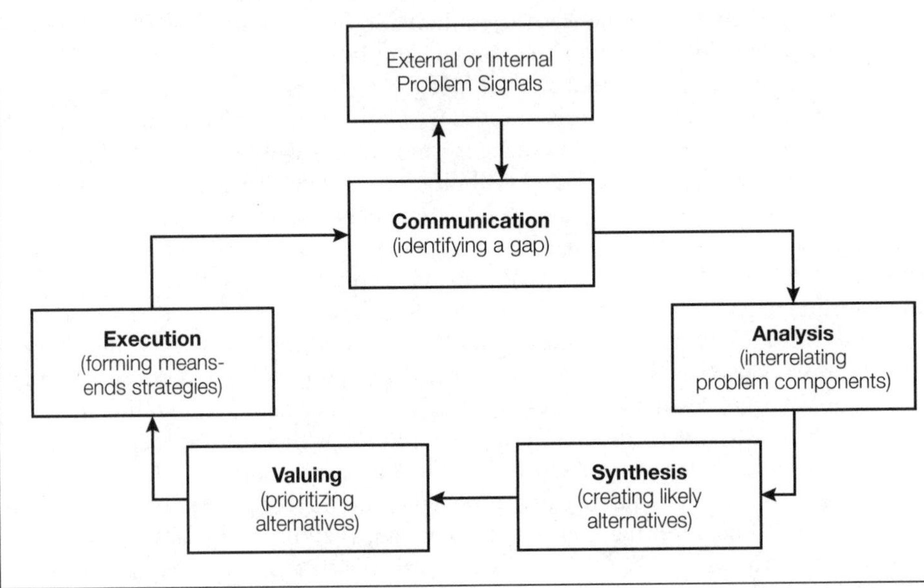

of Communication, Analysis, Synthesis, Valuing, and Execution. The cycle begins with Communication.

Communication or "Knowing I Need to Make a Choice"

In the ***Communication*** phase, individuals become aware that a gap exists between an existing and a desired state of affairs, or where they are and where they want to be. This awareness results from one or more external or internal cues. ***External cues*** may include positive or negative events that occur or input from one or more significant others. ***Internal cues*** may include client perceptions of negative emotions, avoidance behavior, or physiological changes. Clients' growing awareness of a gap creates a tension that stimulates individuals to engage in career problem solving and decision making. It may also provide the motivation necessary for seeking career services. Clients generally seek assistance with a career problem when the discomfort they feel becomes greater than their fear of change. Clients also seek assistance when their existing support resources are inadequate to help them solve their problem. Clients' reasons for seeking help are often clarified in the initial stage of counseling. Clients also become aware of factors related to the gap in the problem space (i.e., the complexity of the decision they are making).

Figure 2.4 | Client Version of the CASVE Cycle: "A Guide to Good Decision Making"

From "A Cognitive Approach to Career Development and Services: Translating Concepts into Practice," by J. P. Sampson, Jr., G. W. Peterson, J. G. Lenz, and R. C. Reardon, 1992, *The Career Development Quarterly, 41*, p. 70.

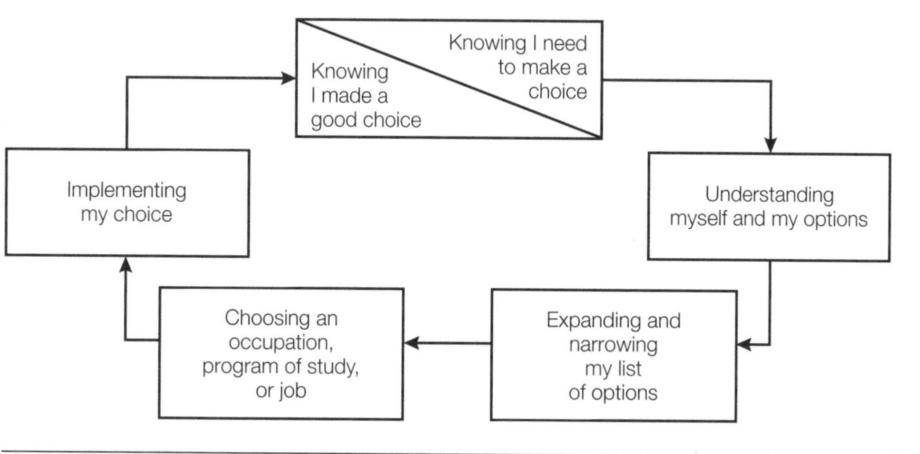

Analysis or "Understanding Myself and My Options"

In the ***Analysis*** phase, clients establish a mental model of the problem and perceive the relationships among the components. The process includes clarifying their self-knowledge in relation to values, interests, skills, and employment preferences. The process also includes enhancing their knowledge of occupations, programs of study, or jobs. Career assessments and computer-assisted career guidance (CACG) systems, as well as personal experience and input from significant others, can be used to inform this type of analysis. In this phase, clients may relate self-knowledge with options knowledge to better understand their personal characteristics in relation to the nature of the occupation or other option they are considering. Clients may also clarify how they typically approach problem solving and decision making, as well as clarify how their positive or negative self-talk influences the choice process. In addition, clients may gain an understanding of how decision-making style influences their approach to career problem solving and acquire a deeper understanding of the nature of their career problem. During the Analysis phase, clients engage in a recurring process of clarifying existing knowledge or obtaining new information, followed by time to reflect on and integrate what has been learned, leading to new or more complex mental models. In almost all cases, clients are adding to existing knowledge they already possess about themselves and their options. Stereotypes that restrict problem solving can be identified and potentially reframed during this phase.

Synthesis or "Expanding and Narrowing My List of Options"

In the *Synthesis* phase, clients expand and narrow the options they are considering. The goal of the Synthesis phase is to avoid missing alternatives while not becoming overwhelmed with options. The two phases of Synthesis are elaboration and crystallization. ***Elaboration*** involves divergent thinking that frees the mind to create as many potential solutions to a career problem as possible. Many assessment measures and computer-assisted career guidance systems generate lists of potential occupations or majors based on various combinations of values, interests, skills, and employment preferences. Individuals can also use their personal experience or recommendations from significant others to generate options. ***Crystallization*** involves convergent thinking that reduces a list of alternatives by eliminating options from consideration that are incongruent with the values, interests, skills, and employment preferences of the individual. Further review of career assessments and information can assist individuals in narrowing their options. At the conclusion of the crystallization process, clients should have narrowed their options to a manageable number of three to five plausible choices (Shahnasarian & Peterson, 1988).

Valuing or "Choosing an Occupation, Program of Study, or Job"

In the *Valuing* phase, clients evaluate the costs and benefits of each of the remaining alternatives to themselves and the potential costs and benefits to their significant others (e.g., friends or family members), their cultural group, community, and society in general. The next step involves prioritizing the alternatives to optimize costs and benefits in relation to the needs of all concerned. After priorities have been established among the three to five options being considered, a tentative primary and secondary choice emerges. Choices at this phase are considered tentative because subsequent preparation, reality-testing, or employment seeking may reveal a choice that is unavailable or inappropriate.

Execution or "Implementing My Choice"

In the *Execution* phase, clients establish and commit to a plan of action for implementing their tentative first choice. This plan may include selecting a preparation program (e.g., planning a program of study, exploring financial aid, or completing a formal education/training experience), reality-testing (working full-time, part-time, and/or as a volunteer, as well as taking academic courses or training programs), and employment seeking (taking the steps necessary to identify, apply for, and get a job). The Execution phase may be completed in a short period of time, as would be the case for an individual making a lateral job change within the same organization. There may be other times when the Execution phase may extend over a period of some years, as would be the case for an adolescent seeking to enter an occupation requiring education in a graduate program.

Communication or "Knowing I Made a Good Choice"

Upon completion of the Execution phase, clients return to the Communication phase to determine whether or not the gap between the existing and desired state of affairs has been effectively removed. If the problem has been resolved, the problem-solving and decision-making process ends. If the gap has not been removed, if external and internal cues indicate that a problem still exists, or if individuals are not taking action to implement their choice, then the process continues through the CASVE cycle again. If a new problem subsequently becomes apparent, then the process continues through the cycle again. Thus, the CASVE cycle is recursive in nature. See Table 2.3 for a summary of the phases of the CASVE cycle.

Cyclical Nature of the CASVE Cycle

The CASVE cycle is a relatively simple schema that is used to describe a complex career problem-solving and decision-making process. A single career decision that evolves over a period of weeks, months, or years may involve numerous iterations of the CASVE cycle. Clients experiencing difficulty in one phase of the cycle would typically cycle through to a previous phase to correct the problem. For example, when clients experience a problem in Valuing, they may cycle through to Analysis again to better understand themselves and their options. A variety of external events (such as another problem or a new opportunity) and personal variables (such as mental health or decision-making style) will influence the speed and the nature of clients' progression through the CASVE cycle. The potential advantage of using this relatively simple and parsimonious schema to represent a complex process is that clients who are anxious and overwhelmed will be more likely to understand and use a simple schema.

Serendipity and the CIP Approach

As individuals progress through Valuing or Execution, chance factors, or serendipity, can result in the identification of new options that may make it necessary to cycle back through Communication, Analysis, and Valuing. Returning to the Analysis and Valuing phases can provide an opportunity to carefully consider new options in comparison to options previously identified in Synthesis-crystallization.

USING THE CIP APPROACH WITH OTHER CAREER THEORIES

The CIP approach is constructed to be used in conjunction with other career theories. As noted earlier in this chapter, the Holland Hexagon (Holland, 1997) can be used as a schema for organizing occupational knowledge. We recognize that no single theory accounts for all of the psychological and social factors in the career development of individuals. Spokane (1991) noted, "Career interventions are rarely designed within the framework of a single theory" (p. 7). "Each [career] theory possesses features that are distinctive and lend themselves to different problems and populations

Table 2.3 | Summary of the Phases of the CASVE Cycle

Communication (knowing that a choice needs to be made)

Become aware that a problem exists, which is a *gap* between a real and desired state of affairs or "the difference between where an individual is and where he or she wants to be."

Become aware of cues that prompted the awareness of a career problem.

Clarify *external cues* that a problem exists, such as positive or negative *events* that occur or input from one or more *significant others.*

Clarify *internal cues* that a problem exists, such as perceptions of *negative emotions, avoidance behavior* when a problem exists, or *physiological changes.*

Awareness of a career problem may prompt an individual to engage in the Analysis phase that follows.

Analysis (understanding self and potential options)

Clarify *self-knowledge* obtained from educational/training experiences, work experience, feedback from significant others, assessment instruments, and CACG systems by considering an individual's *values, interests, skills,* and *employment preferences,* such as seeking opportunities for work-related travel or seeking to avoid heavy lifting at work.

Enhance *knowledge of options.*

Identify important *characteristics* of occupations, programs of study, or jobs obtained from sources such as print and audiovisual materials, CACG systems, information interviews, shadowing, work experience, and academic courses.

Enhance knowledge of the *structure of the world of work* (occupations, programs of study, or jobs) by using an easy-to-understand schema such as the Holland Hexagon.

Engage in a recurring process of clarifying existing knowledge or obtaining new information, then taking time to reflect on what has been learned, leading to a more thorough understanding of self and options being considered.

Clarify the *process typically used* to make important decisions, including the capacity to apply the CASVE cycle or similar approach.

Clarify *metacognitions* used in making important decisions.

Clarify *self-talk* related to career problem solving and decision making ("I always seem to choose a major and then change my mind" is an example of negative self-talk).

Promote *self-awareness* of the career problem-solving and decision-making process by the individual ("I am getting really stressed about making this choice").

Enhance *monitoring and control* of the career problem-solving and decision-making process by the individual ("I am not going to gain anything from getting more information about my options; now is the time to make my choice").

Synthesis (expanding and then narrowing a list of options)

With the insights gained in the Analysis phase, an individual can *elaborate* and *crystallize* his or her occupational, program of study, or employment options.

Table 2.3 *(continued)*

Elaboration involves generating a variety of occupational, program of study, or employment options that fit with an individual's values, interests, skills, and employment preferences. Assessments, CACG systems, personal experience, and input from significant others can be used to generate options.

Crystallization involves narrowing occupational, program of study, or employment options by eliminating alternatives that do not fit with the values, interests, skills, and employment preferences of the individual. Further review of assessments and career information can assist an individual in narrowing down choices to a manageable number of three to five plausible options that are used in the Valuing phase that follows.

Valuing (choosing an occupation, educational or training program, or job)

With the three to five options identified in the Synthesis phase, an individual judges the relative *costs* and *benefits* of each of the remaining options to himself or herself and the potential costs and benefits to his or her significant others (e.g., friends or family members), cultural group, community, and society in general.

Prioritize the three to five options being considered in terms of optimizing costs and benefits in relation to the needs of those concerned.

Make a *tentative primary choice.*

Make a *tentative secondary choice* in case the primary choice becomes inappropriate as a result of reality-testing through education/training or work experience or unobtainable due to job market conditions.

Execution (implementing a choice)

Create and commit to a *plan* of action for implementing the tentative first choice identified in the Valuing phase.

If needed, select an *education/training program* to implement an occupational choice, and then plan a program of study. Financial-aid options can be explored if necessary.

Reality-test an occupational, educational/training, or employment choice by engaging in full-time, part-time, and/or volunteer work experience and taking courses or training.

Seek employment by organizing a job campaign, writing a resume and cover letter, researching specific positions and employers, and preparing for interviews.

Communication (know if an appropriate choice has been made)

After completing the phases of the CASVE cycle, determine if the problem has been solved. Has the gap been resolved between where the individual is and where he or she wants to be?

Determine if the external and internal cues indicate that the problem has been solved.

Determine if the individual is taking action to implement his or her choice.

If the problem still persists, or if a new problem becomes apparent, repeat the CASVE cycle.

with differing effectiveness" (Osipow, 1990, p. 129). The following section provides examples of potential theory integration from the work of Holland (1997), Krumboltz (Mitchell & Krumboltz, 1996), and Super (1990). See Peterson et al. (1991) for a more detailed discussion of the integration of the CIP approach with trait and factor theory, career decision theory, and the work of Roe, Holland, Super, and Krumboltz. Reardon and Lenz (1998) provided an additional detailed analysis of the integration of the work of Holland and the CIP approach.

In terms of self-knowledge, potential examples of theory integration include (a) Holland's constructs, measures, and intervention strategies related to interests; (b) Krumboltz's construct of self-observation generalizations; and (c) Super's constructs and measures of values, work salience, life roles, and developmental stages. In terms of occupational knowledge, potential examples of theory integration include (a) Holland's Hexagon construct, (b) Krumboltz's construct of worldview generalizations, and (c) Super's construct and measure related to the world of work as part of career maturity. With regard to the decision-making skills domain, potential theory integration examples include (a) Holland's construct and measure associated with the need for information and barriers to decision making, (b) Krumboltz's construct and intervention strategies associated with task approach skills, and (c) Super's construct and measure of planning attitudes. In terms of the executive processing domain, potential theory integration examples include (a) Holland's construct and measure of vocational identity, (b) Krumboltz's construct and measure of career beliefs, and (c) Super's construct and measure of attitudes as part of career maturity.

ISSUES OF DIVERSITY AND THE CIP APPROACH

Over time, we have become more aware of important differences in how clients from various ethnic and racial backgrounds engage the respective domains of the pyramid and the phases of the CASVE cycle in career problem solving and decision making. In order for practitioners to gain a sense of how human diversity is managed in the CIP approach, the following discussion presents examples of multicultural considerations according to the domains of the pyramid and the CASVE cycle (Peterson et al., 2002).

The Acquisition of Self-Knowledge

The key concern in the development and refinement of self-knowledge lies in the use of normed measures in the assessment of personality constructs and abilities. Scores from such measures are used to verify or challenge existing self-perceptions of important personality dimensions involved in exploring potential career opportunities. However, the validity of such measures may be called into question when life's experiences that shape the development of self-knowledge schemata, the semantic interpretation of words contained in the measures, or the opportunity to master certain cognitive skills differ appreciably from those of the dominant culture. See Leong (1995) for a more detailed discussion on the use of career assessments with members of diverse racial and ethnic groups.

The Acquisition of Occupational Knowledge

Multicultural issues in the acquisition of occupational knowledge relate to (a) the breadth of experience and opportunity to learn about the nature of the world of work, (b) the meanings and attitudes attached to the knowledge acquired, and (c) the processes through which occupational knowledge is assimilated and stored. If individuals early in life are exposed to restricted environments in which family members and adult role models work, it is likely their firsthand knowledge of the world of work may also be narrow (Robinson & Howard-Hamilton, 2000). In CIP terms, the occupational knowledge schemata may lack differentiation and complexity (Neimeyer, 1988). Furthermore, if occupational knowledge is assimilated and associated with negative attitudes and stereotypic thinking, the world of work will not be seen as a place where one's potential can be realized but as a threatening, oppressive place with few financial or social rewards. Finally, members of certain cultural groups may acquire occupational knowledge more effectively through a social rather than an individual construction process (Lyddon, 1995). Thus, learning about occupations within closely connected family and community groups may be more meaningful and relevant than learning individually from print or other media resources typically available in career centers (Fouad & Arbona, 1994).

The Acquisition of Career Decision-Making Skills

Important multicultural issues are present in each phase of the CASVE cycle. In the Communication phase, members of minority groups must become aware of and explore the affective components in the problem space that result from perceived institutional and cultural bias, racism, and oppression in education and work. In the Analysis phase, members of minority groups may externalize the career problem: "I'm undecided and don't know what to do, but because of society's racism and oppression, it really doesn't matter what I do." In Synthesis, members of cultural or ethnic groups may be drawn either to familiar occupations or to "glamour occupations" in which there may be limited chances for success. In the Valuing phase, an important consideration involves the relative balance in importance between one's own beliefs and the influence of significant others or the cultural group in making a career choice (Fouad & Arbona, 1994). Finally, in the Execution phase, a common issue is confronting and overcoming resistances and constraints of cultural or racial bias and prejudice in the workplace as one reality-tests an occupational choice. At each phase in the CASVE cycle, individuals must identify and resolve cultural issues, if they are present, for effective career problem solving and decision making to happen.

The Executive Processing Domain

Multicultural issues in this domain involve the nature of metacognitions, especially self-talk, that regulate lower-order cognitive processes in the Pyramid of Information Processing Domains. Ultimately, self-defeating or negative self-talk severely limits or distorts the generation and evaluation of career options, which may, in turn, lead to inappropriate actions or inaction. Such phrases as "I can't because I'm . . . " or "Yes, but members of my group . . ." alert a counselor to dysfunction in the executive processing domain. Members of disadvantaged groups need to be aware of any self-imposed metacognitive constraints that inhibit progress through the phases of the CASVE cycle. Cognitive restructuring, as well as systemic interventions such as advocacy, networking with active minority support organizations, and securing legal advice, may help empower individuals to develop and apply more-positive self-statements and feelings of self-confidence in career problem solving and decision making. For example, a more constructive thought might be "In spite of the racism I see in my workplace, there are ways I can network with others to gain support and identify ways of advancing."

MISCONCEPTIONS ABOUT THE CIP APPROACH

As we have discussed the CIP approach with various practitioners, we have sometimes noticed two important misconceptions. Both appear to result from a misperception of the role of "cognition" in our theory.

Cognition and Emotion

The first misconception is that the CIP approach is mostly concerned with cognition (what people think) and is little concerned with emotion (what people feel). Acting on this misconception means that practitioners should pay more attention to cognitions and less attention to emotions. This assumption and the resulting implications are wrong. Emotions may be just as important as cognitions in decision making. Cognition allows us to be able to talk about our emotions. We believe that our emotions are influenced by our cognitions and our cognitions are influenced by our emotions, with both states influencing our behavior (Sampson et al., 1996a, 1996b). Although emotions are an important element in each phase of the CASVE cycle, emotions are particularly important in the Communication phase. In the Pyramid of Information Processing Domains, negative metacognitions can result in depression and anxiety, which, in turn, make it more difficult to clarify self- and occupational knowledge needed for career problem solving. Practitioners should pay careful attention to emotions, as this type of affective data is essential to identifying dysfunctional cognitions that may be impeding problem solving and decision making. It is also important for practitioners to affirm the positive emotions (e.g., happiness and confidence) associated with successful problem solving and decision making. It is worth noting that we use cognition, our thoughts about our feelings, as a way to describe our emotions so that we can communicate information about our feelings to others, which increases our levels of self-understanding and insight.

Rationality and Intuition

A second misconception is that in the CIP approach, rationality and logic are valued over intuition in problem solving and decision making. We believe that intuition is "a different way of knowing." Intuition includes cognitions outside our immediate conscious awareness. Insights gained from intuition are just as valuable as the insights gained from rationality and logic. Although individuals vary in the extent to which they use rationality and intuition in decision making, almost everyone uses some degree of both processes. Rationality and intuition are complementary, not exclusive. A perceived discrepancy between conclusions arrived at by rationality and intuition suggests that the person may need to explore this difference before any final decision is made. The use of intuition is particularly valuable in the Communication, Analysis, and Valuing phases of the CASVE cycle. Good career problem solving and decision making involve both rationality and intuition.

SUMMARY

This chapter explored the use of theory to improve practice, including benefits for both practitioners and persons seeking career assistance. The translation of concepts in the CIP approach for direct use by clients was described, and specific steps to help practitioners apply theory to practice were identified. Constructs from the Pyramid of Information Processing Domains (self-knowledge, options knowledge, decision-making skills, and metacognitions) were explained, and the interrelated nature of the domains of the pyramid was acknowledged. Constructs from the CASVE cycle (Communication, Analysis, Synthesis, Valuing, and Execution) were then explained. Figures were included to illustrate the practitioner and client versions of the pyramid and the CASVE cycle. The use of the CIP approach along with other career theories was described along with related examples. Issues of diversity and the CIP approach were explored in terms of the pyramid and the CASVE cycle. Finally, misconceptions about the CIP approach were identified.

GETTING THE MOST BENEFIT FROM READING THIS CHAPTER

To effectively learn the material in this chapter, complete one or more of the following activities:

- Write down the similarities of and differences between occupational decisions and educational/training decisions.
- In your own words, list the benefits of using career theory for practitioners and clients.
- Write out the terms included in Tables 2.1 and 2.2.
- Review Table 2.3, and think about how you made your current career choice. How might you have done things differently? What would you do in the same way?
- Draw and label Figures 2.1, 2.2, 2.3, and 2.4.
- Identify multicultural issues that may have impacted your career decision making.
- Consider whether you had any of the misconceptions about the CIP approach.

REFERENCES

Brown, D., & Brooks, L. (1991). *Career counseling techniques.* Boston: Allyn & Bacon.

Fouad, N. S., & Arbona, C. (1994). Career in a cultural context. *The Career Development Quarterly, 43,* 96–194.

Gati, I., & Asher, I. (2001). The PIC model for career decision making: Prescreening, in-depth exploration, and choice. In F. T. Leong & A. Barak (Eds.), *Contemporary models in vocational psychology* (pp. 7–54). Mahwah, NJ: Lawrence Erlbaum Associates.

Gelatt, H. B. (1962). Decision-making: A conceptual frame of reference for counseling. *Journal of Counseling Psychology, 9* (3), 240–245.

Gelatt, H. B. (1989). Positive uncertainty: A new decision-making framework for counseling. *Journal of Counseling Psychology, 36* (2), 252–256.

Harris-Bowlsbey, J., & Lisansky, R. S. (1998). *Take hold of your future.* Finksburg, MD: Career Development Leadership Alliance.

Holland, J. L. (1997). *Making vocational choices: A theory of vocational personalities and work environments* (3rd ed.). Odessa, FL: Psychological Assessment Resources.

Johnson, R. H. (1978). Individual styles of decision-making: A theoretical model for counseling. *The Personnel and Guidance Journal, 56,* 530–536.

Katz, M. R. (1966). A model of guidance for career decision-making. *The Vocational Guidance Quarterly, 15,* 2–10.

Kinnier, R. T., & Krumboltz, J. D. (1986). Procedures for successful career counseling. In N. C. Gysbers (Ed.), *Designing careers* (pp. 307–335). San Francisco: Jossey-Bass.

Law, B. (1996). A career learning theory. In A. G. Watts, B. Law, J. Killeen, J. M. Kidd, & R. Hawthorn (Eds.), *Rethinking careers education and guidance* (pp. 46–71). London: Routledge.

Law, B. (1999). Career learning space: New-DOTS thinking for careers education. *British Journal of Guidance & Counselling, 27,* 35–54.

Law, B., & Watts, A. G. (1977). *Schools, careers, and community.* London: Church Information Office.

Leong, F. T. L. (1995). *Career development and vocational behavior of racial and ethnic minorities.* Mahwah, NJ: Lawrence Erlbaum Associates.

Lyddon, W. L. (1995). Cognitive therapy and theories of knowing: A social constructivist view. *Journal of Counseling and Development, 73,* 579–585.

Mitchell, L. K., & Krumboltz, J. D. (1996). Krumboltz's learning theory of career choice and counseling. In D. Brown & L. Brooks (Eds.), *Career choice and development* (3rd ed.) (pp. 233–280). San Francisco: Jossey-Bass.

Neimeyer, G. J. (1988). Cognitive integration and differentiation in vocational behavior. *The Counseling Psychologist, 16,* 440–475.

Osipow, S. H. (1990). Convergence in theories of career choice and development: Review and prospect. *Journal of Vocational Behavior, 36,* 122–131.

Parsons, F. (1909). *Choosing a vocation.* Garrett Park, MD: Garrett Park Press.

Peterson, G. W., Sampson, J. P., Jr., Lenz, J. G., & Reardon, R. C. (2002). Becoming career problem solvers and decision makers: A cognitive information processing approach. In D. Brown (Ed.), *Career choice and development* (4th ed.) (pp. 312–369). San Francisco: Jossey-Bass.

Peterson, G. W., Sampson, J. P., Jr., & Reardon, R. C. (1991). *Career development and services: A cognitive approach.* Pacific Grove, CA: Brooks/Cole.

Peterson, G. W., Sampson, J. P., Jr., Reardon, R. C., & Lenz, J. G. (1996). Becoming career problem solvers and decision makers: A cognitive information processing approach. In D. Brown & L. Brooks (Eds.), *Career choice and development* (3rd ed.) (pp. 423–475). San Francisco: Jossey-Bass.

Reardon, R. C., & Lenz, J. G. (1998). *The Self-Directed Search and related Holland career materials: A practitioner's guide.* Odessa, FL: Psychological Assessment Resources.

Robinson, T. L., & Howard-Hamilton, M. F. (2000). *The convergence of race, ethnicity, and gender.* Upper Saddle River, NJ: Prentice Hall.

Sampson, J. P., Jr., Peterson, G. W., Lenz, J. G., & Reardon, R. C. (1992). A cognitive approach to career services: Translating concepts into practice. *The Career Development Quarterly, 41,* 67–74.

Sampson, J. P., Jr., Peterson, G. W., Lenz, J. G., Reardon, R. C., & Saunders, D. E. (1996a). *Career Thoughts Inventory: Professional manual.* Odessa, FL: Psychological Assessment Resources.

Sampson, J. P., Jr., Peterson, G. W., Lenz, J. G., Reardon, R. C., & Saunders, D. E. (1996b). *Career Thoughts Inventory workbook.* Odessa, FL: Psychological Assessment Resources.

Shahnasarian, M., & Peterson, G. W. (1988). The effect of a prior cognitive structuring intervention with computer-assisted career guidance. *Computers in Human Behavior, 4,* 125–131.

Spokane, A. R. (1991). *Career intervention.* Englewood Cliffs, NJ: Prentice Hall.

Super, D. E. (1990). A life-span, life-space approach to career development. In D. Brown & L. Brooks (Eds.), *Career choice and development* (2nd ed.) (pp. 197–261). San Francisco: Jossey-Bass.

Tiedeman, D. V., & O'Hara, R. P. (1963). *Career development: Choice and adjustment.* New York: College Entrance Examination Board.

Tulving, E. (1972). Episodic and semantic memory. In E. Tulving & W. Donaldson (Eds.), *Organization of memory.* London: Oxford University Press.

Tulving, E. (1984). Précis on elements of episodic memory. *The Behavioral and Brain Sciences, 7,* 223–268.

Yost, E. B., & Corbishley, M. A. (1987). *Career counseling.* San Francisco: Jossey-Bass.

3 CHAPTER Helping Persons Make Employment Choices

This chapter explains how the two core constructs of the Cognitive Information Processing (CIP) approach can be used to help persons make decisions about employment.[1] After reviewing this chapter, the reader should understand how practitioners and persons seeking career assistance could use the CIP approach. The chapter is organized as follows:

- Making Employment Choices
- The Nature of Employment Problems
- The Pyramid of Information Processing Domains (Including the CASVE Cycle)
- A Case Example
- Summary
- Getting the Most Benefit from Reading This Chapter

MAKING EMPLOYMENT CHOICES

This chapter provides theoretical perspectives from the CIP approach for practitioners who are helping individuals and clients make employment choices. As we stated in Chapter 1, an *employment decision* involves choosing and applying for a position with an employer in an industry that is in a

[1]This chapter has been adapted from "A Cognitive Information Processing Approach to Employment Problem Solving and Decision Making," by J. P. Sampson, Jr., J. G. Lenz, R. C. Reardon, and G. W. Peterson, 1999, *The Career Development Quarterly, 48,* 3–18. Copyright 1999 by the National Career Development Association. All rights reserved.

sector of the economy. An employment decision is both the ultimate outcome of career decision making and the starting point for further choices about occupations, education, training, and employment. One employment decision leads to a sequence of future decisions that continue through retirement. Chapter 2 applies CIP constructs to occupational, educational, and training decisions.

THE NATURE OF EMPLOYMENT PROBLEMS

As stated previously, a *problem* is defined as a gap between an existing and a desired state of affairs. Or stated more simply, a gap is the difference between where a person is and where he or she wants to be. The following are examples of gap statements for persons who might be seeking employment.

> "Now that I am about to finish school, I am going to need to get a job."
>
> "I have two job offers and need to decide which one to take."
>
> "This job is not leading anywhere. I need to find an employer who will give me the opportunity to get into management."
>
> "With a new baby, I don't want to work full-time. But we need for me to earn some money. I need a part-time job and good child care."
>
> "My company has been sold, and my job was eliminated in the downsizing. I need a job to survive. What am I going to do?"
>
> "I retire soon, but I don't want to just sit around the house. I want to find a part-time job that will be interesting but not too stressful."

Problem solving involves individuals acquiring information and learning cognitive strategies that enable them to remove the gap between their existing and desired state of affairs. The outcome of the problem-solving process is a choice that has a reasonable probability for narrowing the gap between where a person is and where he or she wants to be. ***Decision making*** involves transforming the choice into specific action steps (Peterson, Sampson, Lenz, & Reardon, 2002; Peterson, Sampson, & Reardon, 1991; Peterson, Sampson, Reardon, & Lenz, 1996). Both processes are needed to make effective employment decisions. An ***employment choice*** is an outcome of the employment problem-solving process, and ***taking action*** is a result of the decision-making process. Taking action requires making a commitment to follow through with a choice. The following section explains how the Pyramid of Information Processing Domains and the CASVE cycle can be used to explain the vocational behavior of persons seeking and securing employment and to provide the foundation for delivering services to individuals and clients seeking assistance with employment problems.

THE PYRAMID OF INFORMATION PROCESSING DOMAINS

The Pyramid of Information Processing Domains in Figure 3.1 shows the content of employment problem solving and decision making (Peterson et al., 1991; Peterson et al., 1996; Peterson et al., 2002). The base of the pyramid is concerned with what clients know about themselves and their employment options. The midlevel of the

Figure 3.1 What's Involved in Career Choice: The Pyramid of Information Processing Domains

From "A Cognitive Approach to Career Development and Services: Translating Concepts into Practice," by J. P. Sampson, Jr., G. W. Peterson, J. G. Lenz, and R. C. Reardon, 1992, *The Career Development Quarterly, 41*, p. 70. Adapted with permission.

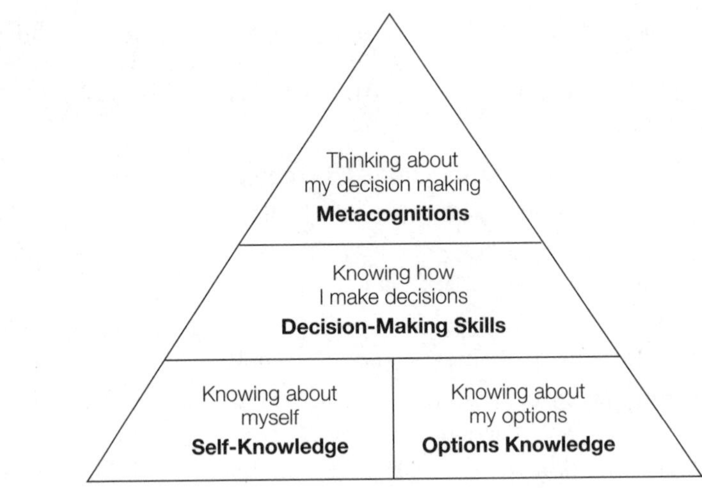

pyramid involves the process individual clients might typically use in solving important problems. The top of the pyramid is concerned with how thinking influences the way clients solve employment problems. These thoughts (positive or negative) influence both how individuals go about problem solving and decision making and what they think about themselves and their options. The next section describes the *content* of employment problem solving and decision making—that is, what individuals need to *know*.

Knowledge of Self

The self-knowledge necessary to make an appropriate employment choice is similar to the knowledge necessary to make an appropriate career choice (Peterson et al., 1991; Peterson et al., 1996; Peterson et al., 2002). Individuals can also apply the values, interests, skills, and employment preferences that they consider in making general occupational choices to a more specific employment choice.

Values Clarifying values in the job search process with instruments, card sorts, and exercises can help individuals identify job targets and potential employers that match their important *values*. Clarifying values also helps clients identify specific positions that are likely to satisfy their values. For example, assume that a client values independence and variety. The client's employer research (recruitment literature, employer Web sites, networking, and interviews) may indicate that a potential employer the client is considering generally encourages independence in making decisions as a method to increase quick responsiveness to customer needs. The specific description for management trainee also indicates that considerable variety is included in the position. The client's self-knowledge and the knowledge gained about a specific employer confirm that this employer is potentially a good match for the client and should be targeted in the job search process.

Interests Another important component of self-knowledge is *interests*. Having clients in the job search process clarify their interests with instruments, card sorts, and exercises helps them identify job targets or specific positions where they can be involved in activities they enjoy. For example, assume that a client is interested in working with people and problem solving. Data from employer research may indicate that the management trainee position with a potential employer involves working with both employees and customers in solving a wide variety of problems. This information about the requirements of the position appears to fit with interests in people contact and problem solving. However, researching the employer also reveals that the management trainee position requires diverse data management skills. It is important to evaluate whether the client currently possesses these skills (or can likely develop them in the training program) and to clarify whether the client has an interest in manipulating data. This type of information can be a stimulus to help clients further clarify their self-knowledge. Thinking about past experiences, an individual may decide that he or she enjoyed the sense of order and control that sometimes results from manipulating data. This clarification of interests helps confirm the client's decision to pursue jobs that involve this type of activity or to continue the selection process with the employer.

Skills In the CIP approach, as well as in many popular job search strategies, clarifying one's *skills* with instruments, card sorts, and exercises helps an individual identify types of jobs or specific positions where he or she will have the opportunity to competently complete specific work tasks assigned to a particular position. For example, assume that a client has skills in training and instruction, especially related to technical topics. Again, data from employer research may indicate that training and instruction skills are very relevant for management positions in a particular organization. This clarification of skills affirms the client's decision to target this organization in the job search process.

Reevaluating Values, Interests, and Skills Reviewing employer recruitment information and position listings and participating in job interviews also influence clients' perceptions of their values, interests, and skills. As a result of new information, individuals may reconsider the relative importance of specific values, interests, and skills. For example, as individuals become more aware of the opportunity to develop diverse skills in a management trainee position, they may then be willing to forgo the higher salary offered for a position that provides less opportunity to develop skills. Individuals may also misunderstand the nature of a particular value, interest, or skill. For example, reviewing employer recruitment information and participating in the job interview process may clarify that the value of independence is often associated with assuming considerable responsibility for success or failure in a job. The individual may decide that the benefit of limited supervision offered by jobs characterized by high independence is not worth the increased responsibility for success and failure in assigned responsibilities.

Employment Preferences Clients' employment preferences and family situation may also influence their employment choices. Potential ***employment preferences*** include such factors as desired salary level, commuting time, physical demands, environmental conditions of work, hours of work, travel requirements, and related items. Clarification of employment preferences may occur as a result of reviewing occupational information and position descriptions and reflecting on past paid and unpaid work experience. For example, an individual imagines what it would be like to work irregular hours after reading an occupational description and conducting an information interview with a retail store manager. Or the individual may remember how working irregular hours in a summer job influenced his or her lifestyle.

Family Situation An individual's family situation may also influence an employment choice. Potential ***family situations*** include the desire to live close to family members; the employment opportunities for a spouse or partner; the preferences (or bias) of family members; family employment contacts; or the existence of a family business. Clients may need to clarify their family situation as it relates to their job search by communicating honestly with significant others and then reflecting on what has been learned. For example, before accepting a promotion that would involve relocation, some clients might view it important to consider the potential impact of such a decision on their spouse, children, and parents. For some cultural groups, it may be very important to include family members in the employment problem-solving and decision-making process. Counselors can help clients balance their desire for family input while being alert to signs that a client's excessive dependence on one or more family members for guidance in the job search process is contributing to the client's indecisiveness or his or her pursuit of an artificially restricted range of options (e.g., "My family says I shouldn't apply for any social services jobs because I'll never make enough money to support myself"). In some cases, it may also be appropriate to use family counseling to resolve clients' employment problems.

Knowledge of Employment Options

The knowledge of employment options necessary to make an appropriate employment choice is similar to the knowledge necessary to make an appropriate occupational choice (Peterson et al., 1991; Peterson et al., 1996; Peterson et al., 2002). Knowledge of specific occupations and of occupational classifications that are used by clients in making general occupational choices can also be applied to making more-specific employment choices.

Knowledge of Specific Industries, Employers, and Employment Positions Although many career counseling services deliver occupational information, it does not always contain employment information. In the CIP approach to employment problem solving and decision making, knowledge about options includes knowledge about occupations, types of jobs within a particular field or industry, and specific employers and positions within various types of organizations. Clients should be encouraged to briefly review occupational information prior to reviewing the information available for a specific position. In essence, occupational information provides the foundation for using employment information. By being familiar with the typical work tasks for particular occupations, job hunters are better prepared to research specific employers and positions. This strategy has the potential advantages of helping applicants clarify missing or conflicting data in employer literature, to ask more-focused questions in employment interviews, and to demonstrate to interviewers that they have the skills needed for the position. Many of the categories used in describing specific occupations also relate to specific positions, such as salary, education and training required, and physical demands. Clients should also be encouraged to use various sources of information, including employer directories, recruitment information (text materials, videos, CD-ROMs, and Internet Web sites), official position descriptions, and information interviews to enable them to identify options that best match their employment preferences.

Knowledge of Employer Classifications Employer classification schemata can help individuals more quickly find and organize the information they need. For example, employers can be grouped into the 10 major categories of the *Standard Industrial Classification* or the 20 sectors of the *North American Industry Classification System* (U.S. Office of the President, Office of Management and Budget, 1987, 1997). Instead of being overwhelmed with numerous options, individuals can begin identifying job options and employing organizations via a manageable number of categories.

Knowledge About Decision Making (the CASVE Cycle)

As noted earlier, the midlevel of the Pyramid of Information Processing Domains includes a problem-solving and decision-making process known as the CASVE cycle, as shown in Figure 3.2. The CASVE cycle is reviewed as a resource for helping individuals obtain and use the right information at the right time in the employment problem-solving and decision-making process. Although the CASVE cycle represents a "generic" decision-making process (Peterson et al., 1991; Peterson et al., 1996; Peterson et al., 2002), it can be easily applied to the job search process. The CASVE cycle depicts the *process* for obtaining employment—that is, what individuals need to *do* to become employed. It is important to note that the CASVE cycle process may be revisited several times during a person's job search, such as during the initial stages of determining appropriate job targets, during a person's focus on specific positions or openings for which he or she is applying, and during the stage of negotiating and evaluating offers when the person is trying to decide which offer to accept.

Communication In the Communication phase, clients become aware that they need to make an employment decision. Internal cues (such as anxiety) or external cues (such as statements from close friends, the impending completion of a training program or degree, or a request from an employer that an offer be accepted or rejected by a certain date) signal that employment problem solving and decision

Figure 3.2 A Guide to Good Decision Making: The CASVE Cycle

From "A Cognitive Approach to Career Development and Services: Translating Concepts into Practice," by J. P. Sampson, Jr., G. W. Peterson, J. G. Lenz, and R. C. Reardon, 1992, *The Career Development Quarterly, 41,* p. 70. Copyright 1992 by the National Career Development Association. All rights reserved. Adapted with permission.

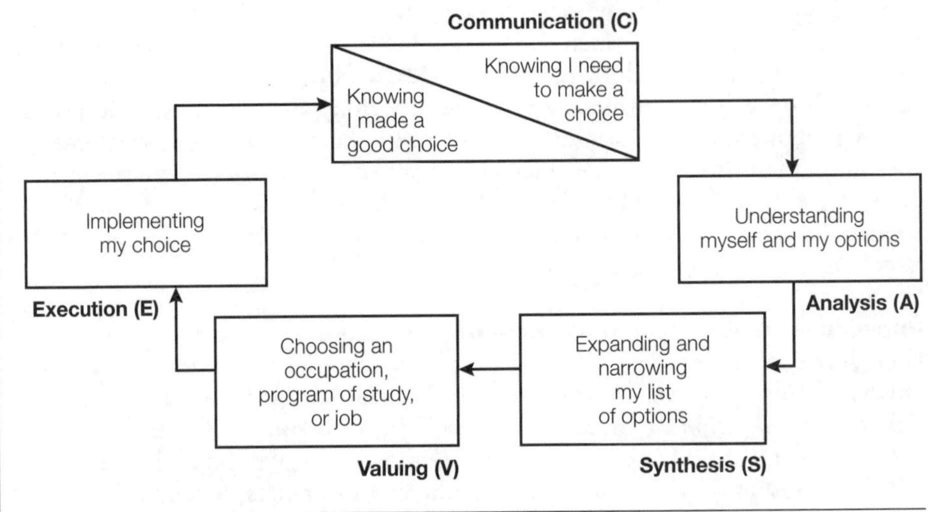

making needs to begin. Internal and external cues create pressure for change. Although some pressure from cues is typically needed to encourage clients to initiate change, too much pressure may cause individuals to use procrastination as a self-defeating coping strategy, resulting in a failure to change when needed. For example, anxiety ("How am I going to pay my student loans if I don't get a job?" or "What if I turn this employer's offer down and I don't get another one?") or recommendations from significant others ("Why not take a sure thing and accept our neighbor's offer of a position?") may be motivational in small amounts, but in large amounts may also lead to procrastination as a defense. Responding to internal and external cues at the appropriate time generally offers the best chance of initiating successful employment problem solving and decision making.

Analysis In the Analysis phase, clients use employment self-knowledge and knowledge of employment options to better understand the gap between where they are and where they want to be. As stated earlier, employment self-knowledge includes values, interests, skills, employment preferences, and family situation. Knowledge of employment options includes knowledge of specific employers, types of jobs, specific position openings, and employer classifications. This type of knowledge is especially critical in evaluating specific job offers. Too often clients accept job offers on the basis of limited information gained through brief interviews and short on-site visits, only to find several weeks or months later that the job does not meet their initial expectations. In the Analysis phase, practitioners can also encourage clients to consider their typical approach to making important decisions and to understand how their positive and negative thoughts influence employment problem solving and decision making. Self-assessment activities and information resources (self-help or provided by a practitioner) may help clients further clarify what they know about themselves and their options. The Analysis phase can be viewed as an ongoing process, where clients reflect on what they know, obtain information, and reflect on what has been learned.

Synthesis In the Synthesis phase, clients typically expand and narrow the employment options they are considering. The goal is to avoid missing potentially appropriate options (expansion or elaboration) while reducing the number of options to a list small enough that clients avoid being overwhelmed when a choice is finally made (narrowing or crystallization). Clients who are going through the CASVE cycle for the purpose of deciding between or among job offers may actually be dealing with a fairly small number of options.

For many clients, however, expanding options are the concern. The clients seek assistance, saying things such as "What else could I do with my major besides teach?" or "I've worked as a sales representative for 10 years but want to start looking for other types of jobs." Clients could explore two methods of expanding their employment options. First, they could be asked to generate a list of potential employers and positions they have considered in the past (similar to their occupational daydreams or aspirations) or even positions they have actually applied for in their current or previous search. Second, they could use an information resource to generate options (such as print or CD-ROM directories or Internet directories or job banks). To narrow their options, clients would apply what was learned in the Analysis phase. From a CIP perspective, they would likely keep as choices only those employers and positions that offer a reasonable chance of helping them eliminate their "employment gap." If none of the options identified provide them with a reasonable chance of eliminating the gap, they may need to expand the number of potential employers or types of positions they are considering or reconsider what is really most important in terms of their criteria for acceptable employment. The outcome of the Synthesis phase is a short list of employment prospects.

Valuing In the Valuing phase, clients finalize their employment options. For some clients, this means specifying the job areas they plan to target. For others, it means they have identified specific positions for which they wish to apply. For still others, this phase involves weighing the pros and cons of specific offers, accepting an employment offer, and beginning work. Clients may consider the costs and benefits of each option to themselves and significant others, such as family. Some individuals may also consider the costs and benefits for their cultural group, community, and society at large. After considering the costs and benefits, clients typically prioritize their options. For instance, in the case of job targets, they may decide, after considering many different areas, that account executive, sales manager, and customer support representative are their three top positions. Other clients, after reviewing multiple position announcements with varied types of employers, may identify those options for which they wish to actually apply. Other job seekers may use the Valuing phase to decide between competing offers, including a scenario that would involve declining one or more offers because they do not appear to be a good match and continuing the job search for a more appropriate employment offer. If clients choose to continue seeking employment options, they would likely return to the Analysis phase to further examine the nature of the employment problem and to generate a new list of options in the Synthesis phase. Being discouraged or perceiving barriers to employment may cause clients to cycle through to the Communication phase to better understand the nature of their employment problem.

Execution In the Execution phase, clients take steps to act on their priority list of options in the Valuing phase. This could include identifying specific organizations where they will send their resumes or informing an employer that a position offer has been accepted (this may first be done verbally, followed by a written acceptance in the form of a letter, fax, or e-mail) and, if multiple employment offers exist, declining the other offers in writing. Other steps might include planning for a transition to new employment. Potential transition issues include relocation, spouse employment, and acquisition of necessary tools and working clothes. The final step involves actually beginning employment or an employer-delivered training program.

Communication The final phase involves a return to Communication to determine if internal and external cues indicate whether or not the original employment gap has been successfully closed. If the cues indicate appropriate employment, then the problem-solving and decision-making process pauses until the next gap is identified. If the cues indicate that the problem still persists (such as the individual does not like an employer training program or the employer withdraws an offer because of a downturn in the economy), then the cycle proceeds to the Analysis phase to better understand the gap and ultimately choose another position or employer.

Understanding How Thoughts Influence Decisions

At the top of the Pyramid of Information Processing Domains is the executive processing domain. From a CIP perspective, the metacognitive skills in this domain influence how individuals think and subsequently act in solving employment problems. The three components of this domain are self-talk, self-awareness, and control and monitoring (Peterson et al., 1991; Peterson et al., 1996; Peterson et al., 2002).

Self-Talk *Self-talk* can be described as the silent conversations clients have with themselves about their past, present, and future capability to complete a specific task—in this case, employment problem solving and decision making. Positive self-talk can help individuals (a) remain motivated when delays occur in obtaining employment, (b) actively seek the employment information needed to make a decision, (c) stay focused on making a good employment choice and avoid being distracted, (d) think clearly and realistically about the good and bad points of employment options, (e) make better use of the opinions of important people in their lives, (f) seek job search assistance when needed, and (g) follow through with an action plan after a decision is made. In terms of employment problem solving and decision making, negative self-talk generally makes it more difficult for clients to (a) clearly write a career objective for a resume, (b) accurately identify skills on a functional resume, (c) be motivated to identify potential employers and position openings, (d) follow through with information interviewing and networking opportunities, (e) be motivated to research an employer, (f) positively articulate potential contributions in an employment interview, (g) respond with clarity and enthusiasm to questions posed by an employment interviewer, and (h) follow through with interview thank-you letters (Sampson, Peterson, Lenz, Reardon, & Saunders, 1996b). Cognitive restructuring, within the context of career service delivery, can be used to help clients identify, challenge, and alter negative thoughts that contribute to the problems identified above (Sampson, Peterson, Lenz, Reardon, & Saunders, 1996a).

For some individuals, employment decision making may provoke more anxiety than occupational decision making because of the relative specificity of each type of decision. Choosing an occupation and related program of study is a more general, future-oriented choice. Failure to obtain an employment position related to an individual's program of study is a possibility but is typically far enough in the future to cause limited anxiety for most persons. Employment decision making, however, offers the possibility of specific and immediate rejection by potential employers. As a result, potential failure is concrete and easily perceived. Most job applicants are aware that they are likely to receive many rejections before actually receiving a job offer. As noted in the section on the Communication phase of the CASVE cycle, a little anxiety may be motivational, but substantial anxiety may lead to self-defeating coping behaviors, such as procrastination.

In summary, if individuals expect to do poorly (or to fail) in employment selection, they have little motivation to prepare for and follow through with the steps in the process. Also, negative self-talk is likely to influence individuals' perceptions of their capabilities to perform successfully in a specific position. Subsequent awareness that the individual is not making good progress in obtaining employment only reinforces negative self-talk—for example, "I knew I wasn't going to get a good job, and it seems I was right." Becoming aware of negative thoughts is a key strategy for limiting the potentially harmful impact of negative thinking on employment choice.

Self-Awareness From a CIP perspective, effective problem solvers are aware of themselves as they are doing a task. Effective *self-awareness* includes an awareness of the interaction among thoughts, feelings, and behaviors, especially the debilitating impact of negative self-talk on employment choice. The following list presents self-awareness factors and sample statements related to the job search process:

- Debilitating negative emotions, such as depression, anxiety, or panic—"I'm really anxious about looking for work after being out of the job market for so long."
- Lack of emotion or caring about an employment problem—for example, lack of motivation—"I'd rather stay in school and change majors than take a job that pays so little."

- Persistent negative thoughts about employment choice—for example, predicting future failure and the use of absolute terminology ("never" and "always")—"I'll never find a good job."
- Failure to initiate or persist with employment problem-solving behaviors—"After so many rejection letters, what's the point of continuing to look?"
- Repeating employment decision-making behaviors when adequate information is available and when a choice needs to be made—"Do you have a test I can take that will determine the types of jobs I'm suited for?"

Self-awareness also includes the reactions of significant others (such as family and friends) to the job hunter's employment problem solving and decision making. The following list presents issues associated with significant others and sample statements:

- Suggestions from significant others that you are proceeding too slowly with employment choice, indicating that action is needed—"It's time to stop reading the classified ads and actually start applying for jobs."
- Feedback from significant others to take just any job, when more caution and careful thought is needed—"There are lots of jobs out there. Why are you being so picky?"
- Failure to seek or consider input from significant others—"My spouse is concerned about health benefits, but I'd rather be my own boss."
- Consideration or selection of an inappropriate employer or position—"I know you've never seen yourself as the sales type, but this seems like too good an opportunity to pass up."

Although it may be important for some clients to consider input from significant others, not all input may be helpful. Counselors can help individuals carefully consider all of the information they have received and then assist them in assuming responsibility for making and following through with an appropriate employment choice. Counselors may also involve clients in cognitive restructuring exercises to improve their self-awareness of the impact of career thoughts on feelings and behavior (Sampson et al., 1996a).

Monitoring and Control *Monitoring* refers to an individual's ability to keep track of his or her progress through the problem-solving and decision-making process—that is, knowing when it is necessary to stop and get more information (e.g., further researching a prospective employer), knowing when a task has been completed successfully enough to continue with the next step in the process (e.g., having an appropriate number of job targets to pursue), and knowing when assistance will be needed to make an appropriate choice (e.g., being overwhelmed by the number of prospective employers in a particular location). *Control* refers to an individual's ability to purposefully engage in the next appropriate problem-solving and decision-making task, including the ability to control negative thinking, such as controlling negative thoughts prior to a job interview, that creates difficulties in problem solving and decision making (Peterson et al., 1991; Peterson et al., 1996; Peterson et al., 2002; Sampson et al., 1996a). Effective problem solvers and decision makers keep track of the "knowing" and "doing" aspects of choice. They are aware of what they know and what they need to know, as well as what they need to do in the sequence of steps associated with employment choice. A brief hypothetical example follows that applies CIP theory to employment problem solving and decision making.

A CASE EXAMPLE

Maria is 46 years old and has two children. Her husband is a local firefighter who has just been promoted to lieutenant. Until recently, Maria was employed as the office manager of a large commercial real estate agency. The agency has been sold and merged with another real estate business, and she has been informed that she will not be needed in the merged organization. Maria has been given three months' severance pay and a positive letter of recommendation but has not been provided with outplacement services. To obtain a similar position in another large agency would likely require her to move to another city. She was reluctant to consider this option in view of her spouse's recent promotion and her children's desire to graduate from the high school they are currently attending. Maria's uncertainty about her future employment prompted her to seek assistance from the career center at the local community college (Communication).

After a brief screening intervention and readiness assessment (Sampson & Reardon, 1998), the counselor judged that Maria had a moderate level of readiness for employment problem solving and decision making and that a brief staff-assisted intervention in the career library would be appropriate. The counselor clarified the nature of Maria's problem as a gap between being unemployed and having a satisfying job that provided adequate income and more time to be with her family. The counselor used printed client versions of the Pyramid of Information Processing Domains and the CASVE cycle (Sampson, Peterson, Lenz, & Reardon, 1992) to orient Maria to the employment problem-solving and decision-making process. Using an Individual Learning Plan (Peterson et al., 1991; Peterson et al., 1996; Peterson et al., 2002), the counselor and Maria collaboratively established goals for service delivery. The counselor then recommended a sequence of assessment, information, and instructional resources to assist Maria in achieving her goals of identifying potentially appropriate jobs and restructuring the negative thoughts identified by the Career Thoughts Inventory (Sampson, Peterson, Lenz, Reardon, & Saunders, 1998) during readiness assessment. The Individual Learning Plan was renegotiated several times as Maria's needs evolved during service delivery.

At the beginning of each session with Maria, the counselor used the pyramid and the CASVE cycle to help her monitor where Maria was in the problem-solving and decision-making process. Maria used a computer-assisted career guidance system to clarify her values, interests, and transferable skills. Maria and her counselor used her previous work experience to clarify her employment preferences and the interaction between her work and family issues (self-knowledge and Analysis). Maria then used a combination of occupational and employer information, along with a computer-assisted job bank, to generate and learn about various local employment options (knowledge of employment options, Analysis, and Synthesis-elaboration). The counselor would occasionally ask Maria to verbalize her thoughts about the options she was considering to determine if negative thoughts were compromising her problem-solving and decision-making process. When negative thoughts were identified, the counselor used a cognitive restructuring exercise (Sampson et al., 1996b) to identify, challenge, and alter Maria's negative career thoughts (executive processing).

With the support of her counselor, Maria used her self- and employment knowledge to narrow down the employment options she was considering (Synthesis-crystallization). Maria then used a theory-based written exercise to evaluate the costs and benefits of her employment options to herself, her family, her cultural group, and her community. She tentatively decided to apply for an administrative position with a local employer (Valuing). Maria then prepared for and interviewed for the position of administrative assistant to the chief operating officer of a large local hospital (Execution). She returned to the career center to inform her counselor that she had received, and accepted, an offer to work as an administrative assistant at the hospital. The counselor briefly reviewed the gap that had prompted Maria to seek career services, and they then mutually agreed that she had achieved her goals (return to Communication). The counselor concluded service delivery by discussing with Maria what she had learned from receiving services and how she might apply this learning to inevitable employment choices that she will make in the future.

SUMMARY

This chapter explored the nature of employment choices and employment problems. Concepts were explored associated with the Pyramid of Information Processing Domains, including (a) knowledge of self (values, interests, skills, employment preferences, and family situation); (b) knowledge of employment options (knowledge of specific industries, employers, employment positions, and employer classifications); (c) the CASVE cycle (Communication, Analysis, Synthesis, Valuing, and Execution); and (d) executive processing (self-talk, self-awareness, and control and monitoring). A case example demonstrated how the Pyramid of Information Processing Domains and the CASVE cycle could be applied to employment problem solving and decision making.

GETTING THE MOST BENEFIT FROM READING THIS CHAPTER

To effectively learn the material in this chapter, complete one or more of the following activities:

- In your own words, describe the nature of your past or present employment problems.
- Write down the similarities and differences between occupational decisions and employment decisions.
- Think about your own employment history. Select one job-seeking experience, and write about it using the Pyramid of Information Processing Domains and the CASVE cycle.

- Draw and label Figures 3.1 and 3.2.
- Talk with a career center staff member, and identify the employment resources and services available to persons with employment problems.

REFERENCES

Peterson, G. W., Sampson, J. P., Jr., Lenz, J. G., & Reardon, R. C. (2002). Becoming career problem solvers and decision makers: A cognitive information processing approach. In D. Brown (Ed.), *Career choice and development* (4th ed.) (pp. 312–369). San Francisco: Jossey-Bass.

Peterson, G. W., Sampson, J. P., Jr., & Reardon, R. C. (1991). *Career development and services: A cognitive approach.* Pacific Grove, CA: Brooks/Cole.

Peterson, G. W., Sampson, J. P., Jr., Reardon, R. C., & Lenz, J. G. (1996). Becoming career problem solvers and decision makers: A cognitive information processing approach. In D. Brown & L. Brooks (Eds.), *Career choice and development* (3rd ed.) (pp. 423–475). San Francisco: Jossey-Bass.

Sampson, J. P., Jr., Lenz, J. G., Reardon, R. C., & Peterson, G. W. (1999). A cognitive approach to employment problem solving and decision making. *The Career Development Quarterly, 48,* 3–18.

Sampson, J. P., Jr., Peterson, G. W., Lenz, J. G., & Reardon, R. C. (1992). A cognitive approach to career services: Translating concepts into practice. *The Career Development Quarterly, 41,* 67–74.

Sampson, J. P., Jr., Peterson, G. W., Lenz, J. G., Reardon, R. C., & Saunders, D. E. (1996a). *Career Thoughts Inventory manual.* Odessa, FL: Psychological Assessment Resources.

Sampson, J. P., Jr., Peterson, G. W., Lenz, J. G., Reardon, R. C., & Saunders, D. E. (1996b). *Career Thoughts Inventory workbook.* Odessa, FL: Psychological Assessment Resources.

Sampson, J. P., Jr., Peterson, G. W., Lenz, J. G., Reardon, R. C., & Saunders, D. E. (1998). The design and use of a measure of dysfunctional career thoughts among adults, college students, and high school students: The Career Thoughts Inventory. *Journal of Career Assessment, 6,* 115–134.

Sampson, J. P., Jr., & Reardon, R. C. (1998). Maximizing staff resources in meeting the needs of job seekers in one-stop centers. *Journal of Employment Counseling, 35,* 50–68.

U.S. Office of the President, Office of Management and Budget. (1987). *Standard industrial classification.* Washington, DC: U.S. Government Printing Office.

U.S. Office of the President, Office of Management and Budget. (1997). *North American industry classification system.* Washington, DC: U.S. Government Printing Office.

4 CHAPTER Delivering Career Services

This chapter explains how the delivery of career services can contribute to career problem solving and decision making. After reviewing this chapter, the reader should have an understanding of the process of service delivery and the conditions for learning that lead to appropriate career choices. The chapter is organized as follows:

- The Use of Career Resources and Services by Individuals and Clients
- The Seven-Step Service Delivery Sequence
- Maximizing Effectiveness in Delivering Career Services
- Integrating Career, Mental Health, and Family Counseling
- Summary
- Getting the Most Benefit from Reading This Chapter

THE USE OF CAREER RESOURCES AND SERVICES BY INDIVIDUALS AND CLIENTS

Almost all persons in our society need to solve career problems and make career decisions over their life spans. People vary, however, in how much they use career resources and services. Some persons make occupational, educational, training, and employment choices without seeking career services. These persons, referred to in this book as ***individuals,*** may use ***career resources*** such as self-help books or Internet Web sites to access the assessments and information they need. Other persons, referred to in this book as

Figure 4.1 | The Seven-Step Service Delivery Sequence

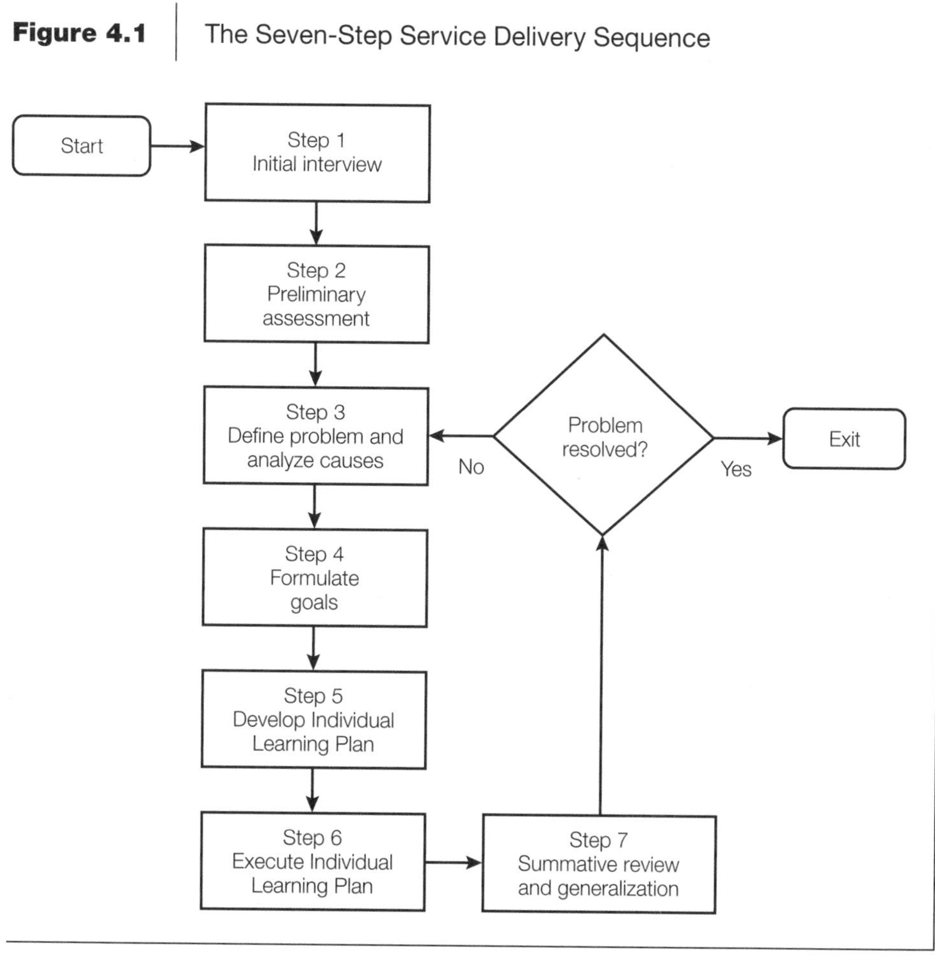

clients, recognize that they require assistance in selecting, locating, sequencing, and using career resources and seek ***career services.*** In the CIP approach, career services include self-help services, brief staff-assisted services, and individual case-managed services. This chapter examines the delivery of career services to clients. Chapter 7 discusses the use of career resources by individuals. This chapter begins with the sequence of steps for delivering career services.

THE SEVEN-STEP SERVICE DELIVERY SEQUENCE

The following seven-step service delivery sequence (shown in Figure 4.1) can be used to guide clients through the process of problem solving and decision making. Clients referred for self-help services complete only step 1, whereas clients receiving brief staff-assisted services and individual case-managed services complete all seven steps in the sequence. In group counseling, prescreening occurs in steps 1 and 2, and input

Table 4.1 The Seven-Step Service Delivery Sequence

Step	Process
1. Initial interview	An interview in which the practitioner gains qualitative information about the nature of the client's career problem.
2. Preliminary assessment	A screening instrument is completed by the client to give the practitioner quantitative information about the client's career problem and readiness for career choice.
3. Define problem and analyze causes	Practitioner and client come to a preliminary understanding of the problem, defined in terms of a gap between a real state and an ideal state. Hypotheses regarding the causes of the gap are established.
4. Formulate goals	Practitioner and client together develop a set of attainable goals to remove the gap.
5. Develop Individual Learning Plan	Practitioner assists the client in developing an Individual Learning Plan (ILP) that will identify the resources and activities necessary to help the client attain his or her counseling goals.
6. Execute Individual Learning Plan	Client carries out the ILP with the practitioner providing encouragement, information, clarification, and reinforcement.
7. Summative review and generalization	When the client has completed the ILP, the client discusses with the practitioner his or her progress toward reaching the goals established in step 4. Plans for the continued use of career services are established. A discussion is held about applying the career problem-solving approach used in this instance to the solving of career problems in the future.

from group members is included in steps 3 through 7. Although the same seven steps are used for both brief staff-assisted and individual case-managed services, the time spent and the activities used vary for each type of service delivery. Chapters 8, 9, and 10 present examples of the use of the seven-step service delivery sequence for the three levels of service. Table 4.1 describes the steps and processes involved with the seven-step service delivery sequence.

Step 1: Initial Interview

This step involves an interview in which a practitioner, with appropriate training and experience, gains qualitative information about the context and nature of the client's career problem. Beginning in the initial interview and continuing through the seven steps, the practitioner (a) attends to both the emotional and cognitive components of the client's problem; (b) develops a relationship with the client using appropriate communication and counseling skills, such as empathy, clarification, summarization, and open-ended questions; (c) uses appropriate self-disclosure to enhance the counseling relationship and to model risk taking and insight; and (d) uses immediacy to enhance the counseling relationship and identify any problems in the relationship that need attention (Peterson, Sampson, Reardon, & Lenz, 1996; Peterson, Sampson, Lenz, & Reardon, 2002). Zunker (2002) noted that specific interview techniques in career counseling include (a) rapport; (b) observation; (c) self-disclosure; (d) open- and closed-ended questions; (e) echoing, restatement, or paraphrasing; (f) continuation; and (g) staying on track.

Clients come to the initial interview in one of several ways. They may refer themselves to a counseling or career center when they become aware of a career problem (see Chapters 2 and 3 for a discussion of the Communication phase of the CASVE cycle). Clients may also accept a referral from a counseling or noncounseling practitioner and present themselves for an interview at a center that provides career services. Some counseling and career centers allow clients to call ahead for an appointment, whereas other centers prefer most clients to be seen briefly by a staff member to collaboratively determine an appropriate level of service delivery in relation to the client's needs.

The initial interview begins with a greeting, such as "What brings you here today?" or "How may I help you?" Although "How may I help you?" may be more common, "What brings you here today?" may be more appropriate by placing the focus from the very beginning of service delivery on the needs of the client as opposed to the actions (helping strategies) of the practitioner. If the client responds to the greeting with a well-focused, concrete question and there is no evidence of a substantial problem, the client may be referred to self-help services, which are described in Chapter 5. For example, if the client responds to the greeting with "I am interested in comparing the starting salaries of accountants and auditors," the practitioner would judge this response to be evidence of a concrete information request with no substantial problem apparent, and referral to self-help services would occur. If the client responds to the greeting with a diffuse question and a substantial problem is apparent, then the practitioner proceeds with a preliminary assessment as described in the following section. For example, if the client responds, "I think I want to change my program of study again, but I am uncertain about what to do or who to see," the practitioner would judge this response as a diffuse information request with a potential problem apparent where preliminary assessment would be appropriate.

During the initial interview, client versions of the pyramid and the CASVE cycle (shown in Figures 2.2 and 2.4 in Chapter 2) are often used to (a) clarify client needs, (b) provide a schema for problem solving and decision making, and (c) provide clients with information they can read after their session, which reinforces concepts discussed in counseling (Sampson, Peterson, Lenz, & Reardon, 1992).

The initial interview provides an opportunity for the client and the practitioner to explore the development of a successful relationship and allows the opportunity to observe the client and begin collecting client information. The interview also helps provide structure and an opportunity to clarify respective responsibilities in counseling (Drummond & Ryan, 1995).

Step 2: Preliminary Assessment

The practitioner can use readiness screening instruments during the preliminary assessment process to obtain quantitative information about the client's problem. The counselor begins by saying to the client, "Please complete this form to give us a better idea of your needs." Readiness measures should be brief and hand-scorable, with a manageable number of scales and appropriate norms to ensure that the measure can be practically used as a screening tool in busy counseling and career centers. If the client's test score indicates a moderate degree of readiness for career decision making and the client concurs, the practitioner can explore brief staff-assisted services, although in a few cases self-help services might be appropriate (see Figure 5.2 in Chapter 5). If the interview data and the client's test score indicate a low degree of decision-making readiness, individual items from the measure should be explored to confirm the level of readiness. If the client and the practitioner collaboratively agree that the client is having substantial difficulty with decision making, then the practitioner may recommend individual case-managed services (see Chapter 5). It is important to note that the discussion and clarification of preliminary assessment data with the client is the ultimate basis for tentatively judging client decision-making readiness. Seeking client perceptions of assessment variables implies that the client's input is valuable to the counseling process, which can make a therapeutic contribution to client self-esteem and self-efficacy.

Preliminary assessment is a key resource for determining an individual's readiness for career problem solving and decision making (Crites, 1974; Fredrickson, 1982; Super, 1983). The Career Thoughts Inventory (CTI) (Sampson, Peterson, Lenz, Reardon, & Saunders, 1996a) is a self-administered, objectively scored 48-item instrument that measures dysfunctional career thoughts. Dysfunctional career thinking limits an individual's capacity to make effective career choices (Borders & Archadel, 1987; Corbishley & Yost, 1989; Dorn & Welch, 1985; Dryden, 1979; Hornak & Gillingham, 1980; Krumboltz, 1983; Lewis & Gilhousen, 1981; Nevo, 1987; Thompson, 1976). The CTI includes items relating to self-knowledge, occupational knowledge, the CASVE cycle, and executive processing (Sampson, Peterson, Lenz, Reardon, & Saunders, 1996b). Although dysfunctional thinking in career problem solving and decision making cannot be directly measured, the existence of dysfunctional thinking can be inferred from the client's endorsement of test items that reflect dysfunctional career thoughts. "Career thoughts are defined as outcomes of one's thinking about behaviors, beliefs, feelings, plans, and/or strategies related to career problem solving and decision making" (Sampson et al., 1996b, p. 2).

The CTI can be used as a screening and needs assessment resource. In screening, the CTI Total Score is used to identify adults, college students, and high school students who are more likely to experience difficulty in career choice as a result of their dysfunctional career thoughts. In needs assessment, the CTI scales of Decision-Making Confusion, Commitment Anxiety, and External Conflict are used to identify specific dysfunctional thinking that was noted during screening (Sampson et al., 1996b). It is important to note that when discussing CTI results with the client, "negative career thinking" or "negative career thoughts" are used in place of "dysfunctional career thinking" or "dysfunctional career thoughts" to avoid inappropriately labeling the client. (See Chapter 6 for a more complete explanation of the CTI.)

The counselor can use a variety of instruments in addition to the CTI during preliminary assessment to provide the practitioner and the client with data necessary to collaboratively plan the type and amount of counseling interventions necessary to meet the needs of the client. Refer to Sampson, Peterson, Reardon, and Lenz (2000) for a review of readiness assessment measures, including the name of the instrument, authorship, the number of items, and the name of each scale. Given that readiness assessment instruments have varying theoretical perspectives, counselors can integrate other career development and personality theories into career counseling by selecting an appropriate theory-based measure.

Preliminary assessment may also include gathering demographic data, as well as a personal, educational, medical, and work history (Drummond & Ryan, 1995; Liptak, 2001; Yost & Corbishley, 1987; Zunker, 2002). These data may be collected during intake or during the initial session, depending on the operational procedures of the service delivery organization. The outcome of preliminary assessment is the collaborative classification of a client into high, moderate, and low states of readiness. Chapter 5 provides a thorough discussion of readiness assessment.

Step 3: Define Problem and Analyze Causes

The practitioner and the client come to a mutual preliminary understanding of the problem (Brown, 2003; Krumboltz & Baker, 1973; Spokane, 1991; Yost & Corbishley, 1987), defined in terms of a gap between a real state of career indecision and an ideal state of career decidedness (Cochran, 1994). The practitioner provides a brief statement that summarizes the nature of the gap and potential causes for the gap, followed by client input regarding the accuracy of the statement. It is important to frame the gap in neutral rather than dysfunctional terms. For example, the gap should be framed as a lack of confidence in decision making and a lack of necessary information (both of which can be corrected), rather than imply that the client is by nature an ineffective decision maker and that there is something inherently "wrong" with him or her. Framing the gap in neutral, learning-oriented terms helps the client perceive the gap as something that the client needs to start or stop doing that is at least partially under his or her control (Peterson et al., 1996; Peterson et al., 2002). In addition, the client and the counselor discuss the causes of the gap and how long it has existed and mutually agree on a mental model of the problem and the "problem space" (Peterson et al., 2002, p. 316). Through the process, the counselor communicates an understanding of the career problem, which, in turn, enhances the working alliance. Liptak (2001) refers to this step as case conceptualization.

Step 4: Formulate Goals

The practitioner and the client collaboratively develop a set of attainable career problem-solving and decision-making goals to remove the gap (Blustein, 1992; Brown & Brooks, 1991; Crites, 1981; Drummond & Ryan, 1995; Gysbers & Moore, 1987; Yost & Corbishley, 1987; Zunker, 2002). Goals are written down on the Individual Learning Plan, which is described more fully in the following section. The practitioner's willingness to collaborate with the client in setting goals provides an important therapeutic message that the client is in control of the service delivery process and is capable of contributing positively to counseling outcomes. For moderate- to high-readiness clients, goals may focus primarily on career choice, whereas goals for low-readiness clients may include both cognitive restructuring to enhance decision-making readiness and goals related to career choice (Peterson et al., 1996; Peterson et al., 2002). Liptak (2001) referred to this step as goal development.

Step 5: Develop Individual Learning Plan

The practitioner collaborates with the client in developing an Individual Learning Plan (ILP) that identifies a sequence of resources and activities to help the client attain his or her goals for career problem solving and decision making. (Refer to Figure 4.2 and to the sample ILPs provided in Chapters 8, 9, and 10.) Given that many clients are often overwhelmed with the content and process of career choice and are unsure of how the counseling process will proceed, the ILP provides a flexible structure that counselors and clients can use to guide the delivery of career resources and services. After the initial ILP is complete, clients should have increased confidence that the practitioner (a) cares about their welfare, (b) is capable of helping them better understand their career problem, and (c) is knowledgeable about specific resources and activities that relate to their problem. This step also establishes mutual expectations for career counseling. A successful ILP is a balance of concreteness and flexibility that evolves with the deepening understanding of the complex nature of client career problems (Liptak, 2001; Peterson et al., 1996; Peterson et al., 2002). Liptak further noted that treatment plans require the counselor to think critically about interventions that are designed to help clients achieve their goals as well as help counselors "stay on track" and not simply "follow the client" (pp. 18–19). Liptak also stated that interventions can be devised from a variety of theoretical perspectives, as we noted in Chapter 2.

The client typically completes the activities and resources included in the ILP independently over time, although there are circumstances where the practitioner and the client collaboratively work on ILP components, as described in Chapter 7. Activities and resources assigned on the ILP can be considered as homework in counseling. Brown and Brooks (1991) stated, "Homework consists of systematic assignments developed collaboratively by counselors and clients and represents a deliberate attempt to intervene in the clients' problems by involving them in appropriate action" (p. 321). Homework provides an opportunity for the practitioner to assess client motivation by examining client follow-through and for clients to see that career counseling is part of a larger process rather than a series of disjointed sessions, to maintain momentum through continuous involvement, and to develop an active approach to counseling that includes regular accomplishments (Brown & Brooks, 1991). In using homework, it is important for the practitioner to prepare the client for completing the homework by explaining the nature of the assignment, the potential benefit, and the relationship to counseling goals. It is important to follow up after the homework is completed in terms of what has been learned (Brown & Brooks, 1991). Additionally, keeping homework objectives concrete and attainable helps to make its completion self-reinforcing.

Creating the ILP involves a modified brainstorming process that promotes a creative elaboration of possible resources and activities, followed by appropriate se-

Figure 4.2 Individual Learning Plan
Career Resource Center

Goal(s): #1 ______________________________

#2 ______________________________

#3 ______________________________

Activity	Purpose/Outcome	Estimated Time Commitment	Goal #	Priority

This plan can be modified by either party based on new information learned in the activities of the action plan.
The purpose of this plan is to work toward a mutually agreed upon career goal.
Activities may be added or subtracted as needed.

______________________________ ______________________________
Student/Client Date Career Adviser Date

quencing of the options. The sequence for completing the ILP involves (a) identifying goals with the client, (b) identifying a resource or activity, (c) noting the purpose of using the resource or completing the activity, (d) noting the estimated time commitment, (e) noting the goal served by using the resource or completing the activity, and after all of the above are complete, (f) selecting a priority sequence for using resources and completing activities. By taking the time to explain the resources, activities, and corresponding purposes, the counselor helps communicate to clients that they are worth the counselor's time to provide the explanation and are capable of understanding the concepts being presented.

The quality of ILPs are improved with a collaborative approach, where the practitioner makes initial recommendations and then asks the client for his or her perceptions. This helps create "buy in" for the client, increasing the likelihood that the client will follow through, complete the assigned activities, and use the assigned resources. Having both the counselor and client sign the ILP further emphasizes the collaborative nature of the service delivery process.

In cases where a counselor perceives that a client may be easily overwhelmed (which is often the case with clients who have low readiness for career choice), the ILP should be limited at the start and grow as the client becomes more familiar and confident in the process. To be effective as a planning and monitoring tool, ILPs need to be easily added to and revised. Montgomery (1984) noted that contracts have the advantage of facilitating client understanding of the counseling process, thus reducing the likelihood of client misunderstandings and unrealistic expectations. Contracts also encourage early client assumption of responsibility in counseling.

The ILP is also a useful tool for staff training, accountability, and research. Managers can review client ILPs and discuss the thinking of trainees regarding the nature of a client's problems and the goals in relation to activities and resources recommended. The existence of client ILPs provides accountability for counselor time and efforts to meet client needs. Periodic review of ILPs also helps managers identify resources that are not being assigned and develop appropriate training or discontinue purchasing the resource. In addition, ILPs provide a rich source of research data that can be used to examine counselor judgment about counseling goals and related activities and resources.

A variety of names exist for the Individual Learning Plan. Although the generic name used in the CIP approach is ILP, other names that have been used include Individual Career Learning Plan (ICLP), which is the name used at the Florida State University Career Center, and Individual Action Plan (IAP), the name used in the *CTI Workbook*. It is important to distinguish between an ILP and an Individual Career Plan (ICP) or an Individual Career Action Plan (ICAP). The ILP has a short-term focus on the resources and services that will be used to solve career problems and make career decisions. The ILP includes resources and services that are delivered in a counseling or career center or that are directly connected to career choice, such as an information interview with an employed person. An ICP typically has a long-term focus on the education and training necessary to achieve employment in an occupation or industry. The ICP or ICAP may also be an official document that is required by organizations in order for an individual to receive funding or services.

Step 6: Execute Individual Learning Plan

The client carries out the ILP with the practitioner providing encouragement, information, clarification, and reinforcement (Peterson et al., 1996; Peterson et al., 2002). During this step, the client versions of the pyramid and the CASVE cycle (shown in

Figures 2.2 and 2.4) and the ILP are used to monitor progress in problem solving and decision making (Sampson et al., 1992). Regular review of the pyramid, the CASVE cycle, and the ILP reinforces client schemata for problem solving, increasing the chances of future gains in problem-solving capabilities. Clients with low readiness for career choice, in comparison to clients with moderate to high readiness, may need more counselor support to effectively complete their ILPs.

In cases where dysfunctional career thoughts have been identified as limiting career problem solving and decision making, clients can use their results from the CTI (Sampson et al., 1996a) to challenge and subsequently alter dysfunctional career thoughts. *Improving Your Career Thoughts: A Workbook for the Career Thoughts Inventory* (Sampson, Peterson, Lenz, Reardon, & Saunders, 1996c) introduces a four-step procedure for cognitive restructuring: identify, challenge, and alter any dysfunctional career thoughts, and then take concrete action to make career decisions. The workbook can also be used to learn about the content and process of career choice from a CIP perspective.

Step 7: Summative Review and Generalization

After completing the ILP, the client discusses with the practitioner his or her progress toward reaching the counseling goals established in step 4, as well as the progress in completing the activities and using the resources agreed to in step 5. During summative review and generalization, the client versions of the pyramid and the CASVE cycle (shown in Figures 2.2 and 2.4) may be used to (a) review progress in resolving the gap that motivated the client to seek career assistance, (b) review follow-up actions that will be part of the continuing Execution phase of the CASVE cycle, and (c) generalize the problem-solving knowledge and skills learned in counseling to other future career problems or to current and future personal and family problems (Peterson et al., 1996; Peterson et al., 2002; Sampson et al., 1992).

Liptak (2001) stated that the final phase of career counseling involved assessing client change and the impact of interventions, followed by termination. Gysbers, Heppner, and Johnston (1998) noted that effective closure in career counseling included (a) review of the content and process of career counseling sessions, (b) review of client strengths in dealing with life issues, (c) evaluation of counseling, (d) examination of important issues that might have gone unexpressed, (e) processing of emotions related to the end of the relationship, and (f) review of next steps for the client. Brown and Brooks (1991) suggested that termination tasks included (a) review of client goals and consolidation of client learning, (b) exploration of affective issues and closure of the relationship, and (c) preparation for postcounseling and transfer of learning.

MAXIMIZING EFFECTIVENESS IN DELIVERING CAREER SERVICES

In order to get the most positive benefit from using the seven-step service delivery sequence, the practitioner needs to competently attend to several counseling strategies. These strategies include (a) using well-developed communication and relationship development skills, (b) modeling and reinforcing information-seeking behavior, (c) using metaphors, and (d) providing a level of support that meets individual needs.[1] The following sections explain these strategies.

Communication and Relationship Development Skills

Basic communication and relationship development skills are essential to the effective delivery of career services using the CIP approach. By developing an effective collaborative relationship and mutual respect, the client is better able to process information and assimilate the expertise of the practitioner. An effective relationship also allows the development of trust, helping clients to have faith that their career problem can likely be solved. In this way, the relationship becomes a bridge that spans the gap between where clients are and where they want to be. Isaacson and Brown (2000) stressed the importance of developing an open, trusting relationship based on mutual respect. Liptak (2001) noted the importance of establishing a relationship quickly given the limited number of sessions typically available in career counseling. The development of an effective relationship initiates therapeutic growth in self-esteem and self-efficacy that is necessary for clients to assume personal responsibility for problem solving and decision making (Crites, 1981). Improved self-esteem and self-efficacy also enhance learning, helping clients to make better use of assessment and career information resources. Drummond and Ryan (1995) suggested that the counselor must create a safe environment for the client where conflicts, ideas, and options can be discussed without pressure. The outcome of this effort is that clients perceive that they have been heard and understood and that it is safe to return for future sessions.

Modeling and Reinforcing Information-Seeking Behavior

Modeling and reinforcement have been shown to stimulate information-seeking behavior (Blustein, 1992; Crites, 1981; Krumboltz & Schroeder, 1965; Reardon, 1984; Thoresen & Krumboltz, 1967). Some clients benefit from observing a model that locates and uses career resources. Brown and Krane (2000) noted, "Modeling involves exposing clients to individuals who have attained success in the process of career exploration, decision making, and implementation" (p. 747). The model can be a fellow client, as in group career counseling (see the case of Juanita in Chapter 9), or a practitioner, as in individual career counseling (see the case of Linda in Chapter 9). Because clients may be using career resources for the first time, they may have no prior experience to draw on in knowing how to obtain and use resources. After clients have observed the initial modeling, they can then replicate the information-seeking behavior for themselves. One technique to apply in modeling is for a practitioner to use a career resource index, resource map, or signage in a career library to

[1] The National Career Development Association (1997) has also developed the *Career Counseling Competencies.*

locate career resources even though the practitioner knows the location of a particular resource and could easily retrieve the item. The client is then knowledgeable about using the index, resource map, or signage to find other career resources. This is a small example of the metaphor of teaching a person to fish rather than giving the person a fish.

Some clients also benefit from reinforcement when they engage in appropriate information-seeking behavior. There are several opportunities to provide reinforcement to clients receiving career services. First, and simplest, the practitioner can ask clients if they are finding the information they need and respond "Good" if a client indicates that he or she has found an appropriate resource. Second, if a client asks a question, the practitioner can respond with "Good question" and then provide an appropriate answer or suggest exploratory behavior. Third, the practitioner can review a client's ILP and provide verbal reinforcement for activities completed and resources used. Each of these examples provides further opportunities to engage in relationship development, indicating that the practitioner has an interest in the welfare of the client.

Use of Metaphors

Practitioners can use metaphors to provide concrete examples of the relationships among constructs. Three examples of metaphors that can be used in the CIP approach include fishing, a building, and cooking. In Chapter 1 of this book, the metaphors of fishing and a building were used. The fishing metaphor provides a concrete example of the aim of the CIP approach. The metaphor of the building communicates the relationships among problem solving, decision making, career development, and lifestyle development. The cooking metaphor in Chapter 2 shows the interaction between the content and process of career choice. These are only examples of metaphors that can be created. Practitioners can develop their own metaphors to help individuals and clients understand concepts in the CIP approach and other career theories.

Providing a Level of Support That Meets Individual Needs

Two clients may enter a counseling or career center with similar gaps (such as indecision about selecting a program of study in college) and yet receive very different career services. Clients vary in their readiness for career choice (Sampson et al., 2000). Clients with low readiness often need the context of a helping relationship to make effective use of career resources. Some clients with low readiness will need encouragement because they lack confidence in their ability to select, locate, and use career resources (for a more complete discussion of the topic of readiness, see Chapter 5). Some clients may have had prior negative learning experiences or had prior difficulty in using a library or the Internet and therefore need assistance to effectively use a career library or Internet Web site. Some clients may be overwhelmed by the sheer mass of information available or by the complexity of their career problem and will need the service delivery process broken down into small, success-oriented experiences (as in the case of Joe in Chapter 8). Other clients may have limited literacy, limited computer skills, a learning disability, or a physical disability that may require a higher level of practitioner support.

INTEGRATING CAREER, MENTAL HEALTH, AND FAMILY COUNSELING

Clients exist as whole people with issues often in multiple arenas of their life. Career issues are sometimes intertwined with mental health and family concerns in the career problem space. Practitioners can use a variety of ways to integrate career services with mental health and family counseling. There are several ways to integrate career counseling with mental health counseling. First, clients experiencing work-adjustment issues in their employment may benefit from career counseling to clarify the relative contribution of career and mental health problems to these issues. Second, clients who are experiencing simultaneous career and mental health problems may benefit from the therapeutic experience of making slow and steady progress in resolving their career problems (with substantial assistance from a practitioner). Third, clients who have experienced a recent traumatic injury may benefit from career counseling to help them evaluate the relative merits of returning to their previous work or taking the opportunity to seek new, potentially more fulfilling career opportunities. Fourth, clients who are transitioning from inpatient or supervised living facilities may benefit from career counseling to help them make a concrete plan for independent living.

There are a number of ways to integrate career services with family counseling. First, students experiencing family conflict over their chosen field of study may benefit from a family counseling session where the respective needs, goals, and values of parents and child are explored. Second, couples in premarital counseling may benefit from career counseling to explore how issues surrounding work and life roles have the potential to influence their relationship. Third, dual-career couples may benefit from career counseling to explore the interaction of life roles and career options. Fourth, couples experiencing relationship problems can use career counseling to determine the relative contribution of career problems to relationship dynamics. Fifth, couples separating or divorcing may benefit from career counseling to resolve career and economic issues of maintaining two independent households.

SUMMARY

This chapter described the CIP approach to delivering career services and clarified the use of career resources by individuals and the use of career services by clients. A description of the seven-step service delivery sequence was provided (initial interview, preliminary assessment, define problem and analyze causes, formulate goals, develop Individual Learning Plan, execute Individual Learning Plan, and summative review and generalization). Figure 4.1 and Table 4.1 depicted the seven steps of the service delivery sequence, and Figure 4.2 presented an ILP. Four counseling strategies for maximizing effectiveness in service delivery were presented (communication and relationship development skills, modeling and reinforcing information-seeking behavior, using metaphors, and providing a level of support that meets individual needs). Finally, opportunities for integrating career, mental health, and family counseling were identified.

GETTING THE MOST BENEFIT FROM READING THIS CHAPTER

To effectively learn the material in this chapter, complete one or more of the following activities:

- Write down the similarities and differences between career resources and career services.
- Draw and label Figure 4.1.
- In your own words, describe the seven-step service delivery sequence.
- Identify the opportunities for counselor-client collaboration in the seven-step service delivery sequence.
- Describe the opportunities for the development of self-esteem and self-efficacy in the seven-step service delivery sequence. Has your own experience with career services included these therapeutic opportunities?
- Describe how communication and relationship development skills, modeling and reinforcement, metaphors, and appropriate support contribute to positive client outcomes. Has your own experience with career services included these counseling strategies?
- Identify opportunities for integrating career, mental health, and family counseling in a future work setting you are considering.

REFERENCES

Blustein, D. L. (1992). Applying current theory and research in career exploration to practice. *The Career Development Quarterly, 41,* 174–184.

Borders, D., & Archadel, K. A. (1987). Self-beliefs and career counseling. *Journal of Career Development, 14,* 69–79.

Brown, D. (2003). *Career information, career counseling, and career development* (8th ed.). Boston: Allyn & Bacon.

Brown, D., & Brooks, L. (1991). *Career counseling techniques.* Boston: Allyn & Bacon.

Brown, S. D., & Krane, N. E. R. (2000). Four (or five) sessions and a cloud of dust: Old assumptions and new observations about career counseling. In S. D. Brown & R. W. Lent (Eds.), *Handbook of counseling psychology* (pp. 740–766). New York: John Wiley.

Cochran, L. (1994). What is a career problem? *The Career Development Quarterly, 42,* 204–215.

Corbishley, M. A., & Yost, E. B. (1989). Assessment and treatment of dysfunctional cognitions in career counseling. *Career Planning and Adult Development Journal, 5* (3), 20–26.

Crites, J. O. (1974). A reappraisal of vocational appraisal. *The Vocational Guidance Quarterly, 22,* 272–279.

Crites, J. O. (1981). *Career counseling: Models, methods, and materials.* New York: McGraw-Hill.

Dorn, F. J., & Welch, N. (1985). Assessing career mythology: A profile of high school students. *The School Counselor, 33,* 136–142.

Drummond, R. J., & Ryan, C. W. (1995). *Career counseling: A developmental approach.* Boston: Allyn & Bacon.

Dryden, W. (1979). Rational-emotive therapy and its contribution to careers counseling. *British Journal of Guidance and Counselling, 7,* 181–187.

Fredrickson, R. H. (1982). *Career information.* Englewood Cliffs, NJ: Prentice Hall.

Gysbers, N. C., Heppner, M. J., & Johnston, J. A. (1998). *Career counseling: Process, issues, and techniques.* Boston: Allyn & Bacon.

Gysbers, N. C., & Moore, E. J. (1987). *Career counseling: Skills and techniques for practitioners.* Englewood Cliffs, NJ: Prentice Hall.

Hornak, J., & Gillingham, B. (1980). Career indecision: A self-defeating behavior. *The Personnel and Guidance Journal, 58,* 252–253.

Isaacson, L. E., & Brown, D. (2000). *Career information, career counseling, and career development* (7th ed.). Needham Heights, MA: Allyn & Bacon.

Krumboltz, J. D. (1983). *Private rules in career decision making* (Special Publications Series No. 38). Columbus: Ohio State University, National Center for Research in Vocational Education, Advanced Study Center (ERIC Document Reproduction Service No. ED 229 608).

Krumboltz, J. D., & Baker, R. D. (1973). Behavioral counseling for behavioral decisions. In H. Borrow (Ed.), *Career guidance for a new age* (pp. 235–283). Boston: Houghton Mifflin.

Krumboltz, J. D., & Schroeder, W. W. (1965). Promoting career planning through reinforcement. *The Personnel and Guidance Journal, 44,* 19–26.

Lewis, R. A., & Gilhousen, M. R. (1981). Myths of career development: A cognitive approach to vocational counseling. *The Personnel and Guidance Journal, 59,* 296–299.

Liptak, J. L. (2001). *Treatment planning in career counseling.* Pacific Grove, CA: Brooks/Cole.

Montgomery, D. J. (1984). Contractual arrangements. In H. D. Burck & R. C. Reardon (Eds.), *Career development interventions* (pp. 108–123). Springfield, IL: Charles C Thomas.

National Career Development Association Professional Standards Committee. (1997). *Career counseling competencies* [On-line]. Available: www.ncda.org/about/polccc.html.

Nevo, O. (1987). Irrational expectations in career counseling and their confronting arguments. *The Career Development Quarterly, 35,* 239–250.

Peterson, G. W., Sampson, J. P., Jr., Lenz, J. G., & Reardon, R. C. (2002). Becoming career problem solvers and decision makers: A cognitive information processing approach. In D. Brown (Ed.), *Career choice and development* (4th ed.) (pp. 312–369). San Francisco: Jossey-Bass.

Peterson, G. W., Sampson, J. P., Jr., Reardon, R. C., & Lenz, J. G. (1996). Becoming career problem solvers and decision makers: A cognitive information processing approach. In D. Brown & L. Brooks (Eds.), *Career choice and development* (3rd ed.) (pp. 423–475). San Francisco: Jossey-Bass.

Reardon, R. C. (1984). Use of information in career counseling. In H. D. Burck & R. C. Reardon (Eds.), *Career development interventions* (pp. 53–68). Springfield, IL: Charles C Thomas.

Sampson, J. P., Jr., Peterson, G. W., Lenz, J. G., & Reardon, R. C. (1992). A cognitive approach to career services: Translating concepts into practice. *The Career Development Quarterly, 41,* 67–74.

Sampson, J. P., Jr., Peterson, G. W., Lenz, J. G., Reardon, R. C., & Saunders, D. E. (1996a). *Career Thoughts Inventory.* Odessa, FL: Psychological Assessment Resources.

Sampson, J. P., Jr., Peterson, G. W., Lenz, J. G., Reardon, R. C., & Saunders, D. E. (1996b). *Career Thoughts Inventory: Professional manual.* Odessa, FL: Psychological Assessment Resources.

Sampson, J. P., Jr., Peterson, G. W., Lenz, J. G., Reardon, R. C., & Saunders, D. E. (1996c). *Improving your career thoughts: A workbook for the Career Thoughts Inventory.* Odessa, FL: Psychological Assessment Resources.

Sampson, J. P., Jr., Peterson, G. W., Reardon, R. C., & Lenz, J. G. (2000). Using readiness assessment to improve career services: A cognitive information processing approach. *The Career Development Quarterly, 49,* 146–174.

Spokane, A. R. (1991). *Career intervention.* Englewood Cliffs, NJ: Prentice Hall.

Super, D. L. (1983). Assessment in career guidance: Toward truly developmental counseling. *The Personnel and Guidance Journal, 61,* 555–562.

Thompson, A. P. (1976). Client misconceptions in vocational counseling. *The Personnel and Guidance Journal, 55,* 30–33.

Thoresen, C. E., & Krumboltz, J. D. (1967). Relationship of counselor reinforcement of selected responses to external behavior. *Journal of Counseling Psychology, 14,* 140–144.

Yost, E. B., & Corbishley, M. A. (1987). *Career counseling: A psychological approach.* San Francisco: Jossey-Bass.

Zunker, V. G. (2002). *Career counseling: Applied concepts of life planning* (6th ed.). Pacific Grove, CA: Brooks/Cole.

Assessing Readiness for Career Choice and Selecting Appropriate Assistance

CHAPTER **5**

This chapter introduces a model for career choice readiness and a strategy for using readiness assessment to make decisions about career interventions.[1] The chapter also presents a decision status taxonomy that is linked to readiness. After reviewing this chapter, the reader should understand how to relate a person's readiness with an appropriate level of service delivery. The chapter is organized as follows:

- A Two-Dimensional Model of Readiness for Career Choice
- Using Readiness Assessment to Make Preliminary Decisions About Career Interventions
- Relating Readiness for Career Choice to Decision Status Taxonomies
- Counseling Strategies for Enhancing Client Readiness for Career Choice
- Summary
- Getting the Most Benefit from Reading This Chapter

---

[1]Portions of this chapter have been adapted from "Using Readiness Assessment to Improve Career Services: A Cognitive Information Processing Approach," by J. P. Sampson, Jr., G. W. Peterson, R. C. Reardon, and J. G. Lenz, 2000, *The Career Development Quarterly, 49,* pp. 146–174. Copyright 1996 by the National Career Development Association. Adapted with permission.

A TWO-DIMENSIONAL MODEL OF READINESS FOR CAREER CHOICE

The preliminary assessment step in the seven-step service delivery sequence described in Chapter 4 includes an assessment of readiness for career choice. The assessment of career choice readiness is based on an additional component of CIP theory. In the CIP approach, ***readiness*** is defined as the capability of an individual to make appropriate career choices while taking into account the complexity of family, social, economic, and organizational factors that influence an individual's career development. Another way of viewing these two dimensions is that *capability* represents *internal factors* and *complexity* represents *external factors* that influence an individual's ability to make appropriate career choices.

Capability

Capability refers to the cognitive and affective capacity of an individual to engage in effective career problem solving and decision making. Individuals who are in a higher state of readiness possess the necessary cognitive capacity and positive affective states to effectively engage in career problem solving and decision making. Individuals who are less ready for effective career problem solving and decision making may be inhibited by dysfunctional thoughts and negative emotions. The following conditions influence individuals' capability to successfully engage in career problem solving and career decision making. First, individuals have a willingness to make an honest exploration of their knowledge of self (e.g., values, interests, skills, and employment preferences) in order to attain a clearer sense of identity (self-knowledge). Second, individuals have motivation to learn about the world of work in order to enhance the development of occupational knowledge (occupational knowledge). Third, individuals have a willingness to learn about and engage in career problem solving and decision making (career decision-making skills). Important components of the ability to think through a career problem and arrive at a career decision include (a) the capacity to think clearly about one's career problem, its causes, and alternative courses of action to solve it;[2] (b) confidence in one's decision-making ability to select a best alternative course of action to solve the problem and the commitment to carry out a plan of action to implement a solution; and (c) an acceptance of personal responsibility for making a career decision. Fourth, individuals have an awareness of how negative thoughts and feelings potentially limit their ability to think clearly and remain motivated to solve problems and make decisions. Individuals are willing to seek assistance when they perceive that personal or external barriers are limiting their ability to choose. Individuals also possess the capacity to monitor and regulate lower-order problem-solving and decision-making processes (executive processing) (Sampson, Peterson, Reardon, & Lenz, 2000). Within the CIP approach, the constructs of decision-making confusion and commitment anxiety from the Career

---

[2]The way in which individuals cope with various problems (such as stress, health, or disability) may make it more difficult for them think clearly about a career problem.

Table 5.1 | Primary Factors for the Capability Dimension

Primary Factors
Willingness to make an honest exploration of values, interests, skills, and employment preferences
Motivation to learn about options
Capacity to think clearly about career problems
Confidence in decision-making ability
Commitment to carry out a plan of action
Acceptance of personal responsibility for problem solving
Awareness of how thoughts and feelings influence behavior
Capacity to monitor and regulate problem solving

Thoughts Inventory (Sampson, Peterson, Lenz, Reardon, & Saunders, 1996) can be used to measure the capability dimension of readiness for career decision making. Table 5.1 summarizes factors for the capability dimension.

Complexity

Complexity refers to contextual factors, originating in the family, society, economy, or employing organizations, that make it more difficult (or less difficult) to process information necessary to solve career problems and make career decisions. The complexity dimension influences the positive or negative nature of an individual's self-talk and approach to problem solving, as well as the content of self- and occupational knowledge. Although complexity impacts each phase of the CASVE cycle, these contextual factors are particularly influential in the Communication and Valuing phases.

Fitzgerald and Betz (1994) noted that most career theories did not adequately address structural and cultural factors. Betz and Fitzgerald (1995) stated that "structural factors are characteristics of the society or organization (including its people) that limit access to or opportunities in the occupational and/or organizational environment. . . . Cultural factors are beliefs and attitudes often found among group members—often these are socialized by society (i.e., occupational and racial stereotypes), but after internalization they serve as self-perpetuating barriers to the individual" (p. 272). The complexity dimension presented here incorporates structural and cultural factors that influence career development.

Individuals who are in a higher state of readiness have fewer negative family, social, economic, and organizational factors to cope with in career problem solving and decision making. Individuals who are less ready may be coping with one severely debilitating factor (e.g., blatant discrimination based on group membership), or they may be coping with a combination of contextual factors that collectively make career problem solving and decision making more difficult (e.g., being a single parent working for a large, diversified employer with numerous positions who is downsizing during a recession). These factors can generate emotional states such as anxiety, depression, and anger that subsequently make it even more difficult to process information necessary for effective problem solving. From a CIP perspective, an individual with a more complex career problem needs to develop more-complex self-knowledge and occupational knowledge schemata to process information effectively in problem solving. For example, an individual who is attempting to balance his or her employment needs with the employment needs of his or her spouse, while also attending to the developmental needs of children and elder care for aging parents, will have to develop schemata that are capable of coping with the large number of variables inherent in a career problem of this complexity. Another approach would involve helping an overwhelmed client cope by dealing with each factor independently and sequentially, sometimes referred to as "chunking." In the previous example, the individual might work with a counselor to process and prioritize the demands associated with balancing multiple work and family issues.

Family Factors *Family factors* can contribute to or detract from readiness for career decision making. Individuals with *few family responsibilities or stressors* have fewer constraints to cope with, which can contribute to reduced complexity in career decision making. Individuals with *supportive family members* typically have more resources for understanding and coping with problems that exist. However, individuals with *multiple family responsibilities or many stressors* may need to develop more-complex schemata or isolate factors independently and manage them one at a time in order to cope with the increased variables in decision making. Family factors can include *deferral,* the decision to compromise one's career development to support the career progress of a spouse or to attend to the needs of children (Raskin, 1998). Career-family conflict may be particularly problematic for women who experience *role overload* as a result of the perception that they have primary responsibility for homemaking and child-rearing (Betz, 1995). Professional women reported that having children makes career development more difficult. They also reported that being a member of a dual-career couple makes career decision making more difficult in reconciling the needs and opportunities of one partner in relation to the needs and opportunities of the other (Betz & Fitzgerald, 1987). The amount of social support present during times of stress can make life transitions easier or more difficult (Solberg et al., 1998). However, input from family members may not always be supportive and may result in increased complexity in decision making. Even in cultures where family involvement in the decisions of a child or spouse is highly valued, *dysfunctional family input* may exist (Leong & Gim-Chung, 1995). The External Conflict scale of the Career Thoughts Inventory (Sampson et al., 1996) is designed to identify the extent to which dysfunctional thoughts associated with input from significant others impedes problem solving.

Social Factors *Social factors* can also contribute to or detract from career decision-making readiness. Whereas *social support* in the form of modeling, mentoring, networking, and caring can greatly facilitate career development, other factors such as discrimination, stereotyping, lack of role models, bias, and harassment make individuals' career decision-making process more complicated. *Stereotyping* occurs when knowledge about another person is based on general characteristics of a group of persons; *discrimination* involves acting on stereotypes in a way that harms another person. Discrimination on the basis of group membership (e.g., age, disability, ethnicity, gender, immigration status, nationality, occupation, physical characteristics, poverty level, race, religion, sexual orientation, and social class) may limit occupational, educational, training, and employment opportunities. As Niles and Harris-Bowlsbey (2002) noted, despite the increased cultural pluralism of society, there is abundant evidence that members of selected groups within society encounter persistent obstacles to their career development. These groups may also be negatively impacted by stereotyping, lack of role models, bias in education, and harassment in education and employment (Betz & Fitzgerald, 1987; Niles & Harris-Bowlsbey, 2002; Pope, 1995; Ridley, Li, & Hill, 1998). Anticipating or directly experiencing these problems may make it more difficult for individuals to develop and integrate self-knowledge and occupational knowledge schemata. Also, individuals experiencing discrimination in education, training, and employment may be denied accurate feedback on their abilities, which complicates the development of self-schemata (e.g., it is uncertain if their failure or success was based on their group membership or their actual ability to perform in class or on the job).

Economic Factors *Economic factors* can support or inhibit readiness for career decision making. The influence of economic factors on readiness can be experienced on a general and a personal level. *General economic factors* include economic trends that influence the rate of change in the labor market. For example, individuals in stable occupations and industries may be able to benefit from the *stable occupational knowledge* that is transmitted from parents, supervisors, or mentors, whereas individuals in rapidly evolving occupations and industries may have to cope with *rapidly changing occupational knowledge* with little informed assistance from parents, supervisors, or mentors. *Personal economic factors* include *inadequate financial resources,* such as poverty, that make it more difficult to obtain housing, transportation, health care, and child care. These problems make it more difficult to think clearly and engage in the complex information processing necessary to solve career problems and make career decisions. Limited personal income may also make it more difficult to fund education and training once an occupational choice is made, reinforcing negative self-talk that educational and occupational success is not possible. On the other hand, having *adequate financial resources* typically makes it easier to complete career transitions.

Organizational Factors *Organizational factors* can help or hinder the readiness of employed adults to make career decisions. The *size* of the employing organization can impact the opportunity structure and the nature of the decision-making variables considered. Large organizations typically have an internal employment market that an employee can explore in addition to seeking a job in a different organization. The *extensive opportunities* for employment in a large organization make the decision more complicated than in small organizations with *limited opportunities.* Ballantine

(1993) noted that individuals need to consider the mission and objectives of the organization in relation to their own sense of purpose and plan of action in making career decisions. In larger organizations, this process of reconciling the individual and the organization is more complex because of the diverse sources of information available. *Organizational culture* influences complexity in relation to the amount of support provided for employee career development. In an organizational culture that *supports* effective mentoring, supervision, and performance appraisal, employees are more likely to have higher readiness to make career decisions. Employees in organizations with a culture that *does not support* employee career development may be less prepared to make career decisions. The *stability* of the organization can also influence complexity. *Stable organizations* with predictable opportunity structures tend to be less complex to negotiate in comparison with *unstable organizations* that are rapidly expanding, being downsized, or taken over.

The family, social, economic, and organizational factors just described may combine to further reduce an individual's readiness for career decision making. For example, an individual experiencing discrimination may also be living with very limited financial resources and many family responsibilities while attempting to negotiate a career change in an organization that is downsizing. The External Conflict scale of the Career Thoughts Inventory (Sampson et al., 1996) can be used to measure some aspects of the complexity dimension in this readiness model. Another assessment tool for measuring the complexity dimension is the Career Attitudes and Strategies Inventory (CASI) (Holland & Gottfredson, 1994). Table 5.2 summarizes factors for the complexity dimension.

USING READINESS ASSESSMENT TO MAKE PRELIMINARY DECISIONS ABOUT CAREER INTERVENTIONS

Practitioners can use the CIP readiness model to link readiness assessment to making decisions about appropriate career interventions. Our intention is to devise a schema that is detailed enough to adequately reflect the diversity of client needs, yet easy enough for busy practitioners to use in actual practice. The cost-effectiveness of career service delivery depends on the level of staff support meeting, but not exceeding, the needs of the individual. Therefore, individuals initially judged to have *high readiness* for career choice generally will be most cost-effectively served by self-help services. Individuals initially judged to have *moderate readiness* for career choice have the potential to be most cost-effectively served by brief staff-assisted services, and individuals with *low readiness* are potentially best served by individual case-managed services. For example, practitioners would rarely sit one-on-one with high-readiness individuals while they use career resources such as an interest inventory, occupational information, or instruction on the job search process. However, practitioners may occasionally need to sit one-on-one with a low-readiness client to help him or her monitor negative self-talk that may be limiting the individual's ability to effectively use a career resource. Figure 5.1 shows the relationship between CIP readiness constructs (capability and complexity) and levels of career service delivery (self-help, brief staff-assisted, and individual case-managed).

Table 5.2 Impact of Primary and Secondary Factors on the Complexity Dimension of Career Choice Readiness

Primary Factor	Impact	Secondary Factor
Family		Family responsiblities or stressors
	positive	Few family responsibilities or stressors
	negative	Multiple family responsibilities or stressors
	positive	Supportive family members, including financial support
	negative	Deferral (compromise career development for needs of family members)
	negative	Role overload (difficulty balancing work with other life roles, e.g., homemaking, parenting, and elder care)
	negative	Dysfunctional family input
Social	positive	Support (caring relationships, financial, modeling, mentoring, networking)
	negative	Discrimination
	negative	Stereotyping
	negative	Lack of role models
	negative	Bias in education
	negative	Harassment in education and employment
Economic		General economics
	positive	Stable occupational knowledge
	negative	Rapidly changing occupational knowledge
		Personal finances
	positive	Adequate financial resources
	negative	Inadequate financial resources
Organizational (employed persons)		Size
	positive	Less complicated internal job market in small organization
	negative	More complicated internal job market in large organization
		Organizational culture
	positive	Supports employee career development
	negative	Does not support employee career development
		Stability of the organization
	positive	More predictable employment opportunities in stable organization
	negative	Less predictable employment opportunities in unstable organization

Figure 5.1 | A Two-Dimensional Model of Readiness for Career Decision Making

From "Using Readiness Assessment to Improve Career Services: A Cognitive Information Processing Approach," by J. P. Sampson, Jr., G. W. Peterson, R. C. Reardon, and J. G. Lenz, 2000, *The Career Development Quarterly, 49,* p. 161.

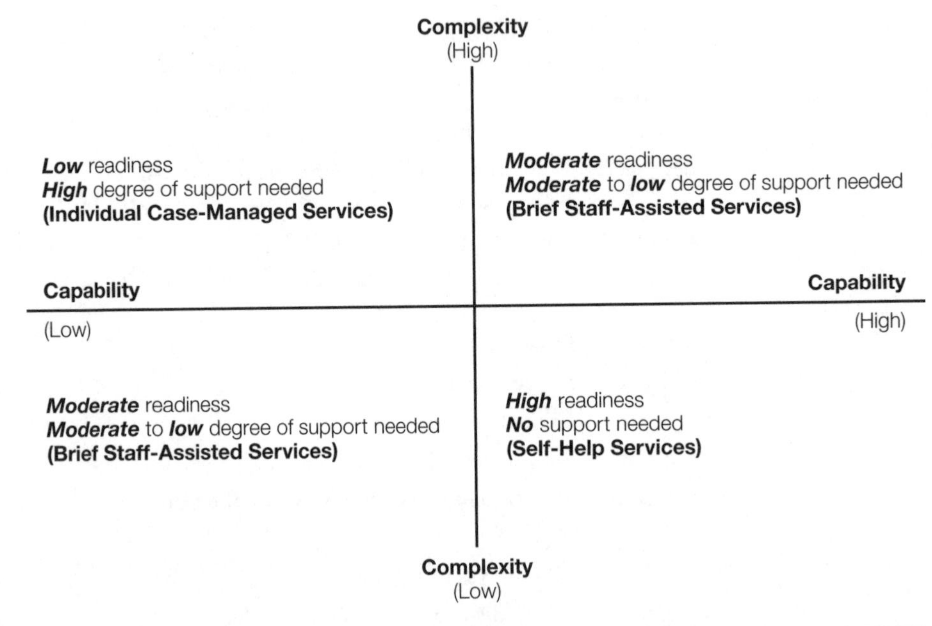

The following discussion explains how the model in Figure 5.1 is implemented in practice. Figure 5.2 illustrates the sequence for screening and selecting service delivery options based on decision-making readiness.

Several assumptions provide a foundation for the model depicted in Figure 5.2. First, a counseling or career center in an educational, agency, or organizational setting is being used to deliver resources and services to individuals seeking assistance with career, educational, training, and employment decision making. "Career resources include assessments, information sources, and instructional media. . . . Career services include varying interventions from practitioners designed to provide individuals with the *type* of assistance (e.g., counseling, career course, or workshop) and the *amount* of assistance (e.g., brief staff-assisted or individual case-managed services) they need to make career, educational, training, and employment decisions" [italics added] (Sampson, 1999, p. 245). Second, the model is based on the assumption that individuals have the option to seek career resources on a self-help basis via the Internet or other self-help resources without being physically present in a counseling or career center. Third, if either clients or practitioners identify a lack of progress in the successful use of self-help resources, readiness assessment may be sub-

Figure 5.2 | Screening and Selection of Service Delivery Options

From "Using Readiness Assessment to Improve Career Services: A Cognitive Information Processing Approach," by J. P. Sampson, Jr., G. W. Peterson, R. C. Reardon, and J. G. Lenz, 2000, *The Career Development Quarterly, 49,* p. 162.

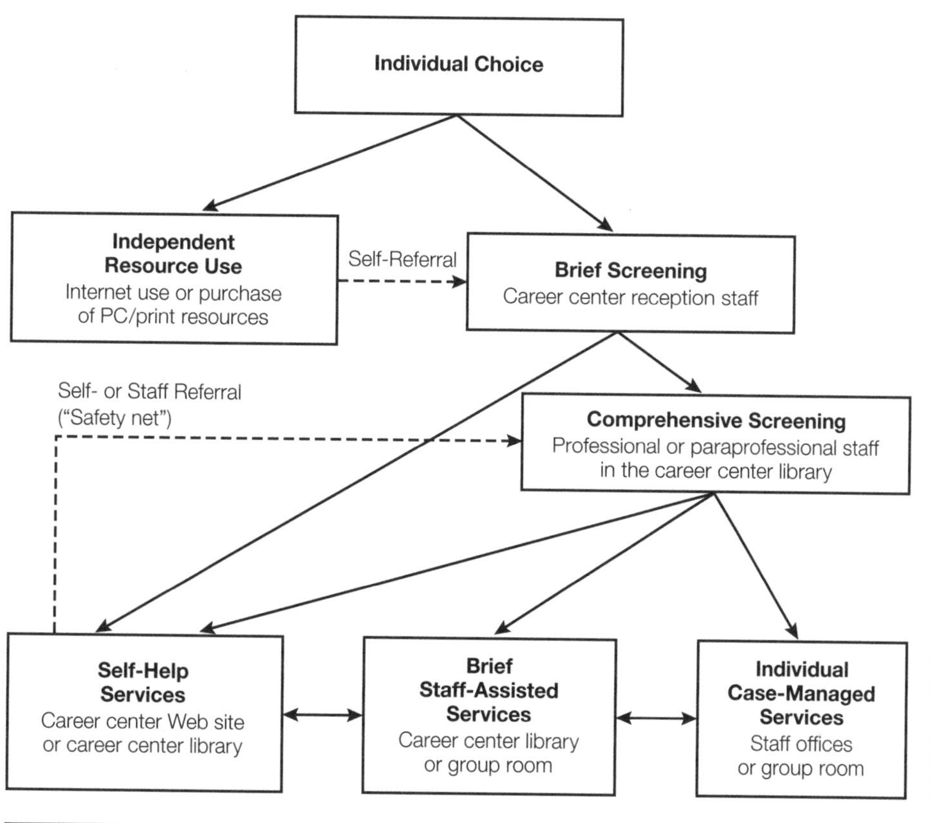

sequently used to better match client needs with service delivery options. Fourth, readiness assessment occurs in one step for some clients and two steps for others. Fifth, clients and practitioners may collaboratively decide to move from one level of assistance to another level to more appropriately meet clients' needs. For example, clients initially receiving individual case-managed services may improve in career decision-making readiness to the point where they move to brief staff-assisted services; or a client initially receiving brief staff-assisted services may be more cost-effectively served with a self-help or an individualized intervention as his or her level of readiness changes or is more accurately assessed.

The first step in this model includes an initial interview and a *brief* screening upon entry to a counseling or career center where clients are greeted and asked their reason for seeking resources or services. If the staff member judges the subsequent response to be a concrete request with no indication of a problem, then self-help access to career resources is provided without further screening. Reception staff with good verbal ability and effective communication skills can perform this brief screening function with on-the-job training.

However, a second screening that is more *comprehensive* occurs if the request for information is vague, if a career problem involves general uncertainty about a decision that needs to be made, or if disabling emotions, confusion, or a complex array of circumstances are present. This second screening involves a preliminary assessment that includes the completion and interpretation of a readiness assessment measure as well as information gained as part of the practitioner's interview with the client. We use the Career Thoughts Inventory (CTI) (Sampson et al., 1996); however, other readiness assessments could be used at this point. (See Sampson et al. [2000] for a listing of available readiness assessment measures.) Using a readiness assessment measure provides clients and practitioners with a common frame of reference for discussing individual needs.

Issues related to complexity factors may be voiced by the client during the interview, or the practitioner may choose to explore family, social, economic, and organizational factors that influence readiness. The following are examples of questions the practitioner could ask:

1. Family factors: Have your family members or other important people in your life influenced your career choices? How?
2. Social factors: Have you ever experienced discrimination in making career choices? How has this influenced your career choices?
3. Economic factors: Have your personal finances influenced your career choices? How?
4. Organizational factors: Have your current or former employers influenced your career choices? How? Has being self-employed influenced your career choices?

After considering assessment and interview results, the practitioner then makes a recommendation for an appropriate level of service (self-help, brief staff-assisted, or individual case-managed) based on the collaborative judgment of the practitioner and the client, using the model shown in Figure 5.1. As stated previously, practitioners should use a combination of test and interview data in discussing readiness with clients. The comprehensive screening function requires a practitioner who has demonstrated knowledge of career development, assessment, and career service delivery along with supervised experience in the use of readiness assessment measures.

If screening is not completed prior to receiving career services, clients with low readiness for decision making may be underserved by staff who are unaware of their substantial need for help, and high-readiness clients may be overserved by staff who deliver costly, individualized interventions when less expensive approaches would likely be as effective. In this model, screening clients at the beginning of service delivery increases the likelihood that the services delivered are congruent with the needs of clients. As a result of better allocation of scarce staff resources (Holland, 1998), staff will have time to serve more clients with briefer interventions and will have more time to deliver intensive, individualized interventions to assist clients with extensive needs (Sampson, Palmer, & Watts, 1999). The nature of self-help, brief staff-assisted, and individual case-managed services is described in the following sections.

Self-Help Services

Self-help services involve self-guided use of self-assessment, information, and instructional resources in a library-like setting or Internet-based remote setting, where resources have been designed for independent use by individuals with a *high readiness* for occupational and employment decision making. Successful use of career service interventions in a self-help mode depends on (a) accurately assessing user needs during brief screening in a career center to ensure that there is a reasonable likelihood that the independent use of career resources will meet the individual's needs; (b) accurately linking individual needs to Internet resources; (c) making available an effective "safety net" that provides reasonable opportunities for identifying individuals who are not making successful use of self-help career resources and then providing a higher level of service (e.g., brief periodic checking with individuals to ask, "Are you finding the information you need?"); (d) having staff available (in person or via telephone, videoconferencing, or e-mail) to respond to basic questions about career resource use (e.g., clarifying interpretation of self-assessment instruments and solving problems related to the use of a specific resource); (e) having available easy-to-understand text and multimedia support materials and signage to assist individuals in selecting, locating, sequencing, and using career resources and services that relate to the individual's needs; and (f) having available text and multimedia career resources that are self-instructional and easy to use, including appropriate readability for the populations being served (Sampson, 1998, 1999; Sampson & Reardon, 1998).

In self-help services, staff provide little or no assistance to high-readiness individuals. Guiding and monitoring the selection, location, sequencing, and use of resources is the responsibility of the individual, with support provided within the resources being used. Resource guides or module sheets (see Appendix A) that suggest selected assessment, information, and instructional options for common career concerns can be used to facilitate the selection process. Appropriate signage, maps, and indexes aid in locating resources. Effective self-help resources are designed to help users understand when and how the resource should be used, including the circumstances when counseling assistance may be needed. Practitioners maintain aggregate data for program evaluation and accountability. It is important to note, however, that self-help does not equate to abandonment. Staff are available to respond to questions from individuals and to periodically check to see if individuals are making good progress.

Brief Staff-Assisted Services

Brief staff-assisted services involve practitioner-guided use of assessment, information, and instructional resources in a library-like, classroom, or group setting for clients with *moderate readiness* for career choice. Successful use of career service interventions in a brief staff-assisted mode depends on (a) accurately assessing user needs during comprehensive screening to ensure that there is a reasonable likelihood that minimally supported use of career resources will meet the individual's needs;

(b) having available an effective "safety net" that provides reasonable opportunities for identifying individuals who are not making successful use of career resources; and (c) having staff available in the career library to respond to basic questions about career resource use.

In brief staff-assisted services, staff provide minimal assistance to moderate-readiness individuals. Practitioners are responsible for working collaboratively with the client to guide and monitor the selection, location, sequencing, and use of resources with the Individual Learning Plan (ILP), which documents goals and resources selected with related outcomes. As with self-help services, practitioners maintain aggregate data for program evaluation and accountability. Examples of brief staff-assisted services include (a) self-directed career decision making, (b) career courses with large group interaction, (c) short-term group counseling, and (d) workshops.

Self-Directed Career Decision Making Self-directed career decision making involves practitioner-guided use of self-assessment, information, and instructional resources in a career resource room. Practitioners complete scheduled periods of service delivery in the career library with clients served on a first-come, first-served basis. Self-directed career decision making provides an opportunity to expand the role of the practitioner from a traditional one-on-one scheduled interaction with one client in the practitioner's office to interaction with several clients simultaneously on a drop-in basis in a career library setting. Continuity in service delivery resides in staff teamwork and collaboratively developed, written ILPs, rather than the action of any single staff member. As a result, the client is not restricted to the available appointment times of any one practitioner. Clients can proceed quickly or slowly, choosing to spend considerable time working with several staff members or choosing to work with one staff member during his or her assigned times in the career library if they value the relationship with one particular practitioner. Clients, with staff input, decide how much time they need to use resources and seek staff assistance. This approach can accommodate two clients who request to receive assistance together and also allows staff to be responsive to periods of high and low client demand by "staffing up" or "staffing down" at peak- or low-demand times. The service delivery system can eliminate the backups and delays in an appointment-based system at times of high demand for services.

Staff members need to be capable of quickly establishing helping relationships, clarifying client progress in completing the ILP, and subsequently revising the ILP if new needs become apparent in working with the client. Staff also need to be able to work with several clients at one time, dividing their time between each client as appropriate. For example, a staff member may help a client interpret a computer printout from a career assessment, then help orient another client to a computer-assisted career guidance system, critique a resume for yet another client, and return to the first client to add exploratory tasks as a follow-up to reviewing the client's assessment results. Common staff training is required to reduce the chances of inconsistent or disjointed service delivery when multiple staff serve one individual (Sampson & Reardon, 1998; Sampson et al., 1999). The availability of practitioners in a library-like setting allows modeling of information-seeking behavior and the provision of timely encouragement and reinforcement of client exploratory behavior (Sampson & Reardon, 1998). Staff can assist clients in selecting, locating, sequencing, and using resources based on the creation and regular review of ILPs. Practitioner availability also provides users with opportunities for relatively immediate follow-up of resource use during the learning event. Reardon (1996) noted that self-directed career decision making could be used to cost-effectively deliver career service interventions at a cost lower than that of individual counseling.

Career Courses with Large-Group Interaction Career courses with large-group interaction involve instructor-guided use of resources in a classroom setting with minimal opportunity for personal interaction among students. Screening is typically accomplished by students self-selecting to register for the course or by having an adviser or instructor recommend the course. Student learning contracts can individualize career resources, or the same career resources can be assigned for all students in a predetermined order. Faculty grading of student assignments (e.g., use of career resources) provides the "safety net" to identify students who may have low readiness for occupational and employment decision making and who therefore may need more individualized assistance.

Short-Term Group Counseling Short-term group counseling involves practitioner-guided use of resources in a group setting with minimal opportunity for sharing information or for developing group cohesion. Screening for career services can occur at the same time as screening for group membership. Members' use of career resources can be linked to specific needs via an ILP for each group member. If practitioners follow a more structured group approach where all members use a common set of career resources, then practitioners can structure group sessions to process members' experience in using specific resources.

Workshops Workshops involve practitioner-guided use of resources in a group setting with little or no opportunity for sharing information or for developing group cohesion among individuals. In this way, workshops are different from group counseling. If a workshop has a predetermined sequence of topics, resource use follows the topic sequencing. If workshop topics vary each time according to participant needs, resource use will also vary in this way.

Individual Case-Managed Services

Individual case-managed services involve practitioner-guided use of assessment, information, and instructional resources in an individual office, classroom, or group setting for clients with *low readiness* for career choice. Successful use of career service interventions in an individual case-managed mode depends on (a) accurately assessing user needs during comprehensive screening to ensure that there is a reasonable likelihood that the supported use of career resources will meet the individual's needs; (b) having staff available in the career library to respond to basic questions about career resource use (e.g., clarifying interpretation of self-assessment instruments and solving problems related to the use of a specific resource); and (c) having practitioners available who are competent to integrate career and mental health counseling in dealing with individuals' low readiness for career choice.

In individual case-managed services, staff provide substantial assistance to low-readiness individuals. As with brief staff-assisted services, practitioners are responsible for collaboratively guiding and monitoring the selection, location, sequencing, and use of resources as documented on the ILP. In comparison with other levels of service delivery, the individualized approach includes the maintenance of individual records to document services. Examples of individual case-managed services include (a) individual counseling, (b) career courses with small-group interaction, and (c) long-term group counseling.

Individual Counseling Individual counseling involves appointment-based, practitioner-guided use of resources in an individual office setting. Individual counseling offers maximum flexibility in relating counseling interventions to the needs of the individual. The time available allows the practitioner to provide more-detailed orientations and follow-up to resource use, as well as assistance in actually using resources (such as occupational information). The nature of an individual's use of career resources provides practitioners with information about factors that may be contributing to low readiness for decision making. For example, an individual's comments about potential occupations resulting from the completion of an interest inventory may indicate specific negative self-talk that can be identified, challenged, and altered. The nature of the supportive relationship established between the practitioner and the client over time may be a key element in client willingness to risk the inevitable change associated with career decision making.

Career Courses with Small-Group Interaction Career courses with small-group interaction involve instructor-guided use of resources in a classroom setting with considerable opportunity for personal interaction among individuals and instructors. The previously described counseling interventions for a career course with large-group interaction apply here as well. The difference is that by meeting with small groups of students in addition to giving large-group lectures, instructors have the opportunity to gain more information about the nature of student decision-making difficulties and can provide more assistance to students in improving their readiness for occupational and employment choice (Reed, Reardon, Lenz, & Leierer, 2001). Dividing the class into small groups of students can improve the capability of students to learn from each other via modeling and reinforcement.

Long-Term Group Counseling Long-term group counseling involves practitioner-guided use of resources in a group setting with considerable opportunity for sharing information and developing group cohesion among members (Corey, 1999). The previously described counseling interventions for short-term group counseling apply here as well. The difference is that the longer duration of the group allows the development of group cohesion necessary to confront and change typically long-established problematic patterns of thinking, feeling, and behaving. The longer duration also provides potential support over a larger proportion of the decision-making process—for example, supporting members in following through on an action plan to implement their goals. This type of group allows for more integration of career and mental health issues for low-readiness clients.

Table 5.3 | Variation in Career Interventions by Level of Service Delivery

	Self-Help Services	Brief Staff-Assisted Services	Individual Case-Managed Services
Readiness of the user	High	Moderate	Low
Assistance provided	Little or none	Minimal	Substantial
Who guides resource use	The user	A practitioner	A practitioner
Where services are provided	Library-like or remote settings	Library-like, classroom, or group settings	Individual office, classroom, or group settings
Selection and sequencing of resources and services	Resource guides	Individual Learning Plans	Individual Learning Plans
Record keeping	Aggregate data for program evaluation and accountability	Aggregate data for program evaluation and accountability	Individual records

In summary, self-help services, brief staff-assisted services, and individual case-managed services vary in terms of the readiness of the user, the level of assistance provided, the person who guides resource use, the place where the services are provided, the selection and sequencing of resources and services, and record keeping. Table 5.3 summarizes the variations among these three levels of service delivery.

RELATING READINESS FOR CAREER CHOICE TO DECISION STATUS TAXONOMIES

A variety of decision status taxonomies have been created to assist practitioners in more readily understanding clients' needs and selecting appropriate interventions.[3] Taxonomies typically integrate varying amounts of theory, research, and practice in describing potential client needs. Some taxonomies also include a specific measure of the elements in the taxonomy (e.g., Gati, Krausz, & Osipow, 1996). See Herr and Cramer (1996) for a review of taxonomies for identifying client problems in career decision making. The CIP decision status taxonomy in career problem solving and decision making (Peterson, Sampson, & Reardon, 1991; Peterson, Sampson, Reardon, & Lenz, 1996) comprises three major categories that include *decided, undecided,* and *indecisive.*

[3]Portions of this section on decision status taxonomies were adapted from "Becoming Career Problem Solvers and Decision Makers: A Cognitive Information Processing Approach," by G. W. Peterson, J. P. Sampson, Jr., R. C. Reardon, and J. G. Lenz, 1996, in D. Brown & L. Brooks (Eds.), *Career Choice and Development* (3rd ed.) (pp. 423–475). San Francisco: Jossey-Bass. Adapted with permission of John Wiley & Sons, Inc.

Decided Individuals

Decided individuals have made a private or public commitment to a specific occupational choice. Three subcategories of decided individuals exist in this taxonomy. First, individuals who are able to specify a choice but wish to confirm or clarify the appropriateness of their choice by contrasting it with other possible choices are categorized as ***decided-confirmation.*** For example, some individuals have a tendency to be careful and systematic in their approach to making any important decision. These individuals wish to ensure that they have completed the Valuing phase of the CASVE cycle to the best of their ability. Second, individuals who are able to specify a choice but who need help in implementing their choice are categorized as ***decided-implementation.*** For example, individuals may need assistance in getting a job or selecting training options related to an occupation chosen in the Valuing phase of the CASVE cycle. These individuals either realize they need assistance before they begin the Execution phase of the CASVE cycle, or they have attempted execution previously and experienced difficulty. Third, individuals who have made a public commitment to a specific choice as a strategy for avoiding conflict with significant others but who are actually undecided or indecisive are categorized as ***decided–conflict avoidance.*** Janis and Mann (1977) referred to "unconflicted change," where a decision maker chooses the most immediately available option in order to reduce stress. In reality, these persons often have the characteristics of undecided or indecisive individuals, described in the following sections.

Undecided Individuals

Undecided individuals have not made a commitment to a specific occupational choice due to gaps in the knowledge necessary for choosing. This taxonomy includes three subcategories of undecided individuals. First, individuals who are unable to specify a choice but have no need to make a choice at the present time are categorized as ***undecided–deferred choice,*** which at times may be an appropriate career choice strategy (Holland & Holland, 1977; Krumboltz, 1992). For example, a college freshman taking general education courses and participating in various campus activities to obtain knowledge and life experience prior to committing to a college major at the end of the sophomore year can appropriately defer a choice until a later date. These types of undecided individuals typically do not seek career services because they lack external and internal cues in the Communication phase of the CASVE cycle that a gap needing resolution exists. Second, individuals who need to choose, are unable to commit to a choice, and who lack self-, occupational, and/or decision-making knowledge are categorized as ***undecided-developmental*** (Chartrand et al., 1994; Fuqua & Hartman, 1983; Larson, Heppner, Ham, & Dugan, 1988). These individuals should not be considered dysfunctional; rather, they have not gained the knowledge or experience necessary to make a choice. In terms of the pyramid, these individuals need clarification or addition of self-, occupational, and/or decision-making knowledge and tend to have metacognitions that are less negative with respect to what is necessary to enable them to make a choice (in comparison with indecisive individuals). Third, individuals who have the characteristics of someone

Table 5.4 Career Decision Status Taxonomy

Decided Individuals
Confirmation
Implementation
Conflict avoidance
Undecided Individuals
Deferred choice
Developmental
Multipotential
Indecisive Individuals

who is undecided, with the addition of having an overabundance of talents, interests, and opportunities, are categorized as ***undecided-multipotential*** (Fredrickson, 1982; Pask-McCartney & Salomone, 1988). These individuals are often overwhelmed with the diversity of available options and may experience pressure from significant others, including family members, for high levels of achievement.

Indecisive Individuals

Individuals who have not made a commitment to a specific occupational choice due to gaps in the knowledge necessary for choosing and who have a maladaptive approach to problem solving in general that is accompanied by a dysfunctional level of anxiety are categorized as ***indecisive*** (Chartrand et al., 1994; Crites, 1969; Fuqua & Hartman, 1983; Herr & Cramer, 1996; Holland & Holland, 1977; Lucas, 1993; Lucas & Epperson, 1990; Salomone, 1982; Savickas, 1989). Indecisive individuals are similar to undecided individuals in terms of knowledge gaps but differ in terms of executive processing. Executive processing deficiencies present in indecisive individuals may include excessive negative self-talk, attention deficits, or confused thought processes. These deficiencies limit the acquisition of decision-making skills and occupational knowledge, as well as the clarity and consistency of self-knowledge. Subsequent awareness of these limitations only serves to reinforce perceived inadequacy in decision making. Table 5.4 summarizes the three levels of the decision status taxonomy.

Determining Decision-Making Status

The first step in determining the decision-making status of clients is relatively straightforward. If the client is able to specify an occupational choice, he or she is tentatively considered decided, whereas the inability of the client to specify a choice leads to a tentative categorization of undecided. Asking clients about their current status or using the Occupational Alternatives Question (Zener & Schnuelle, 1972; modified by Slaney, 1980) provides a quick and effective method of tentatively differentiating decided versus undecided clients. If the client is tentatively judged by the counselor as undecided, the next task is to determine if the client is undecided or indecisive. The undecided-indecisive judgment is more difficult to make than the decided-undecided judgment. Using a brief readiness assessment instrument during the preliminary assessment phase of the seven-step service delivery sequence, described in the previous chapter and earlier in this chapter, is a key resource for distinguishing the undecided-indecisive decision state. For example, a high score on the CTI (Sampson et al., 1996) may (or may not) indicate indecisiveness. After discussing selected item responses with the client, the counselor can make a tentative judgment that the client is undecided or indecisive. This judgment is reevaluated on an ongoing basis as counseling proceeds. Listening for negative client self-talk embedded in client statements (e.g., "I don't think I could learn very much from an information interview") and observing if clients have difficulty following through on the use of assessment and information resources (e.g., consistently missing scheduled appointments on a computer-assisted career guidance system) can provide additional data that may confirm a judgment of undecidedness or indecisiveness.

Relating Decision-Making Status to Services Needed

Individuals categorized as *decided-confirmation* or *undecided-developmental* are most likely to benefit from services that engage the complete CASVE cycle, including developing an awareness of the importance of positive self-talk in successful problem solving. Individuals categorized as *decided-implementation* are most likely to benefit from services that focus on the Execution phase of the CASVE cycle (planning a preparation program, reality testing, and job placement as appropriate). Individuals categorized as *decided–conflict avoidance* are most likely to benefit from assistance to challenge and alter an inappropriate coping strategy, followed by services that fit their actual undecided or indecisive decision-making status. Individuals categorized as *undecided–deferred choice* are most likely to benefit from various career education programs designed to proactively prepare individuals to complete various age-appropriate career development tasks. Individuals categorized as *undecided-multipotential* are most likely to benefit from services that engage the complete CASVE cycle and focus on potential family or cultural issues that may intersect with the career problem-solving and decision-making process. Individuals categorized as *indecisive* are most likely to benefit from services that engage the complete CASVE cycle, with particular attention to the problematic impact of anxiety and negative self-talk on career problem solving. In general, indecisive clients, in comparison with decided and undecided clients, may need more individual assistance from a counselor to make an effective career choice and may also need attention paid to mental health issues. In relation to the readiness assessment model, decided and undecided individuals are most cost-effectively served by self-help and brief staff-assisted interventions, whereas indecisive individuals are most cost-effectively served by individual case-managed interventions (Sampson et al., 2000).

Counseling Strategies for Enhancing Client Readiness for Career Choice

Readiness for career decision making, like career maturity, is not a static individual characteristic. Over time, it is possible for the capability of the individual to increase and the complexity of his or her career problem to decrease. When readiness assessment indicates "that an individual's readiness has been less than optimal, intervention would be directed to remediating those aspects of the individual's readiness that have lagged" (Phillips & Blustein, 1994, p. 65). Savickas and Walsh (1996) stated that career theory needs to go beyond clarifying vocational behavior to include procedures for fostering the career development of clients. Blustein and Flum (1999) stated that "interventions need to help clients attain a readiness to make career decisions and clarify their interests" (p. 362). Levinson, Ohler, Caswell, and Kiewra (1998) noted that a primary goal of career counseling is fostering career decision-making readiness.

The counselor can assist the client in dealing more effectively with the capability dimension of readiness by helping the client view career services as providing a potential opportunity to help him or her become more adept at career problem solving and decision making. As a result, the client will likely be more motivated to identify, challenge, and alter past dysfunctional thoughts that have limited his or her decision-making capability. The client will also likely be better motivated to follow through with the exploratory behaviors necessary to develop the self-, occupational, and decision-making schemata necessary to make an appropriate career choice. The counselor can also assist the client in dealing more effectively with the complexity dimension of readiness by helping the client acquire more-adaptive coping strategies related to family, social, economic, and organizational factors that influence career development. The establishment of an effective helping relationship; collaboration in assessing needs, setting goals, and selecting resources; the use of theory to better understand and manage the decision-making process; the modeling and reinforcement of information-seeking behavior; and framing the problem space in neutral rather than in judgmental terms can help provide the conditions necessary to help clients improve their readiness for career decision making (Peterson et al., 1996).

SUMMARY

This chapter presented a two-dimensional model of readiness for career choice that included capability and complexity (family, social, economic, and organizational factors). The level of client readiness for career choice was then related to three levels of service delivery (self-help services, brief staff-assisted services, and individual case-managed services). A flowchart relating brief and comprehensive screening to the three levels of service delivery was presented. Readiness was then related to a decision status taxonomy (decided individuals, undecided individuals, and indecisive individuals). Finally, counseling strategies for enhancing client readiness for career choice were presented.

GETTING THE MOST BENEFIT FROM READING THIS CHAPTER

To effectively learn the material in this chapter, complete one or more of the following activities:

- Describe the factors associated with the readiness dimensions of capability and complexity.
- Identify how the dimensions of capability and complexity have influenced your own readiness for career choice.
- Draw and label Figure 5.1.
- Draw and label Figure 5.2.
- Describe self-help services, brief staff-assisted services, and individual case-managed services. What has been your own experience with any of these career services?
- Compare and contrast decided, undecided, and indecisive individuals.
- Identify how counseling can help improve an individual's readiness for career choice.

REFERENCES

Ballantine, M. (1993). A new framework for the design of career interventions in organisations. *British Journal of Guidance & Counselling, 21,* 233–245.

Betz, N. E. (1995). Basic issues and concepts in career counseling for women. In W. B. Walsh & S. H. Osipow (Eds.), *Career counseling for women* (pp. 1–41). Mahwah, NJ: Lawrence Erlbaum Associates.

Betz, N. E., & Fitzgerald, L. F. (1987). *The career psychology of women.* Orlando, FL: Academic Press.

Betz, N. E., & Fitzgerald, L. F. (1995). Career assessment and intervention with racial and ethnic minorities. In F. T. L. Leong (Ed.), *Career development and vocational behavior of racial and ethnic minorities* (pp. 263–279). Mahwah, NJ: Lawrence Erlbaum Associates.

Blustein, D. L., & Flum, H. (1999). A self-determination perspective of interests and exploration in career development. In M. L. Savickas & A. R. Spokane (Eds.), *Vocational interests: Meaning, measurement, and counseling use* (pp. 345–368). Palo Alto, CA: Davies-Black Publishing.

Chartrand, J. M., Martin, W. F., Robbins, S. B., McAuliffe, G. J., Pickering, J. W., & Calliotte, A. A. (1994). Testing a level versus an interactional view of career indecision. *Journal of Career Assessment, 2,* 55–69.

Corey, G. (1999). *Theory and practice of group counseling* (5th ed.). Pacific Grove: CA: Brooks/Cole.

Crites, J. O. (1969). *Vocational psychology.* New York: McGraw-Hill.

Fitzgerald, L. F., & Betz, N. E. (1994). Career development in a cultural context: The role of gender, race, class, and sexual orientation. In M. L. Savickas & R.W. Lent (Eds.), *Convergence in career development theories* (pp. 103–117). Palo Alto, CA: Davies-Black Publishing.

Fredrickson, R. H. (1982). *Career information.* Englewood Cliffs, NJ: Prentice Hall.

Fuqua, D. R., & Hartman, B. W. (1983). Differential diagnosis and treatment of career indecision. *The Personnel and Guidance Journal, 62,* 27–29.

Gati, I., Krausz, M., & Osipow, S. H. (1996). A taxonomy of difficulties in career decision making. *Journal of Counseling Psychology, 43,* 510–526.

Herr, E. L., & Cramer, S. H. (1996). *Career guidance and counseling through the life span: Systematic approaches* (5th ed.). New York: HarperCollins.

Holland, J. L. (1998). Debate: New and old perspectives. *British Journal of Guidance and Counselling, 26,* 555–558.

Holland, J. L., & Gottfredson, G. D. (1994). *Career Attitudes and Strategies Inventory.* Odessa, FL: Psychological Assessment Resources.

Holland, J. L., & Holland, J. E. (1977). Vocational indecision: More evidence and speculation. *Journal of Counseling Psychology, 24,* 404–415.

Janis, I. L., & Mann, L. (1977). *Decision making: A psychological analysis of conflict, choice, and commitment.* New York: Free Press.

Krumboltz, J. D. (1992). The wisdom of indecision. *Journal of Vocational Behavior, 41,* 239–244.

Larson, L. M., Heppner, P. P., Ham, T., & Dugan, K. (1988). Investigating multiple subtypes of career indecision through cluster analysis. *Journal of Counseling Psychology, 35,* 439–446.

Leong, F. T. L., & Gim-Chung, R. H. (1995). Career assessment and intervention with Asian Americans. In F. T. L. Leong (Ed.), *Career development and vocational behavior of racial and ethnic minorities* (pp. 193–226). Mahwah, NJ: Lawrence Erlbaum Associates.

Levinson, E. M., Ohler, D. L., Caswell, S., & Kiewra, K. (1998). Six approaches to the assessment of career maturity. *Journal of Counseling and Development, 76,* 475–482.

Lucas, M. S. (1993). A validation of types of career indecision at a counseling center. *Journal of Counseling Psychology, 40,* 440–446.

Lucas, M. S., & Epperson, D. L. (1990). Types of vocational undecidedness: A replication and refinement. *Journal of Counseling Psychology, 37,* 382–388.

Niles, S. G., & Harris-Bowlsbey, J. (2002). *Career development interventions in the 21st century.* Upper Saddle River, NJ: Merrill/Prentice-Hall.

Pask-McCartney, C., & Salomone, P. R. (1988). Difficult cases in career counseling: III. The multipotentialed client. *The Career Development Quarterly, 36,* 231–240.

Peterson, G. W., Sampson, J. P., Jr., & Reardon, R. C. (1991). *Career development and services: A cognitive approach.* Pacific Grove, CA: Brooks/Cole.

Peterson, G. W., Sampson, J. P., Jr., Reardon, R. C., & Lenz, J. G. (1996). Becoming career problem solvers and decision makers: A cognitive information processing approach. In D. Brown & L. Brooks (Eds.), *Career choice and development* (3rd ed.) (pp. 423–475). San Francisco: Jossey-Bass.

Phillips, S. D., & Blustein, D. L. (1994). Readiness for career choices: Planning, exploring, and deciding. *The Career Development Quarterly, 43,* 63–67.

Pope, M. (1995). Career interventions for gay and lesbian clients: A synopsis of practice knowledge and research needs. *The Career Development Quarterly, 44,* 191–203.

Raskin, P. M. (1998). Career maturity: The constructs validity, vitality, and viability. *The Career Development Quarterly, 47,* 32–35.

Reardon, R. C. (1996). A program and cost analysis of a self-directed career decision-making program in a university career center. *Journal of Counseling and Development, 74,* 280–285.

Reed, C., Reardon, R., Lenz, J., & Leierer, S. (2001). Reducing negative career thoughts with a career course. *The Career Development Quarterly, 50,* 158–167.

Ridley, C. R., Li, L. C., & Hill, C. L. (1998). Multicultural assessment: Reexamination, reconceptualization, and practical application. *The Counseling Psychologist, 26,* 827–910.

Salomone, P. R. (1982). Difficult cases in career counseling: II. The indecisive client. *The Personnel and Guidance Journal, 60,* 496–500.

Sampson, J. P., Jr. (1998). *Integrating Internet-based distance guidance with services provided in career centers.* Plenary paper presented at a seminar entitled Guidance in Open Learning Environments in the Finnish Polytechnics, at Espoo-Vantaa Polytechnic, Vantaa, Finland.

Sampson, J. P., Jr. (1999). Integrating Internet-based distance guidance with services provided in career centers. *The Career Development Quarterly, 47,* 243–254.

Sampson, J. P., Jr., Palmer, M., & Watts, A. G. (1999). *Who needs guidance?* Occasional paper, Centre for Guidance Studies, University of Derby, United Kingdom.

Sampson, J. P., Jr., Peterson, G. W., Lenz, J. G., Reardon, R. C., & Saunders, D. E. (1996). *Career Thoughts Inventory.* Odessa, FL: Psychological Assessment Resources.

Sampson, J. P., Jr., Peterson, G. W., Reardon, R. C., & Lenz, J. G. (2000). Using readiness assessment to improve career services: A cognitive information processing approach. *The Career Development Quarterly, 49,* 146–174.

Sampson, J. P., Jr., & Reardon, R. C. (1998). Maximizing staff resources in meeting the needs of job seekers in one-stop centers. *Journal of Employment Counseling, 35,* 50–68.

Savickas, M. L. (1989). Annual review: Practice and research in career counseling and development, 1988. *The Career Development Quarterly, 38,* 100–134.

Savickas, M. L., & Walsh, W. B. (1996). Introduction: Toward convergence between career theory and practice. In M. L. Savickas & W. B. Walsh (Eds.), *Handbook of career counseling theory and practice* (pp. xi–xvi). Palo Alto, CA: Davies-Black Publishing.

Slaney, R. B. (1980). Expressed vocational choice and vocational indecision. *Journal of Counseling Psychology, 27,* 122–129.

Solberg, V. S., Gusavac, N., Hamann, T., Felch, J., Johnson, J., Lamborn, S., & Torres, J. (1998). The adaptive success identity plan (ASIP): A career intervention for college students. *The Career Development Quarterly, 47,* 48–95.

Zener, T. B., & Schnuelle, L. (1972). *An evaluation of the Self-Directed Search* (Research Rep. 124). Baltimore: Johns Hopkins University, Center for Social Organization of Schools (ERIC Document Reproduction Service No. ED 061 458).

Using the Career Thoughts Inventory to Measure Career Choice Readiness

CHAPTER 6

This chapter describes the use and development of the Career Thoughts Inventory (CTI). After reviewing this chapter, the reader should understand how the CTI can be used as a readiness screening measure and as a resource for identifying, challenging, and altering negative career thoughts. The reader should also understand how the CTI was developed. Readers can review information on the CTI at www.career.fsu.edu/techcenter/designing_career_services/. The chapter is organized as follows:

- Background of the CTI
- Use of the CTI and the *CTI Workbook*
- CTI Case Studies
- Development of the CTI and the *CTI Workbook*
- Summary
- Getting the Most Benefit from Reading This Chapter

BACKGROUND OF THE CTI

The Career Thoughts Inventory (Sampson, Peterson, Lenz, Reardon, & Saunders, 1996a, 1998)[1] is a theory-based assessment and intervention

---

[1]This chapter describes the design and use of the Career Thoughts Inventory. Much of the material in this chapter is adapted from *Career Thoughts Inventory: Professional Manual,* by J. P. Sampson, Jr., G. W. Peterson, J. G. Lenz, R. C. Reardon, & D. E. Saunders, 1996b, Odessa, FL: Psychological Assessment Resources. Reproduced by special permission of the publisher, Psychological Assessment Resources, Inc., 16204 North Florida Avenue, Lutz, FL 33549. Further reproduction is prohibited without permission from PAR, Inc.

resource intended to improve the quality both of career decisions made by adults, college students, and high school students and of career services delivered to these individuals. The CTI is a self-administered, objectively scored measure of dysfunctional thoughts in career problem solving and decision making. The CTI and *Improving Your Career Thoughts: A Workbook for the Career Thoughts Inventory* (the *CTI Workbook*) (Sampson, Peterson, Lenz, Reardon, & Saunders, 1996c) are based on a ***Cognitive Information Processing*** (CIP) theoretical approach to career development and career services (Peterson, Sampson, & Reardon, 1991; Peterson, Sampson, Reardon, & Lenz, 1996; Peterson, Sampson, Lenz, & Reardon, 2002) and a ***cognitive therapy*** theoretical approach to mental health and mental health services (Beck, 1976; Beck, Emery, & Greenberg, 1985; Beck, Rush, Shaw, & Emery, 1979).

The CTI was developed to integrate the functions of assessment and intervention within a career service delivery context. The goal was to link the measure and the accompanying workbook in such a way that clients might make more efficient use of their time and their human service practitioner's time, while more effectively incorporating the assessment concepts into intervention strategies for change. As a result, the CTI comprises traditional assessment components (*CTI Test Booklet* and *Professional Manual*) (Sampson, Peterson, Lenz, Reardon & Saunders, 1996b) plus a learning resource (the *CTI Workbook*).

Cognitive Information Processing theory postulates that effective career problem solving and decision making require the effective processing of information in the following four domains: (a) self-knowledge; (b) occupational knowledge; (c) decision-making skills (Communication, Analysis, Synthesis, Valuing, and Execution); and (d) executive processing (Peterson et al., 1991; Peterson et al., 1996; Peterson et al., 2002). In order to simplify the process of instrument development, the above domains and subcomponents were organized into eight Cognitive Information Processing (CIP) *content dimensions* that include the following:

1. Self-knowledge
2. Occupational knowledge
3. Communication
4. Analysis
5. Synthesis
6. Valuing
7. Execution
8. Executive processing

Dysfunctional thinking in any of the CIP content dimensions could impair an individual's ability to solve career problems and make career decisions. For the purposes of this instrument, the terms *thinking* and *information processing* are used synonymously.

Cognitive therapy theoretical concepts (Beck, 1976; Beck et al., 1979; Beck et al., 1985) specify that dysfunctional cognitions have a detrimental impact on behavior and emotions. Through cognitive restructuring, collaborative empiricism, attention to emotions, and the development of an effective helping relationship, clients learn to replace dysfunctional cognitions with functional cognitions, resulting in positive changes in behavior and emotions.

In developing the CTI, the authors made the following assumption: Although dysfunctional thinking in career problem solving and decision making cannot be measured directly, it can be inferred from an individual's endorsement of statements (test items) reflecting a variety of dysfunctional career thoughts. For the purposes of this instrument, ***career thoughts*** are defined as outcomes of one's thinking about assumptions, attitudes, behaviors, beliefs, feelings, plans, and/or strategies related to career problem solving and decision making. Regardless of whether CTI items refer to assumptions, attitudes, behaviors, beliefs, feelings, plans, and/or strategies, all items reflect dysfunctional thinking that inhibits effective career problem solving and decision making.

USE OF THE CTI AND THE *CTI WORKBOOK*

In service delivery, the CTI can be used by practitioners to help adults, college students, and high school students identify, challenge, and subsequently alter dysfunctional thinking that impairs their ability to effectively solve career problems and make career decisions. Specifically, the CTI can be used as an instrument for screening and needs assessment, as well as a learning resource in delivering career services. The *CTI Professional Manual* provides additional details on the use of the CTI and *CTI Workbook,* including specific strategies for individual counseling, group counseling, self-directed career decision making, workshops, and curricular interventions.

Screening

As a screening measure, the CTI can be used to identify individuals who are likely to encounter difficulties in making career choices as a result of their dysfunctional thinking. Individuals identified as having a number of dysfunctional thoughts will likely have lower readiness for career choice and require more assistance in making effective use of career services, whereas individuals identified with fewer dysfunctional thoughts will likely have higher readiness for career choice and require less assistance. The practitioner can use the *CTI Workbook* to facilitate an individual's understanding of how much help he or she will likely need to make effective use of career services.

The CTI Total Score is a single global indicator of dysfunctional thinking in career problem solving and decision making. Lower CTI Total Scores tend to reflect limited dysfunctional career thinking and are best interpreted at the item level. Higher CTI Total Scores tend to reflect greater dysfunctional career thinking and the emergence of specific issues that can be interpreted at both scale and item levels. As CTI Total Scores increase, scale scores tend to function independently.

By comparing the individual's CTI Total Score with normative data, it is possible to determine if the individual's level of dysfunctional thoughts is greater than or less than those of a normally distributed group of adults, college students, or high school students. Organizations or individual practitioners are strongly encouraged to develop local CTI norms to allow more-specific population comparisons, provided expertise is available in calculating norms.

The convergent validity evidence presented in the *CTI Professional Manual* can be used as a starting point for developing interpretive hypotheses. For *all groups,* the CTI Total Score was inversely correlated with vocational identity, certainty, knowledge about occupations and training, and positively correlated with indecision, neuroticism, and vulnerability.

In addition to these correlates, *adults* with high CTI Total Scores tend to have a greater need for information, be less decided, perceive more barriers to choice, and be more anxious. *College students* with high CTI Total Scores tend to be less decisive and more depressed. *High school students* with high CTI Total Scores tend to lack self-clarity.

Any hypothesis about the specific nature of any of the described characteristics for an individual, based on CTI scores, should be considered tentative until verified by interviewing the client (or having the individual complete other diagnostic measures plus an interview). Section 1 of the *CTI Workbook* can be used to aid interpretation of the CTI Total Score. The *CTI Professional Manual* includes specific recommendations for selecting a level of service delivery intervention based on the CTI Total Score.

Needs Assessment

As a needs assessment measure, the CTI can be used to identify the specific nature of dysfunctional thinking noted in the screening process. In problem-solving terms, the CTI helps define the problem space. Practitioners can then recommend career interventions to reduce career choice problems. Using the *CTI Workbook* can also facilitate an individual's understanding of the nature of his or her dysfunctional thoughts. Construct scales include Decision-Making Confusion, Commitment Anxiety, and External Conflict.

Decision-Making Confusion The *Decision-Making Confusion* (DMC) scale reflects an individual's inability to initiate or sustain the decision-making process as a result of disabling emotions and/or a lack of understanding about the decision-making process itself.

Commitment Anxiety The *Commitment Anxiety* (CA) scale reflects an individual's inability to make a commitment to a specific career choice, accompanied by generalized anxiety about the outcome of the decision-making process. This anxiety perpetuates indecision.

External Conflict The *External Conflict* (EC) scale reflects an individual's inability to balance the importance of self-perceptions with the importance of input from significant others, resulting in a reluctance to assume responsibility for decision making.

As with the CTI Total Score, comparisons of construct scale scores can be made with those of a normally distributed group of adults, college students, or high school students. Again, organizations are strongly encouraged to develop local CTI norms to allow more-specific population comparisons.

Learning

As a learning resource, the CTI and the *CTI Workbook* can be used with various counseling interventions in assisting individuals to challenge and alter the specific dysfunctional thoughts identified as problematic in the prior needs assessment process. The primary cognitive restructuring schema (Beck et al., 1979) used throughout the workbook encourages individuals to *identify, challenge,* and *alter* any negative career thoughts and then follow up with *action.* This schema is repeated at several key points in the workbook to reinforce client understanding of the cognitive restructuring process. By reducing dysfunctional career thinking, clients are more likely to effectively process information needed for career problem solving and decision making. By becoming more aware of the negative impact of dysfunctional thinking and by learning the process of cognitive restructuring, clients can become "freed up" to think in more-creative, reality-based ways about their career choices. A theory-based, decision-making checklist, included in the *CTI Workbook,* can indicate potentially useful areas for specific instruction in career decision making. The CTI and the *CTI Workbook* are designed to help clients make current career decisions as well as learn how to be better problem solvers in the future. The workbook includes the following five sections.

Section 1: Identifying Your Total Amount of Negative Career Thoughts: The CTI Total Score The first section is designed to help clients understand that as dysfunctional career thinking increases, the level of practitioner assistance necessary for clients to benefit from career services increases as well. The intended outcome of using this section is that clients will be more motivated to seek a level of service appropriate for their needs.

Section 2: Identifying the Nature of Your Negative Career Thoughts The second section is designed to help clients gain insight into the development and nature of their dysfunctional thinking. The intended outcome of using this section is that clients will be more self-aware, more capable of monitoring and controlling cognitions, and more motivated to cognitively restructure negative career thoughts and take action to make career decisions.

Section 3: Challenging and Altering Your Negative Career Thoughts and Taking Action The third section is designed to improve self-awareness of the detrimental impact of dysfunctional thinking on career problem solving and decision making, to improve client capacity to monitor and control negative self-talk, to facilitate the cognitive restructuring of negative career thoughts through completion of an exercise, and to facilitate the development of an Individual Action Plan (IAP) for using career resources and services. The intended outcome of using this section is that clients will reduce their dysfunctional career thinking and more effectively use career resources and services, ultimately leading to a more consistent reduction of dysfunctional thoughts and more appropriate career decisions. (See the sample cognitive restructuring exercise in Figure 6.1 and Individual Action Plan in Figure 6.2.)

Section 4: Improving Your Ability to Make Good Decisions The fourth section is designed to enhance the present and future decision-making skills of clients through decision-making instruction. The intended outcome of using this section is that clients will be better able to assess and apply their skills in career problem solving and decision making.

Section 5: Making Good Use of Support from Other People The fifth section is designed to help clients better understand how support resources can be used to their benefit in cognitive restructuring, career exploration, and decision making. The intended outcome of using this section is that clients will be more-proactive, knowledgeable consumers in making effective use of available practitioners and significant others.

Appropriate Populations for the CTI

The CTI is designed for the following individuals: (a) 11th- and 12th-grade high school students who may be choosing a postsecondary field of study, choosing an occupation, or seeking employment; (b) college students who may be choosing a major field of study, choosing an occupation, or seeking employment; and (c) adults who are considering an occupational or employment change, seeking employment due to unemployment or underemployment, or reentering the labor market after a substantial period of unpaid work (such as child-rearing).

Using the Harris-Jacobson Wide Range Readability Formula (Harris & Jacobson, 1982), the readability of the CTI and the *CTI Workbook* was calculated to be at a 6.4 and 7.7 grade level, respectively. Thus, the CTI and *CTI Workbook* can be used without assistance by most high school and college students and adults.

Administering and Scoring the CTI

In order to facilitate quick completion, scoring, and profiling of the instrument and avoid unnecessary delays or disruptions in the service delivery process, the CTI combines the inventory, answer sheet, and profile form into one booklet. The *CTI Test Booklet* can be quickly scored by clients, human service practitioners, or clerical support staff. The CTI Profile is printed on the back page of the booklet. (See the scoring and profiling examples in Figures 6.3, 6.4, and 6.5.)

Use of Terminology

Although this book and the *CTI Professional Manual* use the term *dysfunctional* career thoughts, all client materials use the term *negative* career thoughts. It is strongly recommended that practitioners using the workbook with clients use the term *negative* rather than *dysfunctional* when referring to thoughts or thinking that limit career problem solving and decision making.

Figure 6.1 An Exercise for Improving Your Career Thoughts

Item No.	Old Career Thought	New Career Thought
25	Even though I've taken career tests, I still don't know what major or occupation I will like.	There are things I like and dislike. Talking about my past experience is a good place to start to narrow things down.

Item No.	Old Career Thought	New Career Thought
27	I'm so confused, I'll never be able to choose a major.	It's OK to be confused—there are a lot of majors. Using the word NEVER only keeps me stuck! I can learn the steps involved in choosing a major.

Item No.	Old Career Thought	New Career Thought
40	Making career choices is so complicated, I can't keep track of what I'm doing.	Important choices are difficult, but not impossible. I now have help to figure out how to make this choice.

Item No.	Old Career Thought	New Career Thought
41	My achievements must be as good as my brother's.	I can be a success! But I am different from my brother. It's OK for us to be good at different things.

Figure 6.2 Individual Action Plan

Name *Jeff* Date *7/1/03*

Goal *Choose a college major where I can get good grades and then get a good job*

Activities to Help Me Reach My Goal	People or Information Resources Needed	Activity Order	Date	Activity Complete (✔)
Talk with counselor	*Marilyn Abbey*	1	*June July*	
Finish workbook	*CTI Workbook*	2	7/2	✔
Learn how to make better decisions	*Marilyn Abbey*	3	*July*	✔
Identify possible majors	*Computer guidance system*	5	7/8	✔
Identify majors	*Educational opportunities finder*	4	7/3	✔
Learn about possible majors	*Departmental information in career library*	7	7/10	✔
Learn about occupations	*Career guidance system and career library videos*	6	7/8	✔
Talk with people in occupations	*Career center referral list*	8	7/15–7/19	✔
Learn about majors—Talk with advisers	*Dr. Ortez* *Dr. Chu*	9 10	7/22 7/29	✔
Complete change-of-major forms	*Undergraduate studies office*	11	*by* 8/26	

Figure 6.3 | Completing the Career Thoughts Inventory

Currently in school? ☒ Yes or ☐ No If yes, what grade or year? SOPH. Currently employed? ☐ Yes or ☒ No

If yes, current occupation ______________________ Years in current occupation ________

26. My opinions about occupations change frequently. SD D A SA
27. I'm so confused, I'll never be able to choose a field of study or occupation. SD D A SA
28. The more I try to understand myself and find out about occupations, the more confused and discouraged I get. . . . . SD D A SA
29. There are so many occupations to know about, I will never be able to narrow down the list to only a few. . . . . SD D A SA
30. I can narrow down my occupational choices to a few, but I don't seem to be able to pick just one. . . . . SD D A SA
31. Deciding on an occupation is hard, but taking action after making a choice will be harder. . . . . SD D A SA
32. I can't be satisfied unless I can find the perfect occupation for me. . . . . . SD D A SA
33. I get upset when people ask me what I want to do with my life. . . . . SD D A SA
34. I don't know how to find information about jobs in my field. . . . . SD D A SA
35. I worry a great deal about choosing the right field of study or occupation. SD D A SA
36. I'll never understand enough about occupations to make a good choice. . . . SD D A SA
37. My age limits my occupational choice. . . . . SD D A SA
38. The hardest thing is settling on just one field of study or occupation. . . . . SD D A SA
39. Finding a good job in my field is just a matter of luck. . . . . SD D A SA
40. Making career choices is so complicated, I am unable to keep track of where I am in the process. . . . . SD D A SA
41. My achievements must surpass my mother's or father's or my brother's or sister's. . . . . SD D A SA
42. I know so little about the world of work. . . . . SD D A SA
43. I'm embarrassed to let others know I haven't chosen a field of study or occupation. . . . . SD D A SA
44. Choosing an occupation is so complex, I'll never be able to make a good choice. . . . . SD D A SA
45. There are so many occupations that I like, I'll never be able to sort through them to find ones I like better than others. SD D A SA
46. I need to choose a field of study or occupation that will please the important people in my life. . . . . SD D A SA
47. I'm afraid if I try out my chosen occupation, I won't be successful. . . . . SD D A SA
48. I can't trust that my career decisions will turn out well for me. . . . . SD D A SA

Diversity Issues

Consideration of diversity issues is important in the effective use of the CTI and the *CTI Workbook*. The influence of group membership relating to age, disability, ethnicity, gender, immigration status, nationality, occupation, physical characteristics, poverty level, race, religion, sexual orientation, and social class on career thoughts can be an important complexity dimension in readiness for career choice. Group membership may enhance career choice via networking and mentoring, or it may

Figure 6.4 Scoring the Career Thoughts Inventory

Currently in school? [X] Yes or [ ] No If yes, what grade or year? ________ Currently employed? [ ] Yes or [X] No

If yes, current occupation ______________________ Years in current occupation ________

Item	SD	D	A	SA	DMC	CA	EC
26. My opinions about occupations change frequently.	0	1	(2)	3		2	
27. I'm so confused, I'll never be able to choose a field of study or occupation.	0	1	2	(3)	3		
28. The more I try to understand myself and find out about occupations, the more confused and discouraged I get.	0	1	(2)	3	2		
29. There are so many occupations to know about, I will never be able to narrow down the list to only a few.	0	1	(2)	3		2	
30. I can narrow down my occupational choices to a few, but I don't seem to be able to pick just one.	(0)	1	2	3		0	
31. Deciding on an occupation is hard, but taking action after making a choice will be harder.	0	(1)	2	3			
32. I can't be satisfied unless I can find the perfect occupation for me.	0	(1)	2	3		1	
33. I get upset when people ask me what I want to do with my life.	0	(1)	2	3			
34. I don't know how to find information about jobs in my field.	0	1	(2)	3			
35. I worry a great deal about choosing the right field of study or occupation.	0	1	(2)	3		2	
36. I'll never understand enough about occupations to make a good choice.	0	(1)	2	3	1		
37. My age limits my occupational choice.	(0)	1	2	3			
38. The hardest thing is settling on just one field of study or occupation.	0	1	(2)	3		2	
39. Finding a good job in my field is just a matter of luck.	0	1	(2)	3			
40. Making career choices is so complicated, I am unable to keep track of where I am in the process.	0	1	2	(3)			
41. My achievements must surpass my mother's or father's or my brother's or sister's.	0	1	2	(3)			
42. I know so little about the world of work.	0	1	(2)	3			
43. I'm embarrassed to let others know I haven't chosen a field of study or occupation.	(0)	1	2	3	0		
44. Choosing an occupation is so complex, I'll never be able to make a good choice.	0	1	(2)	3	2		
45. There are so many occupations that I like, I'll never be able to sort through them to find ones I like better than others.	0	1	2	(3)			
46. I need to choose a field of study or occupation that will please the important people in my life.	0	1	2	(3)			3
47. I'm afraid if I try out my chosen occupation, I won't be successful.	0	1	(2)	3		2	
48. I can't trust that my career decisions will turn out well for me.	0	1	2	(3)			
		4 + Sum_D	20 + Sum_A	18 Sum_{SA}	DMC_2 sum	CA_2 sum	EC_2 sum
$Total_2 = Sum_D + Sum_A + Sum_{SA}$				42	8	11	3

	Raw score
CTI Total ($Total_1$ 38 + $Total_2$ 42) =	80
DMC (DMC_1 17 + DMC_2 8) =	25
CA (CA_1 4 + CA_2 11) =	15
EC (EC_1 4 + EC_2 3) =	7

Enter the $Total_1$, $Total_2$, DMC_1, DMC_2, CA_1, CA_2, EC_1, and EC_2 sums in the appropriate blanks in the box at the left, and sum as shown. Transfer the CTI Total, DMC, CA, and EC raw scores to the spaces below the appropriate comparison profile (Adults, College Students, or High School Students) on the back of this Test Booklet.

Figure 6.5 Profiles of Three Clients Who Have Completed the Career Thoughts Inventory

Directions: Write the raw scores for CTI Total, DMC, CA, and EC in the spaces beneath the appropriate profile. Circle each raw score on the profile. Then draw lines connecting DMC, CA, and EC.

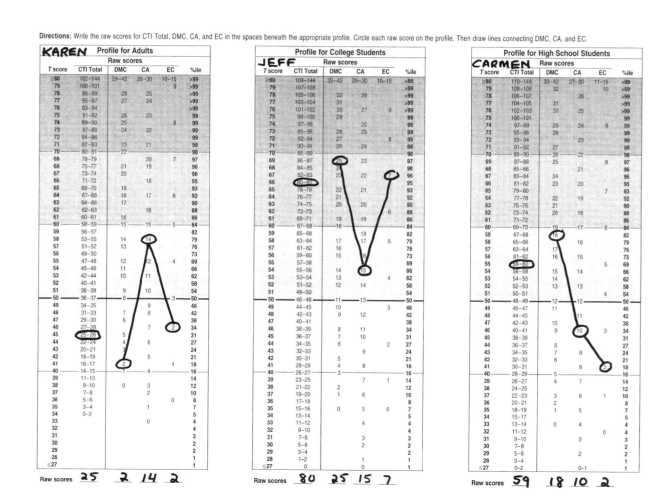

KAREN — **Profile for Adults**

T score	CTI Total	Raw scores DMC	CA	EC	%ile
≥80	102–144	29–42	26–30	10–15	>99
79	100–101			9	>99
78	98–99	28	25		>99
77	95–97	27	24		>99
76	93–94				>99
75	91–92	26	23		99
74	89–90	25		8	99
73	87–88	24	22		99
72	84–86				99
71	82–83	23	21		98
70	80–81	22			98
69	78–79		20	7	97
68	75–77	21	19		96
67	73–74	20			96
66	71–72		18		95
65	69–70	19			93
64	67–68	18	17	6	92
63	64–66	17			90
62	62–63		16		88
61	60–61	16			86
60	58–59	15	15	5	84
59	56–57				82
58	53–55	14	14		79
57	51–52	13	[illegible]		76
56	49–50				73
55	47–48	12	12	4	69
54	45–46	11			66
53	42–44	10	11		62
52	40–41				58
51	38–39	9	10		54
50	36–37	8		3	50
49	34–35		9		46
48	31–33	7	8		42
47	29–30	6			38
46	27–28		7	2	34
45	25–26	5			31
44	22–24	4	6		27
43	20–21	3			24
42	18–19		5		21
41	16–17	2		1	18
40	14–15	1	4		16
39	11–13				14
38	9–10	0	3		12
37	7–8		2		10
36	5–6			0	8
35	3–4		1		7
34	0–2				5
33			0		4
32					4
31					3
30					2
29					2
28					1
≤27					1
Raw scores	25	2	14	2	

JEFF — **Profile for College Students**

T score	CTI Total	Raw scores DMC	CA	EC	%ile
≥80	109–144	33–42	29–30	10–15	>99
79	107–108				>99
78	105–106	32	28		>99
77	103–104	31			>99
76	101–102	30	27	9	>99
75	99–100	29			99
74	97–98		26		99
73	95–96	28	25		99
72	92–94	27		8	99
71	90–91	26	24		98
70	88–89				98
69	86–87	25	23		97
68	84–85	24			96
67	82–83	23	22	7	96
66	80–81				95
65	78–79	22	21		93
64	76–77	21			92
63	74–75	20	20		90
62	72–73			6	88
61	69–71	19	19		86
60	67–68	18			84
59	65–66		18		82
58	63–64	17	17	5	79
57	61–62	16			76
56	59–60	15	16		73
55	57–58				69
54	55–56	14	15		66
53	53–54	13		4	62
52	51–52	12	14		58
51	49–50				54
50	46–48	11	13		50
49	44–45	10		3	46
48	42–43	9	12		42
47	40–41				38
46	38–39	8	11		34
45	36–37	7	10		31
44	34–35	6		2	27
43	32–33		9		24
42	30–31	5			21
41	28–29	4	8		18
40	26–27	3			16
39	23–25		7	1	14
38	21–22	2			12
37	19–20	1	6		10
36	17–18				8
35	15–16	0	5	0	7
34	13–14				5
33	11–12		4		4
32	9–10				4
31	7–8		3		3
30	5–6		2		2
29	3–4				2
28	1–2		1		1
≤27	0		0		1
Raw scores	80	25	15	7	

CARMEN — **Profile for High School Students**

T score	CTI Total	Raw scores DMC	CA	EC	%ile
≥80	110–144	33–42	27–30	11–15	>99
79	108–109	32		10	>99
78	106–107		26		>99
77	104–105	31			>99
76	102–103	30	25		>99
75	100–101				99
74	97–99	29	24	9	99
73	95–96	28			99
72	93–94		23		99
71	91–92	27			98
70	89–90	26	22		98
69	87–88	25		8	97
68	85–86		21		96
67	83–84	24			96
66	81–82	23	20		95
65	79–80			7	93
64	77–78	22	19		92
63	75–76	21			90
62	73–74	20	18		88
61	71–72				86
60	69–70	19	17	6	84
59	67–68	18			82
58	65–66		16		79
57	63–64	17			76
56	61–62	16	15		73
55	59–60			5	69
54	56–58	15	14		66
53	54–55	14			62
52	52–53	13	13		58
51	50–51			4	54
50	48–49	12	12		50
49	46–47	11			46
48	44–45		11		42
47	42–43	10			38
46	40–41	9	10	3	34
45	38–39				31
44	36–37	8			27
43	34–35	7	9		24
42	32–33	6			21
41	30–31		8	2	18
40	28–29	5			16
39	26–27	4	7		14
38	24–25				12
37	22–23	3	6	1	10
36	20–21	2			8
35	18–19	1	5		7
34	15–17				5
33	13–14	0	4		4
32	11–12			0	4
31	9–10		3		3
30	7–8				2
29	5–6		2		2
28	3–4				1
≤27	0–2		0–1		1
Raw scores	59	18	10	2	

constrain career choice via stereotyping and discrimination. The specific nature and consequences of these environmental factors on career choice will likely vary with group membership. As a result, the specific career thoughts of an individual are a product of individual experience, mediated by personal characteristics and by group membership.

It is difficult to develop an instrument that reflects differences in life experience between group cultures, and within subcultures of specific groups, that is brief enough to be hand-scored for use as a screening tool in service delivery. The CTI was designed to specifically measure career thoughts that tend to be common across groups. During development of the CTI, items that might be significantly associated with gender or ethnicity were eliminated from the item pool. It can be helpful, however, to collaboratively use the CTI with the client to identify, challenge, and alter career thoughts of an individual from a specific group. The *CTI Professional Manual* includes specific suggestions for dealing with diversity issues in interpreting the CTI and using the *CTI Workbook*.

Professional Requirements

A variety of practitioners may make effective use of the CTI and the *CTI Workbook*. In addition to general training in human behavior, helping skills, and assessment, practitioners need training in career development, career service delivery, and cognitive-behavior therapy. Practitioners need general experience in the delivery of human services and in the delivery of career services with appropriate supervision. In particular, practitioners using the CTI with clients should be familiar with the *CTI Professional Manual,* personally complete all components of the CTI, and make use of appropriate supervision. They should also explore their own dysfunctional career thoughts in counseling or supervision.

CTI CASE STUDIES

Three case studies with profiles from the *CTI Professional Manual* (Sampson et al., 1996b) can be used to illustrate potential interpretations and implications for use of the instrument in counseling, including screening, needs assessment, and learning. (Refer to the CTI Profile in Figure 6.5.)

Case Study 1: Karen

Karen, who is 38 years old and currently employed, is seeking assistance from a community college career center where services are offered to adults in the community for a minimal fee. After determining that more than a simple information request was involved, a staff member asked Karen to complete the CTI to determine the extent and nature of services she might require. Given the interview with Karen and her somewhat below average CTI Total Score (adult norms are $T = 45$ and percentile rank = 31), the staff member concluded that Karen was not encumbered by substantial dysfunctional thoughts and hypothesized that she had moderate readiness for career choice and would require minimal to moderate assistance in making effective use of career assessment and information resources (screening). The staff member recommended a self-directed approach to using the resources of the center, with professional and paraprofessional support provided to the client as needed. The staff member asked Karen to discuss the nature of her career problem. Karen perceived that she was in a dead-end job with little opportunity for advancing or gaining new skills. She had decided on a new occupation that was congruent with her current skills and educational qualifications but was reluctant to follow through because she was "afraid of making a mistake." The staff member noted that Karen's higher CA score (T = 58; percentile rank = 79) in relation to DMC (T = 41; percentile rank = 18) and EC (T = 46; percentile rank = 34) provided additional evidence that being "afraid of making a mistake" was an obstacle in working through the decision-making process (needs assessment).

Based on the information available, the staff member hypothesized that Karen was decided, as opposed to being undecided or indecisive. As service delivery progressed, this initial hypothesis was confirmed by occasional reviews of Karen's use of resources. After briefly exploring the thoughts and feelings Karen had about committing to an occupation (including item 35 on the CA scale, "I worry a great deal about choosing the right field of study or occupation," and item 38, "The hardest thing is settling on just one field of study or occupation"), the staff member summarized Karen's problem in terms of a gap in self-confidence and in her ability to transform choices into actions. The staff member then recommended that Karen complete the *CTI Workbook* to identify, challenge, and alter specific negative career thoughts (learning). In addition to having Karen focus on *valuing* items on the decision-making checklist, the staff member offered to assist her in completing and carrying out an Individual Action Plan to resolve her career problem.

Case Study 2: Jeff

Jeff is a 20-year-old college sophomore seeking assistance from a college counseling center in choosing a major field of study. The CTI was included as one component of the counseling center intake procedure. Given Jeff's relatively elevated CTI Total Score (college norms are T = 66 and percentile rank = 95) and interview data, the counselor hypothesized that Jeff had low readiness for career choice and potentially required a high degree of assistance in making effective use of career assessment and information resources offered in the center (screening). The counselor recommended individual career counseling as an appropriate service delivery option and scheduled an individual appointment. While discussing the nature of his career problem, Jeff admitted that he had already changed majors three times and was currently unable to identify an appropriate major or subsequent occupations. He admitted that he was overwhelmed with all of his options and was uncertain about how to proceed. He further stated that he found it difficult to make any important decision. The counselor noted that Jeff's higher DMC score (T = 69; percentile rank = 97) in relation to his CA score (T = 54; percentile rank = 66) provided additional evidence that he was more confused and overwhelmed about making a choice than he was anxious about making a career commitment, although some generalized anxiety was still present. When the counselor asked about the potential for conflict with significant others, indicated by his EC score (T = 67; percentile rank = 96), Jeff disclosed that his parents were upset that his progress in college varied so much from that of his more successful older brother (needs assessment). Based on the information available, the staff member hypothesized that Jeff was indecisive. After the client elaborated his responses to DMC and EC items rated "strongly agree," the counselor summarized Jeff's situation as a gap in career decision-making skills influenced by negative thinking. The counselor helped Jeff complete the Individual Action Plan in the *CTI Workbook,* sequencing individual counseling and the completion of Sections 3 and 4 of the workbook (learning) prior to utilizing career assessment and information resources.

Case Study 3: Carmen

Carmen is a 17-year-old high school senior participating with other students in a three-period classroom career guidance unit designed to facilitate school-to-work and school-to-school transitions as part of the social studies curriculum. The CTI was completed as an initial activity in the guidance unit and delivered by a school counselor with teacher support. In the class setting, the counselor used Sections 1 and 2 of the *CTI Workbook* to help the students interpret their scores. Given her somewhat above average CTI Total Score (high school norms are T = 55 and percentile rank = 69), Carmen concluded that she could use some help with her career choice (screening). During a student group discussion of career concerns, Carmen stated that she was undecided about her plans after high school and unsure how to go about making a good choice. She noted that her higher DMC score (T = 59; percentile rank = 82) in relation to her CA score (T = 46; percentile rank = 34) and EC score (T = 41; percentile rank = 18) made sense, given that she felt confused and overwhelmed about the choices before her rather than afraid or at odds with her parents (needs assessment). The counselor suggested to Carmen that she might benefit from some career assistance (moderate readiness). Student peer counselors and parent volunteers were available in the afternoons in the school career resource room to provide information on decision making and to help with accessing appropriate career resources. The counselor then provided all students in the class with an overview of the remainder of the *CTI Workbook* and helped them use the IAP to state initial goals, as well as to list activities, resources, and priorities related to their goals by presenting examples of typical action plans. After the classroom teacher approved a draft IAP, completing the plan became a graded project assignment for students in the class. Carmen included the completion of Sections 3 and 4 of the workbook on her IAP (learning) in addition to resources for assessment and information. The counselor announced her availability to answer any specific questions about the CTI, the *CTI Workbook,* or available guidance resources and services.

DEVELOPMENT OF THE CTI AND THE *CTI WORKBOOK*

This section describes the development of the CTI and the *CTI Workbook* and provides a foundation for understanding how to use the CTI and the workbook.

CTI Item Selection and Scale Construction

The authors used a rational-empirical approach in developing the CTI.[2] After reviewing the theoretical foundations of the CTI and the literature on dysfunctional thinking in career choice, they developed criteria for each of the eight CIP content dimensions. An initial pool of 248 items was then created based on actual client statements from the authors' career counseling experience. After experienced career counselors reviewed the items for clarity and realism, the pool was revised to 195 items and then reviewed by a six-member bias panel to identify and correct any bias related to ethnicity (African American, Hispanic American, Asian American), gender, disability, and age. The 195-item pool plus 13 randomly inserted items from the short form of the Marlowe-Crowne Social Desirability Scale (Reynolds, 1982) was administered to 320 volunteer undergraduate students. Eighty items were retained on the basis of their general psychometric quality; freedom from gender, ethnic, or social desirability bias; item-scale reliability; and content domain coverage. A new sample of 196 volunteer undergraduate students completed this 80-item form. A principal components analysis with Varimax rotation revealed three interpretable constructs that were associated with dysfunctional career thinking: *decision-making confusion* (DMC), *commitment anxiety* (CA), and *external conflict* (EC). Items could then be identified as relating to one of these three constructs as well as contributing to one of the eight CIP content dimensions. The 80 items were also administered to clients seeking services, allowing an analysis of the capacity of individual items to distinguish clients ($n = 68$) from nonclients ($n = 196$). The authors then derived a shortened 48-item version of the CTI on the basis of factor loadings, contribution to scale separation, capacity to discriminate clients from nonclients, and content domain coverage. The 48 items were then administered to a new sample of 145 volunteer undergraduate students. A second principal components analysis with Varimax rotation revealed the same three interpretable constructs noted earlier.

CTI Workbook Development and Pilot Testing

Workbook development began with the cognitive restructuring exercise in Section 3. In order to assist clients in challenging and altering their thoughts, the authors wrote reframing stimulus statements for each CTI item to show clients how negative thoughts interfere with their ability to make career decisions and to provide information on making the best use of time spent on career decision making. (Refer to the sample reframing stimulus statements found in Table 6.1.) Reframing stimulus statements include varying combinations of the following themes:

1. The difficulty often encountered by individuals making career choices
2. The often inherent ambiguities in making career choices

---

[2] Refer to the *CTI Professional Manual* (Sampson, Peterson, Lenz, Reardon, & Saunders, 1996b) for additional details on the development, standardization, and validation of the CTI. Further information on CTI development may be found in Sampson, Peterson, Lenz, Reardon, & Saunders (1998) and Sampson, Peterson, Lenz, Reardon, & Saunders (1996d).

Table 6.1 | A Sample of CTI Items and Reframing Stimulus Statements

If CTI items are endorsed by individuals "Strongly Agree" or "Agree," it may be helpful to challenge and alter their self-defeating career thoughts. Some key words that make thoughts more negative and harmful are underlined. Reframing stimulus statements are provided to suggest potentially more effective ways of thinking to improve career problem solving and decision making.

1. **No field of study or occupation interests me.**

   It's possible that you haven't determined what your likes and dislikes are. You may need more life experience to really understand your interests. You can get more life experience from full-time or part-time jobs, volunteer work, or leisure activities.

2. **Almost all occupational information is slanted toward making the occupation look good.**

   While it is certainly true that some kinds of occupational information are designed to make the occupation "look good," it is likely an overstatement to say this about all information. Occupational information may be biased in both directions, good or bad. Helping professionals, like librarians or counselors, can help you determine the quality of various sources of information. It's important to evaluate the source and purpose of each piece of information and determine its usefulness in your career decision making.

3. **I get so depressed about choosing a field of study or occupation that I can't get started.**

   While it is important to admit that you are feeling depressed about making a career choice, doing nothing about your problem is not a good idea in the long run. You may need to get help for your feelings of depression, or take small concrete steps toward getting the information you need to begin the decision-making process. Such steps might include talking with people in different occupations, reading about occupations, or seeking career assistance to help you develop a plan for taking the next step.

4. **I'll never understand myself well enough to make a good career choice.**

   It is important to be aware of your values, interests, and skills as you make career decisions. Thinking that you must have total understanding of yourself before you can make a good career choice may make you feel discouraged and less likely to think carefully about your options. Going through the career choice process will actually help you better understand yourself. There are resources, including print materials and helping professionals, that can assist you in gathering enough information about yourself to at least take the next step in the career decision-making process.

5. **I can't think of any fields of study or occupations that would suit me.**

   Right now you may feel discouraged and that may cause you to cut yourself off from developing and exploring suitable possibilities. If you think, instead, that it is possible to identify appropriate options, you may free yourself up to explore and discover suitable fields of study or occupations.

6. **The views of important people in my life interfere with choosing a field of study or occupation.**

   The differing views of important people in your life can easily complicate your choice of a field of study or an occupation. Some of the information you may get from important people in your life may be useful, while other input makes you more confused or uncertain. However, no matter what suggestions you get from others, you are ultimately the person who is responsible for and capable of making your career choice.

Table 6.1 (*continued*)

7. **I know what I want to do, but I can't develop a plan for getting there.**

   In knowing what you want to do, you have already made good progress toward completing your career plans. The fact that you are unclear about your next step shows you that you need to find information on career planning, or you need to find a competent person to help you develop a plan, so you can reach your goals.

8. **I get so anxious when I have to make decisions that I can hardly think.**

   Many people feel anxious when making important decisions. Anxiety does make it harder to think clearly. However, avoiding decision making or depending on others to make decisions for you is not a good idea. With help from a competent person, you can get the information you need and learn how to make a good career decision.

Note.

3. The importance of assuming personal responsibility for decision making while also considering input from significant others
4. The importance of linking career choices with other life choices
5. The identification of factors that make it more difficult to think clearly about career options
6. The identification of absolute dichotomous thinking that interferes with career choice
7. The assumption that improved decision-making and information-seeking skills can be learned
8. The value of broad career exploration prior to final choice
9. The value of using a variety of sources of information in career exploration
10. The value of obtaining assistance from a helping professional when individuals experience difficulty in career choice

The reframing stimulus statements were then examined for potential bias regarding ethnicity, gender, disability, and age. The exercise was pilot-tested and subsequently revised for clarity. The authors then added interpretive and decision-making instruction sections to the workbook.

Standardization

The authors collected CTI normative data for adults ($n = 571$), college students ($n = 595$), and 11th- and 12th-grade high school students ($n = 396$), as well as combined data on college student and adult clients ($n = 376$). In general, all groups were representative in terms of geographic distribution, gender, and ethnicity, with the exception that female adults were overrepresented and Hispanic American adults were underrepresented. As stated previously, organizations and individuals are strongly encouraged to develop local CTI norms to allow more-specific population comparisons, provided expertise is available in calculating norms. Analysis of normative data revealed that gender and ethnicity accounted for 0.2% and 0.1% of the variance, respectively, in CTI Total Scores for all groups combined. Therefore, the authors concluded that there is little relationship between gender or ethnicity with respect to CTI Total Scores and that there is no need to provide separate norms for either of these factors.

Reliability

The following section describes the reliability of the CTI in terms of internal consistency (alpha) and stability (test-retest).

Internal Consistency The internal consistency of the CTI Total Score and construct scales was determined by calculating coefficient alphas for each of the respective norm groups. The internal consistency (alpha) coefficients for the CTI Total Score ranged from .97 to .93. Alpha coefficients for the construct scales ranged from .94 to .74.

Stability Stability concerns the extent to which individuals achieve the same CTI scores on two different occasions. The stability of the CTI Total Score and construct scales was determined by having 73 volunteer college students and 48 volunteer 11th- and 12th-grade high school students complete the CTI twice over a four-week interval. Four-week test-retest stability coefficients for the CTI Total Score were high ($r = .86$) for the college student sample, indicating little change in responses to the entire 48 items over the four-week period. The stability coefficients for the construct scales ranged from .82 to .74, following a similar pattern as the data for internal consistency, with lower correlations for scales with fewer items. This pattern was also observed for the high school student sample, with the CTI Total Score at $r = .69$ and the construct scales ranging from .72 to .52, showing that adequate stability exists for the use of the instrument.

Validity

The following section describes the validity of the CTI in terms of content, factorial, convergent, and criterion validity.

Content Validity Content validity concerns the congruence of CTI items, CIP content dimensions, and construct scales with the theoretical basis of the instrument. This congruence was built into the development strategy for the CTI items and scales. Individual items and construct scales are directly linked to CIP theory through content dimensions. CIP content dimensions (self-knowledge, occupational knowledge, communication, analysis, synthesis, valuing, execution, and executive processing) provided specific criteria for developing items. The *CTI Professional Manual* groups all 48 CTI items by content dimension and includes the corresponding criterion number or numbers for each (Sampson et al., 1996b).

Factorial Validity Factorial validity is concerned with the extent to which clusters of empirically associated items that are conceptually consistent with the theory can be identified and reproduced across populations. Evidence of construct validity was established through a series of factor analyses. The constructs of decision-making confusion, commitment anxiety, and external conflict, which were identified in two different samples during CTI development, were replicated for adults, college students, and 11th- and 12th-grade high school students based on normative data. The CTI Total core is highly correlated (r = .89 to .94) with DMC for all groups. These correlations, along with the large percentage of the variance accounted for by DMC (factor 1), suggest that a general predisposition toward dysfunctional thinking strongly influences subsequent specific aspects of dysfunctional career thinking, such as commitment anxiety. External conflict (EC) appears somewhat less related to general dysfunctional thinking, as represented by the lower correlation of EC with the CTI Total Score and DMC. Correlations among construct scales, especially CA and EC, are distinctly lower for the client population than for nonclient adults, college students, and high school students. CA and EC appear to be more distinct from DMC for clients than nonclients.

Given the magnitude of correlations among CTI factors observed for adults, college students, and high school students, a Principal Components Analysis with oblique rotation was used to extract the factor structure of the instrument. A three-factor model was confirmed for the college population, the combined normative sample, and the client comparison group. A two-factor solution (decision-making confusion and external conflict) was the most interpretable solution for the adult sample, whereas a different two-factor solution (decision-making confusion and commitment anxiety) was most interpretable for high school students. Our interpretation of these findings is that for adult, nonclient populations who are almost all employed or not seeking employment, commitment anxiety is not an operative construct when a career problem does not exist, whereas confusion about decision making and external conflict with significant others (such as spouses) are operative. For high school, nonclient populations, external conflict with significant others (such as parents and caretakers) concerning career problems is not yet an issue, whereas confusion about decision making and anxiety about post–high school commitments yet to be made are operative. The three-factor solution, including decision-making confusion, commitment anxiety, and external conflict, was again reproduced for the client population, for which the CTI was designed. We concluded that the three-factor solution is the most appropriate model to use for the instrument, as it is the most generalizable solution across all populations.

What these analyses reveal about the construct validity of the CTI is that there is a single powerful confusion entity that is pervasive in career problem solving and decision making. Beyond this, there are more-specific issues related to one's anxiety about committing to a career choice and to potential conflict with significant others. Therefore, all three constructs may be viewed as indicators of the presence of dysfunctional thinking. This type of thinking constrains the cognitive system that undergirds career problem solving and decision making.

Convergent Validity Convergent validity concerns the extent to which the CTI Total Score and construct scale scores correlate with other measures of similar constructs in a theoretically consistent direction. Convergent validity measures included the following:

My Vocational Situation Identity Scale and Occupational Information and Barriers categories (Holland, Daiger, & Power, 1980)

The Career Decision Scale Certainty and Indecision scales (Osipow, Carney, Winer, Yanico, & Koschier, 1987)

The Career Decision Profile Decidedness, Comfort, Self-Clarity, Knowledge About Occupations and Training, Decisiveness, and Career Choice Importance scales (Jones, 1988)

The NEO PI-R Neuroticism Domain, including the facets of anxiety, angry hostility, depression, self-consciousness, impulsiveness, and vulnerability (Costa & McCrae, 1992)

Evidence of convergent validity was established by administering the above measures to 50 adults, 152 college students, and 151 high school students in the 11th and 12th grades. All samples were representative in terms of geographic distribution in the United States, gender, and ethnicity, with the exception that females slightly outnumbered males (56% to 44%, respectively) across all three groups, and Hispanic American adults were underrepresented.

Across all three groups (adults, college students, and high school students), CTI scale scores were consistently inversely correlated with positive constructs such as vocational identity, certainty, and knowledge about occupations and training, and directly correlated with indecision. The CTI Total Score was consistently directly correlated with neuroticism and vulnerability. Only career choice importance exhibited inconsistency in relationships across groups, as was expected. Although CTI construct scale scores covaried directly with angry hostility, self-consciousness, and impulsiveness, the relatively low magnitude of the correlations has limited practical importance.

The following additional relationships were also noted. CTI scale scores for adults were consistently inversely correlated with comfort with choice, decidedness, and lack of information needs, and positively correlated with anxiety. CTI scale scores for college students were consistently inversely correlated with comfort with choice and decisiveness; the CTI Total Score was positively correlated with depression. CTI scales for high school students were consistently inversely correlated with self-clarity.

Relationships between the CTI Total Score and convergent variables were very similar to the relationships observed between DMC and the convergent variables. This is to be expected given the high correlation between the CTI Total Score and the DMC scale. The number of correlations having practical significance (.50 to .75) were 32 for adults, 21 for college students, and 17 for high school students. This is also to be expected given the slightly lower alpha reliabilities for high school students and college students in comparison with those for adults. These lower reliability coefficients, combined with the lower alpha reliabilities from some Career Decision Profile scales and small numbers of items in NEO facet scales, could explain the lower number of correlations between convergent variables and either CA or EC.

Criterion Validity Criterion validity concerns the extent to which the CTI accurately discriminates between persons seeking career services (clients) and persons not seeking career services (nonclients). Evidence of predictive validity was established by administering the CTI to 199 clients and 149 nonclients at two different universities. Both samples were representative in terms of geographic distribution in the United States and ethnicity, with the exception that females slightly outnumbered males, a greater proportion of clients were sophomores, and a greater proportion of nonclients were seniors. Analysis of the data revealed significant differences in CTI Total and construct scale scores for each group, with clients having higher scores, as predicted. Post hoc CTI item-level comparisons revealed significant differences between clients and nonclients on 26 items, with clients scoring higher than nonclients on all 48 items.

Further CTI Research

Since the publication of the CTI and the *CTI Professional Manual* in 1996, there have been continued efforts to validate the constructs of the instrument as well as to examine the application of the CTI in a variety of populations different from the initial norm groups. One study, in which the factor structure of the CTI was replicated in a Finnish translation of the CTI, underscored the potential cross-cultural use of the CTI (Lerkkanen, 2002). Other studies explored the extent to which the CTI scales were correlated with other psychological constructs. For example, in one study (Saunders, Peterson, Sampson, & Reardon, 2000), the CTI Total Score was significantly ($p < .05$) correlated with career indecision ($r = .78$), trait anxiety ($r = .42$), state anxiety ($r = .36$), and depression ($r = .37$). In another study (Osborn, 1999), the CTI scales were moderately ($rs = .20–.40$) related to perfectionism, concern about mistakes, doubt about actions, and parental criticism. Lustig and Strauser (2002) found a moderate relationship between college students' sense of coherence and the CTI Total Score and construct scales. "Individuals with a strong sense of coherence seemed to have less dysfunctional thoughts" (p. 8). Other studies demonstrated that the CTI scales were not related to either anger (Strausberger, 1998) or to interests (Wright, Reardon, Peterson, & Osborn, 2000). In terms of information processing, the CTI Decision-Making Confusion scale scores were related to the extent to which individuals are able to fully engage printed occupational information (Hill & Peterson, 2001). Finally, the CTI scales were able to differentiate between female first-time offenders, probationers, and repeat offenders (Railey & Peterson, 2000), between persons with diagnosed learning disabilities and those without (Dipeolu, Reardon, Sampson, & Burkhead, 2002), and between persons classified in ego statuses as diffused, foreclosed, moratorium, and achieved (Voight, 1999). The CTI has also proved useful as a pre-posttest to document the impact of a career planning class (Reed, Reardon, Lenz, & Leierer, 2001). Thus, a growing body of research literature continues to support the psychometric properties of the CTI, as well as its application to a variety of populations.

Utility

The utility of a test concerns how well the test achieves its intended purpose within the constraints of "typical" practice. Many career service delivery organizations serve numerous clients. In this type of environment, an instrument used for screening, needs assessment, and learning is most cost-effective when it meets the criteria of quick administration, rapid scoring, easy interpretation, easy integration, and inexpensive use. The CTI was designed to meet these criteria.

1. Quick administration: Most clients complete the 48 CTI items in 7 to 15 minutes.
2. Rapid scoring: The CTI can be hand-scored in 5 to 8 minutes. As a result, the CTI can be used as part of a brief intake procedure or during an initial session.
3. Easy interpretation: The CTI includes a limited number of scales (the CTI Total Score and three construct scales), which simplifies interpretation. The *CTI Workbook* presents interpretive information for all four scales with text, metaphors, and illustrations that practitioners can use to facilitate interpretation of CTI results.
4. Easy integration: The *CTI Workbook* has several components that can be assigned as homework, such as cognitive restructuring of negative thoughts, developing an Individual Action Plan for using career resources and services, and learning about the decision-making process.
5. Inexpensive use: The *CTI Test Booklet* and the *CTI Workbook* are relatively inexpensive to purchase, and the hand-scoring feature eliminates scoring processing fees.

SUMMARY

This chapter examined the use of the Career Thoughts Inventory as a measure of readiness for career choice. The use of the CTI was described in terms of screening, needs assessment, learning, appropriate populations, administration and scoring, use of terminology, diversity issues, and professional requirements. Three case studies were then presented showing different scores and resulting recommendations for career assistance. The development of the CTI was then described in terms of the creation of items and the design of the workbook, as well as the standardization, reliability, validity, and utility of the measure.

GETTING THE MOST BENEFIT FROM READING THIS CHAPTER

To effectively learn the material in this chapter, complete one or more of the following activities:

- Complete, score, and profile the CTI yourself, and have a career practitioner help you interpret the results.
- Complete the *CTI Workbook,* and have a career practitioner help you review your work.
- Discuss the three case studies with a career practitioner who is familiar with the use of the CTI. Focus on the use of the CTI for screening, needs assessment, and learning.
- Compare the use of the CTI in a counseling center versus a career center.
- Compare the reliability, validity, and utility evidence for the CTI with that of another test that you have used in practice.

REFERENCES

Beck, A. T. (1976). *Cognitive therapy and the emotional disorders.* New York: International Universities Press.

Beck, A. T., Emery, G., & Greenberg, R. L. (1985). *Anxiety disorders and phobias: A cognitive perspective.* New York: Guilford Press.

Beck, A. T., Rush, A. J., Shaw, B. F., & Emery, G. (1979). *Cognitive therapy of depression.* New York: Guilford Press.

Costa, P. T., Jr., & McCrae, R. R. (1992). *Revised NEO Personality Inventory.* Odessa, FL: Psychological Assessment Resources.

Dipeolu, A. O., Reardon, R., Sampson, J. P., Jr., & Burkhead, J. (2002). The relationship between dysfunctional career thoughts and adjustment to disability in college students with learning disabilities. *Journal of Career Assessment, 10,* 413–427.

Harris, A. J., & Jacobson, M. D. (1982). *Basic reading vocabularies.* New York: Macmillan.

Hill, S., & Peterson, G. W. (2001). *The impact of decision-making confusion on the processing of occupational information.* Seattle, WA: American Educational Research Association.

Holland, J. L., Daiger, D. C., & Power, G. (1980). *My vocational situation.* Palo Alto, CA: Consulting Psychologists Press..

Jones, L. K. (1988). Measuring a three-dimensional construct of career indecision among college students: A revision of the Vocational Decision Scale—the Career Decision Profile. *Journal of Counseling Psychology, 36,* 477–486.

Lerkkanen, J. (2002). *The relationship between dysfunctional educational and career thoughts, and the success of Polytechnic studies and the students' need for guidance.* Unpublished doctoral dissertation, University of Jyvaskyla, p. 219.

Lustig, D. C., & Strauser, D. R. (2002). The relationship between sense of coherence and career thoughts. *The Career Development Quarterly, 51,* 2–11.

Osborn, D. S. (1999). The relationships among perfectionism, dysfunctional career thoughts and career indecision. *Dissertation Abstracts International Section A: Humanities & Social Sciences, 59* (10-A), 3746.

Osipow, S. H., Carney, C. G., Winer, J., Yanico, B., & Koschier, M. (1987). *Career Decision Scale.* Odessa, FL: Psychological Assessment Resources.

Peterson, G. W., Sampson, J. P., Jr., Lenz, J. G., & Reardon, R. C. (2002). A cognitive information processing approach to career problem solving and decision making. In D. Brown (Ed.), *Career choice and development* (4th ed.) (pp. 312–369). San Francisco: Jossey-Bass.

Peterson, G. W., Sampson, J. P., Jr., & Reardon, R. C. (1991). *Career development and services: A cognitive approach.* Pacific Grove, CA: Brooks/Cole.

Peterson, G. W., Sampson, J. P., Jr., Reardon, R. C., & Lenz, J. G. (1996). Becoming career problem solvers and decision makers: A cognitive information processing approach. In D. Brown & L. Brooks (Eds.), *Career choice and development* (3rd ed.) (pp. 423–475). San Francisco: Jossey-Bass.

Railey, M. G., & Peterson, G. W. (2000). The assessment of dysfunctional career thoughts and interest structure among female inmates and probationers. *Journal of Career Assessment, 8* (2), 119–129.

Reed, C., Reardon, R., Lenz, J., & Leierer, S. (2001). Reducing negative career thoughts with a career course. *The Career Development Quarterly, 50,* 158–167.

Reynolds, W. M. (1982). Development of reliable and valid short forms of the Marlowe-Crowne Social Desirability Scale. *Journal of Clinical Psychology, 32,* 221–231.

Sampson, J. P., Jr., Peterson, G. W., Lenz, J. G., Reardon, R. C., & Saunders, D. E. (1996a). *Career Thoughts Inventory.* Odessa, FL: Psychological Assessment Resources.

Sampson, J. P., Jr., Peterson, G. W., Lenz, J. G., Reardon, R. C., & Saunders, D. E. (1996b). *Career Thoughts Inventory: Professional manual.* Odessa, FL: Psychological Assessment Resources.

Sampson, J. P., Jr., Peterson, G. W., Lenz, J. G., Reardon, R. C., & Saunders, D. E. (1996c). *Improving your career thoughts: A workbook for the Career Thoughts Inventory.* Odessa, FL: Psychological Assessment Resources.

Sampson, J. P., Jr., Peterson, G. W., Lenz, J. G., Reardon, R. C., & Saunders, D. E. (1996d). Negative thinking and career choice. In R. Feller & G. Walz (Eds.), *Optimizing life transitions in turbulent times: Exploring work, learning and careers* (pp. 323–330). Greensboro: University of North Carolina at Greensboro, ERIC Clearinghouse on Counseling and Student Services.

Sampson, J. P., Jr., Peterson, G. W., Lenz, J. G., Reardon, R. C., & Saunders, D. E. (1998). The design and use of a measure of dysfunctional career thoughts among adults, college students, and high school students: The Career Thoughts Inventory. *Journal of Career Assessment, 6,* 115–134.

Saunders, D. E., Peterson, G. W., Sampson, J. P., Jr., & Reardon, R. C. (2000). Relation of depression and dysfunctional career thinking to career indecision. *Journal of Vocational Behavior, 56,* 288–298.

Strausberger, S. J. (1998). The relationship of state-trait anger to dysfunctional career thinking and vocational identity (Doctoral dissertation, Florida State University, 1998). *Dissertation Abstracts International, 59* (10), 3747A.

Voight, L. (1999). Parental attachment and ego identity as antecedents of career identity. (college students). *Dissertation Abstracts International: Section B: The Sciences & Engineering, 60* (6-B), 2992.

Wright, L. K., Reardon, R. C., Peterson, G. W., & Osborn, D. S. (2000). The relationship among constructs in the Career Thoughts Inventory and the Self-Directed Search. *Journal of Career Assessment, 8* (2), 105–117.

Planning and Delivering Career Resources

CHAPTER 7

This chapter explores the selection and use of career assessments, information, and instruction to help individuals and clients solve career problems and make career decisions. The potential contributions of each resource are described, sources for the resource are identified, issues of quality are considered, and strategies for use are examined. After reviewing this chapter, the reader should be better prepared to select and use career resources to meet individual and client needs. The chapter is organized as follows:

- The CIP Approach and the Use of Career Assessment, Information, and Instruction
- Career Assessment
- Career Information
- Career Instruction
- Summary
- Getting the Most Benefit from Reading This Chapter

THE CIP APPROACH AND THE USE OF CAREER ASSESSMENT, INFORMATION, AND INSTRUCTION

The purpose of a career intervention should be to enhance the ability of clients to use assessment information and career information to solve career problems and make career decisions. Career assessment, information, and instruction should be presented in the form of a learning event that results in a change in knowledge, attitudes, or skills (Peterson, Sampson, & Reardon,

1991). In the next section, we present examples of various types of assessments and information in relation to the Pyramid of Information Processing Domains and the CASVE cycle.

The Pyramid of Information Processing Domains

Assessments and information used in career services can be integrated within the Pyramid of Information Processing Domains as illustrated with the following examples.

- *Self-knowledge domain*—The counselor and client review information from career assessments, such as a values card sort, autobiography, computer-assisted career guidance (CACG) system, or an interest inventory.
- *Occupational knowledge domain*—The client obtains a description of a typical working day for an occupation from a CACG system or an information interview. A schema for organizing the world of work, such as the Holland Hexagon (Holland, 1997), is presented via videotape or a printed handout. The counselor discusses with the client the results of a vocational card sort (Peterson, 1998).
- *Decision-making skills domain*—The counselor explains the five steps of the CASVE cycle, which are simulated in a written exercise or a classroom exercise.
- *Executive processing domain*—The counselor obtains information about the client's dysfunctional metacognitions through the use of the Career Thoughts Inventory (Sampson, Peterson, Lenz, Reardon, & Saunders, 1996a), a card sort, or a counselor-conducted structured interview. A counselor may then explain this information and suggest methods for identifying, challenging, and altering dysfunctional metacognitions using print-based materials such as a cognitive restructuring exercise (Peterson et al., 1991; Peterson, Sampson, Reardon, & Lenz, 1996; Peterson, Sampson, Lenz, & Reardon, 2002; Sampson, Peterson, Lenz, Reardon, & Saunders, 1996b).

The CASVE Cycle

Assessments and information used in career services can be integrated within the CASVE cycle as illustrated with the following examples.

- *Communication*—A description of the career and family issues that women typically face in returning to paid employment is presented in a videotaped interview of a currently employed woman or in a panel discussion at a workshop. The client completes an autobiography that includes a sequence of career successes and problems.
- *Analysis*—The counselor provides explanations of basic education requirements for degree programs presented in a community college catalog, and the client then reviews the requirements with an academic adviser. A cognitive map showing the relationships among self- and occupational knowledge variables in a two-dimensional space can be developed.
- *Synthesis*—The client obtains a list of potentially appropriate occupations through use of an interest inventory. A variety of career options in the computer

field are presented at a seminar on emerging occupations in e-commerce. A right-brain activity such as free-form thought listing can also be used.

- *Valuing*—The counselor presents in a CACG system or in a printed handout an exploration of how the roles of parent, spouse, and homemaker would be affected by the assumption of the worker role (Super, 1990).
- *Execution*—The counselor provides a description of a functional resume emphasizing transferable skills, followed by the creation of a resume on a resume-authoring system (Peterson et al., 1991).

CAREER ASSESSMENT

Career assessment is typically used to help persons clarify their knowledge of self and their options. This section begins with an exploration of the potential contributions that career assessment can make to individuals' career choices, then explains a schema for organizing career assessments and presents examples of available career assessments, discusses quality issues, and reviews a model for promoting effective use of career assessments.

Potential Contributions of Career Assessment to Career Choice

Career assessment has the potential to help individuals progress through the CASVE cycle. The following section examines seven potential contributions of career assessment to career choice.

Enhancing Awareness of Career Problems and Promoting the Motivation to Change Readiness assessment can result in increased awareness of a career problem (the gap) and greater motivation to engage in problem solving and decision making (Communication phase of the CASVE cycle). Some clients may be vaguely aware that they have a problem but have poor motivation for working to remove the gap. Our experience has been that when clients see a high score profile from the Career Thoughts Inventory (CTI), their career choice gap becomes concrete, and they better perceive the need for obtaining assistance with their career problem. In addition to the CTI, other readiness assessment measures identified in Sampson, Peterson, Reardon, and Lenz (2000) can be used to promote awareness of a gap that needs attention through problem solving and decision making.

Motivating Persons to Clarify Knowledge of Self Career assessment can motivate persons to expend the effort necessary to clarify knowledge of their values, interests, and skills and employment preferences (Analysis–self-knowledge phase of the CASVE cycle). Many persons are curious about what a career assessment will reveal about themselves. This curiosity can be used to motivate self-knowledge clarification by asking clients how the test results compare with their existing self-perceptions, including what new insights they may have gained. In addition, although all persons have some level of knowledge of their values, interests, skills, employment preferences, personality, and aptitudes, they often do not have the information organized in a way that is easily used in making career choices. Using a simple schema for organizing self-knowledge, such as values, interests, skills, and employment preferences, can make it easier for persons to manage and use the information they have about themselves.

Motivating Persons to Enhance Knowledge of the World of Work Career assessment can also motivate persons to clarify what they know about the world of work (Analysis-options phase of the CASVE cycle). The prospect of reviewing numerous occupations and related education and training options can be overwhelming, especially for persons with low readiness for career choice. Having a simplified schema for organizing the world of work can make the task of learning about options less daunting because all options can be categorized according to the schema. Instead of dealing with hundreds of options, individuals can deal with a handful of occupational categories that relate to almost all occupations. Having a manageable way of effectively organizing what they already know can motivate individuals to add further knowledge. Many interest inventories and CACG systems present assessment results organized by a world-of-work schema, such as the Holland Hexagon (Holland, 1997) in the Self-Directed Search (Holland, 1994a). Card sorts can also be used as a cognitive mapping tool that allows individuals to reveal a personalized schema of the world of work and their depth of occupational knowledge (Peterson, 1998).

Generating Career Options Career assessment can also help persons generate career options that they might not have considered in the past (Synthesis-elaboration phase of the CASVE cycle). Although most individuals have an idea of one or more career options worth considering, they generally are not aware of the full range of occupations or programs of study that are congruent with their values, interests, skills, and employment preferences. Counselors need to be sensitive to clients whose life history, disability, ethnicity, socioeconomic circumstances, and related factors may have limited their awareness of occupational alternatives. Many interest inventories and CACG systems generate career options that fit various combinations of values, interests, skills, and employment preferences. The danger, however, in using career assessments to generate career options for consideration is that persons may view generating options as the end of career exploration rather than as a way to broaden career exploration. Practitioners need to ensure that persons understand that career assessments are not a tool for gaining magical solutions to career problems with little effort. Career assessments are best used to promote rather than limit career exploration; they do not provide "the answer" or "the best option" for the person.

Narrowing Career Options After Generating Career Options Some career assessments and CACG systems provide an indication of the goodness of fit between individuals' characteristics and specific occupations and educational opportunities (Synthesis-crystallization phase of the CASVE cycle). This use of assessment can help individuals decide which alternatives merit further consideration out of all possible options. One problem with the use of goodness of fit is that individuals may assume that the test or computer system is very precise and that poorly fitting options do not warrant further consideration, even when those options may be worth exploring for some other reason. With CACG systems, in particular, it is desirable to complete assessment and search functions several times to examine the impact of changing the individual characteristics on the options generated. The narrowed career options can then be used in the subsequent Valuing phase of the CASVE cycle.

Evaluating Narrowed Options Persons can reconsider or add to self-knowledge needed to choose among options remaining after completing Synthesis-crystallization (and moving on to the Valuing phase of the CASVE cycle). Reviewing values, interests, skills, and employment preferences provides part of the basis necessary for persons to evaluate the relative costs and benefits associated with the final set of career options they are considering. For some clients, weighing their options with respect to family, cultural, and societal factors may be important in narrowing their choices. Careful thought about several competing career options may cause persons to reevaluate their values, interests, skills, and employment preferences, potentially leading to generation of new career options (Synthesis-elaboration).

Preparing for Choice Implementation The results from previous career assessments can help individuals prepare for implementing their choices by clarifying how their characteristics fit with various occupational, educational, or employment options (Execution phase of the CASVE cycle). For example, assessment resources that were previously used to clarify values, interests, skills, and employment preferences can now also be used to provide individuals with a focal point for reviewing employment literature. As a result, individuals are better prepared to articulate, in an employment interview, how their characteristics and preferences fit with the needs and environment of a potential employer. Previous skills assessments can also be used to complete a skills section of a functional resume or the skills component of an educational and work portfolio.

A Schema for Organizing Career Assessments

As we stated in Chapter 1, career assessment can generally be categorized as either self-assessment or practitioner assisted. *Self-assessment* resources are designed to be used without practitioner assistance to select, administer, score, profile, and interpret the measure. This assumes that the self-assessment has been validated for self-help use. Self-assessments include objective instruments and structured exercises. Self-assessment is appropriate for individuals with high decision-making readiness who are seeking independent use of career resources. *Practitioner-assisted assessments* are designed for use within the context of a helping relationship with a practitioner who is qualified to use the assessment. The client and the practitioner collaboratively select an appropriate assessment, with the practitioner supervising or providing administration, scoring, profiling, and interpretation. Practitioner-assisted assessments include objective instruments, structured exercises, card sorts, and interviews (both structured and unstructured). Practitioner-assisted assessment is appropriate for clients with moderate to low decision-making readiness who are using career resources with assistance from a practitioner. Although a self-assessment measure can be ethically used in a practitioner-assisted environment, it is unethical to use a

Table 7.1 Examples of Options Available for Practitioner-Assisted Career Assessment

Clear Stimulus and Clear Response

Career Thoughts Inventory

Self-Directed Search

Strong Interest Inventory

Campbell Interest and Skills Survey

Clear Stimulus and Ambiguous Response

Card sorts

Career-o-Gram

Problem space assessment

Work sample assessment

Structured interview

Assessment center tasks

Ambiguous Stimulus and Clear Response

Occupational Alternatives Question

Ambiguous Stimulus and Ambiguous Response

Unstructured interview

Autobiography

Lifeline

---

practitioner-assisted assessment in a self-help environment because these measures are not typically validated for such use (Sampson, Purgar, & Shy, 2002).

Table 7.1 presents a schema for organizing practitioner-assisted assessment (Peterson et al., 1991). This schema is provided to help practitioners generate a full range of possible options for career assessment. Examples of career assessments can be categorized by the *stimulus* the person receives (clear or ambiguous) and the *response* the person makes to the assessment (clear or ambiguous). Practitioners are encouraged to use all categories of career assessment shown in Table 7.1 and to avoid the assumption that career assessment consists only of objective measures having a clear stimulus and a clear response.

Available Career Assessments

Numerous published and unpublished career assessments are available for use in self-help or practitioner-assisted modes in paper-and-pencil, personal computer, and Internet versions. Kapes and Whitfield (2001) present comprehensive descriptions of 49 career assessments. Kapes and Whitfield use the follow schema for categorizing career assessments: (a) aptitude, achievement, and comprehensive measures; (b) interest and work values inventories; (c) career development and career maturity measures; (d) personality assessments; and (e) instruments for special populations. Information is typically provided on target population, purpose, scales, publication date, languages available, time required, presentation of results, scoring, and costs. Kapes and Whitfield also provide brief descriptive information on 270 additional instruments. Other descriptions of career assessments can be found in Herr and Cramer (1996), Brown (2003), Zunker (2002), and Zunker and Osborn (2002).

Evaluating the Quality of Career Assessments

Career assessment measures range in quality from reliable and valid to unreliable and invalid. Reliability refers to evidence of the consistency of the measure, whereas validity refers to evidence that the test measures what it is designed to measure. Quality career assessments provide evidence of the reliability and validity of the measure. Questionable career assessments may be well developed but lack evidence of quality, or the measure may simply be poorly developed. A lack of documentation of the quality of career assessments delivered on the Internet appears to be a particularly serious problem (Oliver & Zack, 1999). The use of questionable assessments with individuals and clients may negate the potential contributions of career assessment to career choice described previously. Helping professionals who use questionable assessments are in violation of ethical codes.

Kapes and Whitfield (2001) also present reviews of 49 career assessments. Standards governing quality development and use of assessments have been established by the American Educational Research Association, American Psychological Association, and National Council on Measurement in Education (1999); the Joint Committee on Testing Practices (1988); and the Association for Measurement and Evaluation in Counseling and Development (1989).

Promoting Effective Use of Career Assessments

Three basic strategies exist for helping persons make effective use of career resources (assessments, information, and instruction). The three strategies are screening, orientation, and follow-up (Sampson, 1997). *Screening* helps to ensure that career resource use is appropriate for the person's needs. As stated in Chapter 4, screening can be brief (question and answer) or comprehensive (use of a readiness assessment measure). *Orientation* helps ensure that persons make effective use of career resources by promoting a realistic understanding of the potential benefits, limitations, and functioning of the resource in relation to their needs. *Follow-up* helps ensure that persons have appropriately used career resource features to meet their previously identified needs and that they have a plan for future action. Zunker and Osborn (2002) have developed a cyclical and continuous model for using assessment results in career counseling that includes analyzing needs, establishing purpose, determining instruments, utilizing results, and making a decision about work or training/education.

As previously discussed (see Chapter 4), the three levels of service delivery in the CIP approach are self-help, brief staff-assisted, and individual case-managed services.

1. If an individual shows high readiness for career choice during screening, the use of career resources can continue in a self-help mode, with orientation and follow-up provided if requested by the individual.
2. If the screening process indicates that the client has moderate readiness for career choice, then a brief staff-assisted intervention is likely needed, with an orientation provided prior to the use of career resources and follow-up provided after resources have been completed.
3. If the screening process indicates that the client has low readiness for career choice, then an individual case-managed intervention is likely needed, and a recurring cycle of orientation to and follow-up after each resource or resource feature is provided until the individual's needs are met or an appropriate referral is made for other services.

In self-help services, self-assessments are used. In brief staff-assisted and individual case-managed services, practitioner-assisted assessments are used, although self-assessments can also be used. Strategies differ for promoting the effective use of self-assessment and practitioner-assisted assessment and are described in the following sections.

Self-Assessment in Self-Help Services In self-assessment, the individual, the practitioner, or both have decided that a self-help intervention is appropriate (the screening function). Orientation to the self-assessment is typically embedded in the instructions for the instrument being used (for the Self-Directed Search, see Holland, 1994a). Follow-up to the use of self-assessment can also be provided (for the recommended follow-up activities for the Self-Directed Search, see Holland, 1994b).

Practitioner-Assisted Assessment in Brief Staff-Assisted and Individual Case-Managed Services In practitioner-assisted assessment, screening has already occurred because a decision has been made that some assistance with assessment is needed. Orientation begins with the development of the Individual Learning Plan (ILP), as described in Chapter 4. An assessment is listed as one of the ILP activities; and the purpose/outcome of completing the assessment, the estimated completion time, and the way in which completing the assessment relates to ILP goals are briefly discussed. Follow-up occurs when the practitioner reviews assessment results with the client and establishes a plan for using this information in career choice. For a low-readiness client, the practitioner needs to take care that negative thoughts have not interfered with the client's capacity to respond to individual test items. For example, negative thoughts about self can limit responses to inventories of interests or skills. Practitioners can identify potential negative thoughts by asking clients to verbalize the thought process they used to respond to individual items that reflect a perceived lack of interest or skill.

CAREER INFORMATION

Career information is typically used to help persons enhance their knowledge of occupational, educational, training, and employment options. This section begins with an exploration of the potential contributions that career information can make to individuals' career choices. The section then explains a schema for organizing career information and provides examples, identifies available career information, reviews quality issues, and reviews a model for promoting effective use of career information.

Potential Contributions of Career Information to Career Choice

Career information, like career assessment, has the potential to help individuals progress through the CASVE cycle. The following section examines seven potential contributions of career information to career choice.

Enhancing Awareness of Career Problems and Promoting the Motivation to Change Exposure to career information, such as a description of a new high-wage occupation or general employment opportunities in a geographic location, can help persons become aware that they may have a career problem (i.e., gap) that needs attention. The possibility of earning more money or living in a nicer location is an example of such a gap (Communication phase of the CASVE cycle). This type of career information might be utilized by reading a magazine article or Internet Web page, viewing a presentation on television, or listening to information provided by a significant other.

Clarifying Self-Knowledge Career information can be used to clarify self-knowledge by helping individuals reconsider their values, interests, skills, and employment preferences based on what they have learned from occupational, educational, and employment information (Analysis–self-knowledge phase of the CASVE cycle). For example, after using various assessment resources to gain an initial clarification of values, interests, skills, and employment preferences, individuals can use occupational information to identify opportunities for satisfying their values. As a result of using occupational information, individuals may discover that what they thought they wanted (such as being a leader with substantial authority over others) was no longer desirable. The doubts that now exist can motivate individuals to return to the assessment process to further clarify their self-knowledge. Individuals can now respond to assessments with a more differentiated view of what they want or do not want.

Motivating Persons to Enhance Knowledge of Options Career information can be used to increase individuals' motivation for career exploration by increasing their awareness of the nature of available options (Analysis-options phase of the CASVE cycle). Involving at-risk youth in a university-based summer program to heighten their awareness of occupational alternatives in math and science is one example of a programmatic approach to helping persons acquire occupational awareness. An employed adult reading about emerging occupations in a business magazine is an example of a serendipitous approach to promoting awareness. One learning outcome of this use of career information is to motivate the individual to invest the time necessary to engage in further career problem solving and decision making.

Preparing for Assessments That Generate Career Options Career information can be used before the completion of career assessments to better prepare persons to respond thoughtfully to assessments that ultimately generate lists of career options (Synthesis-elaboration phase of the CASVE cycle). Many interest inventories and CACG systems generate lists of occupations or programs of study. Some individuals have difficulty in confidently responding to test items or selecting and rating computer search criteria. By reading the description of one or two occupations before using an assessment, the individual has a concrete example to reflect on regarding personal characteristics related to occupations. This is analogous to warming up the engine of a car in the winter before driving or stretching before exercising.

Narrowing Career Options After Generating Career Options Career information can be used to narrow career options after receiving lists of occupations, programs of study, or educational institutions from various assessments or CACG systems (Synthesis-crystallization phase of the CASVE cycle). This use of information can help individuals decide which alternatives merit further consideration. One problem with Synthesis-elaboration is that individuals can become easily overwhelmed with the number of options presented by assessments and computer systems. Becoming overwhelmed may decrease individuals' motivation to continue with career exploration. One strategy for dealing with this problem is to use a small number of information topics to rapidly sort through options, discarding inappropriate alternatives and retaining potentially satisfactory options. One learning outcome of this use of career information is to increase the motivation necessary to complete a more thorough analysis of occupations that have been identified. Another learning outcome is to make the individual more confident that potentially appropriate options were not missed. A written exercise is available to assist with this process (Sampson & Lenz, 2002).

Evaluating Narrowed Options After the individual has identified three to five options for more detailed analysis, career information can be reconsidered, or added to, so that finer distinctions can be made among potentially appealing alternatives (Valuing phase of the CASVE cycle). This careful review of career information to support evaluation of the costs and benefits of narrowed options can help persons develop more confidence in the selection of a tentative first and second choice. It is possible that after learning further details about occupations, educational institutions, training providers, or employers, individuals may lose confidence in the appropriateness of the options they are considering or in the assessment responses or computer search criteria they used to generate options. In this case, the person will need to return to Analysis–self-knowledge. This is an example of career problem solving and decision making being an iterative or recursive process.

Preparing for Choice Implementation Career information can help persons prepare to implement their career choice, whether it is job placement, an educational pursuit, or retirement (Execution phase of the CASVE cycle). For example, career information can provide a foundation for subsequent review of employer recruitment literature. By having general occupational information on work tasks, income, working conditions, and so forth, persons are better able to evaluate how a particular employer may, or may not, vary from the norm. Career information can also help persons prepare to evaluate job offers in the same manner.

A Schema for Organizing Career Information

A vast amount of career information is available to persons seeking to make career choices. Table 7.2 provides a schema for organizing career information and specific examples for occupational, educational, training, and employment information.

Available Career Information

Career information is available in a variety of media and can be categorized as noninteractive or interactive.

Noninteractive Career Information Information delivered through noninteractive media is generally linear in nature. The structure of the medium influences the selection and sequencing of the information presented. In comparison with interactive media, noninteractive media generally have the advantages of broader and more detailed topic coverage and lower cost; the disadvantage is a reduced potential for motivating further exploratory behavior. The similarities and differences between noninteractive and interactive media presented in this chapter are generalizations, which have the limitation of not applying in all circumstances. This discussion of similarities and differences is intended to provide a frame of reference for comparing and contrasting various types of media. Table 7.3 provides examples of noninteractive career information media.

Interactive Career Information Interactive media are generally nonlinear in nature. The person maintains some control over the selection and sequencing of information. In comparison with noninteractive media, interactive media have the advantage of enhancing motivation for career exploration and the disadvantages of typically higher cost and less detailed topic coverage. Table 7.4 presents examples of interactive career information media.

The greatest change that has occurred in the delivery of career information has been the use of the Internet for dissemination of information. The following Web sites deliver a broad diversity of career information:

1. O*NET at http://online.onetcenter.org/ (U. S. Department of Labor, 2001)
2. ACINet at www.acinet.org/acinet/ (U. S. Department of Labor, 2002)
3. *Occupational Outlook Handbook* at www.bls.gov/oco/ (Bureau of Labor Statistics, 2002)
4. Computer-based career information delivery systems at www.acsci.org/acsci_states.asp (Association of Computer-Based Systems for Career Information, 2001)

Table 7.2 | A Schema for Organizing Career Information

Occupational Information Elements

Nature of the Work

- Abilities/skills of typical workers
- Aptitudes of typical workers
- Interests of typical workers
- Overview/definition
- Pros & cons of the work
- Temperaments of typical workers
- Tools & equipment used
- Values of typical workers
- Work location
- Work tasks/activities
- Working conditions/environment
- Classification data codes (O*NET, SOC, DOT code)
- Related civilian occupations
- Related military occupations
- Sources of additional information

Nature of Employment

- Earnings/wages
- Employment statistics
- Fringe benefits
- Future employment outlook
- Job security
- Opportunities for advancement
- Typical job titles

Requirements for Employment

- Educational/training/apprenticeship
- Licensing/certification

Educational Information Elements

Nature of the Education

- Alternative credit options
- Apprenticeship opportunities
- Contact for further information
- Degree/certificate requirements
- Degrees/certificates offered
- Foreign study options
- Honors courses/program
- Military training opportunities
- Placement of graduates
- Programs of study/majors

Nature of the Institution

- Academic calendar
- Accreditation
- Activities & sports
- Community size/type
- Degree/certificate completion time
- Degree/certificate completion %
- Enrollment
- Faculty characteristics
- Housing/residence
- Institutional affiliation/control
- Pros & cons of the institution
- Student body characteristics
- Student services
- Type of institution

Admissions

- Admissions process
- Admissions selectivity
- Costs
- Entrance requirements
- Financial aid
- Scholarships

Table 7.2 (*continued*)

Training Information Elements

Nature of the Training

- Certification available
- Length of training
- Knowledge obtained
- Skills obtained
- Training content
- Training method—On the job, On-line, Apprenticeship, etc.

Nature of the Training Provider

- Accreditation
- Location of training
- Provider contact information
- Trainer credentials

Admissions

- Application process
- Costs
- Financial aid
- Scholarships
- Training prerequisites

Employment Information Elements

Sector

- Employer types
- Employment statistics
- Future outlook
- Size

Industry

- Employment statistics
- Future outlook
- Size
- Sources of additional information
- Typical employers
- Typical occupations

Employer

- Advancement opportunities
- Employment statistics
- Fringe benefits
- Human resource development offerings
- Location(s)
- Occupations employed
- Recent employer financial performance
- Sector
- Size
- Sources of additional information
- Training policy and opportunities

Position

- Contact person
- Compatibility with co-workers
- Duties
- Educational qualifications
- Experience qualifications
- Fringe benefits
- Licensure/certification
- Local environment
- Location
- Potential use of values, interests, & skills
- Pros & cons of the position
- Recent employer financial performance
- Relocation services
- Salary
- Schedule, hours worked, and travel required
- Security
- Training provided

Table 7.3 | Noninteractive Career Information Media

Medium	Examples
Print	Books, pamphlets, brochures, and files
Microform	Microfiche and microfilm
Audio	Commercially and locally produced audiocassette programs, broadcast and Web-based radio programs
Video	Commercially and locally produced videotape, Web-based, and broadcast television programs
Public presentations	Speeches and panel discussions with limited audience participation
Assessment	Paper-and-pencil, personal computer-based, and Internet-based measures of values, interests, skills, and employment preferences

Table 7.4 | Interactive Career Information Media

Medium	Examples
Internet Web sites	Employer, job bank, occupational, or educational information Web sites
Computer-assisted career guidance systems	Personal computer–based or Internet-based guidance systems
Computer-assisted instruction	Instruction and assistance in resume preparation
CD-ROM or DVD	Reference or descriptive information on various employers
Card sorts	Self- or counselor-guided assessment of values, interests, skills, and employment preferences
Programmed instruction	Job experience kit that provides the opportunity to perform actual job tasks
Structured interview	Interviewing a currently employed worker at the job site or at a career day or career fair
Role playing or games	Classroom or group career-guidance activity that allows students to try out career and life options
Instruction	Classroom activities that allow individuals to try out various work behaviors (e.g., accounting, welding)
Synthetic work environment	A flight training simulator for pilots
Direct observation	Shadowing a worker for a day to observe typical work tasks, or taking field trips to places of employment
Direct exploration	Volunteer work, cooperative education, internships, work-study programs, or part-time employment
Social interaction	Conversations with parents, relatives, peers, school personnel, and acquaintances about various career opportunities

Evaluating the Quality of Career Information

Career information ranges in quality from valid and usable to invalid and unusable. Appearance is not a reliable guide to the quality of the information; bad information is sometimes well presented. As in assessment, the provision of invalid and unusable information to individuals and clients may negate the potential contributions of career information to career choice described previously. Helping professionals who use information with undocumented validity are in violation of ethical codes.

The Career Development Quarterly provides reviews of career information according to the *Guidelines for the Preparation and Evaluation of Career and Occupational Information Literature* (National Career Development Association [NCDA], 1991b). Additional standards for the quality of career information are available in the *Career Software Review Guidelines, Guidelines for the Preparation and Evaluation of Video Career Media,* and *NCDA Guidelines for the Use of the Internet for Provision of Career Information and Planning Services* (NCDA, 1991a, 1992, 1997), available on-line from the NCDA. Another resource, the *Handbook of Standards for the Operation of Computer-Based Career Information Systems,* is available on-line from the Association of Computer-Based Systems for Career Information (1999).

Promoting Effective Use of Career Information

As stated previously in this chapter, the use of career information in career services is a learning event (Peterson et al., 1991). In order to promote learning, persons need to be able to appropriately select, locate, sequence, and use career information (Sampson, 1999). *Selecting* career information involves choosing information that is related to specific needs, such as the needs reflected in the goals and purpose/outcome statement on an ILP. *Locating* career information involves acquiring the career information that has been selected to meet a person's needs. *Sequencing* career information involves ordering information resources to maximize the potential for learning. For example, reading general descriptions of occupations helps persons prepare for an information interview or a job interview, as sequenced on a module sheet or an ILP. It is important to note that not all career information needs to be sequenced. Sequencing is only recommended when ordering enhances learning. *Using* career information involves reading, listening to, or viewing the information as suggested by instructions included with the information or by following recommendations of a practitioner. For example, comprehensive instructions for use are often included in CACG systems. The process of selecting, locating, sequencing, and using career information is a part of the orientation function described earlier in the section on career assessment. Strategies differ for promoting the effective selection, location, sequencing, and use of career information in self-help and practitioner-assisted services (brief staff-assisted and individual case-managed), as well as for screening, orientation, and follow-up, and are described in the following sections.

Career Information in Self-Help Services

Selecting Career Information The practitioner can facilitate a client's appropriate selection of career information by making recommendations for matching career information resources with specific needs that are included on module sheets/resource guides, in a career library index, or on an Internet Web site.

Locating Career Information The practitioner can help the client locate selected career information by use of signage identifying resource locations in a career library, an index of career resources that includes location, a map of a career library showing resource locations, and links on an Internet Web site.

Sequencing Career Information If necessary, the practitioner can provide recommendations on module sheets/resource guides for sequencing the individual's selected career information.

Using Career Information Recommendations for using career information can be included as part of the information resource itself.

Screening, Orientation, and Follow-Up In self-help services, the individual, the practitioner, or both have decided that a self-help intervention is appropriate (the screening function). Orientation to the career information is typically embedded in the instructions for the information being used (see the instructions typically included in a CACG system). Follow-up to the use of career information can also be provided within the information resource (see the recommended follow-up activities for some CACG systems).

Career Information in Brief Staff-Assisted and Individual Case-Managed Services

Selecting Career Information The practitioner can make recommendations and document them on the ILP to facilitate the individual's appropriate selection of career information.

Locating Career Information The practitioner can help the client locate career information by modeling information-seeking behavior, showing the client how to use signage, indexes, maps, and Internet Web sites.

Sequencing Career Information Appropriate sequencing of career information, if necessary, can be included using the priority feature of the ILP.

Using Career Information The practitioner can facilitate the client's use of career information by briefly reviewing usage instructions or demonstrating the use of an information resource. As the practitioner observes information use by the client, positive reinforcement can be provided to further enhance the motivation of the client to increase use of the resource.

Screening, Orientation, and Follow-Up As in career assessment, screening has already occurred because a decision has been made that some assistance with information use is needed. Orientation begins with the development of the ILP. Career in-

Table 7.5 | Relating Screening, Orientation, and Follow-Up to Selecting, Locating, Sequencing, and Using Career Information

Screening
Orientation
  Selecting career information
  Locating career information
  Sequencing career information
  Using career information
Follow-up

formation is listed as one of the ILP activities, and the purpose/outcome of using the information, the estimated completion time, and the way in which the information relates to ILP goals are briefly discussed. Follow-up occurs when the practitioner talks with the client to clarify the nature of the client's learning experience and a plan is established for using what has been learned in making a career choice. For a low-readiness client, the practitioner must also take care that negative thoughts have not interfered with the client's capacity to learn. For example, negative thoughts about self can limit a client's motivation to use information resources. Negative thoughts can also cause clients to perceive that they will not be successful with job tasks associated with an occupation or learning tasks associated with education or training. The practitioner can identify potential negative thoughts by asking clients to verbalize the thought process they are using as they read career information. Table 7.5 presents a schema for relating screening, orientation, and follow-up to selecting, locating, sequencing, and using career information.

Additional Considerations Several additional considerations can contribute to effective use of career information (Peterson et al., 1991). The following section includes brief recommendations on readiness for career choice, decidedness, motivation, verbal aptitude, decision-making style, and balance of presentation. These recommendations represent generalizations that may not be true in a particular circumstance. Practitioners can use these recommendations to suggest how to help persons use career information effectively.

Readiness for Career Choice Persons with higher readiness for career choice need less assistance from a practitioner to use career information, whereas persons with lower readiness need more assistance.

Decidedness Persons who are decided and undecided need less assistance from a practitioner to use career information, whereas persons who are indecisive generally need more assistance.

Motivation Persons who are highly motivated to engage in career choice need less assistance from a practitioner to use career information, whereas poorly motivated clients need more assistance. Using the features of the ILP, as well as modeling and reinforcing information-seeking behaviors, can enhance motivation for career choice.

Verbal Aptitude Persons with higher verbal aptitude need less assistance from a practitioner to use career information, whereas persons with lower verbal aptitude need more assistance. Persons with higher verbal aptitude can make better use of information resources requiring a higher reading comprehension level, and persons with lower verbal aptitude need resources designed for lower reading levels.

Decision-Making Style Persons can have a spontaneous to systematic approach to information gathering and an external to internal approach to information processing (Johnson, 1978). For example, a person with a spontaneous, external decision-making style might benefit from a structured interview with a currently employed person, whereas an individual with a systematic, internal style may prefer to work with self-study materials before engaging in interviews.

Balance of Presentation Persons need access to negative career information describing options as well as positive career information in order to maximize the potential for learning (Reardon, 1984). Information that is overly positive does not facilitate critical thinking about the costs and benefits of career options that takes place in the Valuing phase of the CASVE cycle.

CAREER INSTRUCTION

As stated in Chapter 1, career instruction is also used to help persons clarify their knowledge of self, their options, and the decision-making process. In this way, instruction is similar to career assessment and career information described previously. However, there are also several differences. Instruction integrates several sources of data in a meaningful sequence designed to achieve a specific learning outcome. Instruction also typically includes some type of evaluation of how well persons have mastered the intended learning objectives. In comparison with career assessment and career information, instruction is a less commonly available type of career resource. Instruction most commonly occurs in K–12 schools as part of instruction in specific subjects, in higher education as credit and noncredit courses, and on some occasions as part of continuing education programs or organization-based courses.

Because instruction typically includes career assessment and information, the potential contributions of assessment and information to career choice described previously apply to instruction as well. By its nature, instruction is practitioner assisted for both assessment and information. Folsom and Reardon (2000) provided a comprehensive description of the effects of college career courses on learner outputs and outcomes in higher. A career course syllabus can be viewed on-line at www.career.fsu.edu/techcenter/instructor/undergraduate/.

Screening occurs when an individual decides (sometimes with input from a staff member) that instruction is needed and registers for a course. Depending on the rules of the institution or organization, instructor permission may be required to take the course, and screening can be accomplished by admitting only students with moderate to low levels of readiness for career choice. Orientation occurs as the nature, purpose, time commitment, and relationship to student goals of assignments are discussed in class. Students can use an ILP or similar performance contract to help keep track of class assignments (Reardon, Lenz, Sampson, & Peterson, 2000). Follow-up occurs as the instructor monitors student progress and provides feedback on individual assignments.

SUMMARY

This chapter described the planning and delivery of career resources and presented examples of the use of the Pyramid of Information Processing Domains and the CASVE cycle with career assessment, information, and instruction. Career assessment was examined in terms of potential contributions to career choice, a schema for organizing assessments, available assessments, evaluation of quality, and promotion of effective use. Career information was examined in a similar way in terms of potential contributions, organizational schema, available information, evaluation of quality, and promotion of effective use. The chapter ended with an examination of instruction as a career resource.

GETTING THE MOST BENEFIT FROM READING THIS CHAPTER

To effectively learn the material in this chapter, complete one or more of the following activities:

- Write down the similarities and differences between career assessment, career information, and career instruction.
- In your own words, describe the potential contributions of career assessment and career information to career choice.
- Talk with a career counselor about the range of career assessments he or she uses in practice. Think about other assessment options, if any, that could be added.
- Complete and have interpreted by a counselor several career assessments. Consider how these assessments might have helped with your own career choice.
- Talk with a career counselor about the strategies he or she uses to help persons benefit from career assessment.
- Talk with a career counselor about the range of career information he or she uses in practice. Think about other information options, if any, that could be added.
- Use several career information sources, and consider how this information might have helped with your own career choice.
- Talk with a career counselor about the strategies he or she uses to help persons benefit from using career information.

- Talk with an instructor about the potential contributions that his or her career course has for students. Review the syllabus for the course, paying attention to assignments and resources used.

REFERENCES

American Educational Research Association, American Psychological Association, & National Council on Measurement in Education. (1999). *Standards for educational and psychological testing.* Washington, DC: American Psychological Association.

Association for Measurement and Evaluation in Counseling and Development. (1989). *Responsibilities of users of standardized tests.* Alexandria, VA: American Association for Counseling and Development.

Association of Computer-Based Systems for Career Information. (1999). *Handbook of standards for the operation of computer-based career information systems* [On-line]. Available: www.acsci.org/acsci_pubs1.htm.

Association of Computer-Based Systems for Career Information. (2001). *State sites* [On-line]. Available: www.acsci.org/acsci_states.asp.

Brown, D. (2003). *Career information, career counseling, and career development* (8th ed.). Boston: Allyn & Bacon.

Bureau of Labor Statistics. (2002). *Occupational outlook handbook* [On-line]. Available: www.bls.gov/oco/.

Folsom, B., & Reardon, R. C. (2000). *The effects of college career courses on learner outputs and outcomes: Technical report no. 26* [On-line]. Available: www.career.fsu.edu/techcenter/instructor/undergraduate/.

Herr, E. L., & Cramer, S. H. (1996). *Career guidance and counseling through the life span: Systematic approaches* (5th ed.). New York: HarperCollins.

Holland, J. L. (1994a). *Self-Directed Search* (4th ed.). Odessa, FL: Psychological Assessment Resources.

Holland, J. L. (1994b). *You and your career* (4th ed.). Odessa, FL: Psychological Assessment Resources.

Holland, J. L. (1997). *Making vocational choices: A theory of vocational personalities and work environments* (3rd ed.). Odessa, FL: Psychological Assessment Resources.

Johnson, R. H. (1978). Individual styles of decision making: A theoretical model for counseling. *The Personnel and Guidance Journal, 56,* 530–536.

Joint Committee on Testing Practices. (1988). *Code of fair testing practices in education.* Washington, DC: American Psychological Association.

Kapes, J. T., & Whitfield, E. A. (2001). *A counselor's guide to career assessment instruments* (4th ed.). Tulsa, OK: National Career Development Association.

National Career Development Association. (1991a). *Career software review guidelines* [On-line]. Available: www.ncda.org/about/polsrg.html.

National Career Development Association. (1991b). *Guidelines for the preparation and evaluation of career and occupational information literature* [On-line]. Available: www.ncda.org/about/polcoil.html.

National Career Development Association. (1992). *Guidelines for the preparation and evaluation of video career media* [On-line]. Available: www.ncda.org/about/polvid.html.

National Career Development Association. (1997). *NCDA guidelines for the use of the Internet for provision of career information and planning services* [On-line]. Available: www.ncda.org/about/polnet.html.

Oliver, L. W., & Zack, J. S. (1999). Career assessment on the Internet: An exploratory study. *Journal of Career Assessment, 7,* 323–356.

Peterson, G. W. (1998). Using a vocational card sort as an assessment of occupational knowledge. *Journal of Career Assessment, 6,* 49–67.

Peterson, G. W., Sampson, J. P., Jr., Lenz, J. G., & Reardon, R. C. (2002). A cognitive information processing approach to career problem solving and decision making. In D. Brown (Ed.), *Career choice and development* (4th ed.) (pp. 312–369). San Francisco: Jossey-Bass.

Peterson, G. W., Sampson, J. P., Jr., & Reardon, R. C. (1991). *Career development and services: A cognitive approach.* Pacific Grove, CA: Brooks/Cole.

Peterson, G. W., Sampson, J. P., Jr., Reardon, R. C., & Lenz, J. G. (1996). Becoming career problem solvers and decision makers: A cognitive information processing approach. In D. Brown & L. Brooks (Eds.), *Career choice and development* (3rd ed.) (pp. 423–475). San Francisco: Jossey-Bass.

Reardon, R. C. (1984). Use of information in career counseling. In H. D. Burck & R. C. Reardon (Eds.), *Career development interventions* (pp. 53–68). Springfield, IL: Charles C Thomas.

Reardon, R. C., Lenz, J. G., Sampson, J. P., Jr., & Peterson, G. W. (2000). *Instructor's manual for career development and planning: A comprehensive approach.* Pacific Grove, CA: Brooks/Cole.

Sampson, J. P., Jr. (1997). *Helping clients get the most from computer-assisted career guidance systems.* Paper presented at the Australian Association of Career Counselors 7th National/International Conference, Brisbane, Australia.

Sampson, J. P., Jr. (1999). Integrating Internet-based distance guidance with services provided in career centers. *The Career Development Quarterly, 47,* 243–254.

Sampson, J. P., Jr., & Lenz, J. G. (2002). *Career information exercise.* Unpublished manuscript, Florida State University, Center for the Study of Technology in Counseling and Career Development, Tallahassee.

Sampson, J. P., Jr., Peterson, G. W., Lenz, J. G., Reardon, R. C., & Saunders, D. E. (1996a). *Career Thoughts Inventory.* Odessa, FL: Psychological Assessment Resources.

Sampson, J. P., Jr., Peterson, G. W., Lenz, J. G., Reardon, R. C., & Saunders, D. E. (1996b). *Improving your career thoughts: A workbook for the Career Thoughts Inventory.* Odessa, FL: Psychological Assessment Resources.

Sampson, J. P., Jr., Peterson, G. W., Reardon, R. C., & Lenz, J. G. (2000). Using readiness assessment to improve career services: A cognitive information processing approach. *The Career Development Quarterly, 49,* 146–174.

Sampson, J. P., Jr., Purgar, M. P., & Shy, J. (2002). Computer-based test interpretation in career assessment: Ethical and professional issues. *Journal of Career Assessment, 10* (4), 400–417.

Super, D. E. (1990). A life-span, life-space approach to career development. In D. Brown & L. Brooks (Eds.), *Career choice and development* (2nd ed.) (pp. 197–261). San Francisco: Jossey-Bass.

U. S. Department of Labor. (2001). *O*NET* [On-line]. Available: http://online.onetcenter.org/.

U. S. Department of Labor. (2002). *America's Career InfoNet* [On-line]. Available: www.acinet.org/acinet/.

Zunker, V. G. (2002). *Career counseling: Applied concepts of life planning* (6th ed.). Pacific Grove, CA: Brooks/Cole.

Zunker, V. G., & Osborn, D. N. (2002). *Using assessment results for career development* (6th ed.). Pacific Grove, CA: Brooks/Cole.

8 CHAPTER Case Study for Individual Case-Managed Services

This chapter presents a case study showing how the CIP approach can be used in individual career counseling, which is one form of individual case-managed services. After reviewing this chapter, the reader should understand how the CIP approach could be used in individual career counseling. The chapter is organized as follows:

- Case Study: Joe
- Summary
- Getting the Most Benefit from Reading This Chapter

The case study in this chapter shows how a practitioner in a career center or counseling center might use the CIP approach to develop an Individual Learning Plan (ILP) to help the client become a better career problem solver and decision maker. The case study allows us to illustrate the nature of complex career problems and the way they may be addressed within the CIP approach. Although this case study does not fully represent the cognitive complexity of the client's career problem solving and decision making or depict the full range of service delivery options available, it does demonstrate how the CIP paradigm might be used to deliver individual case-managed career services.

The case studies presented in this book are composite descriptions of hypothetical individuals drawn from the counseling experience of the authors. Any resemblance, therefore, to specific persons is purely coincidental. Although the case study presented in this chapter is hypothetical, the procedures and resources that are used reflect actual practice at the Florida State

University Career Center. The FSU Career Center is a comprehensive facility, providing counseling, experiential education, and placement services to students in local schools, students in higher education, and community-based adults in career transition. We want to emphasize that the assessment, information, and instructional resources used in this case are *not* the only resources that can be used with the CIP approach, as the theory accommodates the use of a wide range of career resources. We have limited the resources depicted in this case study to the actual resources we use in practice in order to present the most accurate picture possible of the application of the CIP approach in real life. The case of Joe is updated from the case presented in Peterson, Sampson, and Reardon (1991). Refer to Chapter 5 for a discussion of the readiness levels and career assistance options that provide the basis for the case studies presented in this book.

CASE STUDY: JOE

Background

Joe Williams is an 18-year-old community college freshman majoring in general studies. He is seeking assistance from the community college career resource center to help him decide what he wants to do in life. Joe's standardized test scores indicate that his mathematical skills are slightly above average and his verbal skills are slightly below average. These results are congruent with his school performance; he has a B average in math, an A average in physical education, and a C average in other subjects. Joe enjoys a variety of sports activities. Basketball is his favorite sport, and he was on the basketball team each year in high school.

Joe has held a variety of jobs. He has been a food service worker at a local fast-food restaurant, a grocery bagger, and a cashier at a local movie theater. His main objective in working has been to earn money for his car and for going out with his friends. When asked by his parents, "What do you want to do now that you've graduated from high school?" he was unable to provide a definite answer. His most consistent occupational aspiration has been to become an air force pilot. However, recently diagnosed limitations in his vision have eliminated this option. He now wears corrective glasses all the time.

In addition to having uncertain career plans, Joe doubts his general decision-making abilities. When making decisions, such as selecting a gift, purchasing clothes, or choosing a date, he often hesitates until forced by some external circumstances to decide. His parents often criticize Joe for his inability to make choices, especially when he delays making a decision so long that only one option remains. After Joe continued to express confusion regarding what he should do about his career, his mother suggested that he talk with a counselor at the community college.

Joe's mother owns and operates an office supply store; his father is a police officer. Joe's mother graduated from high school and has worked in various clerical jobs in the purchasing department of a local aluminum products manufacturer. After working for four years, she began attending community college in the evening to pursue a degree in fashion merchandising. Although her academic performance was satisfactory, she was unable to maintain adequate motivation to complete this program of study. An opportunity to move from her job in purchasing to a bookkeeping job in the comptroller's office resulted in greater job satisfaction. Encouraged by her success, she went on to complete an associate of science degree in accounting eight years ago. With the support of her family, four years ago she opened her own office supply store after working as an assistant manager of a similar business. Her job satisfaction has increased as a result of the greater independence and economic rewards, in spite of the greater time demands and risks that are part of her new job. Joe's mother's avocational pursuits are serving as financial secretary at her church, gardening, and competing regularly in an adult swimming league.

Joe's father has worked as a police officer for the past 21 years. As an adolescent, he thought that being a police officer would earn him respect from his peers and give him an opportunity to demonstrate his capabilities. After graduating from high school, he joined the army and served as a military police officer. This training and experience later enabled him to obtain a job as a police officer in the police department of his hometown. His work performance has been well above average, but the small size of the police department has not allowed for much advancement. In an attempt to improve his opportunities for promotion, Joe's father completed an associate of science degree in criminal justice two years ago. He has been given additional responsibility for supervising beginning police officers in local investigation procedures, but he is still frustrated by the lack of leadership opportunities within the department. Joe's father's avocational pursuits include playing basketball regularly in a YMCA league and coaching a YMCA youth basketball team. He is also an avid fisherman, and he and Joe still enjoy this activity together from time to time.

Several internal and external cues have prompted Joe to become aware of his career problem (the Communication phase of the CASVE cycle). His anxiety about the gap between his real state of affairs and his ideal state has increased considerably as his parents question his lack of future plans. He has received several external cues within the last two weeks. First, his best friend brought him an employment application form from the grocery store where the friend works. Second, the local army recruiter, who had talked with Joe at the community college, called to offer any additional information that Joe might need to decide about leaving college and joining the army. The fact that Joe was considering joining the army as an enlisted soldier, as opposed to completing college and entering the army as an officer, has created considerable conflict with his parents, especially with his father. Finally, Joe's mother told him that they would be finalizing their summer vacation plans within the next month and he needed to let them know what his summer plans were so that reservations could be made. The combination of internal and external pressure led Joe to take an initial step toward making a series of career decisions by making an appointment with a counselor, with the encouragement of his mother.

Joe's Career Counseling Sequence

Let us begin with the initial interview as a vehicle for understanding Joe's problem from a qualitative perspective. Joe and the counselor communicate or interact with the problem—the first step of the CASVE cycle presented in Chapter 2.

Initial Interview An individual assessment interview allows Joe's problem to be analyzed in terms of the characteristics of career problems presented in Chapter 1. These characteristics include (a) a gap, (b) ambiguous and complex cues, (c) interacting courses of action, (d) unpredictability of courses of action, and (e) solutions resulting in new problems. The career resource center's policy is that an individual appointment will be scheduled if sought by a prospective client. If the client and the counselor subsequently agree that individual counseling is not needed, the client will be referred to brief-staff assisted or self-help services. Fifty minutes were reserved for the initial interview and preliminary assessment. Joe arrives for his appointment and meets Marilyn Abbey, a National Certified Counselor with a master's degree in counseling who works as a staff member in the career resource center.

Marilyn began the session by asking Joe, "What brought you in to see me today?" Joe responded by saying, "I'm having a real hard time making a choice about what I'm going to do in the future. And this career thing is really beginning to stress me out." Marilyn then gained information about the nature of Joe's career problem.

Gap Joe enjoys the comfortable lifestyle that has resulted from his parents' economic success. He has observed the respect that his mother receives as a result of starting and maintaining a successful business, and the respect his father receives for his professional attitude and commitment as a police officer. Joe, too, would like to achieve respect as a result of his employment. Joe admires his mother's ability to be decisive and the way she achieves her goals. He also admires the independence his mother has at work and the self-reliant attitude his father has toward his work and avocational activities. Joe becomes anxious and then depressed when he perceives the gap between what he wants out of work and what he is receiving from his present job and future prospects.

Joe's best friend accepted a full-time job immediately after graduation as an assistant produce manager at the grocery store where he and Joe worked the previous summer. Joe often visits the apartments of two of his friends from high school who also graduated last year and are now working full-time in entry-level, semiskilled jobs. He is painfully aware of his friends' lower standard of living in comparison with that of his parents. Joe also perceives his friends' work as not providing the level of respect and independence he wants. Finally, he does not view himself as having the characteristics of decisiveness and self-reliance demonstrated by his mother.

> **COUNSELOR HYPOTHESIS:** Joe senses a considerable gap between his real state of affairs (low-paying job, low self-respect, indecisive) and his ideal state (higher status, greater independence, more self-respect, more decided).

Ambiguous and Complex Cues Joe has been receiving numerous cues from his environment about his career problem. Joe's best friend has been pressuring him to work at the grocery store and to share an apartment and expenses. His friend said, "We can save money by sharing expenses and have a great time at work together just like we did last summer." Joe's other high school classmates are either attending college or working full-time. Many of his friends appear confident in their ability to succeed. His mother often talks about his lack of concrete plans. At times, she asks, "Joe, what are you going to do with your life? Your father and I want to help you, but you've got to decide on something." Sometimes, in frustration, she says, "You're never going to amount to anything by sitting around all the time watching television!" At this point, he usually retreats to his room, anxious and depressed. His father, on the other hand, rarely mentions his opinion of Joe's lack of direction; however, he often states that joining the army when he was Joe's age was an important turning point in his life.

> **COUNSELOR HYPOTHESIS:** Joe has been receiving considerable input, some of it conflicting and much of it confusing. He is trying to please himself, his best friend, his mother, and his father—all at the same time.

Interacting Courses of Action In attempting to solve his problem, Joe is faced with several possibilities. He perceives three options to solving his problem.

1. To drop out of community college and find any employment that offers on-the-job training
2. To continue his education at the community college, which will lead to one or more specified occupations
3. To enter the military and receive specific training that would lead to employment after he completes his tour of duty

> **COUNSELOR HYPOTHESIS:** At this point, none of Joe's options appear very appealing or promising. Each alternative has advantages and disadvantages for him; there is no clear first choice. He could possibly combine two of the three options to form one or two further alternatives.

Unpredictability of Courses of Action In considering his three options, Joe finds it difficult to predict how successful he might be with each one. His uncertainty may be caused by his lack of self-confidence or his lack of knowledge about himself or the world of work. For instance, although he has worked at the grocery store, he is unsure what it would be like doing that type of work 40 to 50 hours a week. He is also unsure what it would be like to live with his friend instead of his family. Although he is passing his present courses at the community college, he is worried that future courses might be too difficult or too boring. Although his father served in the military and talks positively about his experience, Joe knows little of what military life is actually like. He does not know how he would cope if he were hundreds of miles from his family.

> **COUNSELOR HYPOTHESIS:** Joe's lack of confidence in his ability to be a good decision maker further complicates his problem. This lack of confidence is made worse by his lack of specific knowledge about himself and the world of work. When he is particularly anxious about making a decision, he often copes by delaying until only one option remains or by subtly manipulating significant others to make decisions for him.

Solutions Resulting in New Problems Even if Joe selects one of the options just described, new problems become apparent. In the initial interview, Joe asked rhetorically, "If I should decide to work at the grocery store, will I be more successful stocking groceries, where I have some experience, or would it be better to seek more training and become a cashier? Or should I go to work as an apprentice meat cutter?

What if the store doesn't need additional staff right now? If I decide to continue my education at the community college, what course of study should I choose? Should I go to school in my hometown, or should I leave home? If I leave home, how will I pay for all my expenses? I could work part-time, but what kind of work would I do? If I join the army, which training program should I choose? Will I be able to get a civilian job with a skill I learn in the army? Will my choice of training affect where I'll be living while I'm in the service?"

COUNSELOR HYPOTHESIS: It seems that one initial choice leads Joe to numerous subsequent choices. He believes that things will improve after making his decision, but it seems that right now he is even more confused than before.

COUNSELOR'S INTERVIEW SUMMARY: Joe has become aware that his personal resources and the resources of his family and friends are not helping him solve his career problem. He lacks a clear understanding of his values, interests, skills, and employment preferences. His knowledge of occupations, educational options, and training programs is simplistic and sometimes inaccurate, often due to stereotypical beliefs. His decision-making skills seem to be poorly developed, and he doubts his ability to be an effective decision maker. Joe appears at this point to possess many of the attributes of an indecisive individual. He can list alternatives, but they seem to be random and unrelated.

Preliminary Assessment On the basis of information gained from the initial interview and the preliminary assessment, Marilyn should now be able to determine Joe's readiness for beginning the career problem-solving and decision-making process. In order to maximize her effectiveness, the counselor attends to the development of a facilitative counseling relationship (Brown, 2003). At this point, it is important to know if Joe is ready to begin using assessment instruments and career information resources, or if there are other issues that need to be addressed first, such as negative self-talk that may be making decision making more difficult.

Marilyn began by reviewing with Joe the results of the Career Thoughts Inventory (CTI) (Sampson, Peterson, Lenz, Reardon, & Saunders, 1996), which he completed prior to his first counseling sessions as part of the intake process. The CTI is a self-administered, objectively scored measure of negative thinking in career problem solving and decision making that is based on the CIP approach.[1]

Joe received a CTI Total score of 88 (2.0 standard deviations above the mean), a Decision-Making Confusion score of 26 (2.0 standard deviations above the mean), a Commitment Anxiety score of 19 (1.0 standard deviation above the mean), and an External Conflict score of 8 (2.0 standard deviations above the mean). These scores indicate that in comparison to the norm group of college students, Joe has many negative thoughts about making a career choice. More specifically, he is very confused about how to make a career choice, is somewhat anxious about making a commitment to a choice, and is having difficulty reconciling his views about the future with his parents' expectations. Marilyn also determined Joe's readiness by encouraging

---

[1] A variety of other instruments could also be used at this point to aid in determining the client's readiness. See Sampson, Peterson, Reardon, and Lenz (2000) for a description of available readiness assessment measures.

Joe to share his view of the problem and of himself. Specific items on the CTI were used as a focal point for this discussion.

The CTI results confirmed some of the information obtained in the initial interview. Marilyn concluded that, because of his considerable confusion about career choice, his anxiety about making a commitment (low capability), and the conflict he was experiencing with his parents (moderate complexity), Joe had low readiness for career decision making, and individual career counseling would be more appropriate for Joe than self-directed interventions. Although group counseling with other indecisive individuals could be particularly useful, no such groups are currently available. Joe's situation clearly meets the criteria for use of individual career counseling as an appropriate intervention strategy (Sampson, Peterson, Reardon, & Lenz, 2000). Marilyn shared her perceptions with Joe and asked him if he agreed. He said that he did agree and thought that individual counseling sounded like a good idea.

To help orient Joe to the process they would use in career problem solving and decision making, Marilyn provided Joe with two handouts: (a) the client version of the CASVE cycle ("A Guide to Good Decision Making") and (b) the client version of the Pyramid of Information Processing Domains ("What's Involved in Career Choice") (Sampson, Peterson, Lenz, & Reardon, 1992). Marilyn briefly explained the concepts contained in the handouts and told Joe that they would be referring back to the handouts to help him keep track of where he was in the problem-solving and decision-making process, as well as learn more about this process. She asked Joe to bring these handouts to each of their counseling sessions.

Define Problem and Analyze Causes Marilyn summarized Joe's problem as a gap between being frustrated and discouraged by his uncertainty about his future and wanting to be confident about a choice and making progress in his career. Marilyn asked Joe if this was a good summary of his situation, and Joe agreed that it was. Joe and Marilyn then analyzed his problem to identify probable causes of the gap (Yost & Corbishley, 1987). Marilyn suggested (and Joe agreed) that his problem involved (a) a lack of confidence in his decision-making ability and (b) a lack of information about himself, the world of work, and the decision-making process. The counselor helped Joe to frame his problem as a lack of confidence and of information and skill, both of which can be rectified, rather than as his being an ineffective decision maker, which would imply that there was something basically wrong with him.

Formulate Goals Joe and Marilyn collaborated to arrive at the following goals for counseling:

1. To understand what Joe does to help and to hinder his problem-solving and decision-making process (metacognitions)
2. To clarify Joe's knowledge of himself (self-schemata) and his knowledge of occupations (world schemata)
3. To improve Joe's decision-making skills (generic information processing skills)

The goals established by Joe and Marilyn become the basis for developing an Individual Learning Plan (ILP) to guide the selection and use of career information resources (see Figure 8.1). The ILP is incorporated into the contract between Joe and Marilyn. A formal contract has the advantage of providing the client with a general

Figure 8.1 Individual Learning Plan
Career Resource Center—Central Community College

Goal(s): #1 Understand personal barriers to decision making

#2 Clarify self-knowledge and occupational knowledge

#3 Improve decision-making skills

Activity	Purpose/Outcome	Estimated Time Commitment	Goal #	Priority
Individual counseling	Clarify issues and help with resource use	1 hour each session	1,2,3	1
CTI Workbook Sections 1, 2, & 3	Challenge and reframe negative thinking	1 ½ hours	1	2
CTI Workbook Section 4	Enhance decision-making skills	½ hour	3	3
Monitor thoughts related to a real decision	Learn about the decision-making process	1 hour	3	4
Occupational card sort	Clarify self-knowledge and generate options	1 hour	2	5
SDS: CV	(Same as above)	1 hour	2	6
Summary of self-knowledge	Clarify self-knowledge	½ hour	2	7
Career Key	Identify information resources	15 minutes	2	8
Choices	Obtain occupational information	1 hour	2	9
Information interviews with land surveyor and computer programmer	Obtain more specific occupational information	2 hours	2	10

This plan can be modified by either party based on new information learned in the activities of the action plan. The purpose of this plan is to work toward a mutually agreed upon career goal. Activities may be added or subtracted as needed.

Joe Williams	10/16/02	Marilyn Abbey	1/16/02
Student	Date	Career Adviser	Date

understanding of the sequence and scope of career counseling, thus reducing the likelihood of misunderstandings and the development of unrealistic expectations. It also encourages the client to assume an active role at an early stage in the counseling process (Montgomery, 1984). Marilyn referred back to the client version of the Pyramid of Information Processing Domains to show how Joe's goals related to the process of career decision making.

The goals identified by Joe and Marilyn are best viewed as short-range goals. Achieving these goals will help Joe achieve the ultimate goal of making an appropriate career choice as he learns how to be a better career problem solver and decision maker (which are the aims of the CIP approach).

Develop Individual Learning Plan With Joe's general goals for counseling in mind, Joe and Marilyn completed an Individual Learning Plan (ILP). For each counseling goal, the planned activities and their purposes were listed; the activities were ranked according to priority. The ILP is used to guide and to monitor the career counseling process. It is flexible and should be modified as new data become available. Marilyn serves as a mentor to enhance Joe's motivation as he completes various learning activities. By involving Joe in the creation of an ILP, Marilyn encourages his active participation in the counseling process. By seeking Joe's opinion on how to progress through the counseling process, Marilyn is creating the conditions to challenge Joe's dysfunctional belief that he is bad at making decisions. A relatively small number of learning activities were assigned initially—the ILP originally contained three activities, and other activities were added as the counseling process continued—so that Joe did not feel overwhelmed by the amount of work to be done.

Execute Individual Learning Plan The first counseling goal for Joe is to learn what he does to help and to hinder his problem-solving and decision-making process. This is achieved by making him more aware of his metacognitions.

Executive Processing Marilyn began the next session by reviewing Joe's ILP, reinforcing his schema for how the counseling process will proceed. She then asked Joe to talk about what he thinks of himself and his situation. The majority of Joe's self-statements were negative. Marilyn then explained how negative thoughts could result in feelings of anxiety and depression (Beck, 1976). She disclosed how some of her own negative thought processes occasionally limited her effectiveness as a decision maker and increased her own feelings of anxiety. After she was confident that Joe understood how negative self-statements impede problem solving and decision making, she asked Joe to describe a recent decision he had made that was accompanied by anxiety.

Joe described buying a birthday gift for his mother. The choice took several days and involved significant anxiety; he finally selected a book on gardening. Marilyn then helped Joe to identify what he had been thinking in relation to his decision-making process and how his self-talk contributed to his anxiety. Marilyn suggested that before the next session, Joe should complete the first two sections of the *CTI Workbook* (Sampson et al., 1996) to help him learn more about how his thoughts influenced his ability to make a career choice and to complete Section 3 of the workbook, which includes an exercise that was designed to help him identify, challenge, and alter cognitive distortions.

At the beginning of the next session, Joe reviewed his homework exercise from the *CTI Workbook* with Marilyn. A consistent pattern of cognitive distortions and subsequent anxiety began to emerge. Joe often anticipates that his decisions will lead to future disastrous consequences. He is sure that significant others believe he is incompetent in making decisions and successfully completing tasks. He constantly compares himself to very successful people, magnifying their good qualities and minimizing his own abilities.

Keller, Biggs, and Gysbers (1982) stated the following:

> Dysfunctional cognitive career schemata common to clients with career disturbances include drawing conclusions where evidence is lacking (arbitrary inference), making important career decisions on the basis of a single incident (overgeneralization), exaggerating the negative or underplaying the positive aspects of a career event (magnification or minimization), overly self-attributing negative vocational occurrences (personalization), and perceiving career events only in extreme terms (dichotomous or absolutistic thinking). (p. 369)

Joe began to understand that his negative self-statements contributed to his anxiety in general and to his difficulties with career problem solving. He had concluded that he would not be successful in various occupations even though he knew little of the actual work tasks and had no specific experience that suggested that he would fail. He had decided that, because of his vision problems, no occupational specialty in the military would be an appropriate choice (overgeneralization). He had exaggerated the deficiencies of his academic achievement, assuming that it prevented his admission into good colleges (magnification). He also had concluded that if he did not get a really good job, he could not be happy working (dichotomous thinking).

Joe is a prey to the "crystal ball myth." Lewis and Gilhousen (1981) stated that "the crystal ball myth suggests that people who 'have it together' always have clear, concise plans for their lives at all times" (p. 296). This assumption not only contributes to Joe's feeling of inadequacy as a decision maker but also results in feelings of depression, as Joe imagines that the situation is not likely ever to get better. In closing the session, Marilyn suggested that perhaps the problem is not who Joe is, but rather how Joe thinks about himself and how Joe believes the world functions. She asked him to continue with his cognitive-distortions exercise, but this time Joe is to do the exercise while making three important decisions during the week.

At the beginning of the next session, Joe admitted that he had used a variety of cognitive distortions related to important decisions during the week. However, he did not feel as anxious for as long a time because he had recognized what he was doing and had attempted to substitute more positive thoughts. Joe then asked Marilyn, "I understand how my thoughts relate to my feelings, but why am I so negative all the time?" Marilyn said she believed that Joe's negative point of view could be related to his assumptions about himself and the way the world operates.

Krumboltz (1983) suggested that inaccurate self-observation generalizations or worldview generalizations contribute to career decision-making problems. Marilyn perceived that two of Krumboltz's five consequences of unfounded beliefs relate to

Joe. First, Joe fails to exert the effort needed to make a decision or solve a problem. "It is easier to avoid than to face decisions. . . . Beliefs such as these inhibit constructive action, discouraging people from exploring alternatives and actively seeking information, opinions, or advice that might lead them to consider new directions" (Krumboltz, 1983, p. 3). Second, Joe suffers anxiety over a perceived inability to achieve goals; this inability is linked to feelings of low personal worth. "If I choose the wrong job here, it will be awful and I will have ruined my life. . . . People who link their feelings of personal worth to specific experiences in life create potential misery for themselves" (p. 5). Marilyn hypothesized that the following factors identified by Krumboltz contribute to Joe's beliefs:

1. *Self-comparison with a single standard:* "My dad didn't have any problems choosing an occupation. He always knew that he wanted to be a police officer."
2. *Self-deception:* "The reason I'm having trouble choosing an occupation is that I'm not good at making decisions!" In reality, Joe was afraid of failing on the job, but he found it too embarrassing to admit this to himself or others.

Irrational beliefs can also contribute to problems in career decision making (Ellis, 1967). Marilyn perceived that Joe had the following irrational beliefs:

1. It is absolutely necessary for an individual to be loved or approved of by every significant person in his or her environment.
2. It is necessary that each individual be completely competent, adequate, and achieving in all areas if the individual is to be worthwhile.
3. It is easier to run away from difficulties and self-responsibility than it is to face them.
4. Individuals need to be dependent on others and have someone stronger than they are to lean on.
5. Past events in a person's life determine present behavior and cannot be changed. There is always a correct and precise answer to every problem, and it is catastrophic if that answer is not found.

Marilyn asked Joe to evaluate these beliefs.[2] At the next session, Joe admitted that they did not make much sense and that they directly related to his decision-making problems. Marilyn asked Joe to check out these beliefs in the real world (collaborative empiricism) (Beck, 1976). Because Joe has stated that he can talk with his mother easily, Marilyn suggested that for two important decisions during the week, he should (a) monitor and correct his cognitive distortions and (b) check out the appropriateness of his underlying beliefs with his mother. Marilyn received Joe's permission to call his mother and provide her with the information necessary to complete the assignment.

---

[2]Weinrach (1980) and Dryden (1979) provided specific examples of the use of Ellis's ABC theory in disputing irrational beliefs related to career decision making. An alternative cognitive-behavioral intervention would have involved identifying ways that Joe disowns responsibility for his career indecision; identifying the prices paid for that indecision; learning to face the fear associated with making a commitment; owning responsibility for his career choice; making a firm commitment—for example, testing career decision-making skills; and taking specific action to initiate the career decision-making process (Hornak & Gillingham, 1980).

At the following session, Joe reported that he now understands that his decision-making problems are not necessarily a result of his incompetence, but rather a result of his beliefs. His mother was very understanding and supportive of his efforts to change. Joe's father was also encouraging and suggested that Joe practice his decision-making skills by providing an itinerary for the family summer vacation. Marilyn then asked Joe to complete Section 4 of the *CTI Workbook* to help him learn about the content and process of career decision making from a CIP perspective.[3] After completing the workbook, Joe was more inclined to perceive himself as knowing how to solve problems and make decisions, and as a result, be more confident as a decision maker. This demonstrates the important relationship between changes in attitude and changes in knowledge. As Joe becomes more confident of his capacities, his increased knowledge can lead to a more positive attitude.

Over the next week, Joe used what he had learned from the *CTI Workbook* to make his decisions about the vacation itinerary. At the beginning of the next counseling session, he reported that he wanted to try to transfer his improved problem-solving and decision-making skills to his career problem. Marilyn used this opening to review the process of career problem solving and decision making by reviewing the client versions of the CASVE cycle and the Pyramid of Information Processing Domains.

Analysis (Self) and Synthesis (Elaboration) Although Joe was now better prepared to think more positively about himself and his career options, he still had considerable difficulty in articulating self-knowledge and admitted to having little accurate information about the world of work in general. Marilyn suggested to Joe that assessment strategies would now be an appropriate step to foster self-knowledge and career exploration. After providing Joe with an overview of the assessment process, Marilyn actively involved Joe in the assessment decision-making process, encouraging him to see himself as a capable decision maker as well as providing a verbal model of the cognitive aspects of the decision-making process. Joe and Marilyn summarized his needs as follows: Joe needs to clarify and organize his self-knowledge (values, interests, skills, and employment preferences) to provide a basis for expanding the occupational alternatives being considered (Synthesis-elaboration) and narrowing them to a manageable number for further consideration (Synthesis-crystallization).

Marilyn asked Joe to describe his previous assessment experiences. Joe said that he becomes very anxious when taking tests and that he did not learn very much from the interest inventory and aptitude test that he took at the end of his junior year in high school. Joe said that the interpretation was confusing, and he remembered little of what was said. Marilyn reviewed with Joe the data from the score reports from the interest and aptitude assessments that he had brought with him. The interest assessment data were undifferentiated, with no apparent trends in the occupational scales.

---

[3] Additional strategies for decision making are provided by Bergland (1974), Bransford and Stein (1984), Fredrickson (1982), Gati and Asher (2001), Gelatt (1962, 1989), Harren (1979), Janis and Mann (1977), Katz (1966), Krumboltz (1966), Law and Watts (1977), Remer and O'Neill (1980), Tolbert (1980), and Yost and Corbishley (1987).

The inventory showed a high percentage of indifferent responses, which reflected Joe's indecisiveness at the time. The results of the aptitude battery indicated that Joe's mathematical skills were more developed than his verbal skills. These results were consistent with his past grades in mathematical and verbal subjects. On the basis of Joe's past negative experience with testing, Joe and Marilyn decided to begin with an occupational card sort, with additional instruments selected as needed. They selected a brief 36-card sort (Peterson, 1998; Peterson et al., 1991).[4]

Marilyn then explained the procedures for using the card sort. After Joe had sorted the cards into "might choose," "uncertain," and "would not choose" piles, Marilyn observed that in comparison with his interest inventory responses, Joe was using the uncertain category much less often. When asked for his reaction to this observation, Joe stated, "I feel more confident now about my ability to choose. Before, I was focusing more on my uncertainty about choosing rather than on actually having preferences. Now I realize that there are things that I really do like and dislike."

In talking about his reasons for rejecting many of the occupations, he stated, "I don't want to work in a job where I have to deal with people—like helping them with their problems. I like having friends and all; I just don't want to work with people all the time. I also don't want a job that means I have to be in school for a long time, like going to grad school or anything like that. I also don't like doing the same thing over and over again."

In talking about his reasons for placing the eight occupations in the "might choose" pile, Joe stated, "I like the idea of working with my hands and using math in some way in my job. I like it when things are orderly and precise. I also like understanding how things work. Having some variety in what I do would also be nice. And some of these occupations would let me work outdoors."

In order to clarify and organize Joe's self-knowledge, he and Marilyn decided to complete a brief guided fantasy. "Through the relaxation and imagery of guided fantasy, individuals can be stimulated to consider aspects of themselves that may be repressed or ignored" (Jones, 1984, p. 103). Joe imagined events during a typical day 10 years in the future (Morgan & Skovholt, 1977). Joe vaguely described his job as "working outdoors with my hands"; his leisure activities involved spending time with his family, fishing, or woodworking. Joe stated, "Taking my son on a fishing trip, like Dad and I used to go on, would be really great!" In reflecting on his fantasy, Joe stated, "What I did away from the job seemed as important as what I did at work. I never thought that my leisure time meant so much to me. I do spend a lot of time at school daydreaming about fishing or building my own boat. I don't want a job that has a lot of long hours, like owning my own business the way Mom does. She works almost all the time!"

---

[4]In describing the benefits of card sorts, Dolliver (1969) stated that "the counselor can gain an understanding of a client's processes in making choices, as well as identifying the elements which the client uses to make those choices" (p. 153). Dolliver (1982) found expressed and measured interests to have equal predictive validity. Dewey (1974), Peterson (1998), and Slaney and MacKinnon-Slaney (2000) explained how card sorts can be used as a career assessment resource. See Slaney, Moran, and Wade (1994) and Zunker and Obsorn (2002) for a description of other card sorts that might be used in career counseling.

When asked if he felt they were making progress, Joe said he was getting more confident that he knew what he wanted out of a job, but he was not sure how appropriate his list of occupations was for him. Marilyn suggested that he complete the Self-Directed Search (SDS), which is designed to help him learn more about himself and identify potential vocational choices (Holland, 1994).[5] Marilyn offered Joe the choice of using the paper-and-pencil version, the computer version, or the Internet version. In view of his interest in math and computers, Joe selected the computer version (Reardon & PAR Staff, 2001). Marilyn then used the client versions of the pyramid and the CASVE cycle to clarify the progress that Joe had made in solving his career problem. The session ended with Marilyn helping Joe make an appointment to complete the SDS in the career center computer lab.

Joe completed the SDS and received his results, which he read before his next session. Prior to beginning the session, Marilyn reviewed the SDS professional summary to prepare for Joe's test interpretation. After Marilyn asked Joe to describe his experience with the SDS, which was positive, they discussed his results. Joe's SDS-SP code was IRE (Investigative, Realistic, and Enterprising), confirming the results of the card sort. The consistency level of the IRE code was high, which indicated that commonalities existed among the types of activities inherent in the work environments represented by the I and R types. The differentiation among types was average, indicating some distinct likes and dislikes; this was an improvement over the lack of differentiation shown in Joe's previous interest inventory results. The congruence between his SDS occupational daydreams and his SDS final score was high, which indicated a similarity between his expressed and measured interests that enhanced the concurrent validity of the results (similar data produced by multiple assessments). It is also important to note that although Joe had an undifferentiated SDS profile, his three highest Holland codes were RIE (in order); his interest measurements were thus consistent over time. A definite trend existed in the data from the interest inventory, card sort, and SDS-SP, with Investigative, Realistic, and Enterprising types being prominent.

Marilyn asked Joe to write a summary of his self-knowledge as homework, using his card sort results and his SDS-SP Interpretive Report as a stimulus. The summary statement would be organized as follows:

1. Identification of values
2. Identification of interests
3. Identification of skills
4. Identification of no more than five occupations for further exploration[6]

Using the client versions of the CASVE cycle and the Pyramid of Information Processing Domains, Marilyn then showed Joe the progress he had made to date in problem solving and decision making.

---

[5] Other instruments that could have been used to help Joe learn more about himself and identify potential vocational choices are described by Kapes and Whitfield (2001).

[6] Shahnasarian and Peterson (1988) demonstrated that individuals are able to consider effectively only three to five occupational alternatives at one time.

At the beginning of the next session, Joe presented Marilyn with his summary. He had identified the following five occupations for further exploration: forester, land surveyor, landscape architect, computer programmer, and police officer. He had added police officer (which did not appear on his earlier "might choose" list), as he was familiar with the occupation because of his father. Marilyn and Joe then reviewed his ILP in terms of the client version of the CASVE cycle in order to discuss his progress and refine the learning activities associated with obtaining and using career information. Joe reported that he was pleased with his progress, especially because prior to their first counseling sessions, he had not expected counseling to be helpful. Marilyn agreed that progress had been made and said she was pleased with Joe's progress and the quality of their relationship.

Analysis of Occupations In helping Joe formulate a plan for obtaining and using career information, Marilyn suggested two basic steps: (a) reviewing general information on how the world of work is structured, to help Joe discern differences among occupational categories and also to enhance his later recall of information; and (b) reviewing specific information on occupations and educational or training opportunities to help Joe narrow his list of alternatives to tentative primary and secondary choices. These two steps provide Joe with a cognitive schema for understanding how to use occupational information. By helping Joe formulate a concrete, sequential plan for obtaining and using information, his counselor enhances the likelihood that Joe will view himself as capable of success instead of feeling overwhelmed with the task and unsure of where to begin.

An important role for Marilyn at this point in the counseling process is to help Joe select appropriate career information materials (Brown, 2003), taking into account (a) the way in which the information is presented (Herr & Cramer, 1996); (b) the reading level of the information (Brown, 2003; Herr & Cramer, 1996); and (c) the amount of information in relation to Joe's motivation (Brown, 2003). For Joe, Marilyn had concluded that (a) the information should be very interactive initially, progressing to noninteractive materials when he requires more specific and detailed data; (b) the reading level should be no more than ninth grade in view of his verbal performance; and (c) the amount of information should be limited at first so it will not overwhelm him, with additional information introduced at a pace selected by Joe.

Joe's next task is to identify specific sources of career information located in the career resource center. He uses a computer in the center to provide access to Career Key, a computer-assisted index of career materials (Smith, 1983). This type of system is designed to reduce the common frustrations that clients experience when trying to locate specific career information among the vast, often overwhelming amount of data available (Sampson, 1982). See Chapter 13 for a more detailed discussion on organizing career resources. Joe began by selecting five occupations he was considering. The computer searched the database of current materials and generated a list of available materials organized by the type of resource—such as book, CD-ROM, video, or computer application.

Marilyn suggested that Joe review the Holland's typology contained in his SDS Computer Version printout to provide a framework for organizing and evaluating information on specific occupations (Shahnasarian & Peterson, 1988). In terms of Strong's (1968) social-influence model of counseling, the perceptions that Joe had of Marilyn's expertness, attractiveness, and trustworthiness enhanced his capacity to integrate career information into his problem-solving and decision-making process. Research on counselor intervention and information use suggests that the client's interest in a particular source of information will tend to be greater if the counselor explains how the material is relevant to solving the client's career problem (Halpern & Norris, 1968).

Synthesis (Crystallization) Marilyn next suggested that Joe use a computer-assisted career guidance system to learn about typical work tasks, educational or training requirements, the amount of contact with people, variety, leisure time, hours worked in a typical week, and outdoor work for the occupations he is considering. As Joe completed this task, Marilyn recommended that he think back to what he learned from completing the card sort and the "day in the future" guided fantasy. Marilyn suggested that Joe begin with the five occupations on his list and then explore any other occupations that seem interesting. In this way, the task is small enough to be manageable, but the breadth of his exploration is unrestricted. At the end of the session, Marilyn briefly discussed where Joe was in the problem-solving and decision-making process by reviewing the client versions of the Pyramid of Information Processing Domains and the CASVE cycle. A paraprofessional staff member in the career resource center provided Joe with an introduction to the system (Careerware, 2002) and monitored his use of the system, providing support as needed.

At their next session, Joe reported to Marilyn that he enjoyed using the computer, especially being in control of how he received information. He had narrowed his alternatives to two occupations: land surveyor and computer programmer. When Marilyn asked about his reasons for selecting land surveyor and computer programmer, Joe stated that these two occupations would provide him with some variety and opportunity to solve problems but would not require extensive education. Marilyn said she was pleased that Joe was able to make progress in evaluating his alternatives. Joe replied, "I'm really interested in learning more about becoming a land surveyor or computer programmer." Marilyn's verbal acknowledgment of Joe's information-seeking statements further reinforced his information-seeking behavior (Krumboltz & Schroeder, 1965).

Marilyn now suggested that Joe revise the occupational information exploration plan in his ILP to include interviews with a local computer programmer and a land surveyor. If the interviews were successful, it would be useful to follow up by observing the work tasks (shadowing) of a local computer programmer or land surveyor.

Joe said, "It all sounds good to me, but where do I start?" Marilyn suggested that he first view his Choices printouts for each occupation. Reviewing these printouts prior to the information interviews should help him ask well-focused questions in the interview. If he concluded that one or both of the occupations were worth further consideration, then a more intensive shadowing experience would help him gain additional detailed information. Marilyn suggested that he become familiar with the content of the printed materials and then refer to them for answers to specific questions, rather than use them for general reading. By providing Joe with alternatives and discussing the rationale for his planned use of information resources, Marilyn helped to reinforce Joe's positive self-image as a decision maker and to develop his schema for understanding the problem-solving and decision-making process. As the session ended, Marilyn again briefly reviewed the client versions of the Pyramid of Information Processing Domains and the CASVE cycle to clarify where Joe was in his problem-solving and decision-making process.

John White Cloud, a career counseling major working part-time as a paraprofessional staff member in the career resource center, helped Joe review his Choices printouts for "Computer Programmer" and "Land Surveyor." Reviewing his printouts helped Joe with his analysis of the differences between the work tasks in these two occupations. After reviewing his printouts, Joe commented to John: "I really liked what was said about the computer programmer writing programs to solve problems. But on the other hand, it seems like land surveyors move around a lot more. A computer programmer spends a lot of time at a desk." John suggested that Joe could clarify his reactions by asking a computer programmer and a land surveyor how they spent a typical working day.

Salmer (1964) suggested that vicarious role assumption is an important aspect of using occupational information. Clients picture themselves in the work environment, estimate how successfully they can meet the demands of the occupation, and imagine the potential job satisfaction from working. An information interview, especially when conducted at the work site, provides substantial realism and facilitates the client's vicarious role assumption. Lenz (1984) provided a comprehensive examination of the use of various community resources in support of career decision making.

When Joe said he felt that he was ready for an information interview, John provided him with the procedures for completing an interview and a list of typical questions asked by students and then arranged two appointments for Joe during the week. John helped Joe briefly role-play what it would be like to conduct the information interview to help Joe gain confidence with this new skill.

Valuing Joe completed both interviews and returned to talk with Marilyn. He stated: "After talking with the computer programmer and the land surveyor, I think that being a surveyor would be my best choice. Before the interviews, I was leaning toward computer programming, in spite of being cooped up in an office. But then the programmer showed me some of the textbooks she used at the community college. What I figured out was that I like using computers, but I don't think I would like to take all of the programming courses. Anyway, when I talked to the land surveyor, he said that he was now using computers to schedule jobs, process financial records, and even do some graphics work. As a surveyor, I would use the computer to help me do my work, instead of writing programs to help someone else do their job. And I can also work indoors and outdoors."

Marilyn asked Joe if irrational thinking had played a part in his problem solving. After some thought, he replied, "I really liked it when the computer programmer talked about solving problems that other people were having trouble with. My parents think computer programmers are real smart. I really want to prove myself, to show people I can get the tough jobs done! But that's thinking about what others want me to do and not so much about what I want to do. It seems like I still slip back into those old ways of thinking pretty easily. It would have been a bad choice to start taking computer programming courses if all I wanted to do was prove myself to others. I can do that just as well, or better, as a surveyor, and enjoy working a lot more. Given what I know about myself now, forester would be a good second choice, in case land surveyor doesn't work out."

Marilyn asked, "Do you think being a land surveyor would match your values, interests, skills, and employment preferences?" Joe said, "Yes, except that it would be a while before I could get involved with the computer aspects of the business. I would have to learn the basics first." They discussed how Joe's leisure time could be used to supplement his work activities. Needs that are not met at work can be supplemented by pursuing supplemental activities during time allocated to leisure pursuits (Blocher & Siegal, 1981). When asked how he might approach this, Joe said that he might try assembling a home computer from mail-order parts. He could also spend some of his leisure time fishing or woodworking.

Execution Joe needs to determine how to implement his decision. Marilyn asked Joe to identify, through brainstorming, some of the factors involved in implementing his first choice. Joe developed the following list:

- Choosing an educational program for land surveying
- Paying for school
- Deciding where to live
- Getting a job after graduating

An associate degree in land surveying is available from numerous community colleges. The Choices system identified two such programs available in Joe's home state. A community college within commuting distance of the city where he lived had a two-year program in land surveying leading to an associate degree. Joe made an appointment with an academic adviser at the community college to gain specific details on admissions and the nature of the surveying program.

The feedback that Joe received from his parents has been positive. Both have had personal experience at a community college, and they are confident that Joe has the aptitude to succeed in obtaining an associate degree. They are also pleased that he can remain in the area while attending school. Joe's parents are continuing to offer assistance with funding for his community college degree. They offered to pay all of his direct educational expenses, such as tuition, books, lab fees, and equipment. They also agreed to pay for the gasoline needed to commute to and from school. As in the past, Joe will be responsible for working for his own spending money. If Joe decides to move out of the house, he will have to cover all of his room and board expenses because these costs are optional and fully under his control.

Marilyn suggested that Joe might want to seek employment in a minimum-wage position with a land surveying company. During an information interview with a local surveyor, Joe was encouraged to call if he was interested in employment. When Joe followed up on this opportunity, he obtained a job as a general office clerk. Although he would make more money by working at the grocery store, the opportunity to gain direct experience offsets the lower pay. He plans to live at home for the first semester at the new community college, save his money, and then share an apartment with his best friend during the second semester. With regard to getting a job after graduation, Marilyn briefly explained the career planning and placement services available at community colleges.

Joe was still concerned, however, about his father's "real" opinion about his choice of surveying given the conflict that occurred when he was considering joining the army as an enlisted soldier. Marilyn encouraged Joe to address his concerns with his father, especially because his father appeared pleased with Joe's choice of surveyor. When they talked, Joe learned that his father's negative reaction to his considering being an enlisted soldier actually had little to do with Joe himself. His father explained that he regretted not being an officer himself and waiting so long to go to college. His father said he was really pleased with the progress Joe had made and wished that he had talked with a career counselor when he was making decisions at Joe's age. This information from his father further increased Joe's confidence with his choice.

Summative Review and Generalization Marilyn told Joe she has positive feelings about what she thinks she and Joe have accomplished and asked him to let her know how he gets on in the program in land surveying. Joe said that after this positive experience with counseling, he would not hesitate to see a counselor at the other community college if the need arises. Marilyn and Joe reviewed Joe's goals for counseling and the way he had used the CASVE cycle to make a decision. They also reviewed the role of metacognitions and the use of information in problem solving and decision making. Such a review is important to help Joe generalize this experience to other career problems and decisions. At this point, Joe and Marilyn agreed to terminate the counseling sessions.

Although Joe will continue to face various career development issues as he grows older, the particular gap that led him to seek individual career counseling has been resolved. The theoretical and applied courses in land surveying, as well as the part-time job for a surveying company, will provide him with the opportunity to reality-test his occupational choice (Fredrickson, 1982). As he completes his educational program and prepares to begin the job search process, the tentative nature of his choice will be reduced. His experience with career counseling has given him a more fully developed set of functional self-schemata, occupational schemata, and problem-solving and decision-making skills that will enhance his career development in the future.

SUMMARY

This chapter demonstrated how individual career counseling could be delivered using the CIP approach. In the case study of Joe, the counselor helped the client clarify his self-knowledge through a variety of assessments, to acquire occupational knowledge from the use of various career information resources, and to understand the career problem-solving and decision-making process. Services were delivered within the context of an interpersonal relationship that encouraged the development of insight and commitment to implementing career choices. The case showed how a seven-step counseling intervention process could be used to deliver career services. The case study also showed how the Pyramid of Information Processing Domains and the CASVE cycle could be used to structure the counseling process. The next chapter presents three case studies for the delivery of brief staff-assisted career services.

GETTING THE MOST BENEFIT FROM READING THIS CHAPTER

To effectively learn the material in this chapter, complete one or more of the following activities:

- If you have had individual career counseling, how was your experience similar to and different from the approach used to serve Joe?
- Given your knowledge of counseling theory and career development theory, what other strategies might be used to meet the needs of Joe?
- Visit a career center or counseling center, and without violating any confidentiality, ask a staff member to describe how individual counseling is provided to clients. How is the process similar to and different from the CIP approach, especially the seven-step service delivery sequence?
- Talk with a friend about how the counseling strategies described in this chapter can be used to provide individuals with assistance in making career choices.

REFERENCES

Beck, A. T. (1976). *Cognitive therapy and the emotional disorders.* New York: International Universities Press.

Bergland, B. W. (1974). Career planning: The use of sequential evaluated experience. In E. L. Herr (Ed.), *Vocational guidance and human development* (pp. 350–380). Boston: Houghton Mifflin.

Blocher, D. H., & Siegal, R. (1981). Toward a cognitive developmental theory of leisure and work. *The Counseling Psychologist, 9,* 33–44.

Bransford, J. D., & Stein, B. S. (1984). *The ideal problem solver.* New York: W. H. Freeman.

Brown, D. (2003). *Career information, career counseling, and career development* (8th ed.). Boston: Allyn & Bacon.

Careerware. (2002). *CHOICES: Florida version* [Computer program]. Ottawa, Ontario, Canada: Author.

Dewey, C. R. (1974). Exploring interests: A non-sexist method. *The Personnel and Guidance Journal, 52,* 311–315.

Dolliver, R. H. (1969). Card sorts: Combined review. In J. T. Kapes & M. M. Mastie (Eds.), *A counselor's guide to vocational guidance instruments* (pp. 152–160). Washington, DC: National Vocational Guidance Association.

Dolliver, R. H. (1982). Strong Vocational Interest Blank versus expressed vocational interests: A review. *Psychological Bulletin, 72,* 94–107.

Dryden, W. (1979). Rational-emotive therapy and its contribution to careers counseling. *British Journal of Guidance and Counselling, 7,* 181–187.

Ellis, A. (1967). Rational-emotive psychotherapy. In D. Arbuckle (Ed.), *Counseling and psychotherapy.* New York: McGraw-Hill.

Fredrickson, R. H. (1982). *Career information.* Englewood Cliffs, NJ: Prentice Hall.

Gati, I., & Asher, I. (2001). The PIC model for career decision making: Prescreening, in-depth exploration, and choice. In F. T. Leong & A. Barak (Eds.), *Contemporary models in vocational psychology* (pp. 7–54). Mahwah, NJ: Lawrence Erlbaum Associates.

Gelatt, H. B. (1962). Decision-making: A conceptual frame of reference for counseling. *Journal of Counseling Psychology, 9* (3), 240–245.

Gelatt, H. B. (1989). Positive uncertainty: A new decision-making framework for counseling. *Journal of Counseling Psychology, 36* (2), 252–256.

Halpern, G., & Norris, L. (1968). Student curriculum decisions. *The Personnel and Guidance Journal, 47,* 240–243.

Harren, V. A. (1979). A model of career decision-making for college students. *Journal of Vocational Behavior, 14,* 119–135.

Herr, E. L., & Cramer, S. H. (1996). *Career guidance and counseling through the life span: Systematic approaches* (5th ed.). New York: HarperCollins.

Holland, J. L. (1994). *The Self-Directed Search.* Odessa, FL: Psychological Assessment Resources.

Hornak, J., & Gillingham, B. (1980). Career indecision: A self-defeating behavior. *The Personnel and Guidance Journal, 58,* 252–253.

Janis, I. L., & Mann, L. (1977). *Decision making: A psychological analysis of conflict, choice, and commitment.* New York: Free Press.

Jones, L. K. (1984). Self-assessment. In H. D. Burck & R. C. Reardon (Eds.), *Career development interventions* (pp. 89–107). Springfield, IL: Charles C Thomas.

Kapes, J. T., & Whitfield, E. A. (Eds.). (2001). *A counselor's guide to career assessment instruments* (4th ed.). Columbus, OH: National Career Development Association.

Katz, M. (1966). A model of guidance for career decision-making. *The Vocational Guidance Quarterly, 15,* 2–10.

Keller, K. E., Biggs, D. A., & Gysbers, N. C. (1982). Career counseling from a cognitive perspective. *The Personnel and Guidance Journal, 60,* 367–371.

Krumboltz, J. D. (1966). *Stating the goals of counseling.* Fullerton, CA: California Personnel and Guidance Association.

Krumboltz, J. D. (1983). *Private rules in career decision making.* Columbus: Ohio State University National Center for Research in Vocational Education, Advanced Study Center (ERIC Document Reproduction Service No. ED 229 608).

Krumboltz, J. D., & Schroeder, W. W. (1965). Promoting career planning through reinforcement and models. *The Personnel and Guidance Journal, 44,* 19–26.

Law, B., & Watts, A. G. (1977). *Schools, careers, and community.* London: Church Information Office.

Lenz, J. G. (1984). Using community resources. In H. D. Burck & R. C. Reardon (Eds.), *Career development interventions* (pp. 191–211). Springfield, IL: Charles C Thomas.

Lewis, R. A., & Gilhousen, M. R. (1981). Myths of career development: A cognitive approach to vocational counseling. *The Personnel and Guidance Journal, 59,* 296–299.

Montgomery, D. J. (1984). Contractual arrangements. In H. D. Burck & R. C. Reardon (Eds.), *Career development interventions* (pp. 108–123). Springfield, IL: Charles C Thomas.

Morgan, J. I., & Skovholt, T. M. (1977). Using inner experience: Fantasy and daydreams in career counseling. *Journal of Counseling Psychology, 5,* 391–397.

Peterson, G. W. (1998). Using a vocational card sort as an assessment of occupational knowledge. *Journal of Career Assessment, 6,* 49–67.

Peterson, G. W., Sampson, J. P., Jr., & Reardon, R. C. (1991). *Career development and services: A cognitive approach.* Pacific Grove, CA: Brooks/Cole.

Reardon, R. C., & PAR Staff. (2001). *Self-Directed Search Software Portfolio (SDS-SP™) for Windows®* [Computer program]. Odessa, FL: Psychological Assessment Resources.

Remer, E., & O'Neill, C. (1980). Clients as change agents: What color should my parachute be? *The Personnel and Guidance Journal, 58,* 425–429.

Salmer, J. (1964). Occupational exploration in counseling. In H. Borrow (Ed.), *Man in a world at work* (pp. 411–433). Boston: Houghton Mifflin.

Sampson, J. P., Jr. (1982). A computer-assisted library index for career materials. *Journal of College Student Personnel, 23,* 539–540.

Sampson, J. P., Jr., Peterson, G. W., Lenz, J. G., & Reardon, R. C. (1992). A cognitive approach to career services: Translating concepts into practice. *The Career Development Quarterly, 41,* 67–74.

Sampson, J. P., Jr., Peterson, G. W., Lenz, J. G., Reardon, R. C., & Saunders, D. E. (1996). *Career Thoughts Inventory workbook.* Odessa, FL: Psychological Assessment Resources.

Sampson, J. P., Jr., Peterson, G. W., Reardon, R. C., & Lenz, J. G. (2000). Using readiness assessment to improve career services: A cognitive information processing approach. *The Career Development Quarterly, 49,* 146–174.

Shahnasarian, M., & Peterson, G. W. (1988). The effect of a prior cognitive structuring intervention with computer-assisted career guidance. *Computers in Human Behavior, 4,* 125–131.

Slaney, R. B., & MacKinnon-Slaney, F. (2000). Using vocational card sorts in career counseling. In C. E. Watkins, Jr., & V. L. Campbell (Eds.), *Testing and assessment in counseling practice* (2nd ed.) (pp. 371–428). Mahwah, NJ: Lawrence Erlbaum Associates.

Slaney, R. B., Moran, W. J., & Wade, J. C. (1994). Vocational card sorts. In J. T. Kapes, M. M. Mastie, & E. A. Whitfield (Eds.), *A counselor's guide to career assessment instruments* (pp. 347–360). Washington, DC: National Vocational Guidance Association.

Smith, E. (1983). Career Key: A career library management system. *The Vocational Guidance Quarterly, 32,* 52–56.

Strong, S. R. (1968). Counseling: An interpersonal influence process. *Journal of Counseling Psychology, 15,* 215–224.

Tolbert, E. L. (1980). *Counseling for career development* (2nd ed.). Boston: Houghton Mifflin.

Weinrach, S. G. (1980). A rational-emotive approach to occupational mental health. *The Vocational Guidance Quarterly, 28,* 208–218.

Yost, E. B., & Corbishley, M. A. (1987). *Career counseling. A psychological approach.* San Francisco: Jossey-Bass.

Zunker, V. G., & Osborn, D. S. (2002). *Using assessment results for career development* (6th ed.). Pacific Grove, CA: Brooks/Cole.

9 CHAPTER Case Studies for Brief Staff-Assisted Services

This chapter presents case studies showing how the CIP approach can be used in brief staff-assisted services.[1] After reviewing this chapter, the reader should understand how the CIP approach could be used in self-directed career decision making, workshops, and group counseling. The chapter is organized as follows:

- Case Study: Linda
- Case Study: Carla
- Case Study: Juanita
- Summary
- Getting the Most Benefit from Reading This Chapter

The case studies of Linda and Carla are presented in this chapter to show how self-directed career decision making can be an effective intervention to promote career problem solving and decision making (Reardon, 1996). The case study of Linda also shows how workshops can be used in delivering career services. The case study of Juanita shows the delivery of group career counseling (Pyle, 1986). These case studies allow us to illustrate the nature of career problems and the way the CIP approach could be

[1] Although this chapter features self-directed career decision making, short-term group counseling, and workshops, another brief staff-assisted career service (such as career courses with large-group interaction) could have been used to meet the needs of these clients. See Chapter 5 for a description of career courses with large-group interaction.

used to address these problems. Although these case studies do not fully represent the cognitive complexity of each client's career problem solving and decision making, or show the full range of options for service delivery, they do demonstrate how the CIP approach might be used to deliver brief staff-assisted career services.

The case studies presented in this book are composite descriptions of hypothetical individuals based on the experience of the authors. Therefore, any resemblance to specific persons is purely coincidental. Although the case studies are hypothetical, the procedures and resources used reflect current practice at the Florida State University Career Center. (The only exception to this is the case in a high school setting, which we present to show how the CIP approach can be used in a variety of settings.) The Career Center is a comprehensive facility, providing counseling, experiential education, and placement services to FSU students, as well as drop-in career advising and appointment-based counseling to non-FSU students and community-based adults in career transition. We want to emphasize that the assessment, information, and instructional resources used in this case are *not* the only resources that can be used with the CIP approach, as the theory accommodates the use of a wide range of career resources. We have limited the resources depicted in these case studies to the actual resources we use in practice in order to present the most accurate picture possible of the application of the CIP approach in real life. The cases of Linda, Carla, and Juanita are updated from the cases presented in Peterson, Sampson, and Reardon (1991). Refer to Chapter 5 for a discussion of the readiness levels and career assistance options that provide the basis for the case studies presented in this book.

CASE STUDY: LINDA

Background

Linda Johnson is a 32-year-old African American female who is completing the final semester of her senior year in college. While attending high school, Linda worked evenings and weekends in a small, locally owned retail clothing store. After graduating from high school, Linda began working full-time in the clothing store and enrolled part-time in the local community college in a college-transfer associate of arts program. She was very successful in her work at the store and was promoted to assistant manager and then to manager. Her experience at the community college, however, was not as successful. The long and variable hours demanded by her work made it difficult to make progress toward her degree. Linda became frustrated by her slow progress and by the level of her performance, which could be described as average. She believed strongly that she could make very good grades if she could concentrate on her studies for an extended time. Linda's parents could provide emotional support, but they were not able to provide much financial assistance to enable her to attend college full-time. When Linda was promoted to store manager, she stopped taking courses entirely because of her increased workload.

Eight years after graduating from high school, Linda was dissatisfied with her work. The lack of future advancement possibilities, the limited income potential, and the routine nature of her job prompted Linda to seek new employment. She obtained a job as an assistant manager in a larger clothing store that was part of a regional chain of retail stores. In order to increase her future options, Linda continued to save part of her salary for college expenses. After two years, Linda became convinced that she enjoyed retail management but that small retail operations were still limiting. She had been offered a promotion to manager in another city, but it was unlikely that she would progress past the position of local store manager in the company for some time. At the age of 28, Linda enrolled full-time at the local community college, using her savings, student loans, and a part-time retail sales job to pay her expenses. She majored in business administration and graduated with a B+ average in two years. She then transferred to a state university and majored in management in the College of Business, with a minor in merchandising. She has continued to maintain a B+ average while attending the university. Now in her final semester, Linda is using the university on-campus recruitment services. With Linda's situation in mind, let us begin with her initial interview with a career adviser.[2]

Initial Interview

Linda approached the desk at the entrance to the career center and stated that the placement coordinator who schedules on-campus interviews had suggested that she talk with a career adviser. Isabel Garcia, a master's degree student in counseling, invited Linda to sit down. She introduced herself and asked Linda her reasons for seeking career services. Linda stated that last week she completed her first on-campus job interview with a large national retail department store. Before the interview, she had felt confident in her ability to get a good job because of her prior work experience and relatively good grades. After the job interview, she was confused, frustrated, and anxious. She perceived that she was unable to provide good answers to several questions raised by the interviewer. For example, she was asked how her values, interests, skills, and employment preferences fit in with the company's employment opportunities, training options, and priorities for future growth as described in the available recruitment literature. Linda told Isabel, "I came across as though I really didn't know who I am or what I want, and that was really frustrating!" Her negative impression of the interview was confirmed when she received a polite letter thanking her for attending the interview and informing her that she would not be invited for a second interview at the company headquarters.

Preliminary Assessment

Isabel explained that Linda's problem was a reasonably common one, especially for the first interview, and that the career center was designed to provide assistance with this type of concern. She then asked Linda to complete a brief demographic infor-

---

[2] "Career adviser" is used here to indicate a practitioner with varied academic background, including counseling, education, psychology, and human services, who has the training and supervised experience necessary to provide quality career services.

mation form. This form provides accountability data on the nature of the individuals served by the center. Isabel also asked Linda to complete the Career Thoughts Inventory (CTI) (Sampson, Peterson, Lenz, Reardon, & Saunders, 1996a) in order to help Isabel more completely understand the nature of Linda's career concerns. Isabel quickly reviewed the data and noted that Linda's CTI scores were average for the CTI Total, average for Decision-Making Confusion, high for Commitment Anxiety, and low for External Conflict. Isabel used Linda's answers on the CTI as a focal point for a 15-minute unstructured interview to assess the extent to which negative thinking compromised Linda's self-knowledge and occupational knowledge, decision-making skills, and metacognitions.

At this stage of the service delivery process, it is crucial that Isabel exhibit good communication skills, such as empathy, clarification, and appropriate self-disclosure, as well as verbally reinforce Linda's self-disclosures and her quest for further information. Isabel must also be sensitive to any multicultural issues that might impact her work with Linda (Bingham & Ward, 1994). In light of Linda's comments, Isabel concluded that the CTI results appeared to be an accurate representation of the extent of her negative career thoughts. Based on the available data, Isabel stated that she believed that Linda could benefit from the support provided by self-directed career decision making but did not at this time need individual case-managed services. She also stated her opinion that simply gaining access to self-help resources on the job search would not provide Linda with the help that she needed. Isabel asked Linda if she agreed with this recommendation, and Linda replied that this seemed to be a good approach.

Define Problem and Analyze Causes

Isabel and Linda explored the nature of Linda's problem, including gap, ambiguous and complex cues, interacting courses of action, uncertainty of the success of a solution, and career decisions creating new problems. (In defining the problem, all aspects of the CIP perspective would not necessarily be discussed with each individual receiving self-directed career decision-making services. All aspects are discussed in this case study to explore fully the dimensions of the CIP perspective.)

Gap Linda's problem can be conceptualized as a gap between her current situation (difficulty in communicating her self-knowledge in relation to a specific employment opportunity) and an ideal situation (being clear about her self-knowledge and occupational knowledge so she can perform well in job interviews). This conceptualization frames Linda's problem in rational, relative terms, as opposed to Linda's often more emotionally laden, absolute terms, such as, "I'm stupid" or "I just don't interview well."

Ambiguous and Complex Cues Several of Linda's friends also began interviewing on campus, with varying degrees of success. After receiving a second interview with an employer, one of her friends commented, "This interviewing is a piece of cake!" This external input, combined with Linda's conflicting feelings (disappointment over her performance in comparison with her prior confidence in her abilities) contributed to her feelings of being confused.

Interacting Courses of Action Linda has been offered a full-time job where she is now working; she has also been invited to return to the regional retail organization where she worked prior to going back to college. She is therefore certain that she can secure employment, but she doubts that these kinds of jobs will provide the stimulating environment or the opportunities for further advancement that she desires. Finding a more challenging job would seem to be more likely to provide the job satisfaction she seeks, but the path she should take to reach this goal is uncertain.

Uncertainty of the Success of a Solution Even if Linda is able to improve her ability to communicate her self-knowledge in relation to a specific employment opportunity, there is still no guarantee that she will receive a second employment interview. This uncertainty contributes to her anxiety.

Career Decisions Creating New Problems If Linda is successful in obtaining employment with a large national retail department store, she must then cope with planning for relocation while still completing her degree and working part-time. The prospect of so many important, simultaneous efforts contributes to Linda's feeling overwhelmed.

After asking Linda to state her perceptions of the causes of her problem, Isabel supplemented and reframed Linda's statement to be congruent with the CIP approach. Linda is confused about how to relate what she knows about herself (self-knowledge) with what she knows about her options (occupational knowledge—in this case, a job with a specific employer) as part of an overall decision-making strategy. Linda's anxiety related to this situation is made worse by some negative self-talk (metacognitions).

Formulate Goals

Linda and Isabel together arrived at the following goals for Linda's self-directed career decision making:

1. Clarify Linda's self-knowledge and occupational knowledge in order to verify her choice of retail sales management and to help her to more effectively use what she knows about herself and her options in a job interview
2. Identify, challenge, and alter any negative career thoughts that increase Linda's anxiety, which, in turn, can interfere with her job interview performance
3. Expand Linda's knowledge of successful job search strategies
4. Enhance Linda's job interview skills

The use of such terms as *clarify, expand,* and *enhance* is important from a CIP perspective. These terms imply that the individual already possesses some valid information and that the process of service delivery will build on this. Such an approach encourages the development of positive self-talk. Goal statements with terms such as *provide* tend to imply a deficiency and do not facilitate positive self-talk.

Develop Individual Learning Plan

Isabel explained how they would use an Individual Learning Plan (ILP) form to manage the delivery of services (see Figure 9.1). The ILP is essentially a contract between the career center and the client who receives services. The use of a contract in providing self-directed career decision making has several advantages. These advantages include (a) reduced client-counselor misunderstandings resulting from poor communication, (b) improved client understanding of his or her expectations and of the requirements of service delivery, (c) and increased accountability (Montgomery, 1984). From a CIP perspective, the ILP provides the client with a strategy for relating specific career resources to her goals (decision-making skills domain), as well as a means for monitoring the progress the individual is making toward achieving agreed-upon goals (executive processing domain). Because self-directed career decision making may involve a large number of activities, the use of the ILP helps individuals manage more effectively the career problem-solving and decision-making process. In CIP terms, the ILP serves as a mechanism to enable an individual to download material that would normally be carried in working memory, thereby helping the individual to feel less overwhelmed by the size of the task. Some of the learning activities included in the ILP are in the form of instructional modules, sometimes referred to as "resource guides." Each module or resource guide contains a set of objectives and alternative learning activities, such as reading print-based media, viewing audiovisual media, using computer applications, engaging in counselor-client activities, and completing homework assignments. Sample modules are included in Appendix A.

Isabel began by writing down the four goals that she and Linda had just formulated verbally. After putting the goals in writing, Isabel asked if Linda agreed with the goals and if the goals should be reformulated in any way. Linda said she felt satisfied that the attainment of these goals would help solve her career problem. Linda's active participation in this process of clarifying her goals helped increase her motivation for achieving them; it also affirmed that her contributions were valuable, thus reinforcing positive self-talk about her problem-solving and decision-making skills.

For the first goal, clarifying self-knowledge and occupational knowledge for verifying her career choice and preparing for future employment interviews, Isabel recommended that Linda use the computer software SIGI PLUS (Educational Testing Service, 2002). Isabel recommended that Linda use the self-assessment, search for options, and information components of the system. The purpose of this activity is to help Linda confirm her choice of retail sales manager as an occupation by helping her understand how this occupation is potentially congruent with her values, interests, skills, and employment preferences. She also has the opportunity to compare the appropriateness of retail sales management with that of other possible occupations. Such comparisons can confirm her choice, or they may open up the possibility of other occupations that may be more appropriate. Because SIGI PLUS provides the same type of information for each occupation, the similarities and differences between occupations can be explored. This knowledge then serves as a basis for understanding the similarities and differences between specific job opportunities, which can, in turn, be communicated in an initial job interview with a potential employer.

Figure 9.1 | Individual Learning Plan
Career Center—Central University, 215 Parsons Hall

Goal(s): #1 Clarify self-knowledge and occupational knowledge

#2 Restructure negative career thoughts

#3 Expand knowledge of job search strategies

#4 Enhance job interview skills

Activity	Purpose/Outcome	Estimated Time Commitment	Goal #	Priority
SIGI Plus ① self assessment ② search ③ information ④ skills	Clarify choice and obtain information	2 hours	1	1a
CTI Workbook	Identify, challenge, and alter negative career thoughts	2 hours	2	2
Job search video	Clarify job search knowledge	30 minutes	3	3
Resume critique	Improve resume	30 minutes	3	4a
Interviewing video	Improve interview skills	30 minutes	4	5
Interviewing workshop	Improve interview skills	90 minutes	4	6
Book on retailing	Obtain information	30 minutes	1	1b
Information interview	Obtain information	2 hours	1	1c
Employer videos	Obtain information	1 hour	3	4b

This plan can be modified by either party based on new information learned in the activities of the learning plan. The purpose of this plan is to work toward a mutually agreed upon career goal. Activities may be added or subtracted as needed.

Linda Johnson — Student/Client   10/15/02 — Date   Isabel Garcia — Career Adviser   10/15/02 — Date

By verifying her choice of retail sales management, Linda can also increase her confidence in her choice as she searches for a job. This increased confidence results from more-positive self-statements, such as "I have thought about this carefully, and this is the best choice for me right now."

For the second goal, restructuring negative career thoughts, Isabel recommended that Linda complete the *CTI Workbook* (Sampson, Peterson, Lenz, Reardon, & Saunders, 1996b). Isabel suggested that Linda complete Sections 1, 2, and 3 of the workbook in order, gaining an understanding of the nature of her negative thoughts, clarifying how negative career thoughts make it more difficult to make career choices, and restructuring her negative career thoughts with an exercise.

For the third goal, expanding Linda's knowledge of successful job search strategies, Isabel recommended that Linda view a video on conducting a job search campaign. This resource can help Linda clarify, organize, and extend her knowledge of effective job search strategies. Isabel then suggested that Linda have her resume reviewed by a career adviser. This will help to ensure that Linda's resume fully and accurately reflects her background and accomplishments. This review can also contribute to positive self-talk with regard to the thoroughness of her preparation for the job search process.

For the fourth goal, enhancing job interview skills, Isabel recommended that Linda view a videotape on job interviewing and then attend a 90-minute workshop on effective interview skills. This workshop will give Linda an opportunity to practice and receive feedback on her interview behavior. The completed ILP is shown in Figure 9.1. (Note: Some of the activities on the ILP were added at a later time.)

Isabel then summarized Linda's presenting concern and the basic elements of the ILP, noting the progress that Linda had made that day. Isabel made an appointment for Linda to use SIGI PLUS and signed her up for the interviewing workshop (allowing adequate time for Linda to first complete goals one, two, and three). Isabel asked Linda to arrive 20 minutes early for her SIGI PLUS appointment so that she can receive some assistance from a career adviser in making good use of the system. Isabel explained that she will not be on duty at the time of Linda's SIGI PLUS appointment, so another career adviser will be there to provide her with assistance. If at any time Linda wants to talk specifically with her, all she has to do is to leave a telephone message at the career center or stop by during any of Isabel's 15 hours of scheduled time in the center. Isabel also reminded Linda to bring her ILP each time she visits the career center for services. Linda's initial contact with a career adviser lasted 45 minutes.

Execute Individual Learning Plan

Two days later, Linda arrived at the career center for her appointment to use SIGI PLUS. She signed in at the main desk (this sign-in procedure provides accountability data for the career center) and met Susan Franklin, a professional staff member and a National Certified Career Counselor with a master's degree in counseling. Susan asked her to describe briefly her reasons for seeking services and to review her ILP. This procedure allowed Susan to assess the clarity with which Linda understood both her situation and the service delivery approach outlined in the ILP. From Linda's description of the situation, Susan judged that it was appropriate to proceed. Susan then oriented Linda to the use of SIGI PLUS.

Susan reviewed with Linda the assessment variables that she would be examining on SIGI PLUS, made sure that Linda understood how the system would link her personal characteristics with various occupations, and reminded her to review with a career adviser the printouts obtained from SIGI PLUS before reviewing occupational information. Susan then walked with Linda to a room containing several computers and asked Linda to sit at a computer running SIGI PLUS. She provided Linda with a brief orientation to the computer and printer and remained while Linda progressed through the first few displays to ensure that she understood how the computer functioned. She asked Linda to seek her assistance if she had any questions or concerns.

Goal 1: Clarifying Self-Knowledge and Occupational Knowledge Linda used SIGI PLUS to assess her values, interests, skills, and employment preferences (the Analysis phase of the CASVE cycle), making printouts when appropriate. She then used the system to identify occupations that were congruent with her values, interests, skills, and employment preferences (the Synthesis-elaboration phase of the CASVE cycle). Linda developed the following preliminary list of potentially appropriate occupations:

Buyer, retail store
Merchandise manager
Hospital administrator
Human resources manager
Import/export specialist
Labor relations specialist
Manager, sales
Manufacturer's representative
Personnel manager

Susan and another career adviser checked with Linda every 15 minutes to see if she had any concerns or questions. At one point, Linda asked how long the computer will keep records of her use of the system. The other career adviser replied that records are kept for a least one year, in case she returns to use the system again. After completing SIGI PLUS, Linda returned to the main desk to let Susan know she had completed her appointment. They briefly discussed her reaction to using SIGI PLUS, with Susan suggesting that Linda review her printouts before returning to use the system again. Linda requested an appointment for SIGI PLUS when Susan was on duty, as she appeared to be very knowledgeable about the system. Susan scheduled Linda an appointment for later in the week.

Linda arrived 20 minutes early for her next SIGI PLUS appointment so she could discuss her use of the system with Susan, who had helped her at her previous appointment. In their review, Susan paid particular attention both to Linda's efforts to clarify her knowledge and to her understanding of the career problem-solving and decision-making process. Linda was relieved that occupations related to retail sales and management appeared several times on various lists generated by the system, thus reinforcing positive self-talk about her capacities as a problem solver and decision maker. Susan then suggested that Linda return to SIGI PLUS to learn more about the occupations she was considering. She then reviewed with Linda the components within the SIGI PLUS program for obtaining information about the career options she was considering. Linda made an appointment to talk with Susan after she had completed her inquiry on the system.

Using a strategy recommended by Susan, Linda briefly reviewed general information on all of the occupations she was considering, eliminating those occupations that were inappropriate. Linda then used SIGI PLUS to explore buyer, sales manager, and personnel manager in more depth. After she completed her appointment, which lasted 55 minutes, she discussed her reactions with Susan. Linda described two higher-order categories for her occupational options: retailing occupations and personnel occupations. By using SIGI PLUS and then reflecting on what she had learned, Linda was able to further develop her schema for occupational knowledge (see Figure 9.2).

Susan helped Linda to consider the options in terms of costs and benefits (the Valuing phase of the CASVE cycle). Linda stated that although she finds the interpersonal activities in personnel appealing, she thinks retailing would provide a greater diversity of benefits (contact with people and early opportunity for leadership) while having well-defined but manageable costs (long and variable hours). Retailing also has the advantage of allowing her to build more easily on her past experience, providing a sense of continuity that she likes, as well as improving her starting-salary potential. Susan suggested that Linda might want to add to her ILP the reading of a book in the career library that provides a comprehensive description of retailing. Linda agreed.

The next day, Linda returned to the career center to gain additional information. After she signed in at the front desk, Linda asked Karen Wong, a career adviser who was enrolled in a master's degree program in student affairs in higher education, for assistance in locating the book on retailing. After clarifying that Linda was in the process of completing an ILP and needed minimal assistance, Karen helped Linda use the Career Key system (Epstein, Eberhardt, Powers, Strickland, & Smith, 2000; Smith, 1983), a computer-based index of resources contained in the career center library. Karen then helped Linda locate the book and reminded her that she was available to answer questions.

Sitting down at a reading table in the career center, Linda read relevant portions of the book for 30 minutes. Then, closing the book, she thought about what she had read, comparing the information both with what she had learned from SIGI PLUS and with own work experience (cycling back to the Analysis phase of the CASVE cycle). Sensing that Linda might need assistance, Steve Goldberg, the career center librarian, who has a master's degree in library and information science, asked Linda if he could be of any assistance. Linda replied that she was trying to learn more about retailing and had just finished reviewing a book on the topic. Steve asked if she would be interested in talking with someone in the field of retail management. When Linda

Figure 9.2 | Schema Generalization

From *Career Development and Services: A Cognitive Approach* (p. 272), by G. W. Peterson, J. P. Sampson, Jr., and R. C. Reardon, 1991, Pacific Grove, CA: Brooks/Cole.

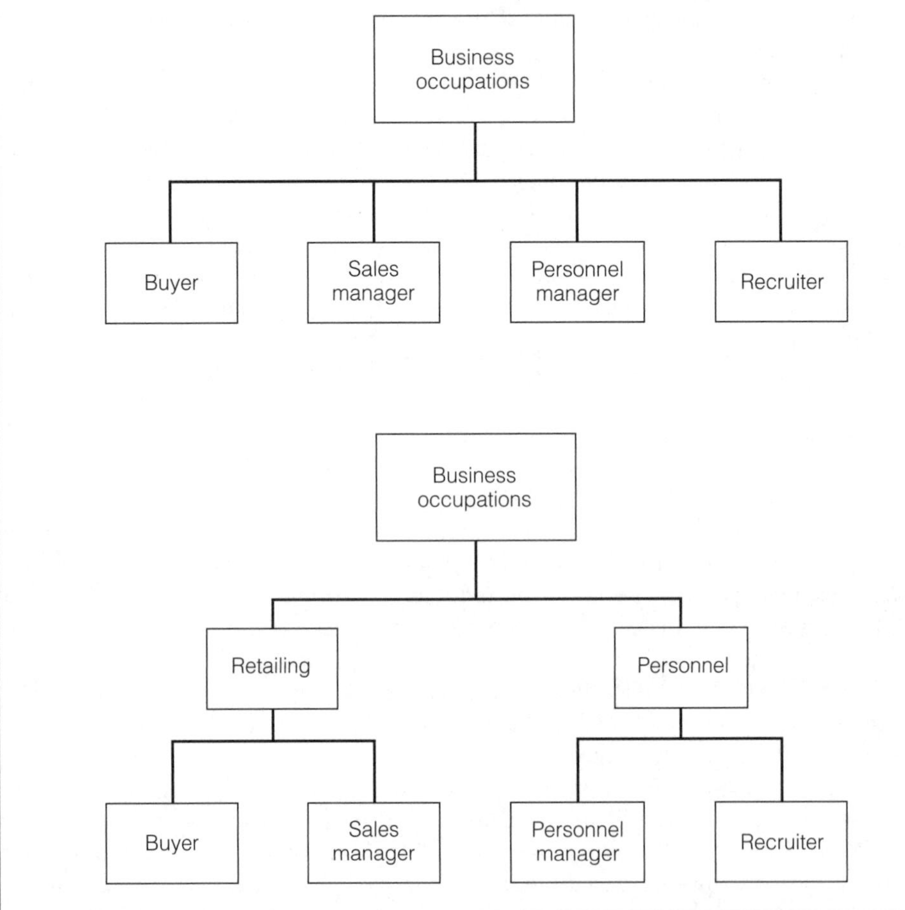

said, "Yes," Steve invited her to sit down at an available computer and access the career center Web site. Linda used the Web site to identify the name of Ingrid Swensen, who was the manager of a large national retail store located at a local shopping mall. Linda expressed interest in an interview with Ingrid, and Steve provided her with a handout with guidelines for scheduling and conducting an information interview. Steve also updated her ILP before she left the center.

Linda prepared a brief list of questions and went to Ingrid's office two days later for the interview. Ingrid asked if Linda had a copy of her resume that she could briefly review to become more familiar with Linda's education and experience. After reviewing the resume, Ingrid provided a brief overview of the company and her specific job responsibilities. Linda then asked questions based on the new insights she had gained from clarifying her self-knowledge and occupational knowledge. With this foundation, Linda then asked how the satisfactions and frustrations of her previous work experience would relate to working as a retail sales manager in a large organization. At the close of the interview, Ingrid gave Linda a tour of the management offices of the store. As Linda was leaving, Ingrid stated that although her company was not currently interviewing for positions at Linda's level, she was impressed with Linda and would like to keep her resume on file. Linda said that would be fine and thanked Ingrid for her time. At this point, Linda's self-talk was enhanced, both in terms of her self-worth ("I do have something of value to offer in retailing") and her confidence in decision making ("My initial decision about retailing was good after all").

The next day, Linda called the career center to ask when Isabel was scheduled to work. The receptionist stated that Isabel was on duty that day from 4 to 8 P.M. and that she would leave Isabel a message that Linda had called. Linda indicated that she would try to stop by the career center after class at 5 P.M.

When Linda arrived at the center, Isabel was helping a student use a card sort. It looked as though Isabel would be occupied for a while, so Linda began browsing through a display of magazines, locating and reading an article on African American women in business. In putting magazines on display, the career center was following the practice recommended by Reardon (1973).[3]

Ten minutes later, Isabel was able to attend to Linda and asked her to sit down and review her progress on the goals in her ILP. Linda described her experiences, with Isabel asking questions to assess how Linda had progressed in terms of self- and occupational knowledge, decision-making skills, and metacognitions. After being briefly interrupted by a telephone call, Isabel then asked Linda to summarize her thoughts about her occupational choice. Linda replied, "As I see things now, my two best options are retail sales manager and buyer. If I had to choose right now, I would choose retail sales manager. The initial position that I want to apply for would be a management trainee position. I found out that because of my work experience, I could move right into a position as assistant buyer with some retailers. I like the idea of the higher pay and the respect for my past work experience, but a structured training program will help me make a better start with the company. After all the time and effort that I've put into this degree, I really want to do this right. A few of the largest retailers offer training programs that rotate you through all of the major operations areas as well as help you network with new and experienced employees. So I think that management trainee would be a better choice now than assistant buyer. After I rotate through all of the areas, I may still be able to move into an assistant buyer position or try for a different position that I like better."

[3] "Career data should be available to students in such a way that they can freely explore or browse according to their interests. The information materials should be easily accessible and promote personal reflections and self-analysis within the student users. The data in the career information service should serve as stimulus materials which promote reflective thought, discussion, and effective decision making among students" (Reardon, 1973, p. 497).

Isabel asked Linda what she thought about her progress on this first goal listed on her ILP. Linda said that she was confident of her tentative choice and was ready to move on to her next goal.

Goal 2: Restructuring Negative Career Thoughts Isabel briefly reviewed how negative self-talk could influence one's job search behavior. Linda stated that she was feeling pretty good about herself now, so why not skip this goal and go on to the next goal. Isabel said, "You could go on to clarifying your knowledge of job search strategies at this point, but I believe it would still be worth the time to explore your self-talk and job search behavior. Even though I am well aware of how my thoughts influence my feelings and behavior, I still let things get out of hand from time to time. Recently I was studying for an exam in statistics that covered three chapters. I was able to answer all of the problems in the book except one that dealt with a particularly abstract concept that was just barely covered in class. I was really anxious about the exam and was not studying effectively at all. Because anxiety is one of my signals that something is wrong, I gave myself permission for a time out, to figure out what was happening. Well, of course, I was doing my usual perfection game, thinking that if I can't work every problem, I'm not going to pass the exam. When I thought about the situation more rationally, I realized that I could miss several problems and still do well enough on the exam to keep my current grade point average. I went back to my studying, concentrating a lot better. As it turned out, I did get the answer wrong on the question related to the abstract concept, but I did well on the rest of the exam. I don't have to be perfect to succeed." Isabel's modeling via self-disclosure encourages Linda's exploratory behavior as well as provides a further concrete example of how cognitions influence feeling and behavior.

Isabel continued, "I suspect that you may have some similar self-talk that limited your success with your first job interview. Being more certain of your occupational choice doesn't necessarily eliminate negative self-talk." Linda agreed that it probably would be useful for her to examine this issue. Isabel now reviewed how Linda should complete the three sections of the *CTI Workbook* that were assigned on her ILP. Isabel informed Linda that she would be out of the center for the remainder of the week because she was making a presentation at the annual meeting of the state counseling association, but that other staff would be available to help her complete her ILP. Linda thanked her and said that she would try to see her next week.

That evening, Linda completed the first two sections of the *CTI Workbook*, learning about the impact of negative career thoughts on career choice and the nature of her scores. She then began the third section, which is designed to help users challenge and alter negative career thoughts. Using CTI items as a focal point, she learned the process of cognitive restructuring. After writing out the original negative career thought, she read a brief reframing stimulus statement that challenged her thinking. With this input, she then altered (revised) her original negative thought to be more rational. She noticed a recurring theme of absolute thinking and perfectionism that made her more anxious and less effective as a decision maker. Even though they were not assigned, she read Sections 4 and 5 of the workbook, reviewing the process of career problem solving and decision making and learning how to make good use of support from other people. Her positive self-talk and decision-making confidence were reinforced as she recognized how much she had learned about problem solving and decision making.

Goal 3: Expanding Knowledge of Job Search Strategies Linda returned the next day to the career center to complete the next goal on her ILP. Steve Goldberg, the career center librarian, asked if he could provide any assistance. Linda responded that she did need assistance, and Steve reviewed her progress in completing her ILP. After commenting positively on her progress, Steve helped her locate the job search video indicated on her ILP. After viewing the assigned video, Linda reviewed her resume and revised the section on work experience. After waiting a few minutes for an available staff member, Linda was able to talk with Susan Franklin, who reviewed Linda's ILP progress, paying particular attention to what she learned from viewing the video. The regular review of a client's ILP by various staff members helps to ensure continuity of service delivery and reinforces the belief that the client's behavior (for example, use of resources and thoughtful reflection) is the primary focus (internal locus of control), as opposed to the client seeking to be "fixed" by a staff member (external locus of control).

Susan critiqued Linda's resume, noting that it was comprehensive and well written. She did suggest that Linda reframe the description of her education by providing more specific details about educational experiences.

Susan suggested that in addition to completing the existing activities identified on the ILP for the third goal, Linda view two employer videotapes from large retail companies that describe the opportunities available in their management training programs. This material could facilitate Linda's preparation for interviewing by enhancing her general knowledge of management training programs and helping her prepare specifically for interviews with the two companies on the videotape, as both of these companies recruit on campus. Noting that Linda was scheduled to attend a workshop on effective interview skills the following Monday, Susan suggested that Linda also view the videotape on effective interview skills as soon as possible.

Goal 4: Enhancing Job Interview Skills With a review of the interview skills videotape as a foundation, Linda attended the scheduled 90-minute workshop on effective interview skills. Dave Collins, a Ph.D. degree student in counseling psychology who is working as a career adviser in the career center, led the workshop. The workshop began with Dave and the 12 participants introducing themselves. The introduction included an identification of prior interviewing exposure, giving Dave an indication of the nature of the participants' actual experience. The process continued with a brief discussion of workshop objectives:

1. Describe how job interviewing skills relate to the total job search process
2. Describe a general strategy for preparing for an effective job interview by clarifying and/or obtaining self-knowledge and occupational and employer knowledge
3. Recognize the typical organization of a job interview
4. Respond directly and assertively to typical interview questions
5. Identify common barriers to effective interviewing

After reviewing the workshop objectives, Dave presented information and answered questions related to the first three objectives. He then modeled answering several typical interview questions. The participants selected partners, and Dave had each pair ask and answer prepared questions by using a role-playing technique. Dave then provided feedback to the participants on their interview performance. In the final part of the workshop, two volunteers role-played interviews, which were videotaped. Linda was quick to volunteer for this option. Her interview consisted of Dave playing the part of the potential employer and Linda responding to questions. Linda was able to answer all of the questions confidently, demonstrating a capacity to relate her values, interests, and skills to the employment opportunities, training options, and priorities for future growth of a hypothetical retail company. The workshop participants viewed and critiqued the videotape, generally approving her performance. One student commented that Linda could have been more animated when discussing issues that were personally important. Dave replayed the tape, asking the participants to pay attention to nonverbal communication. Linda noticed that her laid-back posture was not congruent with her actual interest in the interview. The process was repeated for the second volunteer interviewee.

Summative Review and Generalization

Knowing that Isabel was scheduled to be at the career center, Linda arrived to discuss her progress and review her ILP. Isabel finished helping a student locate a videotape and then sat down with Linda to review her progress. Linda commented that although she was still somewhat anxious about finding a good position with the right company, she was much more confident of both her occupational choice and her job search skills. She said, "Retail sales management really appeals to me. I can build on my past experience, which I like, because it means that all of those years in retailing were helping me to get a better job. I believe this type of work can provide me with the challenge and job satisfaction I'm looking for. I also think I can convince any interviewer that I know what I'm doing in terms of my career. Having the terms to describe how I view the work environment and myself helps a lot! I also think I've been pretty thorough in making my decision—sort of like doing your homework when it really counts!"

Isabel asked about Linda's experience in completing the *CTI Workbook*. "I can see how my negative, absolute way of thinking and perfectionism led me to be so anxious that I didn't do very well in my job interview. I guess I've been thinking pretty irrationally for a long time. It's not easy to change the way you think—sort of like changing a bad habit! At least now I am beginning to catch myself before things get way out of hand." Linda then said, "My resume is better and I know a lot more about interviewing, which is important, because after I get a job, I will eventually be in the position myself of doing a lot of interviewing and hiring."

Linda and Isabel agreed that the goals they had established in the ILP had been met. Isabel suggested that Linda keep all of her materials and printouts for future reference. She explained how the career center could help her process future job interviews. Isabel asked Linda to complete a career center comment card, which allows individuals to provide feedback on the quality of services provided and make suggestions for improvements. Linda thanked Isabel and said that she would let Isabel know about her next job interview experience.

CASE STUDY: CARLA

Background

Carla Phillips is a 21-year-old white female who is in her junior year in college and is majoring in social studies education at the secondary level. She currently has a B− average in college. Her work experience has been limited to service jobs in two fast-food restaurants.

Initial Interview

Carla approached the desk at the entrance to the career center, stated that she is a social studies education major, and asked for information on summer job opportunities related to education or government. Isabel Garcia, a career adviser, invited Carla to sit down. Isabel introduced herself and asked Carla to be more specific about the information she needs. Carla stated that by the end of this academic year, she will have developed teaching skills that she would like to use in a summer job instead of returning to her old job at the fast-food restaurant. Carla was making a concrete request for information, and there was no evidence of a significant problem, so Isabel gave her an instructional module (or resource guide) on gaining work experience and indicated the location of several employment directories.

Isabel moved about the career center library, answering questions and keeping track of the activities of several people that she was assisting. She noticed that Carla had a module sheet, directories, and folders spread out in front of her at a table. Isabel initially thought that Carla was making energetic efforts to obtain information, but after a while, these efforts appeared instead to be hyperactivity. Carla moved rapidly from directory to directory, returned to reading her module sheet, and then looked through several folders. Her reading seemed random and disorganized. Sensing that something was wrong, Isabel sat down at the table and asked if Carla was getting the information she needed. Carla stated that the information was very useful. Noting a discrepancy between Carla's words and her apparent anxiety, Isabel stated that the large amount of information that the career center has available can be overwhelming at times. Carla emphatically agreed and stated that she was uncertain how to use all of the information. Isabel suggested that it would be useful to learn a little more about Carla's needs so she could help her locate the most useful information.

Preliminary Assessment

Isabel asked Carla to complete the CTI (Sampson et al., 1996a) to identify her readiness for career decision making. Isabel quickly scored and reviewed the data, noting Carla's Total CTI score of 88 (2.0 standard deviations above the mean), a Decision-

Making Confusion score of 26 (2.0 standard deviations above the mean), a Commitment Anxiety score of 24 (2.0 standard deviations above the mean), and an External Conflict score of 5 (1.0 standard deviation above the mean). To assess Carla's general approach to decision making, Isabel asked her to describe a recent decision she had made. Carla said, "My roommate told me last weekend that the tires on my car were almost bald and that I needed to buy new tires. I went to a tire store and looked at all kinds of tires. The salesperson was nice and told me about all the different tires available. But it was just too confusing! There was no way that I could decide. My father always used to help me with things like that. I just told the salesperson how much I had to spend and asked her to just pick the best tires for the money. I was so glad to get out of there. If I had chosen the tires, they would have been the wrong type, or they would have gone flat or something!" Carla repeatedly folded and unfolded a piece of paper as she talked.

Isabel asked Carla to describe her current occupational choice of secondary social studies teacher. Carla stated, "Teaching is a really good field. It's important work, and kids really look up to their teachers—at least I really did when I was in school." Isabel asked if anything else influenced her decision to become a teacher. Carla said, "My mom and dad were really happy when I decided to become a teacher. They are really counting on me."

Isabel then explored the extent of Carla's occupational knowledge. When asked to describe the most appealing daily work tasks associated with teaching, Carla was unable to provide a concrete answer. Isabel said, "Carla, I sense that although you find teaching appealing, you have some major doubts that being a secondary social studies teacher is your best choice."

Carla increased her hyperactive behavior, shifting her weight back and forth in her chair while speaking. She said, "I'm really scared about all of this. I really don't know what I want to do about anything! I thought that by getting a summer job in teaching, I'd find out if I've made the right choice. But now I'm not sure that would help me after all. What do you think I should do?"

Isabel formed a working hypothesis that Carla was indecisive and that her negative career thoughts, considerable anxiety, and dependent decision-making style were formidable barriers to effective career problem solving and decision making. Carla was clearly not likely to benefit from self-directed career decision making or a brief staff-assisted service, and a referral was warranted. Isabel stated, "Your confusion and anxiety about making decisions indicate to me that there may be some issues for you that have become barriers to making a career choice. In order to have some time set aside to focus on these issues, I recommend that you schedule an appointment with one of our counselors. Right now, I don't believe that looking at this information on summer job opportunities will be very helpful. Later on, I would be happy to help you locate and use any information that we have available. Does this sound like a good approach to you?"

Carla agreed that the opportunity to talk with a counselor would be a good idea. Isabel helped Carla make an appointment for counseling and provided a brief orientation to the counseling process. Carla then completed a counseling intake form that included an informed consent form. Carla left the career center with a commitment to return for individual career counseling to help her resolve her career problems.

CASE STUDY: JUANITA

The case of Juanita Suarez illustrates how counselors might use the Cognitive Information Processing (CIP) paradigm in conjunction with group career counseling. Juanita is receiving services as part of a high school guidance program.

Background

Juanita Suarez is a 16-year-old Hispanic female who is completing the first semester of her junior year in high school. Her aptitude test scores range from the 65th to the 75th percentile. Her grades in high school indicate a similar pattern, with Bs in all subjects except physical education, where she is consistently an A student. Juanita's parents own and operate a dry-cleaning business. All of Juanita's paid work experience has been in her parents' store, where she has worked in customer service and has operated the machinery.

Juanita has been very active in a wide variety of intramural sports. Much of the time that she spends reading and watching television is also related in some way to sports. Juanita has served as a volunteer at a homeless shelter operated by her church. Juanita's older brother is currently completing a certificate program in heating and air-conditioning repair at the local community college.

Juanita is undecided about her future. The three options that she mentions most often are (a) graduating from high school and continuing to work in the family dry-cleaning business, (b) teaching physical education at the high school level, and (c) working as an athletic trainer in college or professional sports.

With Juanita's situation in mind, let us begin with the initial interview (prescreening) as a vehicle for beginning the career problem-solving and decision-making process. At this phase, Juanita and her counselor communicate or interact with the problem, the first step in the CASVE cycle presented in Chapter 2.

Initial Interview

As part of the high school's career education program, Juanita's social studies teacher, Enrique Martinez, assigned students to write a paper describing an occupational choice that they were considering. After class, Juanita confided to Mr. Martinez that she was having difficulty in selecting an occupation for the assignment. Mr. Martinez suggested that Juanita check with her guidance counselor, Paul Rogers, about career services that were available. He added that completing a guidance activity was one of the optional activities in the career education program for their class that semester.

Before going home, Juanita stopped at the guidance office and asked the secretary for an appointment with her counselor, Paul Rogers, a National Certified Career Counselor with a bachelor's degree in African American studies and a master's degree in counseling. Two days later, Juanita discussed her indecision with her counselor. Her career problem could be framed in terms of gap, ambiguous and complex cues, interacting courses of action, uncertainty of the success of a solution, and career decisions creating new problems, as described in Chapter 1.

Gap Juanita's problem can be conceptualized as a gap between her real state of affairs (inability to specify a choice of occupation) and an ideal state of affairs (being committed to an occupational choice as her brother is).

Ambiguous and Complex Cues Juanita's parents have begun to express concern about her lack of direction but have not applied pressure to make any specific choice. Maria, Juanita's best friend, has suggested that they attend the local community college together without initially declaring a major. Maria says, "Most students change their majors lots of times, so why worry about choosing now?"

Interacting Courses of Action Juanita could easily work in the family business, which would be safe and would please her parents. She also might be successful outside the family business, as her brother is, and he appears to have made her parents happy.

Uncertainty of the Success of a Solution Juanita is confident of her ability to be successful in the family business, but her lack of experience in other work settings and her lack of clarity about which personal preferences are important in making her decision contribute to her uncertainty.

Career Decisions Creating New Problems After deciding on an occupational choice, Juanita will likely face a host of new problems related to implementing her choice, such as financing her education, selecting an educational institution, and obtaining employment. As her counselor discussed these career issues, he briefly explored other issues related to family problems, anxiety, and Juanita's approach to decision making in order to judge if group career counseling would be an appropriate intervention.

Preliminary Assessment

Juanita's cumulative record includes her scores on the CTI: Total CTI score of 70 (1.0 standard deviation above the mean), Decision-Making Confusion score of 19 (1.0 standard deviation above the mean), Commitment Anxiety score of 12 (at the mean), and External Conflict score of 6 (1.0 standard deviation above the mean). Juanita completed the CTI at the beginning of the school year as a career education activity for all 11th-grade students. Paul concluded, based on the interview data and the CTI scores, that Juanita is undecided and would be an appropriate candidate for a career counseling group that is starting next week. He chose group career counseling (Pyle, 1986) as the most appropriate intervention on the basis of *needs* (Paul perceived that Juanita was quiet but observant and would benefit from the social learning opportunities provided in a group), *timing* (a new group was starting next week), and *cost-effectiveness* (group interventions would make good use of the limited amount of time that Paul has for direct service delivery).

Paul explained that the group will include a mixture of 11th- and 12th-grade students who want help in career problem solving and decision making. (The membership of the group reflects the demographics of Juanita's high school, with a 50/50 balance of gender and a racial composite of 40% Hispanic, 30% African American, and 30% white students.) Paul then provided Juanita with an overview of the goals, ground rules, and scheduling of the group. The group is intended to help students make a tentative occupational choice, or create a manageable list of options to consider, and obtain an awareness of the resources that are available to help them make a tentative choice. The seven volunteer group members will meet twice a week for four weeks during the period scheduled for Juanita's social studies class. One extra class period per week in social studies is allocated either to assessment activities in the guidance office or to use of career materials in the school media center. Juanita's teacher, Enrique Martinez, has substituted the group experience for her regular class participation at these times.

Define Problem and Formulate Goals

The sequence for group career counseling continues with the first group session.

First Group Session Paul began the first session—the encounter stage—by welcoming students to the group and introducing himself. He described his current work assignment at the school and his leisure activities. The group members were then invited to introduce themselves and share information about their work and leisure activities. Juanita was initially reluctant to speak; she provided only brief statements. Paul then reviewed the general goals and ground rules for the group, paying particular attention to the importance and limits of confidentiality and the importance of homework assignments related to self-knowledge and occupational knowledge.

After soliciting general questions and providing clarifications, Paul disclosed some of the career concerns he had when he was a high school junior. He asked group members to share their thoughts about choosing an occupation. He was careful not to frame this initial discussion in terms of "problems" that students were having with occupational choice; rather, he implied through his comments that making career choices and seeking assistance are normal aspects of the process of human development. The members mentioned confusion about the career problem-solving and decision-making process: (a) uncertainty about self-knowledge and occupational knowledge, (b) pressure from parents and peers to make a choice, and (c) anxiety about the necessity of making the right occupational choices early in life. (Paul made a mental note that a metacognitive error may exist related to making the right choice; such an error can be dealt with later in the group.) Juanita was surprised that so many students shared thoughts that were similar to her own. She was especially surprised by the comments of two academically gifted students, who she had always assumed knew exactly what they wanted to do with regard to career and educational choices. Juanita began to doubt that she is alone in having career problems and to doubt that there is a deficiency in her that is causing her difficulties.

Paul suggested that it would be useful for the members to clarify and extend their self-knowledge as an initial step in the career problem-solving and decision-making process. (Notice the use of the terms *clarify* and *extend* rather than *provide;* Paul implies that all students have self-knowledge as opposed to being empty and in need of "fixing.") He described the two versions of the Self-Directed Search (SDS) (Holland,

1994) that were available: paper-and-pencil and computer. Paul facilitated student investment in the assessment process by having them participate, if only briefly, in the test-selection process by their indication of preference for administration mode. After a brief discussion of available assessment options, the members indicated which version of the SDS they wished to complete.

Paul then briefly defined the concepts of values, interests, skills, and employment preferences and provided examples from his own experience. He asked the group members to list their initial perceptions of their own values, interests, skills, and employment preferences in order to provide them with an initial frame of reference prior to completing the assigned instruments. Paul then asked the members to schedule time with the guidance secretary to complete the SDS. The session concluded with a discussion of how the members' first experience with the group matched their expectations. Several members expressed surprise that they were not being told what to do. Paul related this comment to his perceptions of effective groups and reminded the members of the next scheduled meeting time for the group.

Second Group Session The session began with a review of the names of group members and a review of the homework assignment to estimate their values, interests, skills, and employment preferences. Paul distributed the handouts "What's Involved in Career Choice" (the Pyramid of Information Processing Domains) and "A Guide to Good Decision Making" (the CASVE cycle) (Sampson, Peterson, Lenz, & Reardon, 1992) to orient the students to the CIP approach (see Chapter 2). Paul then briefly explained the model to the group members. To model self-disclosure, he provided personal examples from his own experience with career problem solving and decision making. Paul then invited the members to discuss any difficulties they were having with occupational choice in terms of the models presented in the handouts. Most students identified their difficulties as a lack of self-knowledge and occupational knowledge. Paul provided additional self-disclosure regarding generic information processing skills and metacognitions, thus encouraging members to explore these areas as well. At this point, to enhance group cohesion, Paul used a linking strategy (Pyle, 1986) to help members understand their commonalities.

Because Juanita was not an active participant in these discussions, Paul encouraged her by asking if she would like to share her thoughts. She said she believes she needs to work on all aspects of the pyramid. One of the members, picking up on several of Paul's earlier interventions, asked Juanita if she could provide any specific examples. Juanita responded, "I think I know a lot about myself. My mother and I talk a lot about what's happening to me at school and at work. I don't understand how to fit what I know about myself with what different jobs are like. I know a lot about the dry-cleaning business, but I don't know much about other jobs, or occupations, or whatever. I have never really thought about decision making, but I have an idea that I put myself down at times and that makes me afraid of trying new things." Paul thanked her for sharing her thoughts. Juanita responded, "I'm not used to talking in a group of people like this!" Paul acknowledged her feelings and asked if other group members experienced the same feeling. Two other group members revealed that talking in a group was difficult for them as well. Paul stated that this feeling is very normal and that it is his experience that by the end of the group, many of the members feel comfortable in group discussions.

Paul then asked the members to state their career problem in terms of a gap; this intervention builds on information discussed in the initial interview (prescreening). Juanita expressed her gap as her inability to choose an occupation, compared with her brother's commitment to an occupational choice. The members were asked to write down their goals for occupational choices, present their goals to the group, receive feedback from the counselor and other group members, and then refine their goals. Paul reminded the group that there are no bad goals, only goals that can be refined or enhanced.

Juanita made the following final statement of goals:

1. Understand more about myself and occupations
2. Learn how my thinking influences my choices
3. Make a plan to implement my choice

To help the group members acquire skill in using the CASVE decision-making paradigm, Paul asked the group members to describe in writing, as homework, a recent decision using the CASVE cycle and to complete the SDS.

Develop Individual Learning Plan

The sequence for group career counseling continues with the development of an ILP.

Third Group Session After reviewing the members' homework and perceptions of the progress of the group, Paul explained how the ILP is used to guide and monitor career counseling and guidance services. Each member received a sample ILP as a model and a blank ILP form and was asked to write in his or her goals, with corresponding activities and purposes or outcomes. Paul asked for volunteers to present their ILPs. As members presented their ILPs, Paul and other group members made suggestions for refinement. Consuelo Ortiz, one of the group members, is a popular student leader that Juanita likes and respects and has been Juanita's friend for the past two years. Consuelo disclosed to the group that making an occupational choice has been difficult for her because of intense pressure from her family to make good use of her academic ability. Consuelo presented her ILP with confidence and energy. For some time, Juanita had engaged in negative self-talk, thinking that there must be something wrong with her because she was unable to make a confident occupational choice. In comparing herself to Consuelo, Juanita had perceived herself as inferior. However, Consuelo's self-disclosure, willingness to seek services, and direct support of Juanita during group sessions is encouraging Juanita to question her previous negative self-talk.

For Juanita's first goal, "understand more about myself and occupations," she will (a) complete the SDS; (b) use the DISCOVER system, an interactive computer-assisted career guidance system (ACT, 2002), as a resource for examining occupational options; (c) use the school career library with the assistance of the media specialist to obtain career information (more details to be added to the ILP later); and (d) attend the group on a regular basis. For her second goal, "learn how my thinking influences my choices," Juanita will complete the *CTI Workbook* (Sampson et al., 1996b) and attend the group on a regular basis. For her third goal, "make a plan to implement my choice," Juanita will complete the *CTI Workbook* and attend the group on a regular basis. Figure 9.3 shows Juanita's completed ILP (some of the activities were added at a later stage. Paul asked the group members to review, as a homework assignment, a handout on the Holland Hexagon (Holland, 1997) to provide a structure for understanding the world of work.

Execute Individual Learning Plan

Group career counseling continues with an examination of self-assessment data.

Fourth Group Session After reviewing the members' homework and perceptions of the progress of the group, Paul asked for a volunteer to summarize his or her SDS results and compare these results with initial perceptions of his or her values, interests, skills, and employment preferences (the Analysis–self-knowledge and Synthesis-elaboration phases of the CASVE cycle). Consuelo volunteered and began discussing her SDS results and the way these data matched her previous perceptions of her interests. Paul supplemented and occasionally modified Consuelo's statements, also integrating concepts from the handout that was assigned as homework. As Consuelo discussed her results from the SDS, Paul referred back to the Holland Hexagon (Holland, 1997) as a schema to help organize the group members' thinking about themselves and the world of work (the Analysis-occupations phase of the CASVE cycle). Paul then asked Consuelo to share personal, work, and leisure experiences that support or contradict the test results. Other group members then presented their results, with Paul and others providing feedback. Paul paid particular attention to linking shared values, interests, skills, and employment preferences among group members, thus facilitating further development of group cohesiveness.

The results from Juanita's completion of the SDS: Computer Version showed that her interests were similar to those of individuals who tended to be Realistic and Social (SDS classifications). Paul asked Juanita to comment on her results. Juanita stated that the part of her current job that she liked most was helping the customers, which related to her Social score on the SDS.

Paul asked each of the group members to complete, as homework, an exercise for identifying the occupations identified by the SDS Occupations Finder that would be appropriate for detailed exploration. This type of exercise helps individuals to structure and organize the process of determining the most appropriate occupations for exploration, thus avoiding the confusion that individuals often experience when faced with long lists of occupations on various printouts. Paul suggested that detailed exploration be conducted on three to five occupations, optimizing the capacity of working memory. Following completion of the exercise, each member was to begin completing his or her ILP for using occupational information (the Analysis-occupations phase of the CASVE cycle). Paul informed the group members that he, along with the school media specialist and several parent volunteers, would be available to assist them to identify and use various information resources.

Later that evening, Juanita reviewed her assessment printouts and her handout on the Holland Hexagon. Using the exercise distributed in her group, she evaluated each occupation on her printouts and either (a) eliminated the occupation from further consideration, (b) wrote the name of the occupation in a column indicating

Figure 9.3 | Individual Learning Plan
Guidance Office—Central High School

Goal(s): #1 *Understand more about myself and occupations*

#2 *Learn how my thinking influences my choices*

#3 *Make a plan to implement my choice*

Activity	Purpose/Outcome	Estimated Time Commitment	Goal #	Priority
Complete the SDS	*Learn about myself and identify occupations*	*1 hour*	*1*	*1*
Use Discover to learn about occupations	*Learn about occupations*	*1 hour*	*1*	*2*
Complete the CTI Workbook	*Identify, challenge, and alter negative career thoughts*	*2 hours*	*2 and 3*	~~3~~ *6*
Career videos	*Learn about occupations*	*30 minutes*	*1*	*3*
Read biographical descriptions	*Learn about occupations*	*30 minutes*	*1*	*4*
Interview two workers	*Learn about occupations*	*3 hours*	*1*	*5*
Read community college catelog	*Learn about EMT program*	*30 minutes*	*3*	*7*
Make appointments with counselor and academic advisor	*Learn about admissions and registration*	*2 hours*	*3*	*8*

This plan can be modified by either party based on new information learned in the activities of the learning plan. The purpose of this plan is to work toward a mutually agreed upon career goal.
Activities may be added or subtracted as needed.

Juanita Suarez	*11/27/02*	*Paul Rogers*	*11/27/02*
Student/Client	Date	Career Adviser	Date

uncertainty about the need for further exploration, or (c) wrote the name of the occupation in a column indicating a strong interest in further exploration. Juanita used her personal perceptions and test scores to assist her in making these judgments.

The next day, Juanita went to the media center and talked with Bonnie Patterson, the school media specialist. Bonnie asked to see Juanita's ILP in order to more fully understand her needs. She noticed that DISCOVER was indicated as an activity. Bonnie introduced Juanita to Margaret Scott, a parent-volunteer who had completed a training program on helping students use DISCOVER. After determining Juanita's reasons for using DISCOVER, Margaret oriented her to the system. Then, using Juanita's completed exercise for identifying occupations for further study, Margaret showed her how to use the occupational information component of DISCOVER to explore briefly the occupations on her exercise that she was not sure warranted further exploration.

Because DISCOVER provided a common structure of information for all occupations, Juanita could quickly compare typical work tasks, entry requirements, income, and other pertinent information and decide whether to retain the occupation for more detailed exploration or to eliminate it from further consideration. In addition to helping the individual manage the exploration process, this exercise can facilitate positive self-talk (for example, "I considered a lot of occupations before I made my decision. This was not a spur-of-the-moment choice!"). When Juanita had completed her use of DISCOVER, Margaret asked which of the occupations she would like to explore in more detail. Remembering Paul's suggestion that her final list for exploration should contain no more than three to five occupations (the Synthesis-crystallization phase of the CASVE cycle), Juanita identified the following occupations for more detailed study: emergency medical technician, respiratory therapist, and physical education teacher.

Margaret suggested that Juanita add activities to her ILP that would help her learn more about each of the three occupations she had listed. Margaret went to the computer where Career Key is available (Epstein et al., 2000; Smith, 1983), explaining that Juanita could use this comprehensive index of media center career materials to identify specific resources for occupational and educational information. After explaining how the system operated, Margaret moved on to assist another student with DISCOVER, leaving Juanita to use Career Key. When Juanita had completed her use of Career Key, Bonnie offered to help her to select from among the available resources the items that will be most appropriate for her needs. After explaining how information relates to problem solving and discussing the resource options that are available, Juanita and Bonnie added the following activities to Juanita's ILP: (a) view videotapes that provide general occupational descriptions, (b) read biographical descriptions of individuals engaged in each occupation, and (c) conduct a structured interview of individuals employed in the two occupations that appear most promising based on her previous review of video and printed materials. Bonnie then showed Juanita where to locate the video and print materials and how to operate the video equipment.

Fifth Group Session After reviewing the members' homework and perceptions of the progress of the group, Paul asked each of the group members to identify the three to five occupations that seemed most appropriate out of the options considered and to briefly state his or her reasons for each choice. After each group member had spoken, Paul asked the members to describe the modifications they had made to their ILPs. Consuelo began, eagerly describing how she would like to learn more about the occupational options she had identified. Paul responded that the activities Consuelo proposed in her revised ILP should provide useful information to assist her problem solving and decision making. Paul's positive response to Consuelo's disclosure provided group members with the verbal reinforcement described by Reardon (1984) as enhancing client motivation to use information resources.

At this point, Paul discussed the barriers to effective problem solving and decision making that result from negative self-talk. After introducing the basic concepts and providing relevant examples, Paul briefly disclosed how he had identified and corrected negative self-talk related to his decision to become a high school guidance counselor. Paul asked if anyone would like to share how negative self-talk had been a barrier to his or her own problem solving and decision making. Consuelo described how her thoughts predicting defeat almost caused her not to run for vice president of the junior class. Paul helped Consuelo elaborate and frame her example in CIP terms and then complimented her for taking the risk of sharing such information about herself with the group. Such reinforcement by the counselor can help other group members confront their own dysfunctional thinking.

Paul then initiated a word-association exercise related to sex-role stereotyping (Pyle, 1986). Paul stated an occupational title and then asked the members to describe the type of person that came to mind. After repeating this process for several occupations, Paul asked if particular occupations had been associated with males or females. Members of the group quickly got the idea, with Paul adding concepts relating to sex-role stereotyping where appropriate. Paul then asked the members if sex-role stereotyping, or any other stereotypes, limited the range of occupations that they would consider. Juanita admitted that her dislike of occupations involving math was related at least in part to stereotyping.

Paul continued by discussing how families can be both a resource for and a barrier to effective problem solving and decision making. In Juanita's case, it may be important, as Fouad (1995) has noted, to explore the impact of parents and other family members on her decision making. After providing general examples of positive and negative family influence, Paul disclosed how his parents, as educators, were both a help and a hindrance to him in making his initial occupational choice. Paul then invited members to share positive and negative family influences. Several members shared how parental expectations, sex-role stereotyping, and divorce may have influenced their career problem solving and decision making. After Paul prompted a discussion of positive influence, the members identified role modeling, financial resources, and general support as positive factors. Paul concluded the discussion by explaining how societal stereotyping and family dynamics influence self-talk (executive processing), values, and beliefs. Paul stressed that once the group members become aware of these forces that shape their perceptions of themselves and occupations, they become free to make career choices on a more rational basis.

Paul concluded the session by reviewing the Valuing process as a component of the CASVE cycle, using a brief personal example to explain and model the concept.

Finally, Paul discussed homework assignments, which included the continuing use of career information resources and the establishment of priorities (from most appropriate to least appropriate) based on exploration to date. If possible, a tentative first choice and a second choice should be specified. Paul also reviewed the purpose and use of the *CTI Workbook*.

That evening, Juanita completed the *CTI Workbook*. The next day, she went to the media center to continue her use of information resources. Bonnie asked her about her progress, and Juanita showed her the completed *CTI Workbook*. Bonnie asked if Juanita's negative self-talk had resulted in her inappropriately dismissing any occupations for consideration. Juanita responded, "I've always done fairly well in math, but I avoided occupations that involve a lot of math. In fact, I took secondary mathematics teacher off my list because of the math involved. My mom is the one who is really good at math; she keeps the books for our business. I've convinced myself that I won't ever be successful even though I get Bs in math and I do fine in dealing with math problems at work, like closing out the cash register at the end of the day. It doesn't really make sense." This represents a faulty generalization and self-comparison with a single standard, as described by Krumboltz (1983).

Bonnie suggested that Juanita view the videotape on secondary mathematics teaching to determine if the occupation should be added to her list of occupations being considered. This particular videotape portrays a female math teacher, which was useful in providing Juanita with a possible role model. Over the next two days, Juanita completed her use of video and print materials. After viewing the videotape on math teachers, Juanita concluded that the occupation was not a good fit for her values, interests, and employment preferences. On one occasion, Juanita and Consuelo sat together in the media center and compared notes and reactions to what they were learning.

Later during the week, Juanita talked with her parents about her career problem-solving and decision-making activities in the group. She began by providing an overview of some of the concepts she had learned and by relating her use of information resources, using the CASVE cycle to provide a common understanding of the choice process. Juanita then stated, "One thing that bothers me, though, is whether both of you will be really disappointed if I don't decide to work in the store with you. I know that you have put a lot of work into the business, and because Carlos has decided to do air-conditioning repair work, what will happen to the business if I choose a different occupation?"

Juanita's parents assured her that they did not want to limit her career options to working in the family business. Her mother said that the dry-cleaning business has its ups and downs, and she thought they could hire someone to help manage the business if necessary. Her father went on to say that they had considered selling the business in a few years anyway. Her mother said that it is more important for Juanita to enjoy what she does and to provide an adequate income for herself than it is to keep the family business going forever. Juanita expressed great relief at hearing this point of view from her parents.

With renewed motivation to explore her options, Juanita returned to the media center to ask Bonnie about the process for setting up structured interviews for the occupations of emergency medical technician and respiratory therapist. Using the Career Key system, Bonnie helped Juanita identify the names of two local individuals who are willing to be interviewed. Juanita called from the media center to make appointments to talk with the two individuals the next afternoon. Bonnie provided Juanita with guidelines on how to conduct an effective information interview. The following day, Juanita went to a large local hospital and interviewed an emergency medical technician and a respiratory therapist.

Sixth Group Session After reviewing the members' perceptions of the progress of the group, Paul invited the members to share their list of priorities from most appropriate to least appropriate (the Valuing phase of the CASVE cycle). Five of the members, including Juanita and Consuelo, were able to list priorities and indicate a tentative first and second choice. Two of the members expressed the need for additional time for exploration. The five members indicating specific choices received generally positive feedback from group members regarding the specific choices that were made; for example, "I could really see you doing that!" Juanita listed the following priorities:

1. Emergency medical technician (EMT)—tentative first choice
2. Respiratory therapist—tentative second choice
3. Physical education teacher

Juanita explained that being an EMT had the best chance, in her opinion, to satisfy her values, interests, skills, and employment preferences. With some prompting from Paul, Juanita then discussed her choice in terms of the impact on her family and society.

Paul described options for the Execution phase of the CASVE cycle (the action phase). Using Consuelo as an example, Paul asked a series of questions to draw from the group a potential strategy for becoming a secondary school science teacher. (In conducting groups, it is important for the leader to draw on the resources of the group whenever possible.) Paul asked each member to share a potential plan for executing his or her decision, with the group providing feedback. When the discussion was completed, Paul asked the members to revise their ILPs to reflect the Execution phase of the CASVE cycle; or for those needing more time for exploration, their ILP could include revisions related to the Analysis, Synthesis, and Valuing phases of the CASVE cycle.

Summative Review and Generalization

Continuation of the Sixth Group Session Paul then asked the members to think about the Communication phase of the CASVE cycle and to reexamine the gap that existed previously. Juanita stated that although she is a little apprehensive about failing in the EMT program at the community college, she feels committed, as her brother is, to completing her education and to starting work. In response to Paul's question about how the group experience had influenced the members, Juanita stated that she was confident that she could make a good career choice; talking in groups was a little easier now; and she had learned a lot about decision making.

Paul concluded the session by stating that the CASVE cycle they had applied to career choice could be used for other problem-solving and decision-making issues as well. He went on to state that the most important outcome of the group was not whether each member had made an appropriate career choice by the time the group had ended, but whether each member understood and could use a problem-solving scheme to help solve complex problems. Paul reminded the members that there would be a three-month follow-up session for the group to provide further assistance and to review members' progress. He also stated that he would be available for individual counseling sessions during the remainder of the school year.

Later that evening, Juanita added the following activities to her ILP: (a) review print-based information describing the local community college, (b) make an appointment with a local community college counselor to discuss admission, and (c) make an appointment with a community college instructor in the Allied Health program to discuss the curriculum for an emergency medical technician major. As suggested in the group, Juanita discussed her plan with her parents. They were very supportive and suggested that her hours working in the store could be flexible, depending on her schedule of courses at the community college.

SUMMARY

This chapter demonstrated how brief staff-assisted career interventions could be delivered using the CIP approach. In the case of Linda, several staff members used a self-directed career decision-making strategy to help Linda solve her career problem. In the case of Carla, a brief intervention was inappropriate given her low readiness for career decision making, and a referral was made for individual case-managed services. The case of Juanita showed how the CIP approach could be used in group career counseling. In all three cases, the development of a collaborative interpersonal relationship was essential for promoting successful career problem solving. In the cases of Linda and Juanita, the seven-step service delivery sequence and various career resources were used in applying the CIP approach. The next chapter presents a case study for the delivery of self-help career resources and services.

GETTING THE MOST BENEFIT FROM READING THIS CHAPTER

To effectively learn the material in this chapter, complete one or more of the following activities:

- If you have experienced self-directed career decision making (a brief staff-assisted service), how was your experience similar to and different from the approach used to serve Linda?
- If you have had group career counseling, how was your experience similar to and different from the approach used to serve Juanita?
- Given your knowledge of counseling theory and career development theory, what other strategies might be used to meet the needs of Linda and Juanita?

- Visit a career center or counseling center, and without violating any confidentiality, ask a staff member to describe how brief career interventions and group career counseling are provided to clients. How is the process similar to and different from the CIP approach, especially the seven-step service delivery sequence?
- Talk with a friend about how the brief interventions described in this chapter can be used to provide individuals with assistance in making career choices.

REFERENCES

ACT, Inc. (2002). DISCOVER [Computer software]. Hunt Valley, MD: Author.

Bingham, R. P., & Ward, C. M. (1994). Career counseling with ethnic minority women. In W. B. Walsh & S. H. Osipow (Eds.), *Career counseling for women* (pp. 165–195). Hillsdale, NJ: Lawrence Erlbaum Associates.

Educational Testing Service. (2002). SIGI PLUS [Computer software]. Princeton, NJ: Author.

Epstein, S., Eberhardt, J., Powers, B., Strickland, K., & Smith, E. (2000). *Career Key: A tool for finding and managing career resources—manual for technical, cataloging, and database procedures.* Tallahassee: Center for the Study of Technology in Counseling and Career Development, Florida State University.

Fouad, N. A. (1995). Career behavior of Hispanics: Assessment and career intervention. In F. T. L. Leong (Ed.), *Career development and vocational behavior of racial and ethnic minorities* (pp. 165–191). Mahwah, NJ: Lawrence Erlbaum Associates.

Holland, J. L. (1994). *The Self-Directed Search.* Odessa, FL: Psychological Assessment Resources.

Holland, J. L. (1997). *Making vocational choices: A theory of vocational personalities and work environments* (3rd ed.). Odessa, FL: Psychological Assessment Resources.

Krumboltz, J. D. (1983). *Private rules in career decision making.* Columbus: Ohio State University National Center for Research in Vocational Education, Advanced Study Center (ERIC Document Reproduction Service No. ED 229 608).

Montgomery, D. J. (1984). Contractual arrangements. In H. D. Burck & R. C. Reardon (Eds.), *Career development interventions* (pp. 108–123). Springfield, IL: Charles C Thomas.

Peterson, G. W., Sampson, J. P., Jr., & Reardon, R. C. (1991). *Career development and services: A cognitive approach.* Pacific Grove, CA: Brooks/Cole.

Pyle, K. R. (1986). *Group career counseling: Principles and practices.* Ann Arbor: University of Michigan, ERIC Counseling and Personnel Services Clearinghouse.

Reardon, R. C. (1973). The counselor and career information services. *Journal of College Student Personnel, 19,* 495–500.

Reardon, R. C. (1984). Use of information in career counseling. In H. D. Burck & R. C. Reardon (Eds.), *Career development interventions* (pp. 53–68). Springfield, IL: Charles C. Thomas.

Reardon, R. C. (1996). A program and cost analysis of a self-directed career decision-making program in a university career center. *Journal of Counseling and Development, 74,* 280–285.

Sampson, J. P., Jr., Peterson, G. W., Lenz, J. G., & Reardon, R. C. (1992). A cognitive approach to career services: Translating concepts into practice. *The Career Development Quarterly, 41,* 67–74.

Sampson, J. P., Jr., Peterson, G. W., Lenz, J. G., Reardon, R. C., & Saunders, D. E. (1996a). *Career Thoughts Inventory.* Odessa, FL: Psychological Assessment Resources.

Sampson, J. P., Jr., Peterson, G. W., Lenz, J. G., Reardon, R. C., & Saunders, D. E. (1996b). *Career Thoughts Inventory workbook.* Odessa, FL: Psychological Assessment Resources.

Smith, E. (1983). Career Key: A career library management system. *The Career Development Quarterly, 32,* 52–56.

10 CHAPTER

Case Study for Self-Help Career Resources and Services

This chapter presents a case study showing how the CIP approach can be used in a self-help mode. After reviewing this chapter, the reader should understand how the CIP approach could be used in designing and delivering self-help career resources and services. The chapter is organized as follows:

- Case Study: Catherine
- Summary
- Getting the Most Benefit from Reading This Chapter

The case study of Catherine is presented in this chapter to show how self-help resources and services can be effectively used to promote career problem solving and decision making and how these resources and services can be used in a career center. As with the previous case studies in Chapters 8 and 9, this case study allows us to illustrate the nature of career problems and the way in which the CIP approach can be used to address these problems. Although this case study does not completely represent the cognitive complexity of Catherine's career problem solving and decision making or show the full range of options for service delivery, it does demonstrate how the CIP approach could be used to deliver self-help career resources and services.

The case studies presented in this book are composite descriptions of hypothetical individuals that are based on the experience of the authors. Any resemblance to actual persons is, therefore, purely coincidental. Although the case study presented in this chapter is hypothetical, the procedures and resources used reflect current practice at the Florida State University Career

Center. As we have stated previously, the Career Center is a comprehensive facility, providing counseling, experiential education, and placement services to FSU students, as well as drop-in career advising and appointment-based counseling to non-FSU students and community-based adults in career transition. We want to emphasize that the assessment, information, and instructional resources used in these cases are *not* the only resources that can be used with the CIP approach, as the theory accommodates the use of a wide range of career assessments and information resources. We have limited the resources depicted in these case studies to the actual resources we use in practice in order to present the most accurate picture possible of the application of the CIP approach in real life. Refer to Chapter 5 for a discussion of the readiness levels and career assistance options that provide the basis for the case studies presented in this book.

CASE STUDY: CATHERINE

Background

Catherine Yang is a 19-year-old Asian American female who is completing the first semester of her sophomore year in college. Catherine has been a successful student, maintaining a B+ to A− average. Her standardized test scores consistently show that she is well above average in both verbal and quantitative performance. This pattern of performance on aptitude and achievement tests is also reflected in her performance in high school and college courses.

While attending college, Catherine works part-time as a student assistant in the college library to help with the costs of her education. She is also active in her sorority, serving as an officer responsible for several charity functions benefiting local social service agencies. She is also active in a campus religious organization where she co-leads a weekly discussion group. During high school, Catherine was active in numerous school and community groups. In her senior year of high school, she received an award as "Volunteer of the Year" from a local charitable group. She also worked during summer vacations for the local newspaper.

Catherine's parents are supportive, providing almost all of the funds she needs to pay for her college expenses. Catherine's parents are also emotionally supportive, providing regular opportunities for Catherine to discuss her school, social, and church activities. Although they believe that Catherine should obtain a college degree, they have not pressured her to complete any particular program of study. Catherine's mother is a high school English teacher, and her father is a machinist.

Catherine has become increasingly aware of the need to finalize her selection of a major field of study (the Communication phase of the CASVE cycle). During a recent phone call with her parents, her father asked if she had made any more progress toward choosing a major. She has also talked with her roommate, who appears pleased and excited after recently choosing a major (external input from significant others). Catherine recently received a notice of registration times for spring semester classes, which caused her to think about the need for choosing a major (external event). She felt a mixture of excitement and anxiousness about the possibility of majoring in nursing to "make a contribution in the world" while also helping her to be "economically self-sufficient" (internal cue of emotions). Her career problem can be described in terms of gap, ambiguous and complex cues, interacting courses of action, uncertainty of the success of a solution, and career decisions creating new problems, as presented in Chapter 1.

Gap Catherine's career problem can be viewed as a gap between her real state of affairs (an inability to commit to nursing as a program of study) and an ideal state of affairs (being satisfied with a choice of major as her roommate is).

Ambiguous and Complex Cues The college Catherine is attending offers numerous major fields of study, including nursing, that are briefly described in the college catalog. Faculty members teaching her classes occasionally describe other courses that are required for a particular major. Many of Catherine's friends have chosen majors that they describe with varying degrees of satisfaction.

Interacting Courses of Action There are many majors in addition to nursing that would allow Catherine to make a contribution in the world and be economically self-sufficient. The number of options available makes it more difficult to make a choice.

Uncertainty of the Success of a Solution Even though Catherine is generally confident of her ability to make good grades, she is uncertain if she will like nursing well enough to remain motivated to do her best.

Career Decisions Creating New Problems After choosing a major, Catherine will need to deal with several new problems associated with implementing her choice, such as selecting major courses and elective courses in nursing and selecting a clinical rotation related to her interests.

Initial Interview

During a discussion of Catherine's need to finalize her choice of a major, Catherine's roommate suggested that she go to the campus career center, which provides assistance to students who are choosing or changing majors. Catherine remembered that the services provided by the career center were described during her freshman orientation and that specific details were available on the center's Web site. Using a computer in her residence hall, she learned that assessment and information resources were available, as well as counseling, to help students choose majors. She printed information from the Web site that described the resources and services available in the career center that are typically used to help students choose a major when they are undecided or to clarify a major choice they are considering. This information helped Catherine visualize how she might decide if nursing was an appropriate choice and increased her motivation to seek assistance at the career center.

When she entered the career center, Catherine was greeted by Alan Richardson, an intern completing a master's degree in career counseling. Alan asked, "What brings you here today?" Catherine responded that she wanted to look at information about employment options for nurses. Alan asked her to sign in, explaining that demographic data was being collected for accountability. Noticing that she was a sophomore with an undeclared major, he asked if she would also like information on selecting a major. She said that would be helpful. Alan judged that self-help services would be an appropriate starting point for Catherine's use of resources and services in the career center. He based this judgment on the fact that Catherine had provided a concrete request for information and had not indicated that a problem existed that would compromise her independent use of resources.

Alan selected a book that included information on employment opportunities in nursing. After giving Catherine the book, he showed her the display rack of module sheets/resource guides that she could use to help her select other resources in the library related to her needs. He selected three module sheets that she might find useful: Module IV—"Information: What's Available Out There and Where to Find It"; Module V—"Matching Majors and Jobs"; and Module XVI—"Choosing a Major" (for a more detailed description of the module sheets, see Appendix A). He also gave her a quick orientation to the career library by indicating the signs available and by reviewing the map on the back of Module IV showing the location of specific resources. He also showed her Career Key (Epstein, Eberhardt, Powers, Strickland, & Smith, 2000; Smith, 1983), the center's computer-based index of resources contained in the library.[1] Before moving to help the next person at the reception desk, Alan asked if Catherine had any questions. After she responded, "No," he suggested that she speak with him or another staff member if she needed assistance with any of the resources.

Use of Self-Help Resources

Catherine sat at one of the tables in the library and began reading the book Alan had provided (the Analysis–occupational knowledge phase of the CASVE cycle). She took notes on the relevant portions, thinking to herself that nurses were involved in more diverse work settings than she had imagined. After about 15 minutes, Alan stopped by her table and asked, "Are you finding the information you need?"[2]

Catherine responded, "Yes, the information is great," and Alan moved on to another person in the library to monitor his progress in using resources. Catherine stopped reading and reflected on what she had learned. Nursing, particularly working in a hospital that provided a lot of variety and excitement appealed to her, but she was still uncomfortable with proceeding. Catherine felt anxious about making a

---

[1]Instead of simply delivering information and potentially fostering dependency on the part of the learner, the staff member also helps the learner understand how to select and locate additional information that may be relevant to the needs of the learner. By incorporating learner-specific orientation along with the delivery of information, the staff member is operationalizing the old adage, "Give people a fish and they eat for a day, but teach them how to fish and they eat for a lifetime."

[2]This is an example of the "safety net" that potentially identifies individuals with medium to low readiness for career decision making who are inappropriately referred to self-help services. When the level of readiness is more accurately identified through interaction with a staff member, a more intensive level of service can be recommended that has a greater likelihood of meeting the needs of the individual.

premature choice, remembering some past mistakes from making impulsive decisions without fully understanding what she was choosing. Catherine remained confident that she could make a good choice if she took the time to carefully think about her options.

Remembering the module sheets that Alan had provided earlier, Catherine selected "Choosing a Major" and began reading. The objectives listed on this module sheet (linking personal factors and potential majors, enhancing knowledge about specific majors, and enhancing decision-making skills) fit her needs to make an informed, rather than an impulsive, choice. She reviewed the activities and decided it would be best to begin by reading the career center booklet, "Choosing a Major or a Career." As suggested on the module sheet, she asked a staff member to help her get a copy of the booklet. Alan showed her where the booklets were located and provided the copy that she requested, while also showing her other booklet titles that she might find useful.[3]

Catherine read the booklet on choosing a major, noting that she had completed several of the recommended steps. She felt better knowing that she had intuitively recognized some of the necessary steps in the process of selecting a major (Analysis–decision-making skills phase of the CASVE cycle). She also felt better knowing what some of the remaining steps were that needed to be completed. With renewed energy and confidence, she began to make a list of things that needed to be accomplished. As she was completing her list, Alan again stopped briefly and asked her if she was getting the information she needed. Catherine responded that she was and that she wanted to learn more about several options she had considered in the past—nursing, speech pathology, and clinical psychology. Noting that it was time to leave for class, Catherine decided to return to the career center to begin her exploration of the three options she was considering.

The next afternoon, Catherine returned to the career center library and began exploring nursing, speech pathology, and clinical psychology. After signing in at the reception desk, Catherine introduced herself to Delores Sanchez, the director of the career center who was the career adviser on duty. Catherine explained to Delores that she wanted to get information on several occupations. Delores asked if she needed any help in locating the information, and Catherine said, "No." Delores said that she would be on duty for the next two hours and to talk with her if Catherine had any questions or needed any assistance.

Catherine returned to the module sheet on finding information in the career center to develop a strategy for accessing the information she needed. The Career Key library indexing system was mentioned on the module sheet, and Catherine remembered that Alan Richardson had briefly explained how she could use the index to select and locate resources in the library. As she approached the computer where Career Key was available, the career center librarian, Steve Goldberg, asked if he could be of any assistance. Catherine responded that she was looking for specific informa-

---

[3] Again, the staff member's goal is to deliver information and, at the same time, orient the learner to additional resources that may be appropriate.

tion on nursing and some other related occupations. Steve showed Catherine the menu options for locating occupation-specific information and reminded her to check with him if she had any further questions. Catherine then generated a printout identifying information sources for each of the three occupations that interested her.

Catherine reviewed the information sources indicated on her Career Key printout for each occupation, which indicated that several books and files were available in the library. Looking around the room, she noticed signs labeled "Books" and "Files." She was then able to locate the information she needed and read descriptions for each of the three occupations, confirming what was important to her in an occupation (the Analysis–self-knowledge phase of the CASVE cycle). Based on what she had learned, she was able to eliminate clinical psychology, one of the three options she was considering (the Synthesis-crystallization phase of the CASVE cycle).

As Catherine finished her use of the print resources, Delores stopped by her table and asked if she was finding the information she needed.[4] Catherine responded that the information was very helpful, but she did have a question: "Do you have comparative descriptions of nursing and speech pathology majors?" Delores replied that these descriptions existed and indicated where the information was located. Catherine made copies of relevant information and thanked Delores for the assistance that she had provided. Later that evening in her room, she reflected on what she had learned about herself and the two options she was still considering, occasionally referring to her notes or computer printouts. As she considered the costs and benefits of each option for herself, her family, and her cultural group, she decided that nursing would be a good tentative first choice (the Valuing phase of the CASVE cycle). She also decided that speech pathology would be a good secondary choice if it became clear that nursing was not a good option. In order to obtain further institutional-specific information on nursing, Catherine read the description of the major that she found in her college catalog. She then went to her residence hall computer lab and printed additional descriptive information on the major from the School of Nursing Web site.

Although she was pleased with nursing as a tentative choice of major and with nurse as a tentative choice of occupation, she was still slightly anxious about making a commitment to nursing given her lack of experience with nursing classes and clinical work in the field. What would help her, she thought, would be information on what she could do with a nursing degree that did not involve the practice of nursing. Remembering that one of the module sheets dealt with this question, she reread

[4] Occasional interaction between staff members and individuals being served increases the likelihood that individuals will ask questions of staff members that promote effective learning. In the CIP approach, self-help services delivered in a career library do not involve isolation from practitioners. The atmosphere cultivated by staff should be warm, supportive, responsive, helpful, and competent. What differentiates self-help services from brief staff-assisted services is that in self-help services, individuals themselves make decisions about selecting, sequencing, and using resources; in brief staff-assisted services, individuals use resources on the basis of staff recommendations. Another way of differentiating the two services is that use of resources in self-help services is guided by an individual's use of module sheets/resource guides, whereas the use of resources in brief staff-assisted services is guided by the collaborative development of an Individual Learning Plan by a client and a practitioner.

"Matching Majors and Jobs," noting that the "Undergraduate Academic Program Guide" might be helpful. Returning to the career center, she read the entry for nursing, which indicated that graduates with this degree could also work in several related fields. This helped her to be more confident that majoring in nursing was her best option at this time. She decided not to review the career information for speech pathologist at this time because she could return later to the career center and locate the information in the library if necessary.

Now that she had decided on nursing as a major field of study, she had to take action (the Execution phase of the CASVE cycle). She remembered her roommate saying that Catherine needed to talk to an academic adviser about admission procedures and course scheduling. Although she could just go to the nursing department and ask for help, she thought that the career center might have a contact person that would save her some time. Catherine approached Alan Richardson and asked if he could provide the name of a contact person in the School of Nursing. Alan checked a directory of academic advisers and provided Catherine with a name, office location, and phone number. Catherine collected her books and thanked Alan for the help he had provided. Alan said, "You're welcome. Stop by again in the future if we can be of any further service. If you have a minute, we would appreciate it if you would fill out our brief comment card about the services you received." Catherine agreed and filled out the card, noting that she was able to find the information she needed and that the staff was helpful. As Catherine left the career center, she reflected that she was confident that she had made a good tentative choice of nursing as a major, as well as relieved that this important task had been completed (a return to the Communication–internal cue phase of the CASVE cycle). The subsequent positive reaction to her choice by her parents and her roommate further increased her confidence in her choice (Communication–external cue).

SUMMARY

This chapter demonstrated how self-help career resources and services could be delivered using the CIP approach. In the case study of Catherine, she had a high level of readiness for career choice. The brief screening she received on entering the career center indicated that self-help career services were appropriate. Subsequent brief follow-up interactions between Catherine and various staff members indicated that the self-help approach remained an appropriate intervention choice. Catherine was able to select the resources that she needed by using the module sheets/resource guides that were available. Career Key was also useful in helping her select needed resources. The map of the career library, the location data on the Career Key printout, and the signage in the library helped Catherine locate the resources that she had chosen. In addition to monitoring her readiness for decision making, the brief interactions she had with various staff members helped her access resources with minimum difficulty. These staff interactions also created a caring atmosphere in the career center. Having the combination of a supportive atmosphere and resources that were designed to work in a self-help fashion increased her confidence that she could get the information she needed to make the decisions that she was facing.

11 CHAPTER

Developing a Career Services Program

This chapter explores the multiple roles of the career counselor in delivering services to persons with differing needs. The chapter also examines the delivery of career services from a systems perspective, incorporating CIP theory and instructional systems design. After reviewing this chapter, the reader should be able to (a) understand the varied strategies that counselors can use to help individuals advance their career problem-solving and decision-making skills, (b) relate client needs to the level of complexity of career interventions and the level of counselor and staff competence to meet those needs, (c) understand some basic concepts of social systems, and (d) apply the principles of instructional systems design (ISD) to the design and development of career guidance programs. The chapter is organized as follows:

- Multiple Roles of the Counselor in Service Delivery
- The Scope of the Problem
- Policy Issues
- A Systems Approach to Program Development
- Applying CIP to Career Program Design
- Instructional Systems Design
- An ISD Model for Career Guidance Services
- Summary
- Getting the Most Benefit from Reading This Chapter

GETTING THE MOST BENEFIT FROM READING THIS CHAPTER

To effectively learn the material in this chapter, complete one or more of t ing activities:

- If you have had self-help career services, how was your experience sim different from the approach used to serve Catherine?
- Given your knowledge of counseling theory and career developme what other strategies might be used to meet the needs of Catherine?
- Visit a career center or counseling center, and without violating any tiality, ask a staff member to describe how self-help resources and s provided to individuals. How is the process similar to and different fro approach?
- Talk with a friend about how the self-help strategies described in this c be used to provide individuals with assistance in making career choic

REFERENCES

Epstein, S., Eberhardt, J., Powers, B., Strickland, K., & Smith, E. (2000). *Career Key: A too and managing career resources—manual for technical, cataloging, and database proce* hassee: Center for the Study of Technology in Counseling and Career Development, I University.

Smith, E. (1983). Career Key: A career library management system. *The Career Developmen 32*, 52–56.

MULTIPLE ROLES OF THE COUNSELOR IN SERVICE DELIVERY

As individuals solve career problems and make career decisions, they are often faced with a vast and bewildering sea of information about the world of work, including facts and data about training requirements, supply-demand ratios, and salaries. They must also consider facts and data about themselves, such as their interests, goals, values, needs, abilities, skills, and employment preferences. Given the potentially overwhelming amounts of occupational and personal information available, what can we as counselors do to present information in such a way that it can be used by individuals to enhance their career problem solving and decision making?

All of us have an image of who a career counselor is and what career counseling entails. One typical image is that of a counselor sitting in an office, face-to-face with a client, listening, talking, making helpful suggestions, being supportive, clarifying feelings, and exploring ideas. According to this image, a career counselor is someone who intervenes directly with people and who uses special communication skills and techniques to help individuals learn, grow, and become what they want to become.

But there are other images of career counseling that emphasize less direct roles and activities. Morrill, Oetting, and Hurst (1974) were among those who systematically addressed this issue in past years. Besides counseling, they identified other helping activities, including the following:

- Planning group guidance programs for special groups of students, teachers, parents, or alumni
- Consulting with teachers or parents in their places of work or on the phone
- Collecting and analyzing evaluation and research studies to learn more about the special career needs of persons in a particular organization or setting
- Reviewing reports on the effectiveness of tests, computer-based career guidance systems, or programs that others have already developed and evaluated
- Deciding which materials to purchase for a career information center
- Training and supervising paraprofessionals or career guidance technicians who also work with clients
- Marketing and advertising career services to encourage potential clients to make use of them
- Writing reports on the effectiveness of current programs or proposals for new career programs
- Meeting with administrators, organizational decision makers, and other persons who can provide funds and resources to help develop and improve career programs
- Visiting with employers to learn more about jobs in the community

More recently, Sampson, Vacc, and Loesch (1998) surveyed National Certified Counselors (generalists) and National Certified Career Counselors (specialists) to learn more about the actual professional practice of career counseling. They identified the career counseling work behaviors unique to the career counseling specialization and those that are an element of general counseling practice. They found that career counseling work behaviors related to assessment and counseling were fundamental to the general practice of counseling. Interestingly, they also found that career counseling work behaviors related to program management, information, and consultation were fundamental to the specialty practice of career counseling.

The counselor activities identified by Morrill et al. (1974) and Sampson et al. (1998) are intended to help clients make better career choices. The image of the counselor's role that goes beyond the traditional one-on-one facilitative role is the focus of this chapter and those that follow.

Career counselors can be helpful in many ways, both direct and indirect (Niles & Harris-Bowlsbey, 2002; Whiston, Sexton, & Lasoff, 1998; Zunker, 2002). Our experience is that the majority of clients seeking career assistance want easily accessible information about themselves and about the occupational world. Moreover, most clients are able to function quite well on their own with minimal direct career or personal counseling. Therefore, career counselors must be able not only to attend to individual clients but also to develop and manage career information services that allow for and even encourage independent self-exploration.

THE SCOPE OF THE PROBLEM

We will now change the focus for a moment. We have been thinking about clients making career choices and your role as a counselor in that process. But first, what about your own career? Think about the job ahead of you on completion of your training or continuing education. You may be employed in a school, a private agency, or a human resources department. What would you do and how would you feel if the following job assignments were given to you by your director?

- Review the career resources in our center, and purchase $2,000 worth of new print or audiovisual materials within 10 days.
- Prepare a small-group employability skills program for below-average students who will graduate next month.
- Make a recommendation for purchasing the least expensive, most effective computer-assisted career guidance system for our school.
- Develop a plan for increasing the use of an expanded career library.
- Formulate a program to help undecided college sophomores choose a major field of study.
- Help Sally Jones decide which college to attend when she graduates.
- Assist a woman who is recently divorced and has two small children find a job as soon as possible. She is 28, a high school graduate, and has very little work experience.

These assignments address an organization's obligation to provide career assistance. The managers and program directors who assign tasks such as these are really defining the goals of the career service center and the range of career development interventions it ought to provide. You, as a professional, will take increasing responsibility for identifying and carrying out these career services goals in response to organizational needs.

However, besides thinking about your own career behavior, what about the needs of the clients you seek to help? One comprehensive career center compiled a list of 50 typical client questions or concerns. The list is shown in Table 11.1. Read it carefully. Each of these questions or concerns could include numerous subquestions or problems. In some cases, the need for information must be inferred. But each of these items, and hundreds more, can be positively addressed by a comprehensive career information program. Such client questions and concerns are the essence of career counseling—there are no easy ways out for you as a counselor, no ways to duck these client statements of need—and they represent the basic starting point in career problem solving, as indicated earlier. Designing the information delivery system that will enable career counselors to respond fully to such client questions and concerns is a focus of this chapter.

There is one more point to be made about the scope of the problem. The Florida State University Career Center routinely collects catalogs, flyers, and other announcements of new or revised career programs, products, or materials from various sources. These give a somewhat cloudy picture of the state of the art in this field. At the last count, there were over 435 separate folders for these items (and many of the folders contain multiple products or materials). The typical career course in a community college or university may contain 50 to 75 different career learning activities, such as conducting job interviews or taking interest inventories. All of these materials and activities are designed to assist clients in developing occupational and self-schemata that will help them solve career problems and make better career decisions. Therefore, the problem may be reframed as a question: "What can I do as a prospective counselor to help individuals, with diverse needs and motivations, to use appropriate information in a timely and efficient manner to enhance their career problem-solving and decision-making skills?"

Thus far, we have argued that (a) career counselors can be and are helpful in many ways in addition to direct one-to-one counseling; (b) organizations and individuals have diverse yet specific, pressing needs for career assistance, especially information; and (c) the range and number of potential career interventions and available products are vast. Nevertheless, the first task in developing responsive services, before forging into the design of a comprehensive career development program, is to become aware of organizational, philosophical, or policy issues. The second task is to learn how to use a systems approach to design an effective and efficient career services program in light of these policies. Counselors have an important stake in the development of policies that will enable them to function as effective, helpful professionals and to meet their own life and career goals.

POLICY ISSUES

The method that organizations sometimes use to develop the goals and plans to manage their affairs may be called policy analysis (Quade, 1977). It is not a familiar topic to most counselors. It is a matter of politics, pressure, criticism, conflict, and compromise. But the development of policy represents the molding of idealized values or goals and the reality of practical limits and constraints. It is not possible to meet

Table 11.1 | Fifty Typical Client Questions or Concerns

1. I'm thinking about majoring in psychology. What can I do when I finish school?
2. I want to make a career change, but I'm not sure about what kind of discrimination I will face because I'm almost 55. I think I need to pick something that's really hot. What would that be?
3. I'm trying to find information on a career as a behavioral specialist.
4. I may not be admitted to the FSU Nursing School, but I still want to be a nurse. What can I do?
5. I want to find a summer job on a cruise ship. Do you have a list of addresses?
6. I was told you could give me an interest test. Can I take one now?
7. I'd like to get a job with an oil company overseas. How do I get into such a position?
8. I've been working as a secretary for the State of Florida for 13 years, and I'm tired of it.
9. I want to use the computer to find out what my skills are.
10. My grade point average is 2.6. Can I still major in public relations?
11. I'm good in math and like finance but am wondering if engineering would be more challenging.
12. I'm not sure which area of business to go into. Can you help me?
13. I'm going to attend law school. Do you have anything that tells students what law students should take in college? Where can I find a listing of law schools and their admission requirements?
14. I have a job interview next week. Do you have some materials that can help me prepare?
15. I'm not doing too well in school, and I'm thinking about going to work.
16. I'm really unsure about what to major in. Can you help me?
17. I would like to look through a book that lists cost, entrance requirements, and addresses for graduate programs in environmental policy.
18. How do I go about getting a job in state government? Is there anything special that I need to know?
19. I'm thinking of majoring in modern languages. What would be a good minor or second major?
20. What salary can I expect to make with a major in information studies?
21. I would like to find out about job opportunities in the Atlanta area. Can you help me?
22. I really like working with people, but I really want to make a good salary.
23. How much can I expect to earn working for the federal government?
24. Do you have a list of Internet sites where I can find criminology jobs?
25. I really enjoy my interior design class, but how can I tell if it's the right major for me?
26. What majors get the most job offers these days?

Table 11.1 *(continued)*

27. I don't want to be a doctor or a nurse. Are there other medical careers that I can enter? How many years of college do I need for these careers?
28. I'm majoring in social work. Can you help me find some employers?
29. My adviser told me you could test me to determine my aptitudes.
30. How does one go about getting information on the cinematography business—both production and direction—and other related careers?
31. What's the best way to have my resume reproduced? I need to write one.
32. I need to declare my major this week. I've been thinking of psychology or accounting.
33. What courses should I take for a career in oceanography? Also, who can I talk to about careers in oceanography?
34. I thought I was going to major in accounting, but I'm not doing well in my class. Can you tell me if I have the potential to succeed?
35. I want to set up my placement file. What other services do you provide for FSU graduates who are job hunting?
36. I'm thinking of getting an MBA. What universities in Georgia have a program?
37. I'm not satisfied with my present job.
38. I'd like to study in France. Do you have any information?
39. I know what I want to do—physical therapy—but how do I find out what to major in to do it?
40. My parents think I should major in computer science, but I hate math. Is there something I can do to please them and me?
41. I'm trying to find a communications internship in New York. Do you have directories with this information?
42. As an international student getting ready to graduate, I'm not sure how to proceed regarding the job search.
43. I need to pick up a copy of a federal job application.
44. I took this test to help me choose my major, but it didn't help. I'm more confused than ever.
45. Can you help me find a Web site where I can post my resume?
46. I can't pursue my first choice of a major, engineering, because of my learning disability. I'm not sure what else to consider.
47. I'm a Ph.D. student in electrical engineering and need to write a CV. Do you have any examples or information I could look at?
48. I'm thinking about majoring in English, advertising, or public relations but want to take one of those career tests to see which one might be best.
49. I've heard you have a database of jobs—can you find me a database of jobs in sales in South Carolina?
50. I received a job offer but would like to negotiate for a higher salary. What should I say?

Figure 11.1 Synthesis of Three Career Guidance Dimensions: Client Needs, Intervention Complexity, and Staff Competencies

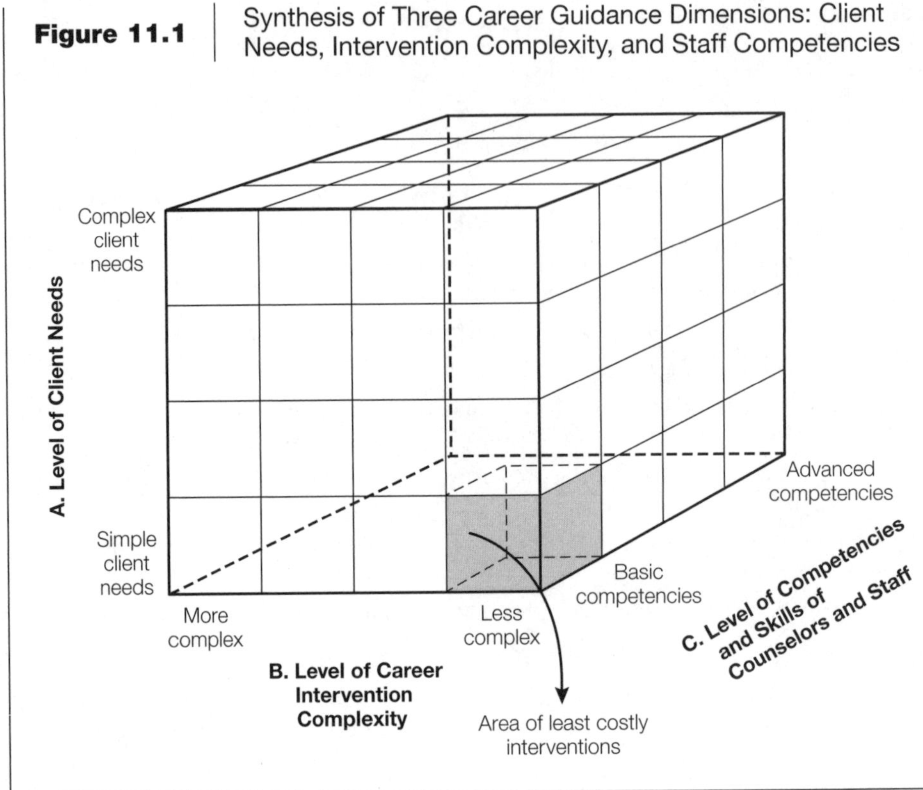

everyone's needs, to be completely helpful, or to have all of the necessary resources. There are almost always limitations in the availability of trained staff, physical space, dollars to meet expenses, and the knowledge of what intervention might be effective and helpful. Therefore, choices have to be made and priorities must be set—not everything that is needed or that could be done will be done.

Figure 11.1 shows a three-dimensional cube that will help you grasp some of the policy issues inherent in designing career development programs. The three dimensions—level of client needs, level of career intervention complexity, and level of staff competencies—relate to one another in various ways. Note that each dimension presents a continuum: from simple to complex client needs, from less to more career intervention complexity, and from basic to advanced staff competencies. The shaded part of the cube is the functional area characterized by the simplest client needs, the least complex interventions, and the most basic staff competencies. This is the point of lowest cost for interventions in terms of staff time and resources to meet the client's need for information.

The continuum for each of the three dimensions is described next, to point out how the cube may be used to guide program planning and policy development.

Level of Client Needs

Client needs for career assistance are complex and varied (Campbell & Cellini, 1981; Tiedeman, Katz, Miller-Tiedeman, & Osipow, 1978). Table 11.2 lists examples of these needs, beginning with the simpler needs and progressing to the more complex. Also, refer to Chapter 5 for a description of a four-quadrant readiness model for assessing client needs in relation to self-help, brief staff-assisted, and individual case-managed career services.

In general, young people tend to have simpler career needs; adults may have more complex situations, including both a greater number and a greater range of needs. A comprehensive career guidance program serving young people and adults should be able to respond to all levels of needs. Complex needs may have multiple causes and may be urgent as well.

Level of Career Intervention Complexity

The state-of-the-art career interventions are also complex and varied. *Career Guidance and Counseling Through the Life Span* by Herr and Cramer (1996) described more than 150 career interventions, many of which have been researched for their effectiveness. Table 11.2 presents examples of interventions corresponding to the various needs.

In general, the more complex the intervention, the more specialized the career counselor must become. The level of non-counselor-mediated interventions can also increase in complexity—for example, the use of multiple print and nonprint media, specialized referral resources, and interventions of longer duration. Less complex interventions generally are less costly, are of shorter duration, and may be delivered with the assistance of less experienced and less trained staff members, such as paraprofessionals.

Level of Staff Competencies

Career development associations, state government agencies, and individuals have specified various competencies needed by teachers, parents, and counselors to deliver career guidance. The National Career Development Association (NCDA) (1997) has provided a complete statement of 11 broad competencies for professional counselors (available at www.ncda.org/about/polccc.html). These are also shown in Appendix B. Teachers, peer counselors, parent volunteers, and guidance paraprofessionals would most likely possess basic skills. Career development facilitators (Splete & Hoppin, 2000) would demonstrate competencies in helping skills, diversity, ethics, career theory, assessment, computer applications, career information, employability skills, instruction, and program design and implementation. Career counselors would have advanced career skills, such as ability to train and supervise staff, to carry out research and evaluation, and to engage in specialized individual or group counseling (Loesch & Vacc, 1986). Examples of competencies and skills corresponding to

Table 11.2 Client Needs, Career Interventions, and Counselor Skills

Client Needs	Corresponding Career Intervention	Corresponding Counselor Skill
1. Become aware of career fields.	1. Browse through the *Occupational Outlook Handbook*.	1. Locate and monitor use of the *Occupational Outlook Handbook*.
2. Obtain a list of courses for a specified training program.	2. Read a course list and descriptions for a college major.	2. Provide a list of courses, and make appropriate referral for more information.
3. Acquire information describing an occupation.	3. Read an occupational brief.	3. Locate and provide occupational briefs and more information if needed.
4. Learn about how to apply for a job.	4. View a videotape on job application procedures.	4. Introduce and process the use of a video-tape player or other audiovisual equipment.
5. Identify personal strengths and weaknesses relevant to career choice.	5. Take an interest inventory, or complete a card sort and then confer with a career counselor.	5. Supervise the use of an interest inventory or other self-assessment materials, and make referrals to special assistance as needed.
6. Learn career decision-making skills.	6. Complete a computer-assisted guidance system.	6. Introduce and process use of a computer-assisted guidance system, and provide follow-up counseling if needed.

7. Increase motivation for career or work success. **8.** Accept personal responsibility for career behavior. **9.** Overcome barriers to employment, such as lack of academic skill, minority group membership, poor work history, offender status, physical disability, displaced worker.	**7, 8, 9.** Obtain specialized career counseling, individual or group.	**7, 8, 9.** Provide specialized group or individual career counseling.
10. Find a solution to a dual-career problem, such as relocation or child care.	**10.** Obtain specialized individual or group counseling, or attend a special workshop.	**10.** Provide specialized family counseling for dual careerists, or refer.
11. Cope with a history of personality or emotional problems in a career choice.	**11.** Obtain psychotherapy to understand one's motives and life experiences.	**11.** Administer intensive or specialized psychotherapy.

the aforementioned needs and interventions are also noted in Table 11.2. The NCDA (1991) has created ethical standards that govern the delivery of career services. Elements addressed in the standards include general issues, the counseling relationship, measurement and evaluation, research and publication, consulting, private practice, and procedures for processing ethical complaints. The NCDA (n.d.) has also developed consumer guidelines for selecting a career counselor.

Given this continuum of counselor and staff competencies, it is obvious that differentiated staffing arrangements and both direct and indirect counselor interventions are required to address the wide range of needs that clients may bring to a career services program. This model underscores the fact that individual counseling may be a highly specialized function that may not be required for many career interventions. Paraprofessionals have long occupied a key role in the offering of career interventions (Lenz & Panke, 2001). Simple client needs, which require less complex interventions, may not require direct or intensive counselor attention. However, the design of comprehensive career services programs requires the professional judgment and input of highly trained counselors.

The cube shown in Figure 11.1 provides a way to describe program activities, to set goals, to choose alternative interventions, and to allocate resources—that is, to develop policy. Policy development shapes the direction, scope, and level of career services programs and can help address the following familiar issues.

- When should career interventions be offered to clients? At the point of first contact to all clients in order to prevent later problems, or to a limited number of clients with special needs?
- Where should the emphasis in interventions be? On the remedying of chronic problems, or on the general, primary prevention of problems?
- Who are the primary clients? Who is entitled to be served? Is everyone entitled to be helped? Or only a few people? Freshmen through seniors? Adults from the community?
- How will human and nonhuman resources be allocated? How much staff time and expense dollars should be spent on different kinds of interventions? Should groups, classes, or individual conferences be used? Should a fee be charged? How should services be funded? Should the intervention include paraprofessionals, professionals, self-help print materials, or computers? Are space and other facilities available?
- Why will the programs be offered? Who are the stakeholders? Individual clients? The organization? Or ourselves as professional counselors?
- What are the desired goals? What are the benefits in comparison to the costs? How are the goals identified?

Wrestling with these policy issues involves coming to terms with one's personal and professional values. The mark of a successful career services professional is knowing one's values and being able to act consistently and systematically on the basis of those values. Referring again to the cube in Figure 11.1, can you begin to assess how your professional goals and personal values match with different kinds of career service interventions and their required counselor competencies? For example, you might decide that prevention of career problems is more important than treating them and that you want to devote your professional efforts to programs that stop or prevent career problems from ever occurring in the first place (Romano & Hage, 2000).

A SYSTEMS APPROACH TO PROGRAM DEVELOPMENT

From the very earliest days of the vocational guidance movement in the early 1900s, program development has been the hallmark of the profession (Parsons, 1909; Stephens, 1970). Frank Parsons, a moderate socialist, social reformer, educator, lawyer, prominent Boston citizen, and the father of vocational guidance, is considered an exemplary program developer, even by today's standards. In *Choosing a Vocation,* Parsons described in detail his work in creating the Boston Vocations Bureau (we would call it a career center today) in the Civic Service House (a settlement house that today we would probably call a neighborhood community center).

One is struck by the ways in which Parsons was sensitive to the education, training, employment, and career needs of Boston youth and other citizens. American cities at the turn of the 20th century often contained urban ghettos populated with southern European immigrants who did not speak English, had little training for industrial work, and were unfamiliar with American citizenship responsibilities (Stephens, 1970). There were powerful "robber barons" who controlled the new wealth from railroads, banks, and industry. Public education was under fire, and the high school drop-out rate was 90% in some cities (Parsons, 1909). Child labor and other social ills were being exposed by muckrakers and other social reformers. Vocational education to prepare citizens with skills and knowledge for the new jobs in industry was nonexistent. In this social context, Parsons developed his programs; and vocational guidance was born to help persons select and secure jobs. It is important to remember this context, because many of these forces still exist in this nation and throughout the world, and they continue to influence the development of career guidance programs today. Persons interested in learning more about the conditions leading to the development of the career counseling profession may read Zytowski's (2001) article "Frank Parsons and the Progressive Movement." This article provides an excellent analysis of the social factors that influenced Parson's thinking and work in developing the Vocations Bureau.

Since the early 1970s, career guidance professionals have become increasingly aware of the importance of broad social and environmental factors in the development and operation of career services programs (Hoyt, 1981). O'Brien (2001) recently called attention to the legacy of social change inherent in the work of career counselors. She challenged career counselors and vocational psychologists to extend Parsons' compassion and vision in ways that enhance people's lives and contribute to the creation of a more just society. Career services program developers and administrators are aware that career services operate within an organizational and social system. A systems approach undergirds the strategies for the development of beneficial career services programs.

Important Systems Concepts

In this subsection, we first examine some of the basic concepts of a systems approach; later, the focus is on a particular application of the systems approach drawn from instructional systems design (ISD) in educational psychology, which has special relevance for the development of career services programs.

Although we frequently use the term *program* in casual and professional discussions, it is important to spend a few moments defining this term. As we have already established, career interventions can cover a wide variety of activities, from career counseling to career education, and from career information to organizational career development. Patton and McMahon (2001) explored matters related to the definition of *career programs,* and we will borrow from their work. For our purposes, a career program is a planned sequence of learning experiences in education, training, and related settings designed to develop knowledge, skills, and attitudes that assist persons in making informed decisions about study and/or work options for effective participation in working life.

Social System A *social system* may be defined as a structure or organization of an orderly whole, showing the interrelationships of the parts to each other and to the whole (Bertalanffy, 1968; Silvern, 1965). An example of a social system could be a high school guidance department composed of a director, six counselors, three secretaries, three student assistants, and five volunteers. A system may be further described as the parts (the staff and helpers) working interdependently, as well as interactively, to accomplish something. The purpose of the system (in this case, a guidance department) is to achieve previously specified performance goals. Thus, a social system is characterized by Silvern as (a) a structure or organization, (b) forming an orderly whole, (c) with parts working interdependently, (d) with parts working interactively, (e) the parts being related to the whole, and (f) with an intent to achieve previously specified performance goals.

Objectives Applying the concept of a social system to the development of career guidance programs, a systems approach therefore leads to several additional concepts (Hosford & Ryan, 1970). The system outputs of guidance programs can be described in terms of ***behavioral objectives.*** This means that the product or output of the system (the guidance program) is defined in terms of observable behaviors or performances.

The following are examples of program outcome objectives:

- A library of career materials will be established for teacher, staff, and student use.
- A new part-time secretary will be employed in the career guidance department within 12 months.

The following are examples of behavioral objectives:

- After completing a career values card sort, the client can name the three values that are most important to his or her career planning.

- An employee will be able to identify three sources of career information to learn more about jobs appearing on the list of jobs posted by the company.

A learner-oriented behavioral objective addresses the question, "As a result of participating in this guidance program, what measurable behaviors should the client be able to perform?" Through such objectives, we seek to describe new capabilities that will ultimately help clients become better problem solvers and decision makers.

Analysis and Synthesis *Analysis* is breaking down the whole into its parts and making explicit the relationships of the parts to one another and to the whole. In analysis, the components of a system are studied and evaluated to identify the causes of performance gaps. A problem, whether an individual's or a program's, is defined in terms of a gap between an existing level of performance and the desired level. In analysis, we seek to identify components and their interrelationships that interfere with the desirable level of operation of the system (for example, the guidance program). In ***synthesis,*** the component parts are added, modified, combined, or reconfigured into new relationships so that a new system or unit is created. Analysis and synthesis should be conducted in a scientific, disciplined, methodologically sound way, and not by guesswork or trial and error.

Feedback Information about the output of the system that is incorporated back into the system is referred to as ***feedback.*** The feedback loop assures that information about the worth or value of the system outputs is channeled back into the system so that continual system changes and improvements can be made. Feedback ensures constant monitoring of the performance of the system.

Flowchart A *flowchart* is a diagram that shows the inputs, the component parts, and the way they interrelate; it shows how information about outputs is looped back into the system; and it shows the system's relationship to the larger environment. Figure 11.2 depicts a simple flowchart of a career guidance intervention. In this example, a student sought help with the following question: "What do astrogeophysicists do?"

Open Versus Closed Systems Much of our thinking about general systems theory comes from the work of Ludwig von Bertalanffy (1968), a theoretical biologist. He observed that an ***open system,*** or living system, constantly interacts with its environment. For example, a single-cell protozoan with its permeable membrane constantly draws nutrients from the surrounding water and gives off waste. A ***closed system,*** on the other hand, such as a piece of steel, does not have this relationship with the environment that would permit it to grow and change. The steel is said to be in a state of entropy—that is, tending toward a static, steady state of equilibrium, or toward gradual disorder. The protozoan, on the other hand, is in a state of negative entropy as long as it maintains its positive interaction with its environment. The protozoan, as a living, growing organism, tends toward higher degrees of order. Social systems, such as persons, families, guidance departments, schools, and even nations,

Figure 11.2 Career Intervention Flowchart

From *Career Development and Services: A Cognitive Approach* (p. 325), by G. W. Peterson, J. P. Sampson, Jr., and R. C. Reardon, 1991, Pacific Grove, CA: Brooks/Cole.

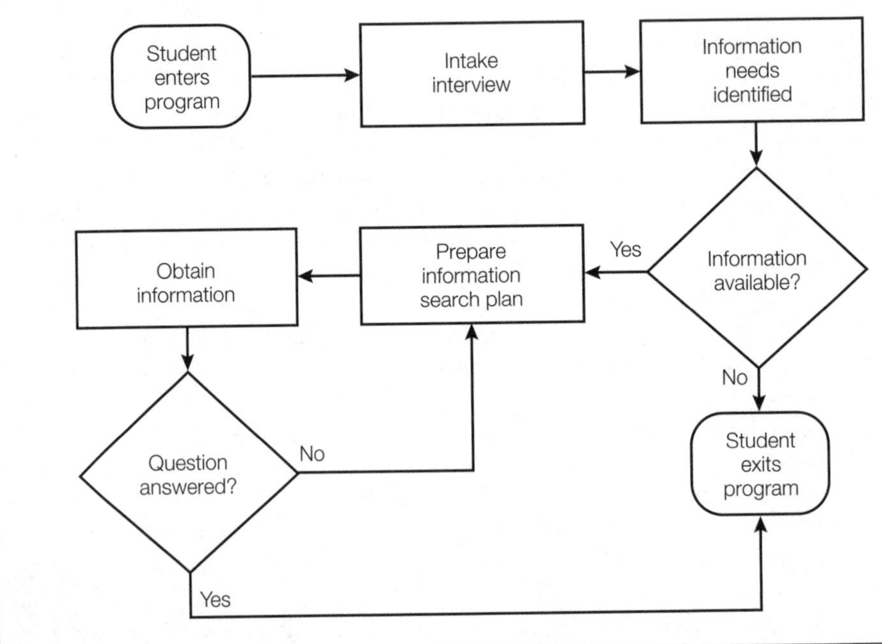

can also be characterized as open systems so long as they engage in positive, growing, interactive relationships with their environments.

Figure 11.3 shows a simple flowchart of a social system. The system exists and functions in a wider environment; for example, a career guidance department functions in an environment that includes the school, the community, and even the state and the nation. The environment also includes the history, policies, and mission of the school; the teachers, administration, and parents and their views of the department; the physical plant and the tax base of the community and state; the state and national laws pertaining to education; and the state of the art in guidance interventions—all that we know about how to operate effective guidance programs. The career guidance program constantly interacts with this environment.

A complex array of information from the environment is screened, analyzed, and fed into the system in the form of inputs. For example, information from the environment could include reports of student needs or school priorities, such as to reduce the drop-out rate or to comply with new state laws or school board policies affecting guidance; or it could include information about new, effective career interventions. Inputs involving resources could include budget allocations, changes in office space

Figure 11.3 | Social System Flowchart

From *Career Development and Services: A Cognitive Approach* (p. 326), by G. W. Peterson, J. P. Sampson, Jr., and R. C. Reardon, 1991, Pacific Grove, CA: Brooks/Cole.

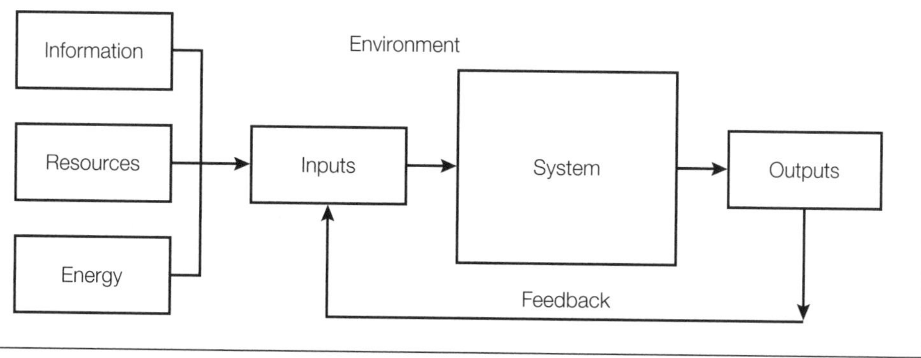

or facilities, or the departure or arrival of new staff members. Energy inputs in guidance service might include everything from the motivation the superintendent has to instill, to the electricity necessary to light the building or to run a computer.

Control Functions The outputs of the system are constantly monitored and evaluated. Information is fed back to the system in a feedback loop, which serves a ***control function***, helping to determine whether the system should grow, shrink, or remain the same. As with a protozoan, the guidance program will counteract the forces of entropy and remain an open system so long as it engages in meaningful, productive interaction with its environment. If the program fails in this function, it will become a closed system—the guidance department will be shut down.

Hierarchy An additional word can be said about the guidance system in relation to other systems. As the focal system, it conducts meetings; provides services to many kinds of clients, including students, parents, teachers, and administrators; possesses a structure (which may be represented in an organization chart); maintains a schedule and calendar of activities; trains new staff and supervises other staff; and performs public relations activities to inform various groups in the environment about the services it offers. The guidance department is actually part of a larger system, the school; the school is part of an even larger system, the local school district; and so forth. These larger systems encompassing the guidance department are called suprasystems; subordinate systems are called subsystems. Any system exists within a ***hierarchy*** of subsystems and suprasystems. An example of a subsystem in a guidance department might consist of the director and one of the counselors, who collaborate to produce reports on the use of career materials within the guidance department.

Figure 11.4 The CASVE Process of Program Development

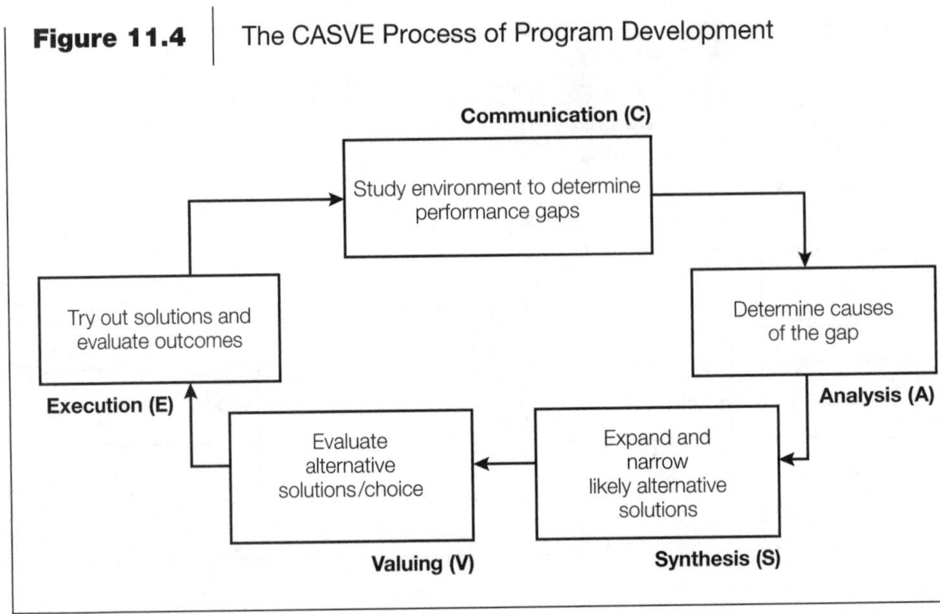

APPLYING CIP TO CAREER PROGRAM DESIGN

The systems concepts that have been introduced thus far are intended to help professional counselors approach the task of designing effective career guidance services in a more effective and orderly way. According to Vaupel (1977), this approach results in better plans and decisions than habit, which is the most commonly used method of program development.

The flowchart shown in Figure 11.4 shows six steps, which are analogous to the phases of the CASVE decision-making cycle discussed earlier. The components of the CIP pyramid and the CASVE cycle can be used to guide practitioners in designing effective career programs. The CIP approach and CASVE cycle provide a systematic approach to program development. By using this CIP framework, practitioners are more likely to be aware of the key issues involved in successful program development.

Peterson, Sampson, and Reardon (1991) provided an early discussion of CIP theory in relation to program development. Another example of the CIP approach to program development is provided in Reardon and Lenz (1998). In that example, CIP is applied to the development of a middle school career assessment program. The remainder of this chapter provides an update to these earlier descriptions, reflecting advancements in CIP theory and research, and uses the redesign of a university-based career service center to accommodate adult distance learners as a means of illustrating the application of CIP theory to career program design. Some of the material in this chapter reflects earlier work by Lenz, Reardon, Peterson, and Sampson (2001).

Self- and Option Knowledge

As noted earlier, the base of the CIP pyramid focuses on self-knowledge and knowledge of options. These concepts can be applied to organizations and programs because they also have a sense of identity. Self-knowledge may include the organization's self-perceptions in terms of its history and values, its view of its mission and goals, and the sense of organizational culture. Organizations and programs may reflect the values of their leaders by what activities they deem important, what services they emphasize, and where they concentrate their staff time and resources. What principles guide the organization? Organizations or programs may be known for doing certain things well or they may have certain strengths—for example, they are known as providers of quality instruction. Organizations may get a sense of satisfaction from the services or programs they deliver—for example, they may help unemployed adults receive retraining and return to gainful employment.

In addition to self-knowledge, program planning and design requires the consideration of knowledge related to options. The programs and services pursued at an earlier time by the organization may need to be revised in light of internal or external forces that now impact the organization. Part of the program design and development process may involve reconsidering the organization's role and purpose and the options available for carrying out this purpose or for a newly identified purpose. We will elaborate on this more when we review the steps in the CASVE cycle, which require the consideration of self-knowledge and option knowledge from an organizational or programmatic perspective.

CASVE Cycle

Each phase of the CASVE cycle raises key issues and topics that program developers must consider. In this section, we discuss each phase of the CASVE cycle with reference to a gap in career service delivery for adult distance learners. The readers of this chapter may wish to reframe the questions and issues to reflect the particular setting and population of interest to them.

Communication The need for an innovation or change in program service delivery derives from several possible situations, each of which involves a need to remove the gap between the present situation and a more ideal situation. The gap may have been identified by a higher-level administrator in the organization, by an internal or external task force, by the collective wisdom of the current staff, or by the felt need of one individual. The agency or organization may have also received feedback from the users of its services, either formally or informally. Whatever the source of this feedback, it typically reflects a desire to improve the current situation. There is often both written information, or in some cases, "hard data," and a certain level of "emotion, energy and motivation to make things better, to reduce the gap between the real and the ideal" (Reardon & Lenz, 1998, p. 208).

Information about career service delivery gaps can come from many varied national and local sources. For example, a series of national surveys (Brown & Minor,

1989, 1992; Hoyt & Lester, 1995) conducted by the Gallup Organization provided information about career guidance gaps in the United States. Only one third of adults were in their current jobs as a result of deliberate planning, whereas most were employed as a result of chance or the influence of other people, or it was the only job available. Not surprising, two thirds of adults had never consulted a career counselor about their careers, although about that many had used newspapers or television to obtain career information. Hoyt and Lester found that 28% of workers anticipated job changes in three years, and 9% (between 3 million and 18 million people) had needed assistance in the past year regarding employment. Isaacson and Brown (2000) provide extensive documentation about gaps in career service delivery in the contemporary United States for those who might be interested in reading more in this area.

How might a program developer seek to close the gap in career services? We offer the following example. A university career services office found itself using a more traditional service delivery model that was not providing an optimum level of service to all constituents. The career office had for many years geared its services to more traditional-aged students, and the emphasis had been primarily on individual appointments. Many of the services had been provided in a face-to-face mode (e.g., career planning classes, workshops, individual counseling) and had been delivered during traditional work-week hours (i.e., 8 to 5).

In recent years, the university had seen a significant increase in the enrollment of adult distance learners. The average age of students had increased from 20 to 28. The career services office had recently hired a staff person with experience in a setting where she had been a direct recipient of distance-learning programs, and she had also held an assistantship as a graduate student in an office that was designed to address the needs of adult learners. In addition, the university's provost and president had allocated new resources for and placed a new emphasis on the delivery of distance learning.

This brief scenario highlights some possible key internal and external cues that signify the existence in the Communication phase of a gap related to organizational effectiveness. With the input of the new staff member, the career services office began to raise questions about the extent to which it was meeting the needs of new student populations, particularly adult distance learners. At this point, it is essential that an individual or a group of concerned persons assume a leadership role in the program design and development process. Reardon and Lenz (1998) outlined some questions that may be useful for these leaders to consider in program planning in order to understand the nature of the gap:

1. Is it reasonable to assume that the gap can be removed? Is this task worth undertaking?
2. What is the history of the gap in this setting? How long has it existed?
3. Does this gap exist in other places? What has been done in other places to remove the gap?
4. Who in the organization or community is concerned about the gap?
5. How do various stakeholders feel about the gap? How badly do they want it removed?

6. What data are available (e.g., survey results, internal reports, accountability studies) that provide specific information about the nature and extent of the gap?

The information gathered in the process of addressing these questions, along with additional external and internal cues, provides the content that is considered in the Analysis phase of this program development model.

Analysis The Analysis phase of the CASVE cycle involves considering all of the causal elements and circumstances that led to the creation of the gap, along with determining the relationships between the gap and possible solutions. Whether in individual career decision making or organizational program planning, there is too often a rush to the Execution phase without careful consideration of all the relevant information and conditions that led to the gap. It is the "quick fix" to the problem that is sought rather than careful reasoning and a deliberate use of a sound program-planning model. These quick-fix approaches ignore the key aspects of strategic planning, which involve both doing the "right things" and "doing things right." As Peterson et al. (1991) noted: "Good problem solvers and decision makers resist the pressure to act impulsively; instead they engage in a period of thoughtful reflection to gain a better understanding of the problem and of their ability to respond" (p. 34). This occurs in the Analysis phase of the CASVE cycle.

Using the previous six questions as a guide, we will examine the types of information that a program developer in our example setting might want to consider. The gap in services delivery identified by this career office is one that can be removed, or at least minimized to some degree. In an initial meeting with the staff, the center's director heard several ideas about how these concerns regarding distance learning and adult learners might be addressed. The gap in services was of relatively recent origin, but the pressure to address that gap had increased quickly. Other academic and student services offices were facing similar pressure from various university administrators, policymakers, and vocal constituents. A key activity undertaken by the career office at this point involved meeting with other department heads in student services, as well as the chief student services person, to discuss possible solutions. The center's director was aware that top university officials considered the provision of services to nontraditional distance learners a high priority. The career services director also wanted to remove the gap in career services to adult learners. There had been a trend in university funding patterns toward the increasing allocation of resources to make services more accessible, both in terms of location and hours, and to move learning resources to a format suitable for distance learners. Legislative reports and student satisfaction surveys from adult learners also provided information on the nature of the gap. The Analysis phase emphasizes the gathering of as much information as possible about the nature of the problem. In the next section, we discuss the Synthesis phase of the CASVE cycle.

Synthesis In the Synthesis phase, the question is asked: "What courses of action might solve the problem?" (Peterson et al., 1991). As Reardon and Lenz (1998) noted, the Synthesis phase asks program developers to "specify solutions that will remove the gap, synthesizing information obtained from Communication and Analysis to identify old and/or new resources and activities to remove gaps" (p. 210). Career office staff members may specify doing familiar tasks in similar or new ways or creating completely new activities. As noted earlier, there are two phases of the Synthesis stage: Synthesis-elaboration and Synthesis-crystallization.

The Synthesis-elaboration phase allows for divergent thinking, and no options are rejected out of hand; this allows for the widest possible consideration of alternatives. The program leader or task force working on removing a gap may solicit input in various ways, such as arranging open meetings or focus groups, consulting with colleagues individually, brainstorming, gathering information through internal or external listservs, or posting surveys electronically. A key point to keep in mind when engaging in the Synthesis phase of program development is to carry forward what was learned from the previous phases—that is, Communication and Analysis. This helps the persons involved in program development stay focused on the needs of the individuals being served and the needs of the organization or agency (Reardon & Lenz, 1998).

In the Synthesis-crystallization phase, the program developer begins to develop a written report, planning document, or proposal outlining the nature of the program intervention being contemplated. This is a critical step in the program development process, because it begins to formulate a strategy for action that can be read, contemplated, discussed, dissected, and criticized by various stakeholders. Quite literally, this written document "crystallizes" the thinking that has taken place earlier in the CASVE cycle.

Perhaps a task force or committee could be given the assignment to develop a specific program proposal for addressing the problem or need. It may involve one or more persons stepping forward and taking leadership in producing documents that move the process forward in the career office. Ultimately, this will lead to writing a document in the form of a need statement ("specifying the nature of the gap") or a program proposal. These need statements or gaps are translated into program goals, which may reflect both intervention process goals and learner outcome goals (Reardon & Lenz, 1998). Process goals could include the following: "Provide access to Web-based career assessments for adult distance learners." Learner outcome goals might include this statement: "Non-campus-based learners will be able to develop effective resumes and cover letters by accessing Web-based formats of the content for existing career center workshops."

Goal statements of this nature outline how things will be different as a result of the introduction of a proposed career services program, how the gap identified in the Communication phase and elaborated in the Analysis phase of the CASVE cycle will be removed or reduced (Reardon & Lenz, 1998). Whereas the Analysis and Synthesis-elaboration phases allow for fairly wide-ranging discussion of information and options, the Synthesis-crystallization phase of the CASVE cycle begins to focus in a more concrete manner on specific options or alternatives that may be used to address the needs and goals identified in the Analysis phase.

Reardon and Lenz (1998) identified key questions to consider during this Synthesis-crystallization phase of program planning. Raising these questions and focusing on possible answers in relation to our example problem of career services to adult distance learners may help in the evaluation and elimination of potential options for the program intervention being contemplated to remove the gap. The ultimate question is whether or not the program development proposal addresses the causes of the gap identified in the Analysis phase.

1. How might staff roles change as services to adult distance learners are increased? Will an existing job description be rewritten to staff this new programmatic effort, or will no changes be needed?
2. Are procedures explained regarding staff selection and training? Does everyone need to be trained? Do different types of staff receive different types of training? Can some staff opt out of the program? What do staff need to understand about the needs of the population being served (e.g., adult learners)? What information will be communicated by staff to these individuals when they call the career center requesting specific services or information?
3. What space and equipment will be needed for the program, if any? Will other service delivery locations, such as a university library or student union, be created on campus? Will there be extended phone hours or in-person service hours to meet the needs of those being served?
4. What resources (e.g., technology, funds, staff) are available to remove the gap? Are these resources readily available on site or do they have to be obtained elsewhere?
5. How will the program be introduced to staff and clients? Will descriptions of these services be included in current publications? Will there be a special section of the career office's Web site devoted to these adult learners?
6. How will the proposed program be supervised and managed on a daily basis? Is there one designated contact person who will be responsible, or are some or all staff cross-trained in order to provide services to new populations being served?
7. What are the daily, weekly, monthly, and quarterly time frames for program operation? Will it operate during breaks and holidays? In the evenings or weekends?
8. Will there be costs associated with the program? What consultation, technical assistance, and human resources support does the proposed program need? How will these costs be paid, or how will these resources be acquired? Will additional staff be paid to work in the evenings and on weekends? Will funds be provided to hire technical personnel to redesign the center's Web site with new populations in mind?
9. How will the proposed program change the current procedures and related programs in the career office? Will some other program be eliminated or curtailed if this new program is added?
10. How will the program be evaluated? What special forms and materials, if any, will be needed to evaluate the program? Who will do this? When will they do it? How will clients and staff provide feedback regarding their experiences with the changes in service delivery resulting from implementation of the program?
11. Will the information collected by the program and in the evaluation process enable the staff to determine if the original gaps identified in the Communication phase have been removed or reduced?

12. How and when will information about the success of the program be shared with others in the organization—for example, potential future clients, staff, top administrators? In the larger community? In the profession—for example, journal articles, conference presentations?

This list of questions specifies the kinds of information that a program developer might review during the Synthesis-crystallization phase of the CASVE cycle. Work in this phase of program development requires staff to become quite specific regarding who will be involved in the program, when they will be doing things, how they will be operating, what they will be doing, and why they will be doing it. Addressing these questions in the program proposal means that the program will more likely operate smoothly when introduced and more likely be effective. If these questions are not addressed in the proposal before actual program operations begin, it is likely that staff confusion and resistance will result in an unsuccessful program. This latter point cannot be overemphasized. Our experience as career services practitioners includes "painful" memories of numerous examples of programs failing because of a lack of careful planning.

Valuing In the Valuing phase of the CASVE cycle of program development, basic questions about the worth and merit of the proposed program are raised and answered. Issues related to questions 8 and 9 in the Synthesis-crystallization phase are especially relevant in the Valuing phase. The basic issue in this phase boils down to this question: "Is this proposed program worth doing, given the costs?" A positive response from key persons affected by the proposed program, including supervisory and support staff in career services, the individuals being served, and higher-level administrators, means that the organization wishes to make a commitment to establishing the program as has been proposed either by the program planning task force or the agency head.

In the case of our career services example, we would hope that the decision to implement the proposed program of new services for adult learners involved in the distance-education program was right for the career center, the university, all students, and the broader community. A positive response might mean any or all of the following:

- The philosophy of the proposed program is the right one.
- It is more important to do this proposed program than some other one.
- The costs are reasonable.
- The likely outcomes of the program are desirable.
- Most stakeholders favor the proposed program.
- The career center and university will be more effective in meeting overall goals as a result of implementation of the proposed program.

After considering all of the questions and information gathered in the Synthesis phase, and after reflecting on the information obtained in the Communication and Analysis phases, the program planners and administrators in charge commit to a specific course of action that reflects a consensus about how to proceed and what option or options are likely to produce the desired results to remove the gap in career services to adult learners. However, any plan about how to proceed is only as effective as the means used to execute the program plan. The next section describes how the Execution phase of the CASVE cycle is applied in program development.

Execution In the Execution phase of the CASVE cycle of program development, the organization or agency staff take action steps to implement the program plan or option specified in the Valuing phase. "It is time to try the program in a real-life setting, to see how it works with real individuals" (Reardon & Lenz, 1998, p. 213). Issues related to questions 1–7 in the Synthesis-crystallization phase are especially important to cover now in the Execution phase. This phase is often governed by a specific set of steps and time lines so that all individuals know what is likely to happen and by when. Key tasks are assigned to the individuals involved in program implementation. If a program development task force was formed, it may be dissolved at this point, unless it was given specific roles associated with the implementation process. For example, if the new services to adult distance learners are to be marketed, this task may revert back to the center's promotions and publicity committee or information specialist. If one person provided leadership throughout the program development process, that person might continue to provide leadership in directing the implementation of the program in the Execution phase of the CASVE cycle, as reflected by his or her revised position description.

Another key element of the Execution phase may be a limited tryout with a select group of clients to determine whether the procedures and resources actually work as expected (Reardon & Lenz, 1998). Going back to our example, one important group of distance learners at the university is made up of persons completing degrees in information studies. The activities and services that came out of the program proposal could be pilot-tested with this group. The experiences and feedback of the group members would allow staff to collect information about program procedures and possibly return to an earlier phase of the CASVE cycle to potentially rethink and redesign some of the program activities (Reardon & Lenz, 1998). In some program development and evaluation models, these kinds of activities are described as formative evaluation or process evaluation—that is, "Are we doing things right?"

Communication Finally, the CIP approach to program development specifies returning to the Communication phase of the CASVE cycle to determine if the gap specified earlier in career services to adult distance learners has been removed following the introduction of the new program. Issues related to questions 10–12 noted earlier in the Synthesis-crystallization phase are important to review now in this Communication phase. Program evaluators are familiar with this general area as product evaluation or outcome evaluation—that is, "Are we doing the right things?" The list of original needs and goals specified in the Communication and Analysis phases is reexamined in light of data collected in the Execution phase to determine if the program is achieving worthwhile goals in a cost-effective way. If it is, then the program would likely be described as a successful career service intervention, and our adult distance learners would be receiving services deemed desirable by the persons being served, the career office staff, the university administration, policymakers, and other constituents.

Executive Processing

In the previous sections, we examined how the base of the pyramid and the CASVE cycle could be applied to the process of program design and development. We noted in an earlier chapter that the executive processing component of CIP theory, with respect to individual career problem solving and decision making, is concerned with how individuals think and feel about career choices or "thinking about thinking." This concept can also be applied to how individuals in organizations approach program design and development, especially when it involves a significant change in how things get done.

When approaching the design and delivery of new programs and services, the collective and individual thinking of staff can play a key role in how successful that process will be. Most readers are aware of how positive thinking contributes to the success of an individual or an organization. This might be reflected in statements such as "We can do this"; "We know what it takes to accomplish this task"; or "We're excited about this new challenge we're facing." In contrast, most of us have also experienced the impact of negative thinking within an organization, reflected in statements or questions such as "We've always done it this way"; "What if we try this, spend all this money, and it doesn't work?"; "Things are working well the way they are, so why change?"; or "That's not in my job description." Negative thinking in individuals tends to shut down the problem-solving and decision-making process. The same can be said of negative thinking in organizations. A key aspect of program design and development from a CIP perspective is to be aware of the potential for negative thinking and to help minimize its impact on the organization's ability to change and develop in order to meet new programmatic needs.

Organizations can use a variety of methods to provide a detached, objective view of their functioning. Following are several examples relevant to our university career services office example:

1. Use an advisory board consisting of members of various stakeholder and constituent groups, such as career center staff, students, employers, faculty, and distance-learning staff.
2. Focus on the formative or process evaluation results of career services related to adult learners involved in distance education.
3. Use external consultants with expertise in career services for adult learners and distance guidance programs.
4. Conduct staff retreats and workshops using innovative staff development techniques to "unfreeze" career center staff thinking so that staff can consider new ways for removing the gap in career services to adult learners.

Thus far, we have explored the logic of a systems view in helping counselors develop more-effective career development programs. In the next section, we focus on how a special application of the systems approach, instructional systems design (ISD), can be used to create a career information delivery system.

INSTRUCTIONAL SYSTEMS DESIGN

The systems approach to the design of effective instructional activities has grown rapidly over the past 30 years. Dick and Carey (1985) described a model that may be considered a systems approach because it is composed of interacting components, each having its own input and output, which together produce predetermined outputs. The instructional system also collects information, which is fed back into the system so that the quality of the output can be monitored and evaluated. The Dick and Carey model will be examined in greater detail later in this chapter.

Returning to the high school guidance program example mentioned earlier, many of the expressed student needs for career assistance may be tied to the development of self-knowledge and occupational knowledge. "What are my interests and abilities?" "How will I decide whether to attend a community college or university?" "How much does a biologist make?" "What does a respiratory technician do?" "How do I get a job now that will pay for a new car?" The guidance department could offer a wide variety of career services activities that would enable students to answer questions such as these, as well as hundreds of others. For example, students could do the following:

- Talk to a counselor or parent volunteer
- Read a book about occupations or a book about decision making
- Take an interest inventory
- Use a computer-assisted career guidance system
- Watch a CD in which a performing artist describes her work
- Talk to a community resource person in a specific occupation
- Create a completely new way to acquire the information needed to solve a career problem

A career service center has a variety of learning resources to help clients acquire knowledge and problem-solving skills to make career decisions. The systems approach to the design of career information services helps counselors transform human and nonhuman resources into dynamic learning processes to meet individual learning styles in an effective and efficient manner. The instructional systems design (ISD) process offers a valuable guide to structure program design activities.

Modules

Modules are the units of instruction that have been designed to help a learner (the client) obtain specific knowledge or skills. We may describe modules as self-contained units of instruction that have an integrated theme, learning objectives, and the information needed to acquire specified knowledge and skills. A module serves as one element of an instructional system (Dick & Carey, 1985). There is no fixed rule about how long a module may take to complete, how many alternative modes of learning are offered (such as reading a book, viewing a film, or talking with a resource person), whether learners should know in advance about the desired performance outcome, or whether teachers or counselors should be incorporated into the module. However, there is agreement that the module should be validated—that is, that clients using it are able to achieve the performance objectives specified in the module. The Florida State University Career Center uses instructional modules to help counselors and clients quickly identify learning resources that will meet identified learner behavioral outcomes.

Counselors

From an ISD point of view, the counselor is an instructional designer. The role of the counselor, as a designer of instruction, is to help clients learn to use information to enable them to become independent problem solvers and decision makers. The counselor also manages the implementation and integration of this instruction into the guidance program and then evaluates its impact on the attainment of program goals and on the environment. Direct counseling activities, from an ISD perspective, are viewed as alternative learning activities or instructional components and are used to accommodate the unique learning styles of individual clients. As indicated in previous chapters and in the analysis of the cube earlier in this chapter, interventions are selected on the basis of client needs, optimal learning styles, available resources, and lowest cost. Some interventions are too expensive and time-consuming to be used with all clients seeking career services. A modular approach to career service delivery is an organized way of developing and delivering the most cost-effective interventions.

AN ISD MODEL FOR CAREER GUIDANCE SERVICES

The instructional systems design model described in this section may be viewed as a guideline to enhance the Execution phase of the CASVE problem-solving cycle described earlier. It provides a metacognitive framework for developing a plan to implement the solutions selected in the Synthesis phase. For example, if it has been decided that the career center should provide activities related to developing a resume, the ISD approach provides a heuristic method for developing a sequence of learning activities to help clients acquire the necessary knowledge, skills, and metacognitions.

We have modified the ISD model developed by Dick and Carey (1985) in order to make it relevant to designing a career guidance program. Figure 11.5 presents a flowchart of the model.

Identify and Prioritize Instructional Goals (1.0)

A learning objective is a statement of an ability or capability that will enable the individual to become a more independent and responsible career problem solver and decision maker. At the program level, goals are statements that subsume the related clusters of skills and knowledge (i.e., objectives) that clients need to develop. In the idiom of ISD, career service interventions are learning events that facilitate the acquisition of knowledge and skills. The first step is to determine what clients should be able to know or do to solve the career problems they bring to the career service center.

Figure 11.5 Flowchart for Designing a Career Services Program

From *Career Development and Services: A Cognitive Approach* (p. 331), by G. W. Peterson, J. P. Sampson, Jr., and R. C. Reardon, 1991, Pacific Grove, CA: Brooks/Cole.

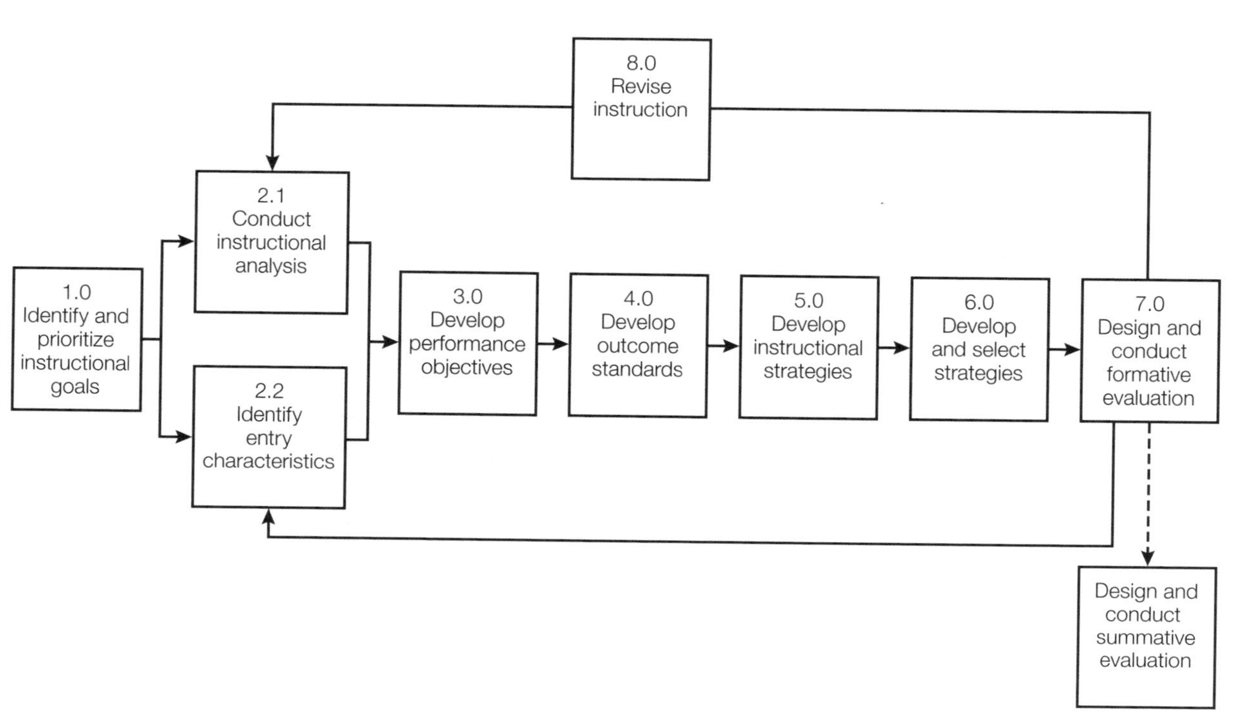

There are many ways to identify such goals and objectives for learning events. Perhaps you notice that many students using the guidance program inquire about how to identify their interests or abilities, which major fields of study are available at your college, or how to get a job after graduation. Besides using such day-to-day experience, the guidance office could conduct a formal assessment of student needs using questionnaires and methodologically sound surveys, or it could respond to administrators who may have targeted certain groups of clients for priority attention (e.g., potential dropouts). Identifying instructional goals may also be related to policies that have been set by committees at the national, state, local, or organizational levels. For example, a parent task force appointed by the parent-teacher organization may have recommended that all graduating seniors in the high school develop a career plan; or a private agency may have adopted the *National Career Development Guidelines* (Kobylarz, 1996). (Additional information about these *Guidelines* is available through the International Career Development Library at http://icdl.uncg.edu/ft/120899-04.html#table, and a copy of the "Career Development Competencies by Area and Level" is shown in Appendix C.) Detailed information on career development competencies and indicators from the *Guidelines* can be found in Appendix D. The NCDA (1993) has established policy on the career development of children, adolescents, adults, and retired persons.

Conduct Instructional Analysis (2.1)

After a goal is specified, the counselor and other team members must thoroughly analyze it in terms of its component parts—that is, its knowledge and skill components. What lower-order skills are needed to achieve higher-order skills? What is the sequence of learning activities for most persons? What resources are available to enable persons to achieve mastery of lower-order and higher-order skills? This analysis could involve holding group meetings, sharing points of view about how learners could be helped, or consulting with an ad hoc client advisory group.

Identify Entry Characteristics (2.2)

Besides the objectives and learning activities of the modules, counselors must know the particular characteristics of clients that bear directly on learning. Important entry characteristics may include learner abilities, motivation, expectations, prior learner, and anxiety level. At this step we must ask, "What psychological characteristics do clients bring to the learning process that must be incorporated into the design and use of learning modules or career interventions to handle most students?" The development of a list such as the 50 client questions presented in Table 11.1 will help you assess the entry-level characteristics and needs of clients.

Develop Performance Objectives (3.0)

Following the instructional analysis of client needs and client entry characteristics, the counselor must develop specific performance objectives for the instructional goals assigned to the various modules. A performance objective is a statement of what clients should be able to do on completion of each module. The performance objectives for each module should describe the specific skills the clients will learn, the conditions under which these skills will be demonstrated, and the criteria for successful performance. For example, after completing the module on clarifying interests and after taking Holland's Self-Directed Search (Holland, 1994), a client should be able to list at least two appropriate Holland interest codes and several characteristics of persons in each code.

Develop Outcome Standards (4.0)

In this step, the assessment procedures are specified to measure whether clients have mastered the performance objectives. In the area of counseling and guidance, these assessments are often self-administered and self-evaluated to alleviate stress and to encourage self-responsibility for learning. For example, an outcome standard could be either a client's improved vocational identity score on a career development inventory or a simple verbal report of an increased level of certainty about occupational interests.

Develop Instructional Strategies (5.0)

Information collected in the preceding steps of this systems design model will assist the counselor in developing alternative instructional strategies to enable clients to achieve a module's performance objectives. The strategies or plans for learning activities adopted for the modules should be based on the knowledge and skills to be learned, the characteristics of the clients, the resources available (human and nonhuman), and the setting in which help can be provided.

Develop and Select Strategies (6.0)

In this step, the strategy is used to select a set of instructional modules to enable clients to achieve their goals. There are common pathways that most students use to achieve certain goals. These pathways can be set forth in a series of modules. Each of the modules may include pretests and/or posttests, a counselor guide or user manual, multimedia materials, and other learning activities. Learning activities may include direct or indirect interventions or a combination of the two, using originally developed materials or preexisting materials already in stock in the guidance department. It is important to note that practical constraints often compel counselors to select from among alternative interventions—it is almost never possible to do everything that is desired.

Design and Conduct Formative Evaluation (7.0)

Following the development of prototype drafts of a module, the counselor conducts a series of process evaluations—referred to as formative evaluations—to determine whether a module is effective in enabling learners to achieve its objectives and how it might be improved. Formative evaluations may include one-on-one, small-group, and field settings. Each type of evaluation provides the counselor with a different type of information and feedback for improving the module. In some cases, the counselor may simply watch some clients go through the module, interview them after completing the module, or ask them to complete a feedback form.

Revise Instruction (8.0)

The final step in the development of a series of modules is revising the instruction or career intervention. Evaluation data are used to assess the impact of learning activities on the clients, to identify any client difficulties in meeting the performance objectives, to reassess assumptions about client characteristics, and to determine if the performance objectives are properly stated. Revisions are made to improve the modules as suggested by the data.

Design and Conduct Summative Evaluation

The dotted line in Figure 11.5 indicates that this step is not part of the instructional design process for each individual module; rather, it is an evaluation of the effectiveness of the modules as a whole. This is the point where the career services program or career information delivery system provides information to the larger environment about its effectiveness and impact. A more comprehensive review of program evaluation and accountability is given in later chapters of this book.

These steps in the design of learning events represent the application of a systems approach to the design of career service interventions and career information delivery systems. Conceptualizing career interventions, especially the presentation of information, as instructional events leading to clients learning new problem-solving capabilities is a departure from the ways counselors usually think about their role and the use of career information. The next two chapters provide detailed examples and applications of this model to a typical career guidance program and discuss how to locate and utilize the information resources necessary to install such a comprehensive career development program.

SUMMARY

This chapter described the roles of the counselor as a program developer and instructional designer and identified some of the career needs experienced by individuals and organizations. The wide range and scope of career-related needs were explored, along with the potentially varied responses available to counselors for successful interventions. The need to set priorities and policies that will direct programs was also pointed out, and a three-dimensional model was used to frame policy options. Program development in career guidance was described from a historical perspective, and current efforts to utilize a systems approach to program development was explained. The CIP approach and CASVE cycle were applied to career program design. Important systems concepts were introduced along with an instructional systems design (ISD) model applicable to the development of career guidance programs. The chapter concluded with the proposition that career information delivery can be viewed as providing a series of learning events that foster more-effective career problem-solving and decision-making skills and knowledge.

GETTING THE MOST BENEFIT FROM READING THIS CHAPTER

To effectively learn the material in this chapter, complete one or more of the following activities:

- Study the list of 50 client information questions in Table 11.1. Pick one question of interest to you, and analyze the question or gap as carefully as you can. What assumptions underlie the question or problem? What information do you need, and what responding questions would you ask in order to begin to think about ways you might be helpful? Could you answer the question or solve the problem if you had no media resources? What if you could use the public or school library? What media resources would you use in the nearest career center? Write your answers to these questions. Pick four more questions, and analyze them in a similar way. Discuss your analyses with other students and/or a professional career counselor.
- Select an occupation that you know little about and that you would not be interested in pursuing or for which you lack the required skills or training. Identify a person in that field, and conduct an information interview to broaden your occupational knowledge and to refine your information acquisition skills. Conduct a second interview with a person in a field you would like to enter. Use the following sample questions to help you prepare your interviews:

    1. *Background:* Tell me how you got started in this field. What was your education? What educational background or related experience might be helpful in entering this field?
    2. *Work environment:* What are the daily duties of the job? What are the working conditions? What skills and abilities are utilized in this work?
    3. *Problems:* What are the toughest problems you handle? What problems does the organization as a whole have? What is being done to solve these problems?
    4. *Lifestyle:* What obligation does your work put on you outside the work week? How much flexibility do you have in terms of dress, work hours, and vacations?
    5. *Rewards:* What do you find most rewarding about this work, besides the money?
    6. *Salary:* At what salary level would a new person start? What are the fringe benefits? What are other forms of compensation (bonuses, commissions, or securities)?
    7. *Potential:* Where do you see your work going in a few years? What are your long-term goals?

8. *Promotion:* Is turnover high? How does one move from position to position? Do people normally move to another company/division/agency? What is your policy about promotions from within? What happened to the person who last held this position? How many have held this job in the last five years? How are employees evaluated?
9. *The industry:* What trends do you see for this industry in the next three to five years? What kind of future do you see for this organization? How much of your business is tied to the economy, government spending, weather, supplies, and so forth?
10. *Demand:* What types of employers hire people in this line of work? Where are they located? What other career areas do you think are related to your work?
11. *Hiring decision:* What are the most important factors used to hire people in this work (education, past experience, personality, special skills)? Who makes the hiring decisions for your department? Who supervises the boss? If I apply for a job, whom should I contact?
12. *Job market:* How do people find out about your jobs? Advertisements in the newspaper (which newspaper?), word of mouth (who spreads the word?), or the personnel office?

- Study the flowchart in Figure 11.2, and then visit a career center, counseling center, or other human services office to collect information about how basic services are provided. Interview a staff member in that setting about how services are provided; then see if you can draw a flowchart that shows how basic client services are provided in that office.
- Imagine that you are a professional counselor at work in a setting of your choice. It may be a setting you have worked in before or a new one. Your director has asked you to begin planning for a program to remedy some problem in that setting. Study the flowchart in Figure 11.4, and prepare a six-step outline for developing the program.
- Pick one of the questions in Table 11.1, and use the ISD model in Figure 11.5 to describe how you might go about the process of creating a simple module to solve the client's problem. Use a sentence outline that covers each step in the model, including issues or questions that are unresolved. Ask for feedback from your instructor or a classmate following his or her review of your outline.

REFERENCES

Bertalanffy, L. von. (1968). *General systems theory: Foundation, development, applications.* New York: Braziller.

Brown, D., & Minor, C. W. (Eds.). (1989). *Working in America: A status report.* Alexandria, VA: National Career Development Association.

Brown, D., & Minor, C. W. (Eds.). (1992). *Career needs in a diverse workplace: A status report on planning and problems.* Alexandria, VA: National Career Development Association.

Campbell, R., & Cellini, J. (1981). A diagnostic taxonomy of adult career problems. *Journal of Vocational Behavior, 19,* 175–190.

Dick, W., & Carey, L. (1985). *The systematic design of instruction* (2nd ed.). Glenview, IL: Scott, Foresman.

Herr, E. L., & Cramer, S. H. (1996). *Career guidance and counseling through the life span: Systematic approaches* (5th ed.). New York: HarperCollins.

Holland, J. L. (1994). *Self-Directed Search* (4th ed.). Odessa, FL: Psychological Assessment Resources.

Hosford, R. E., & Ryan, T A. (1970). Systems design in the development of counseling and guidance programs. *The Personnel and Guidance Journal, 49,* 221–230.

Hoyt, K. (1981). *Career education: What it is and where it is going.* Salt Lake City, UT: Olympus.

Hoyt, K., & Lester, J. L. (1995). *Learning to work: The NCDA Gallup survey.* Alexandria, VA: National Career Development Association.

Isaacson, L. E., & Brown, D. (2000). *Career information, career counseling, and career development* (7th ed.). Boston: Allyn & Bacon.

Kobylarz, L. (1996). *National Career Development Guidelines: K–adult handbook.* Stillwater, OK: National Occupational Information Coordinating Committee Training and Support Center.

Lenz, J. G., & Panke, J. (2001). *Paraprofessionals in career services* (Technical Report No. 32) [On-line]. Available: www.career.fsu.edu/techcenter/designing_career_services/practical_strategies/.

Lenz, J. G., Reardon, R. C., Peterson, G. W., & Sampson, J. P., Jr. (2001). Applying cognitive information processing (CIP) theory to career program design and development. In W. Patton & M. McMahon (Eds.), *Career development programs: Preparation for life-long career decision making* (pp. 46–57). Camberwell, VIC: Australian Council for Educational Research (ACER) Press.

Loesch, L. C., & Vacc, N. A. (1986). *National counselor certification examination: Technical manual.* Alexandria, VA: American Association for Counseling and Development.

Morrill, W. H., Oetting, E. R., & Hurst, J. C. (1974). Dimensions of counselor functioning. *The Personnel and Guidance Journal, 52,* 355–359.

National Career Development Association. (1991). National Career Development Association ethical standards [On-line]. Available: www.ncda.org/about/poles.html.

National Career Development Association. (1993). Career development: A policy statement of the National Career Development Association board of directors [On-line]. Available: www.ncda.org/about/polcdps.html.

National Career Development Association. (1997). Career counseling competencies [On-line]. Available: www.ncda.org/about/polccc.html.

National Career Development Association. (n.d.). Consumer guidelines to selecting a career counselor [On-line]. Available: www.ncda.org/about/polscc.html.

Niles, S. G., & Harris-Bowlsbey, J. (2002). Career development interventions in the 21st century. Upper Saddle River, NJ: Merrill/Prentice-Hall.

O'Brien, K. M. (2001). The legacy of Parsons: Career counselors and vocational psychologists as agents of social change. *The Career Development Quarterly, 50,* 66–76.

Parsons, F. (1909). *Choosing a vocation.* Boston: Houghton Mifflin.

Patton, W., & McMahon, M. (2001). Career development practice: A refocus and renewal. In W. Patton & M. McMahon (Eds.), *Career development programs: Preparation for life-long career decision making* (pp. 2–9). Camberwell, VIC: Australian Council for Educational Research (ACER) Press.

Peterson, G. W., Sampson, J. P., Jr., & Reardon, R. C. (1991). *Career development and services: A cognitive approach.* Pacific Grove, CA: Brooks/Cole.

Quade, E. S. (1977). Analysis for public decisions. In S. S. Nagel (Ed.), *Policy studies: Review annual* (pp. 28–39). Burly Hills, CA: Sage.

Reardon, R. C., & Lenz, J. G. (1998). *The Self-Directed Search and related Holland career materials: A practitioner's guide.* Odessa, FL: Psychological Assessment Resources.

Romano, J. L., & Hage, S. M. (2000). Prevention and counseling psychology: Revitalizing commitments for the 21st century. *The Counseling Psychologist, 28,* 733–763.

Sampson, J. P., Vacc, N. A., & Loesch, L. C. (1998). The practice of career counseling by specialists and counselors in general practice. *The Career Development Quarterly, 46,* 404–415.

Silvern, L. C. (1965). *Systems engineering of education: I. Evolution of systems thinking in education.* Los Angeles: Education and Training Consultants.

Splete, H. H., & Hoppin, J. M. (2000). The emergence of career development facilitators. *The Career Development Quarterly, 48,* 340–347.

Stephens, W. R. (1970). *Social reform and the origins of vocational guidance.* Washington, DC: American Personnel and Guidance Association Press.

Tiedeman, D. V., Katz, J., Miller-Tiedeman, A., & Osipow, S. (1978). *The cross-sectional story of early career development.* Washington, DC: American Personnel and Guidance Association Press.

Vaupel, J. W. (1977). Muddling through analytically. In S. S. Nagel (Ed.), *Policy studies: Review annual* (pp. 44–56). Beverly Hills, CA: Sage.

Whiston, S., Sexton, T. L., & Lasoff, D. L. (1998). Career-intervention outcome: A replication and extension of Oliver and Spokane (1988). *Journal of Counseling Psychology, 45,* 150–165.

Zunker, V. G. (2002). *Career counseling: Applied concepts of life planning* (6th ed.). Pacific Grove, CA: Brooks/Cole.

Zytowski, D. G. (2001). Frank Parsons and the progressive movement. *The Career Development Quarterly, 50,* 57–65.

Developing and Implementing a Career Services Program: A Personal Case History

CHAPTER **12**

In the late 1960s, staff counselors in the university counseling center frequently convened for several hours in open-ended group sessions to freely and candidly exchange views on personal and organizational performance. These were called "encounter groups" and they were common at the time. On one memorable day when we were discussing staff roles and responsibilities, the director turned to me and said, "And what do you do here?" I was shocked, hurt, and embarrassed but finally stammered that I thought everyone knew I was the career counseling specialist. But he persisted, "What are you doing?" I was at a loss—he clearly wanted a better explanation of how I was contributing to the goals of the center. I needed to figure out how to have more of an impact as a career counselor.—**Robert Reardon**

There are various organizational needs that provide a basis for implementing a career services program, but that personal experience more than 30 years ago was a primary motivator for this counselor (and chapter author). Program development and implementation ultimately depend on an individual picking up a challenge, getting personally involved, and making a personal and professional commitment. Many other resources are needed to build a good career development program; but in the final analysis, one

---

Chapter authored by Robert C. Reardon.

person makes the difference by choosing to be a program developer and leader. This person defines the career services to be offered in the organization.

This chapter describes, in a personal way, the experience of the author in designing, developing, and operating a career services program. Many of the ideas for this chapter are based on elements of Cognitive Information Processing theory; others are based on the unique circumstances at Florida State University (FSU) in the late 1960s and early 1970s. After reviewing this chapter, the reader should be able to (a) think more concretely about the personal commitments required to develop career programs; (b) analyze more thoroughly, using the CASVE model, the factors operating in a work setting that might influence career program development activities; (c) use modules to deliver career interventions; and (d) align personal career development with the mission and operation of a career services program. The chapter is organized as follows:

- The Organizational Context
- Establishing a Career Services Program: A Personal Account
- Ongoing Program Development
- Some Personal Reflections
- Summary
- Getting the Most Benefit from Reading This Chapter

THE ORGANIZATIONAL CONTEXT

Effective career interventions, including self-help, brief staff-assisted, and individual case-managed approaches, require facts and data about occupations—for example, occupational descriptions and outlooks. Individuals in decision-making situations transform these facts and data into personally relevant knowledge structures (schemata), which are useful in solving career problems and making career decisions. The professional career counselor seeks to design a career services program or system in which clients can easily locate and process information for career problem solving and decision making. The physical setting for this activity is often a career center, which might also be called a career laboratory, a career information center, a career resource center, a career and life planning center, a career dynamics laboratory, a career planning and placement center, an information room, or even a futures shoppe. (In 1909, Frank Parsons called it a Vocations Bureau.) For consistency, we will use the term ***career center*** in this book to refer to the organizational entity (space plus personnel) in which career services are offered. In Chapter 11, typical questions and concerns were listed from clients who came to the Curricular-Career Information Service (CCIS) at FSU. A review of these questions prompted a group of staff to think about the facts and data required in a career center to help clients identify useful information for their career problem solving and decision making. In other words, these questions framed gaps to be remedied through career interventions or programs.

Clients come to a career center by many pathways. For example, a client might be completing a research assignment for a course, doing personal research for a decision he or she is facing, following through on a referral from a faculty member, or returning after an earlier visit. Some clients come to the career center with a friend or parent, and some arrive alone. Some are confident and self-directed; others are anxious and need reassurance.

Whatever the circumstance, the career center must present a positive, accepting, attractive, neat, organized, helpful public image. Everything about the career center's operation should promote and reinforce client problem-solving behavior by assisting the clients to seek and find information that will help them identify and explore career possibilities. A study several years ago at the University of Missouri showed that career counseling conducted in a career resource center was much more effective in promoting career exploration and problem solving than career counseling conducted one-on-one in a counselor's office or an interview room (Kerr, 1982).

A cube (see Figure 11.1) was presented earlier as a device for depicting the policy issues inherent in career program design. The shaded portion of the cube, which represents the most cost-effective interventions, was the focus of our program development efforts. The career service we wanted to implement was based on the following premises: (a) respond first to the simplest, basic client information needs; (b) provide the least complex interventions; and (c) draw on basic staff competencies or skills. Later, more-complex career service interventions were integrated into the offerings in this career center, and these will be described at the end of this chapter.

ESTABLISHING A CAREER SERVICES PROGRAM: A PERSONAL ACCOUNT

How do counselors get involved in organizing an array of materials and resources into a comprehensive program of career services? Perhaps John Holland's (1997) RIASEC theory can provide us with some clues to ponder. The code for counselor is SAE, project director is ESI, department manager is ESA, training and education manager is EIS, grant coordinator is SEI, and program manager is EIR. Given these occupational titles and codes, the summary code for program developer is EIS.[1] For career counselors to become successful program developers and managers, it seems clear that they must draw heavily on their skills and interests in the "Enterprising" and "Investigative" areas. This can be a personal and professional challenge.

In 1969, Florida State University took the first steps toward creating a novel career services program, later called the Curricular-Career Information Service (Reardon & Minor, 1975). Following the staff encounter described earlier, I began to increasingly invest myself in improving career services in significant ways. [Because this history of the establishing of the center is a personal account by one of the authors of this book, the first person singular is being used for this section of the chapter.] This meant that I began to get angry about the lack of quality of career services available for students and the poor performance of counselors and advisers at the institution. It also meant that I was willing to become known as the vocational person

[1] A summary code for a list of occupations can be created by counting the number of times each letter appears in the first, second, or third column and giving a score of 3, 2, or 1 point. Given the occupations of project director, ESI; department manager, ESA; training/education manager, EIS; grant coordinator, SEI; and program manager, EIR, then a summary code for program developer could be inferred as EIS (R, 1; I, 6; A, 1; S, 8; E, 14; C, 0).

among the other counselors. This was significant because "career stuff" was not a high-prestige area among the other counselors, who were generally more interested in gender issues, stress management, and sensitivity training (Burck, 1984). Coincidentally, during this time I was asked to write several instructional modules and was the recipient of some workshop training in instructional systems design. The convergence of these two personal experiences led to the conceptualization of a career information delivery system based on an instructional systems design (ISD) model.

Although the 30+-year development of CCIS has been marked by various organizational and administrative accidents, I have found that the CASVE cycle, Holland's RIASEC theory, and the ISD model provide useful guides for the continuing operation and growth of the program. The CASVE decision model used in this book will be employed as a metacognitive framework to trace the history of CCIS. The purpose is to show how the model can be successfully adapted and used as a problem-solving strategy for counselors in designing and developing a career services program.

Communication

Even the casual observer could see gaps in the career services provided at the university in the late 1960s. These were some of the incidents that I noticed signaling a need:

- On an intake form, 75% of the students coming to the counseling center wanted career planning assistance.
- Most of the entering students at the university expressed a need for career information—it was their most frequently identified need.
- Several studies of academic advising showed strong student dissatisfaction, especially with regard to career advising.
- The counseling center resources for career information were minimal, consisting of two file drawers of occupational folders and approximately a dozen books, which were accessible to students only after an intake interview.

On closer inspection, several other findings emerged. A volunteer research assistant interviewed 50 academic administrators, faculty and student leaders, and student services staff and found a strong consensus that something dramatic and different needed to be done to improve academic and career advising in the university.

- Several dissertations; a previous Louis Harris survey of faculty, staff, and students; and an accreditation self-study report were located. All of these showed dissatisfaction in the way in which sources of career and academic information were made available to students needing to make career decisions.
- Novel approaches were being attempted in other places to provide career information to students. Tom Magoon at the University of Maryland used an old jukebox to provide students with information about majors (Magoon, Milburn, & Celio, 1971). Some developers, such as David Tiedeman at Harvard and Martin Katz at Educational Testing Service (ETS), were experimenting with computer-based career information systems (U.S. Department of Health, Education,

and Welfare, 1969). Student paraprofessionals were being trained to help other students with a variety of academic and personal problems (Brown, 1965). Some counseling centers were experimenting with outreach programs to provide career services (Morrill & Banning, 1973).
- Career placement, career counseling, and academic and career advising were isolated, administratively separate units within the organization (Hale, 1973–1974).

Therefore, a study of the organizational history and environment revealed numerous indicators of a gap between the real and ideal state of affairs regarding the collection and presentation of career information and services for college students seeking to make educational and career decisions. The nature of the gap was that there was neither sufficient educational and occupational information available for students nor assistance available to help them use such information to make career decisions. The few information materials that were available were inaccessible and not used in a way to enhance the development of career problem-solving and decision-making skills. However, there was evidence of readiness within the organization to change this state of affairs.

Analysis

These problems had existed for a long period of time. They were complex, and there were no ready-made solutions. I began a thoughtful and time-consuming review of the situation. I read books and articles on career decision making. I talked with anyone I could find about the problem and what I might do about it. Coincidentally, David Tiedeman spent several summers teaching at FSU during this time, and he proved to be an inspiring mentor who reinforced my motivation to do something about the problem. He had just concluded development of the computer-based Information System for Vocational Decisions (Tiedeman, 1968) and was a veritable storehouse of knowledge about career information delivery problems and possible solutions. John Holland also visited our campus for a symposium during this period and brought a novel point of view regarding self-directed career assistance (Holland, Hollifield, Nafziger, & Helms, 1972). A senior faculty member on campus, Joyce Chick, had written a monograph on innovations in the use of career information (Chick, 1970), which provided some fresh ideas on the subject.

In talking with academic deans and other leaders about the problem, I discovered that many faculty members and administrators tended to make a distinction between academic or curriculum information and occupational or career information. Indeed, one key academic dean thought it highly inappropriate that non-Ph.D. staff or student paraprofessional counselors be allowed to transmit academic information to students—that is, to discuss majors and career possibilities. Inquiring further, I discovered that although much of the information needed by students was available, there was no roster of faculty resource persons who would be available to discuss major field requirements. Moreover, there was no easy way to make such a roster available to students; nor did anyone really want to take responsibility for such an endeavor.

Finally, in this stage of Analysis, I discovered that (a) several faculty in the counselor education program in the College of Education were highly interested in creating a career counseling or career development emphasis in the master's and bachelor's degree programs; (b) other postsecondary schools around the nation were experiencing similar problems in presenting career information; (c) several colleges on campus were successfully using trained graduate students as paraprofessional academic advisers, although this was strongly resisted in the other colleges; and (d) many of the student information needs for career problem solving were recurring and repetitive in nature. To make some sense of this review, I wrote an article on what the counselor's role in career information might include; the article was eventually published (Reardon, 1973). This writing activity allowed me to put my thoughts together in a coherent manner, setting the stage for the Synthesis phase.

Synthesis

In the process of collecting data and thinking about the problem, I generated many ideas that helped me frame possible solutions. In the Synthesis phase, these potential solutions began to become more concrete with respect to possible implementation at the university.

Emerging ideas for a possible program intervention included the following:

- Given the students' extensive need for information and their image of the counseling center as exclusively a mental health and therapy unit, one idea was to establish small career information centers in residence halls or in the lobby of the student union.
- The university library had some potential—it already had some limited career resources in a reading room, it was open many hours each week, it had some space, and it was experienced in the information business. However, it was not quite ready for a career service center to move into its space.
- The notion of a self-help program had some attractiveness. Such a program would not involve case records, intake interviews, or appointments. It would be truly client centered; that is, services would be matched to specific client needs according to the cube presented in Chapter 11.
- The idea of developing a multimedia career information delivery system with computer terminals, audio- and videotapes, filmstrips, slide-tapes (synchronized color slides and cassette tapes depicting specific occupations), brochures, and handouts seemed worth pursuing. Appropriate use of media capabilities was thought to be cost-effective, but, more important, it would foster the development of independent career problem-solving skills.
- It was important that both educational and occupational information be included in the resources. Campus and community referral contacts for additional information or support services would complement the information resources and activities of the career center.
- It seemed as though such a career center could be staffed by student paraprofessionals and preprofessional career counseling interns—this would help separate it from the clinical image of the counseling center.
- Instructional systems design, including the use of modules, seemed to offer a useful process for the development of program components.

Reactions from others within the organization began to emerge in response to these ideas. As Urie Bronfenbrenner (1966) once said, "If you really want to understand a system, just try to change it." First, the dean of academic affairs was uncomfortable about delegating some of the responsibilities for academic advising to the division of student services, in which the counseling center was administratively located in the university. Second, there was extensive support elsewhere for doing something about the problem, including the president's office and all of the student affairs offices. Third, it was becoming apparent that the new program would need to be centered in the shaded part of the cube; that is, it would have to offer simple, low-cost interventions for as many students as possible. Fourth, program accountability and opportunities for research must be evident from the outset.

Valuing

In the Valuing phase, I began thinking about the consequences and the advantages and disadvantages of intervention alternatives for myself and others who were important to me. I then developed specifications for optimal solutions to the problems; Kaufman (1972) referred to these specifications as solution requirements. I found that the development of a career service delivery system at FSU involved some very difficult choices. My decisions were ultimately reflected in policy (or rules) for the design and operation of the system.

First, I made the decision to use instructional systems design (ISD) as a procedure for structuring the program development process. That is, the design began with an appraisal of client learning needs. This meant that the role of the counselor or paraprofessional could be significantly altered in accordance with the targeted client needs. Thus, the delivery of information for career problem solving may not always be controlled by the counselor. From an ISD perspective, I saw interacting with a counselor simply as one possible learning activity among others, such as reviewing audio- or videotapes or interacting with a computer-assisted career guidance system. The important consideration was to identify the most efficient means of helping clients master explicit learning objectives to meet their needs. Thus, for most persons the program would function more like a learning resource center or a comprehensive modern library than a traditional counseling center. In traditional counseling centers, the organizational structure, staffing, and physical facilities are all designed to provide environments for the establishment of confidential counseling relationships; this would not be the case in the career center I envisioned.

Second, I decided that the program would be located in student living areas and high-traffic areas such as the student union, and not in the counseling center. In this way, information would be more accessible to clients.

Third, the primary clients should be lower-division undergraduates who require information to choose majors and to plan careers. Lower-priority clients should include high school and community college students anticipating transfer to the university. The program would be informal and developmental in nature. The program mission—that is, the specific client needs the program sought to address—would not include helping students who are job hunting, students who are experiencing a personal crisis or who are in an intense emotional state such as acute depression or anxiety, or students with specific academic questions involving the interpretation of academic rules and policies. Referrals to other appropriate campus or community services should be provided to those students. (It should be noted that full-time and part-time employment assistance and mental health counseling were included later in a comprehensive FSU Career Center in 1979 and 1990, respectively.)

Fourth, the program would attempt to develop information resources that could complement the work of professionals external to the system, such as financial aid advisers, personal counselors, and faculty or academic advisers. The career service center should not require a large professional staff.

Fifth, the program should strive to be innovative and to extend our knowledge about how to use information creatively in career services. Even though the program would address local needs, it would also seek to serve as a model for the offering of career services beyond this setting. I believed that the client needs addressed by CCIS were not unique to Florida State University. This research and development function seemed consistent with the mission of a graduate, research-oriented university.

Finally, the Valuing phase involved my personal commitment to build a professional career identity around this activity—to select and train staff, to write and conduct research in the area, to be vigilant in pursuing internal and external funds for the development of the program, and to become more deeply involved in learning about and implementing a career service using the principles of instructional systems design.

All of these choices involved making personal and organizational value commitments to a particular course of action, and at the same time deliberately not choosing other alternatives. Indeed, I assumed considerable risks. What if this new ISD algorithm for the design and development of career service did not work? It had not yet been applied to the counseling and guidance area. What if students did not come in? Could they and would they use self-help without the direct involvement of a professional counselor? What about the unintended effects from this intervention? Would students with low grade point averages come in and explore information about becoming a physician and then try to pursue that occupation as a career? What if the program failed? And for myself, could an academic career be successfully built around this activity with a reasonable chance for promotion and tenure?

Execution

In the spring of 1972, the vice president for student affairs mandated that a pilot career information program be developed and located in a residence hall. Consequently, I procured resources to support development costs from a variety of sources: furniture was donated from other student affairs offices; funds for two student assistants were allocated by the counseling center; the student government provided funds for audiovisual equipment and for listening and viewing carrels; an unpaid doctoral student looking for a dissertation project agreed to use an evaluation model to assess the impact of the pilot program; a professor of library science volunteered to have students in a cataloging class create an indexing system for our materials; the career placement office asked IBM to donate funds for furniture; the president's office provided $15,000 in additional operating funds; and the vice president provided funds for a half-time project coordinator. Six months were to be devoted to developing the pilot program, and another six months to testing it.

I secured funds and directed the development of five instructional modules (Reardon & Domkowski, 1977):

1. "CCIS Introduction," which included a slide-tape overview of the program goals and a user orientation to the program's operating procedures
2. "Decision Making," which included two slide-tapes on common myths about career decision making, a model strategy for making a career decision, and several booklets on career decision making
3. "Self-Assessment," which featured Holland's recently published Self-Directed Search as an activity for exploring interests and personal characteristics and for identifying occupations for further exploration
4. "Information Resources," which featured a card catalog and a small library of audiotaped occupational information interviews and faculty interviews on majors, a four-drawer cabinet of folders of occupational and academic department information, reference books on careers, and education directories
5. "Referral Resources," which included community and faculty resource directories

These basic modules have been modified over the years; at present, there are 16 modules that facilitate the development of the knowledge and skills identified in the CASVE model. [It is interesting to speculate how this start-up might be different in today's environment with the Internet and personal computers.]

The pilot program was formally launched in January 1973 and concluded in May 1973. Following a review of the evaluation report, the university established the Curricular-Career Information Service as an ongoing program in the fall of 1973. I opened a second CCIS center, in addition to the residence hall location, in the student union (Reardon, 1977) and made plans to establish a third center in an academic building on the opposite side of the campus. However, an unexpected series of budget and administrative crises from 1974 through 1979 eventually led to only a single CCIS center in 1979, which was located in the Department of Career Development Services. This new unit, which became the Career Center in 1984, included career placement and cooperative education; it is now located in the University Center building. However, in spite of these administrative changes, CCIS has maintained and enhanced its activities consistent with the original program mission and design. The CASVE problem-solving process has continued to guide the evolution of the program.

ONGOING PROGRAM DEVELOPMENT

The present scope and function of the career services program at the university is described in this section. The purpose is to show how a small career services program, developed by means of a systems approach over a 30-year period, has grown into and merged with a more complex university program with many varied products and services. The purpose is to illustrate how a "living" social system, in this case the CCIS career services program, has adapted to changing conditions in the external environment—that is, facility relocation, personnel, technology (Internet), and university structure. During this time, the use of the CASVE model has helped focus our efforts. We believe today that the same CASVE problem-solving heuristic model we use to address our organizational problems can be generalized to other organizational settings, including the public schools, community colleges, four-year colleges, universities, public libraries, and private corporations.

In this section, we provide an example of a mission statement for a career services program and discuss the nature of its development. The mission statement is a capsule statement of the philosophy of a social system. We then move to a description of the four alternative functional areas in a career services program and indicate where our Career Center is aligned on these four continua. Next, we examine the theory base for a program of career services—in our case, Holland's (1997) RIASEC theory and our own CIP theory (see our Web site at www.career.fsu.edu/techcenter/designing_career_services/). Finally, we examine the matter of fundraising, which is a concrete example of the application of the feedback loop in a social systems model, and two new program initiatives, electronic career portfolio and Web site redesign, which illustrate the operation of a living social system in a university environment.

Mission of the FSU Career Center

"The mission of the FSU Career Center is to provide comprehensive career services, train career services practitioners, conduct life/career development research, and disseminate information about life/career services and issues to the university community, the nation, and the world" (Florida State University, 2002, p. 6). The adoption of an explicit statement of 12 program goals, as well as 56 related performance objectives, is an additional indication of the comprehensive nature of the FSU Career Center. The *Career Center Manual* (Florida State University, 2002), used in staff training and management of the Center, includes over 60 pages of information about the philosophy, policies, and procedures of the Career Center. Space does not permit a description of the management and governance activities of the Center, but a copy of the manual is available at www.career.fsu.edu/techcenter/designing_career_services/practical_strategies/.

There are many benefits in aligning and integrating a career center with the larger mission of the university, in this case a graduate-oriented research university of over 33,000 students. The FSU Career Center has adopted and adhered to the mission of the university, which is centered on service, teaching, and research. Teaching both undergraduate and graduate students, research, and service to the local community, state, nation, and the world are the three traditional elements of a large research university such as FSU. At times, the Career Center has been referred to as a "teaching career center" (Lenz & Reardon, 1997), an indication of the intrinsic links between service, teaching, and research. As a result of the connection between these three areas of activity, the quality of services provided is augmented, and research and teaching benefit from practical application and analysis in a real service delivery setting (Lenz & Reardon, 1997). There are numerous positive outcomes resulting from the integration of service delivery, teaching, and research at the FSU Career

Center. The cooperation and collaboration among staff members at different levels promote new methods for integrating career services.

The composition of the professional staff of the FSU Career Center is reflective of the nature of the activities in which they are engaged. At present time, three faculty members, two faculty affiliates, and one university librarian are involved as staff members at the Career Center. The presence of five doctoral-level staff, including three licensed psychologists, contributes to the attainment of goals typically associated with faculty work. The staff also includes five National Certified Counselors and three National Certified Career Counselors. The concept of "seamless" service is facilitated by the involvement of individuals representative of the teaching and research elements of the university.

A Systems Perspective of the Mission

A large, residential, research university such as Florida State traditionally has a threefold mission: (a) teaching undergraduate and graduate students; (b) research; and (c) service to the local community, the state, the nation, and the world through professional associations, workshops, presentations, and so forth. Of these three mission areas, a career center most easily contributes to the *service mission,* especially to assisting current students and perhaps alumni. But a career center in a university has a unique, boundary-spanning role: It serves constituents outside the university, such as parents, employers, prospective students, and government agencies. Those of us who are involved in the design of a comprehensive career services program want to address the needs of the suprasystem in the development and operation of our program.

A systems approach suggests that a career center could interact with the suprasystem—namely, the university. The following are examples of how our Career Center as a social system supports the *teaching mission* of the university:

- Career Center staff teach 12 sections of a variable-credit, career planning class enrolling 100 to 350 students annually. CCIS modules are incorporated into the course, and Career Center resources serve as a course laboratory. Articles by Lee and Anthony (1974); Gerken, Reardon, and Bash (1988); Reardon and Regan (1981); and Reed, Reardon, Lenz, and Leierer (2001) describe the history, organization, and evaluation of the course.
- The Career Center supports undergraduate instruction by providing educational and career-advising assistance to help some students decide on which field of study they wish to pursue. For example, students enrolled in the Freshman Year Experience course spend one class period in the Career Center. Such services have been shown to increase the retention of students in postsecondary schools (Noel, Levitz, Saluri, & Associates, 1985).
- The Career Center supports graduate-level instruction by training 25–40 graduate students in career advising and counseling each year (Saunders, Reardon, & Lenz, 1999). The availability of practicum and internship students to deliver brief staff-assisted and individual case-managed interventions contributes to the service delivery mission of the Career Center. Besides internship and practicum training, the Career Center provides an opportunity for supervised research, supervised teaching, and directed individual studies for graduate students.

Figure 12.1 Career Center Continua

From "Integrating Service, Teaching, and Research in a Comprehensive University Career Center," by S. Vernick, J. Garis, and R. Reardon, 2000, *Career Planning & Adult Development, 16*, p. 9. Copyright [2000] by the Career Planning & Adult Development Network, 4965 Sierra R, San Jose, CA 95132. Reprinted with permission.

- Cooperative education (a related Career Center program) provides field or employer-based learning experiences that are directly related to the instructional mission of the university. Placement and co-op staff contacts with employers provide access to external teaching resources for regular university faculty.

This Career Center has also made a contribution to the *research mission* of the university. The faculty of FSU place a great emphasis on scholarly creativity. Recognizing the importance of research at Florida State, CCIS sought to establish its credibility, both internally and externally, through the inclusion of research in its mission. More than 35 scholarly, peer-reviewed, or refereed articles on various aspects of career services have been published. In addition, dozens of presentations describing various aspects of the program have been made over the years at state and national meetings.

But research, production, and the procurement of external grants function as a double-edged sword for a career services program—they can take energy and attention away from direct services to students. To avoid this danger, virtually all of the external grants and gifts obtained by the Career Center since 1978 have ultimately been used to provide better client services; some grant opportunities were not pursued because they would conflict with the primary service mission of the Career Center. Grant funds were limited because they are generally not provided to a public institution to provide basic client services; grant-funding agencies think that the university should be providing such services out of its own internal funds.

The following are some examples of the ways that the Career Center has contributed to the research mission of the university:

- It served as a field test site for the adult versions of SIGI PLUS (Educational Testing Service, 2002) and DISCOVER (American College Testing Program, 2002), with the help of Project LEARN and the W. K. Kellogg Foundation.
- It developed a career center evaluation model with funding provided by a state grant (Reardon, Domkowski, & Jackson, 1980).
- It demonstrated the efficacy of a career planning program for visually impaired students with funding provided by the U.S. Office of Education (White, Reardon, Barker, & Carlson, 1979).
- It has conducted research on the comparative effectiveness of the paper, computer, and Internet versions of the Self-Directed Search (Lumsden, Sampson, Reardon, & Lenz, 2002; Reardon & Loughead, 1988).
- It has supported dissertation research by more than 15 doctoral students on the career behavior of college students, the effectiveness of career interventions, and other topics.
- It assisted in the creation of a novel research and development center, the Center for the Study of Technology in Counseling and Career Development, which provides a vehicle for research on the study of computer-based career interventions and the application of Cognitive Information Processing theory (see www.career.fsu.edu/techcenter/).
- It has demonstrated the feasibility of telephone-based career counseling outreach from CCIS (Roach, Reardon, Alexander, & Cloudman, 1983).

In summary, the CASVE problem-solving model and the use of instructional systems design have provided conceptual schemata for designing and implementing career services that offer basic career services, teaching, and research. We believe such theoretical bases can help create and maintain a viable career service center. The CASVE cycle and ISD have already been discussed. A third paradigm, strategic planning, which helps a career center staff prepare for the future, is discussed in Chapter 15.

Program Structure and Function

The delivery of career services in college or university settings can be categorized along four continua, as outlined in Figure 12.1 (Vernick, Garis, & Reardon, 2000). The *first continuum* reflects the degree to which the career center holds the mission for providing career development services through career advising, counseling, assessment, and information. At many institutions, the mission for career counseling and assessment resides in the student counseling center rather than the career center. In such instances, the career center may provide assistance with employability skills but does not offer programs for academic/career choice or career indecision. Such a career center would fall at the far left of the career development continuum. At other institutions, counseling and assessment for career choice may be shared among a variety of offices, such as the student counseling center or academic advising center. Such offices would fall in the middle of this continuum. Finally, some career centers include advising, counseling, assessment, and provision of information supporting career decision making in their mission and fall to the right of the continuum on this dimension. The mission of the FSU Career Center is characterized by complete involvement in all facets of career development services and, therefore, falls to the far right on this continuum.

The *second continuum* addresses the degree to which the career center provides experiential career education services as part of its mission—for example, externships, internships, and cooperative education programs. Part-time, work-study, volunteer, or summer job programs could also be included in this area. At many institutions, internship or cooperative education programs reside in academic units rather than career centers, placing them to the left on this continuum. Commonly, the institutional mission for delivering experiential education is shared among colleges, academic departments, financial aid, and career centers. Such programs would fall in the middle of the continuum. Fewer schools located to the right of the model have career centers shouldering the complete responsibility for experiential education programs. The FSU Career Center is charged with the responsibility for cooperative education and internship services through its Career Experience Opportunities (CEO) unit, but other academic departments also provide internship programs. The Financial Aid Office has the responsibility for administering part-time jobs and work-study, and the Center for Civic Education and Service assists students with volunteer opportunities. Therefore, given these departmental assignments of responsibilities for experiential career education, the FSU Career Center would fall between center and right on this continuum.

Placement, or employer relations services, shown on the *third continuum*, range from decentralized to centralized. Many institutions have several decentralized placement offices residing in academic colleges and fall to the left on this continuum. Other institutions have fully centralized career centers charged with the college or university-wide mission for placement. Commonly, schools fall toward the middle of this continuum with the career center providing most placement and campus recruiting services, although certain "vocationally oriented colleges," such as business or engineering, have their own placement offices. It is common for professional schools—for example, law or MBA programs—to have separate placement services. At FSU, placement services are essentially centralized across the university in the Career Center. One Career Center satellite placement office is located in the College of Business, and another satellite office is in the College of Engineering. The latter is jointly administered by Florida A&M University and FSU. Therefore, the FSU Career Center would fall between center and right on this continuum.

Finally, the degree to which the career center is funded by the institution can be plotted on a *fourth continuum.* At some colleges and universities, the operating budget for career services is not funded by the institution. These career centers must generate their funding base completely through charges and fees to students, alumni, and employers, as well as through fund-raising. At other institutions, the career center operating budget is fully supported by the institution, and any income from fees or contributions is used as enhancement funds. Like many career services, the FSU Career Center receives significant institutional/state funds but charges some fees to students, alumni, and employers to augment operating costs, especially those related to providing comprehensive services with technological applications. This combination of funding places the FSU Career Center between center and right on this continuum.

College and university career services falling on the right side of the four continua reviewed would generally be considered to be comprehensive career centers and would offer the following core programs and services:

1. Career advising and intake
2. Individual and group career counseling
3. Assessment and computer-assisted guidance
4. Career information
5. Career planning classes for credit
6. Career education outreach
7. Experiential education
8. Career expositions
9. On-campus recruiting
10. Job listings and resume referral services

The FSU Career Center offers these core services and monitors the level of most of these programs with three-year activity-level comparisons.

Theory-Based Services

The FSU Career Center has incorporated Holland's typological theory of career development into many of its programs and materials. The Self-Directed Search (SDS) (Holland, 1994) is used in three levels of service delivery: (a) self-help services, (b) brief staff-assisted services, and (c) individual case-managed services (Sampson & Reardon, 1998; Sampson, Peterson, Reardon, & Lenz, 2000). An important element of Holland's theory is the idea that all individuals are characterized by a personal career theory (PCT). A PCT is "a collection of beliefs, ideas, assumptions, and knowledge that guides individuals as they choose occupations or fields of study, explains why they persist in them, and is used by people as they go about making career decisions" (Reardon & Lenz, 1999, p. 103). At the FSU Career Center, career advisers and professional staff consider an individual's PCT in assessing the client's level of needs and structuring career interventions.

Career advisers and professional staff use Holland's RIASEC theory and the SDS as lenses through which they may gain a better understanding of each individual client's PCT. Holland's schema permits a relatively quick and easy method by which to explain the process of matching the person and the environment, and a method by which practitioners may assess an individual's readiness for setting his or her PCT into action in the career development process (Reardon & Lenz, 1999).

A second career theory is also used extensively in the FSU Career Center. Cognitive Information Processing theory (CIP) was developed by faculty members at the FSU Career Center (Peterson, Sampson, Lenz, & Reardon, 2002; Peterson, Sampson, & Reardon, 1991; Peterson, Sampson, Reardon, & Lenz, 1996; Sampson, Lenz, Reardon, & Peterson, 1999; Sampson et al., 2000). The goal of the theory is to teach individuals new methods of career problem solving and decision making (Lenz & Reardon, 1997). This theory is applied in practice at the Career Center, especially in career counseling and advising. Both *Career Development and Services: A Cognitive Approach* (Reardon, Lenz, Sampson, & Peterson, 2000a, 2000b) and the *Career Thoughts Inventory* (Sampson, Peterson, Lenz, Reardon, & Saunders, 1996) are the result of the development and application of CIP theory. The manner in which career theory is applied to both service delivery and training is an additional manifestation of the three-part mission of the FSU Career Center. Information on key elements of the CIP approach is available at www.career.fsu.edu/techcenter/designing_career_services/ and www.career.fsu.edu/techcenter/designing_career_services/practical_strategies/.

Fund-Raising

FSU Career Center staff are involved in multiple efforts to develop proposals for external funding. Such gifts are tangible evidence of the value accorded to the career program services and products in the external environment. If the social system is functioning well, then positive feedback will come in the form of gifts and rewards for the works produced. These gifts from alumni, employers, and friends of the Career Center, in turn, provide resources for services to students and community members, as well as to employers. Fund-raising programs include Placement Partners, Named Rooms, the Career Advisor Scholarship Program, Friends of the Career Center, and other programs for major gifts. Employing organizations may elect to become a Placement Partner (www.career.fsu.edu/placement_partner.html) by contributing to the Career Center, or they may have a room in the Center named for their organization. The Career Advisor Scholarship Program is aimed at individuals wishing to provide support to graduate students pursuing careers in the field of career counseling and human resources. This program is a unique and important initiative of the Career Center because it helps fund the education of students who will someday become professionals in the field of career development. It includes four endowed funds with named scholarships. Over the last 30 years, external gifts to sponsor Career Center initiatives have totaled over $500,000, with more than $235,000 provided to scholarship endowments.

Current Projects

Career Portfolio In 1998, FSU's president invited the Career Center to consider development of a program to assist students in chronicling and communicating professional skills to employers. In response, the Career Center, in cooperation with the university Administrative Information Systems unit (AIS), developed an on-line FSU Career Portfolio system (Lumsden, Garis, Reardon, Unger, & Arkin, 2001). This on-line service (a) educates students on the importance of developing professionally relevant skills throughout college while providing information regarding the array of programs, activities, and services available on and off campus to develop these skills; (b) provides a system for students to chronicle their skills throughout their collegiate experience; and (c) allows students to develop an on-line portfolio available to employers or graduate/professional schools. Preview materials and documentation about the FSU Career Portfolio system are available at www.career.fsu.edu/portfolio/index.html.

After an introduction to the FSU Career Portfolio system, students can document up to 10 skills relevant to their individual experiences. Skill areas in this system include (a) Communication, (b) Creativity, (c) Critical Thinking, (d) Leadership, (e) Life Management, (f) Research/Project Development, (g) Social Responsibility, (h) Teamwork, (i) Technical/Scientific, and an (j) Optional Skill directly related to the student's academic program or career goals. Categories of experiences supporting development of the above skills include (a) Courses, (b) Jobs/Internships, (c) Service/Volunteer Work, (d) Memberships/Activities, and (e) Interests/Life Experiences. Students can manage the FSU Career Portfolio with support from career advisers/counselors, academic advisers, and faculty/staff advisers to student organizations. The student can then make the resulting portfolio available on-line to employers or graduate/professional schools.

Web Site Redesign Tech Center staff have collaborated with the Career Center staff on a project to redesign the Career Center Web site. This redesign features a need-based format (Sampson, 1999; Sampson et al., 2001) that provides a more user-friendly Web page design. The Career Center Web site is an integral part of service delivery at the Career Center because it provides much information for all groups who may seek the Center's services. In effect, the Career Center is adding a "virtual career center" to the existing facility. As such, a user-focused site that is easy to navigate adds to the quality of the Center's service delivery. Information about the conceptual principles undergirding this Web site design is available at www.career.fsu.edu/techcenter/computer_applications/internet_based_models.html.

SOME PERSONAL REFLECTIONS

I have learned some lessons (and will no doubt learn more) from this experience of developing a career services program.

- Clients will take a great deal of responsibility for finding and using career information if helpful people and an effective career information delivery system are available. Career counselors can confidently promote self-help methods.
- The instructional systems design model provided a useful guide for designing instructional units in which human, print, and electronic resources are coordinated to help clients achieve learning objectives.
- Career clients want information—they view it as absolutely essential to career problem solving—and a good system, encompassing both physical and virtual formats, must be attractively packaged to present it to them.

- Delivery of career information via print, computer, or other media (as opposed to person-to-person delivery) is attractive to many administrators; the hardware is tangible evidence that a system exists, and it facilitates program accountability. An effective career programs delivery system needs to connect with the goals of the larger organization in as many ways as possible for both strategic political reasons and pragmatic service delivery reasons.
- And on the personal level, the design and implementation of a career services program such as CCIS and the comprehensive Career Center at Florida State University can become an all-encompassing life and career venture where opportunities continually emerge for the application of creativity and vision.

SUMMARY

This chapter provided a personal case study of the 30-year involvement of one counselor and institution in implementing a career service delivery system to meet the specific needs of clients with certain characteristics. This case history showed how the personal and institutional commitment of time and resources, together with a problem-solving approach using the CASVE cycle and an instructional systems design (ISD) model, led to the creation of CCIS, a career services program. The successful operation of this program in the larger environment was traced to the ongoing development of the larger Career Center at FSU. Our belief is that the CASVE problem-solving paradigm and ISD can be successfully applied to the design, development, and evaluation of career programs in other organizational settings.

GETTING THE MOST BENEFIT FROM READING THIS CHAPTER

To effectively learn the material in this chapter, complete one or more of the following activities:

- From a review of the personal case history on the development of the career services program in this chapter, identify three of the most critical or important assumptions, premises, values, or environmental influences described by the author that you think had a bearing on the program's success. Name one thing that might have been important that the author did not mention. Compare your lists with those of two classmates, and determine where you agree or disagree and why.
- "The establishment and operation of a successful career service center has more to do with history and with external, environmental forces than with a person." Prepare a case for or against this proposition, and debate the issue, with two teams taking opposing views.
- Identify an organizational setting different from the one in this chapter, perhaps an elementary school, high school, library, adult education center, or factory. Work with a team of classmates to construct a hypothetical case study about the development of a career service center for the setting chosen. Use the conceptual frameworks and guides (such as CASVE and ISD) employed in this chapter to

guide your work. Outline the results of your work, and share them with your class and instructor.

- Identify a person who has developed a successful guidance or human services program over a period of years. Using the personal case history in this chapter as a guide, interview this person to learn more about the personal commitment and environmental resources needed to develop a successful program.

REFERENCES

American College Testing Program. (2002). DISCOVER for colleges and adults [Computer program]. Hunt Valley, MD: Author.

Bronfenbrenner, U. (1966). *The ecology of education.* Keynote address given at the annual convention of the American Educational Research Association, San Francisco.

Brown, W. E. (1965). Student-to-student counseling for academic adjustment. *The Personnel and Guidance Journal, 18,* 821–830.

Burck, H. D. (1984). Facilitating career development: Past events, current scenes, and the future. In H. Burck & R. Reardon (Eds.), *Career development interventions* (pp. 5–24). Springfield, IL: Charles C Thomas.

Chick, J. M. (1970). *Innovations in the use of career information.* Boston: Houghton Mifflin.

Educational Testing Service. (2002). *SIGI PLUS* [Computer program]. Princeton, NJ: Author.

Florida State University Career Center. (2002). *Career center manual.* From the Center for the Study of Technology in Counseling and Career Development Web site [On-line]. www.career.fsu.edu /techcenter/designing_career_services/practical_strategies/.

Gerken, D., Reardon, R., & Bash, R. (1988). Revitalizing a career course: The gender roles infusion. *Journal of Career Development, 14,* 269–278.

Hale, L. (1973–1974). A bold, new blueprint for career planning and placement. *Journal of College Placement, 34* (2), 34–41; (3), 68–76.

Holland, J. L. (1994). *Self-Directed Search* (4th ed.). Odessa, FL: Psychological Assessment Resources.

Holland, J. H. (1997). *Making vocational choices.* Odessa, FL: Psychological Assessment Resources.

Holland, J. H., Hollifield, J. H., Nafziger, D. H., & Helms, S. T. (1972). *A guide to the self-directed career program: A practical and inexpensive vocational guidance system* (Report No. 126). Baltimore, MD: Johns Hopkins University Press.

Kaufman, R. (1972). *Educational system planning.* Englewood Cliffs, NJ: Prentice Hall.

Kerr, B. A. (1982). The setting of career counseling. *The Vocational Guidance Quarterly, 30,* 210–218.

Lee, J., & Anthony, W. (1974). An innovative university career planning course. *Journal of College Placement, 35,* 59–60.

Lenz, J. G., & Reardon, R. C. (1997). Improving career services: A student affairs and academic affairs collaboration. *Australian Journal of Career Development,* 6 (3), 3–4.

Lumsden, J., Garis, J., Reardon, R., Unger, M., & Arkin, S. (2001). Developing an on-line career portfolio. *Journal of Career Planning and Employment,* 62 (1), 33–38. Also available at www.naceweb .org/pubs/journal/fa01/lumsden.htm.

Lumsden, J. A., Sampson, J. P., Jr., Reardon, R. C., & Lenz, J. G. (2002). *A comparison study of the paper, personal computer (PC), and Internet versions of Holland's Self-Directed Search* (Technical Report No. 30) [On-line]. Available: www.career.fsu.edu/techcenter/designing_career_services /Holland_theory/.

Magoon, T., Milburn, J., & Celio, D. (1971). Multiple message information in a university counseling center (1970). In T. Magoon & T. B. Scott (Eds.), *Innovations in counseling.* Washington, DC: American Personnel and Guidance Association Press.

Morrill, W. H., & Banning, J. H. (1973). *Counseling outreach: A survey of practices.* Boulder, CO: Western Interstate Commission for Higher Education.

Noel, L., Levitz, R., Saluri, D., & Associates (1985). *Increasing student retention.* San Francisco: Jossey-Bass.

Parsons, E. (1909). *Choosing a vocation.* Boston: Houghton Mifflin.

Peterson, G. W., Sampson, J. P., Jr., Lenz, J. G., & Reardon, R. C. (2002). A cognitive information processing approach to career problem solving and decision making. In D. Brown (Ed.), *Career choice and development* (4th ed.) (pp. 312–369). San Francisco: Jossey-Bass.

Peterson, G. W., Sampson, J. P., Jr., & Reardon, R. C. (1991). *Career development and services: A cognitive approach.* Pacific Grove, CA: Brooks/Cole.

Peterson, G. W., Sampson, J. P., Jr., Reardon, R. C., & Lenz, J. G. (1996). Becoming career problem solvers and decision makers: A cognitive information processing approach. In D. Brown & L. Brooks (Eds.), *Career choice and development* (3rd ed.) (pp. 423–475). San Francisco: Jossey-Bass.

Reardon, R. (1973). The counselor and career information services. *Journal of College Student Personnel, 14,* 495–500.

Reardon, R. (1977). Campus location and the effectiveness of a career information center. *Journal of College Student Personnel, 18,* 240–241.

Reardon, R., & Domkowski, D. (1977). Building instruction into a career information center. *The Vocational Guidance Quarterly, 25,* 274–278.

Reardon, R., Domkowski, D., & Jackson, E. (1980). Career center evaluation methods: A case study. *The Vocational Guidance Quarterly, 29,* 150–158.

Reardon, R., & Lenz, J. G. (1999). Holland's theory and career assessment. *Journal of Vocational Behavior (Special Issue), 55,* 102–113.

Reardon, R. C., Lenz, J. G., Sampson, J. P., Jr., & Peterson, G. W. (2000a). *Career development and planning: A comprehensive approach.* Pacific Grove, CA: Brooks/Cole.

Reardon, R. C., Lenz, J. G., Sampson, J. P., Jr., & Peterson, G. W. (2000b). *Student handbook for career development and planning: A comprehensive approach.* Pacific Grove, CA: Brooks/Cole.

Reardon, R., & Loughead, T. (1988). A comparison of paper-pencil and computer versions of the Self-Directed Search. *Journal of Counseling and Development, 67,* 249–252.

Reardon, R., & Minor, C. (1975). Revitalizing the career information service. *The Personnel and Guidance Journal, 54,* 169–171.

Reardon, R., & Regan, K. (1981). Process evaluation of a career planning course. *The Vocational Guidance Quarterly, 29,* 265–269.

Reed, C., Reardon, R., Lenz, J., & Leierer, S. (2001). Reducing negative career thoughts with a career course. *The Career Development Quarterly, 50,* 158–167.

Roach, D., Reardon, R., Alexander, J., & Cloudman, D. (1983). Career counseling by telephone. *Journal of College Student Personnel, 24,* 71–76.

Sampson, J. P., Jr. (1999). Integrating Internet-based distance guidance with services provided in career centers. *The Career Development Quarterly, 47,* 243–254.

Sampson, J. P., Jr., Carr, D. L., Panke, J., Arkin, S., Minvielle, M., & Vernick, S. H. (2001). *Design strategies for need-based Internet Web sites in counseling* (Technical Report No. 28) [On-line]. Available: www.career.fsu.edu/documents/technical reports/Technical Report 28/TR-28.htm.

Sampson, J. P., Jr., Lenz, J. G., Reardon, R. C., & Peterson, G. W. (1999). A cognitive information processing approach to employment problem solving and decision making. *The Career Development Quarterly, 48,* 3–18.

Sampson, J. P., Jr., Peterson, G. W., Lenz, J. G., Reardon, R. C., & Saunders, D. E. (1996). *Career Thoughts Inventory.* Odessa, FL: Psychological Assessment Resources.

Sampson, J. P., Jr., Peterson, G. W., Reardon, R. C., & Lenz, J. G. (2000). Using readiness assessment to improve career services: A cognitive information processing approach. *The Career Development Quarterly, 49,* 146–174.

Sampson, J. P., Jr., & Reardon, R. C. (1998). Maximizing staff resources in meeting the needs of job seekers in one-stop centers. *Journal of Employment Counseling, 35,* 50–68.

Saunders, D. E., Reardon, R. C., & Lenz, J. G. (1999). Specialty training for career counselors: Twenty-five years at Florida State University. *Career Planning and Adult Development Journal, 15,* 23–33.

Tiedeman, D. V. (1968). *Information system for vocational decisions* (Annual Report). Cambridge, MA: Harvard University, Graduate School of Education.

U.S. Department of Health, Education, and Welfare, Office of Education. (1969). *Computer-based vocational guidance systems.* Washington, DC: U.S. Government Printing Office.

Vernick, S. H., Garis, J., & Reardon, R. C. (2000). Integrating service, teaching, and research in a comprehensive university career center. *Career Planning and Adult Development Journal, 16,* 7–24.

White, E., Reardon, R., Barker, S., & Carlson, A. (1979). Adapting a career center for the blind. *The Personnel and Guidance Journal, 58,* 292–295.

The Career Resource Library: Development and Management Issues

CHAPTER 13

This chapter applies strategies used in professional libraries to the design and use of a career library. After reviewing this chapter, the reader should be able to (a) identify various aspects of developing and managing a comprehensive career resource library, (b) consider how an organization's philosophy, goals, and objectives influence all aspects of library development and management, (c) distinguish the complementary roles of counselor and librarian in a comprehensive career library, and (d) recognize the importance of using a career classification scheme to organize library resources. The chapter is organized as follows:

- Comprehensive Career Resource Libraries
- Administration
- Technical and User Services
- Summary
- Getting the Most Benefit from Reading This Chapter

COMPREHENSIVE CAREER RESOURCE LIBRARIES

The primary purpose of a career resource library in a career service center should be to provide relevant, accessible, timely career information to help individuals solve career problems and make career decisions. To effectively

---

Chapter authored by Susan Epstein and Kirsten Kinsley, who share the position of librarian at the Florida State University Career Center.

manage a modern career resource library, the resource manager (who may be a professional librarian in large centers or a counselor in small centers) must constantly gather, evaluate, systematize, store, retrieve, and update career information. In a comprehensive career resource library, these functions may even require special knowledge and training. By the term ***comprehensive career resource library,*** we mean the collection of a wide range of career information resources, covering varied subjects that are organized for easy access. Such a library also provides varied media delivery options (such as print, video, interactive CD-ROMs, etc.) and is staffed by both professionals and paraprofessionals in a large, multipurpose physical space.

The establishment of a comprehensive career resource library raises some difficult questions. How does one design a career information library? Where should the library be located? Who should be in charge of the library—a career counselor or a professional librarian? A discussion of these questions and other issues regarding the development and management of a comprehensive career library is the focus of this chapter. An in-depth treatment of career resource libraries is included in this text so that the reader will be prepared to function in any career library, no matter how complex. The chapter draws on the authors' experiences and vision regarding the operation of a comprehensive library to support a multimedia career information delivery system; an earlier work by Peterson, Sampson, and Reardon (1991); and *Small Libraries: Organization and Operation* (Sager, 2000).

ADMINISTRATION

We begin by exploring some of the administrative issues associated with the operation of a comprehensive career resource library, including library governance and organization, staffing and human resources, and collection development policies.

Library Governance/Organization

Ideally, a career resource library's location and physical layout, as well as its development and management, should reflect the goals and objectives of the career service center it supports. The career resource library is a type of special library, which serves a specific organization or institution. Special libraries "provide focused information to a defined group of users on an ongoing basis to further the mission and goals of their parent organizations" (Porter & Christianson, 1997, p. 2) and seek "to gather all of the experiences available with regard to that institution's problems, to classify it [sic] in such a way as to make it [sic] quickly available, to digest and prepare the same in usable form, to study the actual problems which confront the institution, and to attempt to bring the information gathered to the right man at the right place, so that it may function in the work of the institution which it serves" (Lapp, 1996, p. 261).

The location and floor plan of the career resource library are important considerations in the delivery of career information services. The choice might be to locate the library within or adjacent to the main library, where it can be directly supported by the existing library staff and services, or it might be located in the heart of the career resource center. Minor (1984) noted that the location of a career library can have a major effect on its use, and it should be located in an area that is easily accessible to clients as well as to counselors. The library's physical layout ideally will also provide easy access to different types of library resources, which should be located on shelves, in carrels, on tables, and so forth to facilitate their use. Concerns such as providing space for the changing balance of print and electronic resources, accessibility to resources for people with disabilities, and proximity of staff offices to the library must also be addressed when deciding on a library's floor plan. Sampson (1999) provided an overview of design considerations, including furnishings, environmental concerns, and equipment, which may be helpful in planning effective facilities. Several books (Dancik & Shroder, 1995; Fraley & Anderson, 1990; Freifeld & Masyr, 1991; Mount, 1988) contain practical guidelines for planning library space. Reviewing samples of career and other special library floor plans may also generate ideas and images for developing a unique library layout to support institutional goals and objectives. For example, the Florida State University (FSU) Career Center (2000) Library's floor plan allows easy access for self-directed use, as well as for supervised groups such as classes. Other special library floor plans may be found in Kreizman (1999) and Mount (1988).

The role that a career resource library plays in the career service center depends on the nature of the center and thus may vary greatly from library to library. Representative staff members from throughout the career service center can provide vision and direction for developing and managing a comprehensive career resource library. A library team, or committee, may be formed to create or review library goals, objectives, policies, and procedures. This diverse group, in addition to its advisory and/or administrative function(s), also serves as a liaison between library personnel and the overall career service center. At The FSU Career Center Library, the library committee determines policies to review the collection and recommends resources or types of resources to improve the collection. The librarian originally chaired the committee, but currently another staff member performs that function so that the librarian may function as a consultant. Recent activities of the committee include creating a Web site collection policy and reviewing professional collection resources.

Human Resources Management

To effectively provide career information services, three roles must be considered: (a) counselor, (b) resource manager or librarian, and (c) technical assistant. Depending on the size of the service, these roles may be performed by one or many staff members. Ideally, due to the different level and type of education required for each role, an information service should have both a professionally trained librarian and one or more career counselors on staff. The librarian, in order to accomplish technical and reference objectives, should have an assistant to help clients locate resources, answer basic questions about the collection, shelve books, and process library materials.

Paraprofessionals can also be used extensively in comprehensive career centers and career libraries (Lenz & Panke, 2001; McKenzie & Manoogian-O'Dell, 1988). In colleges and universities, paraprofessionals may include graduate interns and assistants from counseling or student personnel training programs or undergraduate students with majors in business, psychology, or social science. The training and supervision of paraprofessionals is a matter of concern. Johnston and Hansen (1981) described a complex, differentiated staff of peer paraprofessionals in career services programs at the University of Missouri. Axelrod, Drier, Kimmel, and Sechler (1977) also discussed a differentiated staffing plan for a career resource center, including descriptions of professional, paraprofessional, and clerical staff positions. The reader may also wish to review the paraprofessional training program described by Lenz (2000) in *Paraprofessionals in Career Services: The Florida State University Model.*

Career counselors help clients make the best use of information to solve career problems and make decisions. Sometimes the counseling role overlaps the librarian role, especially when an information search interacts with the counseling process (such as the clarification of career planning problems and issues). Sometimes the librarian role overlaps the counseling role; for example, in many public libraries, employment information and assistance are available to adult patrons who are victims of structural unemployment caused by the decline of some industries. Do librarians offer career self-assessments to unemployed patrons who want to find out how their interests might relate to new career fields in demand? What about self-help books or computer-assisted career guidance systems available in some libraries? These issues raise complex questions about the professional functions of librarians and counselors in the career services area, and they also draw attention to the need for organizations to develop policies that clarify mutual professional responsibilities.

Librarians are specifically trained to operate information centers, including specialized collections such as career libraries. They are experts in setting up systems to help people locate and retrieve information resources. A comprehensive career resource library, which supports the development of career problem-solving skills, will likely require the services of a professional librarian. This assistance may be in the form of periodic review of the service by a technical services librarian or, in some cases, the employment of a full-time, professional librarian. As the scope of a career service center increases, in terms of either function or resources (or both), there is a greater need for the specialized role of a librarian. The more a counselor is required to assume the resource manager role, the more he or she should consult a professional librarian when creating a career information system.

Counselors and librarians each make unique contributions in offering comprehensive career information services; and where both are present in the organization, collaboration is essential. On the one hand, the librarian's role focuses on technical procedures for acquiring, cataloging, arranging, displaying, securing, updating, operating, and evaluating the career information materials in the library collection. Librarians also assist clients in locating and retrieving information. Balancing technical and reference responsibilities may be the librarian's greatest challenge. On the other hand, the counselor's role calls for helping clients use information for solving career problems or making career decisions. Thus, in comprehensive career information libraries, the roles of librarian and counselor may be complementary.

There are also several practical reasons for counselors and librarians to collaborate in organizations where they work in separate areas of service. Public schools and colleges budget special or categorical dollars expressly for the purchase of library and media materials, and if these funds are earmarked for expensive hardcover books, films or videotapes, computer software, or subscription services, a librarian might agree to allocate some of these funds for career resources. Some schools, especially community colleges, have located their career counseling program, including counselor offices, in buildings that house the college library. In these situations, the career library could exist as a subunit of the larger library and hence share in the same budget allocation. Because libraries are designed to serve many persons at once, they are often open evenings or on weekends and have procedures to help prevent the loss of materials. These features can increase the use of career information resources.

Chapter 2 presented a hierarchy of information processing domains in career decision making. Librarians can be of special assistance in helping individuals develop ways of organizing information about occupations. In Cognitive Information Processing (CIP) terms, they can help develop schemata in the respective knowledge domains. Additionally, librarians may help foster the development of problem-solving and decision-making skills. Counselors and librarians should cooperate to integrate the career information search with the development of self-knowledge, occupational knowledge, decision-making skills, and metacognitions. Thus, the information processing paradigm can serve as a framework to describe the respective functions of librarians and counselors in the modern comprehensive career information library.

Orientation and training of library personnel, whether they are counselors, librarians, or technical staff, must be thorough and continuous in order to provide the best library service possible. Depending on the number and type of resources and organization systems used within the library, staff development activities will require time for effective learning. Orientation and training activities should be hands-on, reflect realistic staff-client interactions, and help the staff become as self-sufficient as possible. Developing one or more library training and procedure manuals can document staff development activities and increase consistency in providing effective service.

Career resource managers, due to the changing nature of both libraries and the field of career development, should devote substantial time to professional development activities. These include continuing-education courses that help a career resource manager keep up to date with new technology and gather helpful tools for the management of career resources. Belonging to professional associations, such as the Career Resource Managers Association (CRMA), Special Libraries Association, or American Libraries Association, allows managers to discuss pertinent issues with networks of other professionals. For example, using the CRMA's mailing list, a resource manager may send and receive e-mail to find out what resources are used by other managers regarding certain subject areas. Professional associations also offer workshops and conferences, some even on-line.

Collection Development Policy

The library's collection development policy lays out the library's plan for effectively meeting the information needs of its service clientele and allows the career resource manager to make decisions that truly carry out the library's mission. Specific library goals and objectives shape the collection development policy, whose scope "describes in detail the subject areas and formats collected" (Coughlin & Gertzog, 1992, p. 186). Each library's policy should be unique, as is each library's clientele. A collection development policy precisely articulates who selects which resources, what kinds of resources are selected, and for whom they are selected (Coughlin & Gertzog, 1992). In addition, the policy includes details on collection maintenance and timetables for a periodic and systematic evaluation and review of resources in the collection, and guides the career resource manager to retain or weed/discard materials. Conducting an inventory of what resources are current, out of date, and in need of replacement is a part of this process. A written policy can help ensure that consistent criteria are used to develop and maintain resources so that the needs of the users are effectively met (Coughlin & Gertzog, 1992). The collection development policy is ultimately influenced by the overall philosophy of the library. For example, the FSU Career Center collection development policy reflects the fact that our library is open to community members as well as students and is a noncirculating, self-help career resource library. Additional factors to consider in the collection of materials for a career library are described by Brown (2003).

TECHNICAL AND USER SERVICES

We continue our exploration of issues associated with the operation of a comprehensive career resource library by focusing on the processes that give clients access to library resources. These activities include the acquiring and cataloging of career resources, also known as technical services, and providing user services, including reference and circulation.

Acquisitions

The acquisitions process involves ordering, discarding, and replacing print or multimedia resources. In essence, acquiring resources follows and puts into practice the goals and objectives of a collection development policy (Coughlin & Gertzog, 1992). The collection development policy can guide the career resource manager's acquisitions activities and also provide continuity of service by guiding future career resource managers. Resources may be collected in a multitude of formats based on the subject area, scope of the collection, and client preference. They may be free, given as gifts, or purchased. Possible formats include books, paper files, periodicals/ magazines, videos, CDs, Web sites, audiotapes, and computer software. The choice of medium involves decisions about the type of equipment purchased for the library.

Aside from handling the continuous stream of resource requests from clients, counselors, and other staff, the career resource manager must replace missing items and order new editions of tried-and-true resources. The resource manager must address many issues. For example, in an educational setting, the resource manager might consider the following: What areas of study are offered at the university or college where the library is located? What items are heavily used and frequently requested? Where are the gaps in the collection? What formats are needed? What is the most affordable means to gather resources? Ideally, a task force of staff and counselors may address the aforementioned questions and even review recent publication catalogs to help select new resources. All staff should be involved in acquiring career information from miscellaneous sources, such as newspaper and magazine articles, expired job notices, information interviews, or employer literature. Once materials have been identified, the next step is to evaluate their appropriateness for inclusion in the library collection. Evaluation is a critical step because clients expect to find accurate, current, attractive, and comprehensive information in a career library. Reviews of career materials in various professional publications can be a valuable resource for career resource managers.

The evaluation of career materials involves the application of professional standards to the selection of career information, as well as input from counselors and clients. Circulation statistics, user surveys, and on-site studies can give the career resource manager valuable guidance in the purchase of materials. The National Career Development Association (NCDA) (2001b) provides both general and content guidelines to evaluate career and occupational information. The NCDA (2001a, 2001c) has also created guidelines for evaluating multimedia resources. Career information that does not meet professional standards should be used with caution.

When ordering materials, the resource manager checks to see whether or not a resource is already in the collection, then determines the most recent available edition of the item and which vendor can supply it. Coughlin and Gertzog (1992) recommended that small libraries find a vendor for bulk orders because it is less time-consuming and expensive, rather than order resources through many different agencies. Maintaining a publisher file may be useful to collect, organize, and store ads and publishers' catalogs for new or replacement materials. It may be organized alphabetically by publisher and/or by specialty topics, such as occupations, job hunting, or industry. A spreadsheet file for ongoing subscriptions and one-time orders of print and multimedia resources may be helpful for verifying the order status of resources, showing renewal dates for subscriptions, and keeping costs within a certain budget. Once the received item has been confirmed and recorded, it is ready for integration into the collection.

Subscriptions in a career resource library may be in the form of newspapers, magazines, occupational briefs, directories, or job opportunity listings. When deciding whether to order a print subscription, obtaining a sample issue can be very informative. On-line subscriptions generally have a user name, password, and provisions to restrict the use and distribution of log-in information; a policy on how to handle these types of resources can assure providers that only those affiliated with the career resource center have access to their service. To ensure that all subscriptions get renewed in a timely manner, it may be helpful to set one or two times each year for renewals and use a spreadsheet for subscriptions, showing renewal dates and costs.

Once resources have been acquired, they should be integrated into a collection that has been organized for staff and client access. An information management system can provide the structure necessary to keep track of the collection and ensure the availability of a resource. To be most effective, the information system should be based on a classification scheme that meets the needs of the library's targeted clientele.

Cataloging

In this section, we discuss several historical schemes for organizing career information and present a sample classification scheme developed by a career center.

The Career Information Knowledge Base When Frank Parsons developed the Vocations Bureau in Boston in the early 1900s, he spent considerable effort trying to create a classification of industries in order to help young persons have a better understanding of the world of work. Parsons (1909, p. 65) derived the following groupings:

1. Agencies and office work
2. Agricultural
3. Artistic
4. Commercial
5. Domestic and personal service
6. Fishing
7. Manufacturing
8. Mechanical, building, and construction
9. Professional and semiprofessional
10. Transportation
11. Miscellaneous industries

Parsons noted that these categories were not fixed and would probably change over time. This view was indeed prophetic—scores of other classifications of industrial, occupational, and career information have been created since 1909. All of these efforts have sought to help us better understand the nature of the labor force and ultimately to use career information for more effective career problem solving and decision making. Since the 1970s, the U.S. government has developed numerous distinct classification systems, based on unique data, for economic planners and researchers. Government classification schemes have included the Census Code, Classification of Instructional Programs, Dictionary of Occupational Titles, Guide for Occupational Exploration, Occupational Employment Statistics, Standard Occupational Classification, and the Standard Industrial Classification. These separate systems discouraged information sharing among government agencies until recently, with the revision of the Standard Occupational Classification system. Nongovernmental classification systems developed since the 1970s include the Higher Education General Information Survey, Holland Codes, the Worker Trait Group Guide, and the World-of-Work Map. Many of these classification systems can be cross-referenced by utilizing crosswalk files developed by the National Crosswalk Service center (www.xwalkcenter.org). Several different systems may be used to classify occupations, and the most current are annotated in Table 13.1.

Using one or more of these classification systems to manage occupational information in a career library allows the librarian to relate local resources easily to state or national information and integrate published materials seamlessly into the local collection. In addition, a professional classification system provides more validity than a homemade one. Determining which specific scheme to use might be based on factors such as the needs of the local setting, the philosophical principles of those in

Table 13.1 | Occupational Classification Systems

Standard Occupational Classification (SOC) (U.S. Bureau of Labor Statistics, 1999): The SOC system, revised from the 1980 version to be utilized by all federal statistical agencies, classifies workers into occupational categories for collecting, calculating, or disseminating data. Organized into categories by similar job duties, skills, education, or experience, the SOC contains over 800 occupations. The *Occupational Information Network* (O*NET) utilizes the SOC structure to provide information on over 950 occupations. Originally, the O*NET was designed to update and replace the 1991 version of the *Dictionary of Occupational Titles,* which classified over 12,000 occupational titles. The *Occupational Employment Statistics* uses the SOC structure to provide information on staffing patterns and projected employment in U.S. industries and occupations.

Classification of Instructional Programs (CIP) (U.S. Department of Education, 1990): The CIP classifies instructional programs at the secondary and postsecondary levels and lists 52 programs in two-digit codes, further subdivided into four-, five-, or six-digit program codes.

Holland Codes (Gottfredson & Holland, 1996): Holland codes focus on the work environment to classify occupations, using the RIASEC typology based on Holland's theory of vocational choice. The six types are Realistic, Investigative, Artistic, Social, Enterprising, and Conventional, combined into three-letter Holland codes, then cross-referenced to other classification systems.

North American Industry Classification System (NAICS) (U.S. Census Bureau, 1997): The NAICS classifies business establishments by type of product or service and covers the entire range of economic activity. It is a numerical, hierarchical coding system that replaces the Standard Industrial Classification (SIC) system.

Guide for Occupational Exploration (GOE) (JIST Works/U.S. Department of Labor, 2001): The GOE, first developed in the 1970s to help people explore career options based on their interests, organizes occupations into 14 broad interest areas and their major work groups.

charge of the career information system, and the size of the library collection. Another factor may be the classification scheme's level of interoperability—that is, the extent to which it has been cross-referenced to other systems. Some career development professionals suggest using the three-letter codes developed by Holland (1994), which apply to approximately 1,300 occupations identified in the *Occupations Finder* of the Self-Directed Search and ultimately to the entire *Dictionary of Occupational Titles* (DOT) (Gottfredson & Holland, 1996). The problem with this system is that the retrieval of information may be unwieldy. For example, if a career center had only 3 pieces of information for each of the 45 RIE occupations in the *Occupations Finder,* users would have 135 pieces of material to search through when looking for a specific RIE occupation.

A Modern Classification Scheme Despite the preponderance of industrial and occupational classification systems, the career development process comprises much more than researching industries or occupations and requires a more inclusive scheme for conceptualizing career information. Librarians and career counselors have struggled since the 1940s to develop classification schemes for cataloging career information materials. Around 1968, career guidance, which had been concentrated in high schools, began to appear more prominently in college and university settings. In these new settings, the emphasis was not only on occupational information but also on career decision making, employability skills, women in the job market, and self-awareness. Peterson et al. (1991) provided more detailed information on the evolution of the modern career classification schemes.

Counselors have recently acknowledged that the presentation of career information needs to go beyond the traditional collection of clippings, pamphlets, catalogs, books, and homemade index-card filing systems. Career resource managers, therefore, have developed various ways to organize resource libraries, depending on the nature of the collection and the expertise of the manager. Green (1979) explored the issues involved in developing a library system for organizing and retrieving career materials. She noted that three factors make information readily accessible to users: (a) form, or the type of medium used, such as book, videotape, or brochure; (b) location, as in an open reading room or closed stacks; and (c) content, such as occupational information or job hunting strategies. These three factors should be taken into account in designing a career library so users of the systems can, with minimal assistance, identify and locate the information that meets their needs.

The physical form of materials—for example, print, audio, video, computer—can be an issue in matching information to a client's individual capabilities or preferences. Format is an important consideration in deciding where in the facility both information and complementary hardware could be stored. For example, video players should be in a secure place, and computers should be in an area that can be supervised. Resources may be grouped by physical properties such as size or medium (e.g., books and videotapes), or by their content. Most libraries use a subject classification to organize resources by content, but they separate print and nonprint materials.

Using a subject-matter classification can facilitate access for many information seekers, who browse collections and expect materials on a particular topic to be clustered together. Classification schemes should do two things: (a) guide users to where materials are located in the center and (b) convey, in general terms, the content of the materials. Career resources may be classified according to Library of Congress or Dewey subject headings if they constitute part of a larger library collection; however, if they form a special collection, the arrangement may be by Holland codes, college majors, or a homemade subject-categorization scheme.

Classification schemes must describe the contents of resources in a way that permits clients to ascertain if the resources relate to their career problems. Content can be conveyed two ways in the classification scheme: (a) notation, where numbers and/or letters reference certain subjects; or (b) terminology, where keywords or standard phrases indicate a subject-matter domain. The advantage of using a classification code rather than a subject-heading system is that it eliminates problems of syntax, semantics, and synonymy inherent in the English language. Because terminology and classification systems are often in a state of flux, thesauri and subject-heading lists (keywords and phrases describing a field) have been created to standardize the terminology employed in referencing career information. A career resource library's choice of classification schemes depends on the amount and breadth of information to be included in the library; the types of persons who will access the information (client, counselor, or librarian); and the career center's approach (self-help versus counselor help). A comprehensive career center that emphasizes self-help services requires a more sophisticated classification scheme than a counseling center that emphasizes counselor-client relationships, where counselors actively guide clients to the materials.

In order to cope with the amount of available career information and to organize it in a useful way for self-help clients, the Career Center at Florida State University developed in the early 1980s a taxonomy with six broad categories of career information. The taxonomy, called Career Key: A Career Library Management System (Smith, 1983), was revised in 1998 and the name modified to Career Key: A Tool for Finding and Managing Career Resources (see Table 13.2). This career classification scheme took into account the local university context and the specific existing career information delivery system in the career center. The following six categories of career information are housed in this comprehensive university career library:

I Career and Life Planning
II Occupations
III Education and Training
IV Work Experience
V Job Hunting
VI Employer Information Resources

When a piece of information is received into a career library, a series of events must occur to ensure its availability to users. Cataloging is the process by which brief descriptions of materials are developed in order to provide access to them (Coughlin & Gertzog, 1992). Cataloging not only helps the career resource manager keep track of resources but helps clients and staff find them. For each resource in the library collection, a record containing a brief description of the item is created. This record of information may be stored in print (as in card catalogs) or electronic (database) format. "Each time a resource is received, it must be checked against existing cataloging records to determine if the resource is already in the collection" (Epstein, Eberhardt, Powers, Strickland, & Smith, 2003, sec. III.A.3). If no record of the resource appears, then a new record is created. If the resource is a new edition or version of something already in the collection, then only changes or modifications are made on the pre-existing record. Each resource, no matter what format (e.g., books, videos, or files), must consistently follow standard rules for processing every time an item is cataloged.

Describing a resource through the cataloging process consists of two parts: (a) physical characteristics and (b) intellectual contents. The first step in cataloging a resource includes the process of identifying and describing it in terms of its physical characteristics. This is called descriptive cataloging and includes format/media, number of copies, volumes, general location, author, title, edition, copyright date, publisher, place, price, and so forth. The next step in the process of cataloging is called classification. Classification refers to indexing or assigning categories from a classification scheme to a resource, based on its subject contents. A function of the cataloging process is a scheme of resource arrangement that determines where resources will go in a library (Coughlin & Gertzog, 1992).

Table 13.2 | Career Key Subject Headings and Codes

I Career and Life Planning

- IA Career Choice (examining interests, values, and abilities)
- IB Career Transitions (exploring and adjusting to new work situations)
- IC National Job Outlook (employment trends, labor statistics, and salaries)
- ID Local/Regional/State Job Outlook (employment trends, labor statistics, and salaries)
- IE Work Environment (working hours, work attitudes, and job satisfaction)
- IF Lifestyle (marriage, leisure time, and other lifestyle issues)
  - IF1 Dual-Career Couples
  - IF2 Lifestyle Alternatives
  - IF3 Leisure Time
- IG Special Groups (career planning for ethnic and other minorities, older adults, etc.)
  - IG1 Minority Groups
  - IG2 Older Adults
  - IG3 Persons with Disabilities
  - IG4 Women

II Occupations

- IIA Multiple Occupations (resources with information on a lot of different occupations)
- IIB Specific Occupations (used with an occupational code)
- IIC Occupations by Program of Study (used with a major code)

III Education and Training

- IIIA Training Programs (corporate training programs, apprenticeships, etc.)
- IIIB Vocational/Technical Schools
- IIIC Colleges/Universities
  - IIIC1 Undergraduate School
  - IIIC2 Graduate and Professional Schools
  - IIIC3 The College Experience
- IIID Specific Local Area Academic and Training Programs
- IIIE Alternative Education (continuing education, distance learning, overseas study)
  - IIIE1 Adult and Continuing Education
  - IIIE2 Correspondence Programs
  - IIIE3 Overseas Study Programs
- IIIF Financial Aid (scholarships, loans, grants, etc.)

Table 13.2 (*continued*)

- IIIG Special Groups (education and training for ethnic and other minorities, older adults, etc.)
  - IIIG1 Minority Groups
  - IIIG2 Older Adults
  - IIIG3 Persons with Disabilities
  - IIIG4 Women
- IV Work Experience
  - IVA Cooperative Education Programs
  - IVB Internships
  - IVC Summer Jobs
  - IVD Volunteering
- V Job Hunting
  - VA Resume Writing
  - VB Interviewing
  - VC Letter Writing
  - VD Job Hunting Methods
- VI Employer Information Resources
  - VIA Employment Leads
  - VIB Employer Information by Career Fields
    - VIB1 Business Employers
    - VIB2 Social Sciences and Government Employers
    - VIB3 Education Employers
    - VIB4 Health Employers
    - VIB5 Science and Technology Employers
    - VIB6 Art, Entertainment, and Communications Employers
  - VIC International Employment
  - VID U.S. Employers by Location
  - VIE Trade and Professional Associations

From "Career Key: A Tool for Finding and Managing Career Resources," by S. Epstein, J. Eberhardt, B. Powers, K. Strickland, & E. Smith, 2003, Tallahassee: The Florida State University Career Center. Copyright 2002 by the Florida State University Career Center. Adapted from "Career Key: A Career Library Management System," by E. Smith, 1983, *The Vocational Guidance Quarterly, 32,* pp. 52–56. Copyright 1983 by the American Association for Counseling and Development. Reprinted with permission.

Classification "also refers to the process of assigning a resource a call number, which gives it a unique location within the collection" (Epstein et al., 2003, sec. III.C.2.a). Coding resources with call numbers serves two principal purposes. Because call numbers are based on a classification scheme, they allow resources to be arranged according to subject area. They are unique identification codes as well and allow for fast, accurate access of resources in a database or on the shelves (Epstein et al., 2003). Not all career libraries use a formal and comprehensive classification scheme, preferring to organize their resources with color codes, in alphabetical order, or by another general system. Therefore, they may not use call numbers to physically locate materials.

A resource's descriptive and classification data, recorded in standardized format on cataloging cards or into a database, function as a surrogate for the physical entity. Cards or database records become symbolic representations (or schemata) of the resource's information, a portrayal of the information in a manageable form. The use of surrogates theoretically allows unlimited access points to potentially relevant information for a client's career problem solving and decision making. In general, the access points a client may search by are title, author, subject, or format. In the case of a card catalog, a card is duplicated as many times as necessary and arranged in alphabetical files according to title, author, subject, or format. An electronic database eliminates the need for creating multiple surrogates for a resource. For the career resource manager, an electronic database of library resources can reduce the number of processing steps because multiple access points are embedded in one database record. Even though the use of surrogates is vital to maximize access to information in a library, it is an element often overlooked in the development of a comprehensive career library.

Keyword searching is another feature provided by electronic databases. If a client looks for resources on school counselors and cannot find that occupation, the individual may use a keyword search to look for an alternative term, such as *guidance counselor.* Keyword searching is a good tool to use if clients remember only a word in the title or part of an author's name. Having a user-friendly database catalog with features such as keyword searching may be an important factor in enhancing self-help activities in the career resource library.

At the FSU Career Center Library, resources are cataloged into a database called Career Key: A Tool for Finding and Managing Career Resources and classified into one of six subject areas: Career and Life Planning, Occupations, Education and Training, Work Experience, Job Hunting, and Employer Information Resources. Occupational content gets further categorized and organized by the utilization of the Standard Occupational Classification (SOC) system (U.S. Bureau of Labor Statistics, 1999). Using SOC codes to organize occupational information maximizes browsing in career fields, which would be impossible in an alphabetical arrangement of resources.

Reference

Career resource managers perform reference duties when they become the link or mediator between the client or counselor in need of information and the printed or electronic source where the career information is found (Bopp & Smith, 1995).

Reference also encompasses making counselors and career center staff aware of new resources that come into the collection. Resource managers mediate through conducting reference interviews, creating reference tools, or presenting workshops. These activities assist counselors in the career resource library by modeling how to find information and involving the client as much as possible in the research process. The reference activities of career resource managers may ultimately provide a framework for clients to seek out information independently, by focusing on teachable moments rather than serving information on a silver platter.

Through the reference interview, the career resource manager helps identify what career information a client needs. The first step in this process can be likened to identifying the Communications gap in the beginning of the CASVE cycle. If the gap has been identified as a lack of career information, the reference interview can help further clarify what information is needed. Career resource managers may also help clients secure career information throughout the entire CASVE cycle. Sometimes, clients' questions are clear, and the clients merely need to be directed to a particular resource. In some cases, however, the client may find it difficult to properly articulate his or her information requests. The interview helps determine the context of the question (why the question is being asked), format, quantity, prior search history, and level of information that is needed or preferred from the client (Bopp & Smith, 1995). Many of the skills a counselor uses in the counseling interview process apply in the context of a reference interview. A career resource manager who clarifies, paraphrases, or summarizes back to the client the information request can further understand what the client is seeking. Last, following up or asking clients if they found a resource that answered their Communication gap "may be the most important behavior in improving reference performance" (Bopp & Smith, 1995, p. 45).

Career resource managers frequently create and use tools and workshops to help clients and counselors better locate, understand, and utilize information and resources. Reference tools often provide the foundation for a self-help library and encourage self-help interventions for clients. They create better structure and access to many different types of information and may include guides/handouts, cross-reference lists, bibliographies, Web pages, e-mail, and signage. For example, a guide on researching employers may give someone a schema for what kinds of company information to look for or even where to find it. A cross-reference list may help a client understand how information from or about government agencies and departments is organized within the files. Workshops may be developed to teach a client how to acquire effective search skills using reference tools, such as print or electronic indexes, directories, and databases, or how to better evaluate career information (whether it is in electronic or print format). "Helping an individual understand the organization and use of the library's collection is the oldest and still most commonly practiced form of instruction" (Bopp & Smith, 1995, p. 12).

Circulation

Career center libraries may choose to circulate their resources, depending on the library's philosophy, type of resources, and clientele. A circulation policy communicates the scope of availability of resources by determining when and if they may leave the career center facility, what kinds of materials may circulate and for how long, and what procedures are in place for dealing with resources not returned (Coughlin & Gertzog, 1992). Circulation also protects the availability of resources by making sure that they are in good physical condition and in their proper location. If materials do circulate, then a system for charging them out and ensuring their return needs to be in place.

Whether or not resources are checked out of the career resource library, a resource manager has to make decisions about how to protect the collection from vandalism and theft. This may be embedded in the charging system (e.g., a person may not get his or her student identification card back until the item is returned) or in the physical setup of the library (e.g., there is only one exit and entrance into the library). Some career resource libraries have security systems; at the FSU Career Center Library, the open view of all tables and seating arrangements discourages theft.

Providing full access to noncirculating resources presents a constant challenge for career resource managers. Photocopying information may offer clients an alternative to checking resources out. Career resource managers should be aware of copyright law and cognizant of the general parameters of fair use, which defines what clients may do with copied material so that they do not violate the rights of the copyright holder or author. For example, one is free to photocopy material if used for educational purposes such as teaching, learning, and research, but not for commercial use (Katz, 1997). The FSU Career Center Library has chosen not to circulate resources from the library because they are so integral to the counseling process (see Chapter 7 for more details). However, these clients do have free access to many comprehensive career guides in paper or on-line format.

SUMMARY

This chapter advocated the application of information management techniques used in the professional library field to the development and management of a career information system. Basic issues related to the development and management of a career library were reviewed, including library governance and organization, human resources management, collection development policies, acquisition of resources, the career information knowledge base, modern classification schemes, cataloging processes, reference service, and circulation procedures.

GETTING THE MOST BENEFIT FROM READING THIS CHAPTER

To effectively learn the material in this chapter, complete one or more of the following activities:

- Visit a career service library on-line or in person, and determine how resources are organized. Identify a career planning topic or occupation of personal interest to you, and conduct a search of all available materials in the collection. What kind of classification system does the library use? Is it easy to access information?
- Visit the Bureau of Labor Statistics Web site (http://stats.bls.gov/soc/home.htm) to familiarize yourself with the U.S. government's Standard Occupational Clas-

sification (SOC) system and view its general structure. Identify three occupations of interest to you, and find them (or their nearest equivalent) on the site. Is it easy to navigate the Web site?

- Via the ACQWEB Web site (http://acqweb.library.vanderbilt.edu /acqweb/cd _policy.html#academic), view the "Directory of Collection Development Policies on the Web." Note especially the examples of collection development policies of "Academic Libraries: Special Collections." Compare two of the policies, noting their similarities and differences. Would one or both of them be appropriate as a model for a career resource library's collection development policy?
- Interview two professional librarians about how they help people locate and retrieve career-related materials. Use the topics in this chapter as a guide in developing your interview questions. Compare the skills, systems, and approaches used by each librarian, and decide which aspects you would add to your skills set.
- Assume you are the assistant director of a career services program in the setting of your choice. You have been given $5,000 to establish or upgrade a career library. Use publisher catalogs and/or library catalog lists to determine which resources to include in your library. Review several resources on planning and setting up a library. On graph paper, design a career library floor plan to house the resources you have chosen.

REFERENCES

Axelrod, V., Drier, H., Kimmel, K., & Sechler, J. (1977). *Career resource centers.* Columbus: Ohio State University, Center for Vocational Education.

Bopp, R. E., & Smith, L. C. (1995). *Reference and information services* (2nd ed.). Englewood, CO: Libraries Unlimited.

Brown, D. (2003). *Career information, career counseling, and career development* (4th ed.). Boston: Allyn & Bacon.

Coughlin, C. M., & Gertzog, A. (1992). *Lyle's administration of the college library* (5th ed.). Metuchen, NJ: The Scarecrow Press.

Dancik, D. B., & Shroder, E. J. (1995). *Building blocks for library space: Functional guidelines.* Chicago: American Library Association.

Epstein, S., Eberhardt, J., Powers, B., Strickland, K., & Smith, E. (2003). *Career Key: A tool for finding and managing career resources.* Tallahassee: Florida State University Career Center.

Florida State University Career Center. (2000). *Career center library ~ room A4101* [On-line]. Available: www.career.fsu.edu/library/map.html.

Fraley, R. A., & Anderson, C. L. (1990). *Library space planning: A how-to-do-it manual for assessing collecting and reorganizing collections, resources and facilities.* New York: Neal-Schuman Publishers.

Freifield, R., & Masyr, C. (1991). *Space planning in the special library.* Washington, DC: Special Libraries Association.

Gottfredson, G. D., & Holland, J. L. (1996). *Dictionary of Holland occupational codes* (3rd ed.). Odessa, FL: Psychological Assessment Resources.

Green, C. (1979). Managing career information: A librarian's perspective. *The Vocational Guidance Quarterly, 28,* 83–91.

Holland, J. L. (1994). *The occupations finder.* Odessa, FL: Psychological Assessment Resources.

JIST Works/U.S. Department of Labor (2001). *Guide for Occupational Exploration* (GOE). Indianapolis, IN: JIST Publishing.

Johnston, J., & Hansen, R. (1981). Using paraprofessionals in career development programming. In V. Harren, M. Daniels, & J. Buck (Eds.), *Facilitating students' career development* (pp. 81–97). San Francisco: Jossey-Bass.

Katz, W. A. (1997). *Introduction to reference work: Volume 1.* New York: McGraw-Hill.

Kreizman, K. (1999). *Establishing an information center: A practical guide.* London: Bowker Saur.

Lapp, J. A. (1918/1996, September/October). The growth of a big idea. *Special Libraries, 87,* 260–263.

Lenz, J. G. (2000). *Paraprofessionals in career services: The Florida State University model* (Technical Report 27) [On-line]. Available: www.career.fsu.edu/techcenter/designing_career_services/practical_strategies/.

Lenz, J. G., & Panke, J. (2001). *Paraprofessionals in career services* (Technical Report 32) [On-line]. Available: http://www.career.fsu.edu/techcenter/technical_reports.htm.

McKenzie, I., & Manoogian-O'Dell, M. (1988). *Expanding the use of students in career services: Current programs and resources.* Alexandria, VA: American Association for Counseling and Development.

Minor, C. (1984). Developing a career resource center. In H. Burck & R. Reardon (Eds.), *Career development interventions* (pp. 169–190). Springfield, IL: Charles C Thomas.

Mount, E. (Ed.). (1988). *Creative planning of special library facilities.* New York: Haworth Press.

National Career Development Association (2001a). *Career software review guidelines* [On-line]. Available: www.ncda.org/about/polsrg.html.

National Career Development Association. (2001b). *Guidelines for the preparation and evaluation of career and occupational information literature* [On-line]. Available: www.ncda.org/about/polcoil.html#content.

National Career Development Association (2001c). *Guidelines for the preparation and evaluation of video career media* [On-line]. Available: www.ncda.org/about/polvid.html.

Parsons, F. (1909). *Choosing a vocation.* Boston: Houghton Mifflin.

Peterson, G. W., Sampson, J. P., Jr., & Reardon, R. C. (1991). *Career development and services: A cognitive approach.* Pacific Grove, CA: Brooks/Cole.

Porter, C. A., & Christianson, E. B. (1997). *Special libraries: A guide for management* (4th ed.). Washington, DC: Special Libraries Association.

Sager, D. J. (2000). *Small libraries: Organization and operation* (3rd ed.). Atkinson, WI: Highsmith Press.

Sampson, J. P., Jr. (1999). Elements of an effective career resource room [On-line]. Available: www.career.fsu.edu/techcenter/designing_career_services/practical_strategies/.

Smith, E. (1983). Career Key: A career library management system. *The Vocational Guidance Quarterly 32,* 52–56.

U.S. Bureau of Labor Statistics. (1999). *Standard occupational classification* [On-line]. Available: http://stats.bls.gov/soc/.

U.S. Census Bureau. (1997). *North American Industry Classification System* (NAICS). Washington, DC: Author.

U.S. Department of Education. (1990). *Classification of Instructional Programs.* Washington, DC: Author.

Accountability and Evaluation in Career Services

CHAPTER 14

This chapter explores accountability by focusing on the outputs and outcomes of career service interventions and their costs. The chapter also examines the effectiveness of career service interventions, determined by how well individuals acquire self-knowledge, occupational knowledge, and problem-solving skills, as well as an understanding of metacognitions. After reviewing this chapter, the reader should be able to (a) describe the results of career service interventions in terms of primary effects (outputs) and secondary effects (outcomes); (b) provide general information about the effectiveness of career interventions; (c) state the assumptions on which a CIP accountability model is based; (d) describe the five factors that determine the effectiveness of career service intervention; (e) describe a method for determining the costs of career development interventions and programs; (f) show the relationships between costs and effectiveness; and (g) identify four principal requirements to implement a CIP accountability approach. The chapter is organized as follows:

- The Need for Accountability
- Defining Career Development
- Effects of Career Interventions
- Assumptions and Propositions
- The Five Components of Effectiveness
- Determination of Costs
- Requirements to Implement a CIP Approach

- Implications
- Summary
- Getting the Most Benefit from Reading This Chapter

THE NEED FOR ACCOUNTABILITY

Accountability is defined as the establishing of responsibility for certain outcomes, given a set of human and nonhuman resources (Crabbs & Crabbs, 1977; Henderson & Shore, 1974; Knapper, 1978). There has been a hue and cry for accountability in public education and human service programs since the early 1970s, when the long growth trend in tax dollars that were made available to human services began to level off and even decline. Sometimes managers and public officials use "accountability" as an excuse to make organizational changes of a political nature; at least, employees may view the changes in this way. The National Association of Colleges and Employers (NACE) (1995) described program evaluation as an essential element of professional practice in career services.

In spite of the continuing public demands for accountability, there has been little progress toward the development of accountability models that would enable human service programs to collect and aggregate data that effectively relate program costs to results. In economic terms, we are still very limited in our ability to link inputs (i.e., resources invested in career service, expressed in dollar amounts) to outputs (i.e., the results of the service). However, the reality is that unless we as career counselors can demonstrate such relationships in economically defensible ways, our career programs will likely have considerable difficulty in competing for funds.

One major difficulty behind this apparent lack of progress in the development of useful accountability and evaluation models has been the absence of conceptual and operational constructs that define the outputs of career service interventions. Career counselors have failed to specify in precise terms how career development services effectively change the minds and hearts of our clients so that they may lead more satisfying and productive lives. This chapter presents an accountability model, based on Cognitive Information Processing (CIP) theory, that seeks to define more clearly the products of career development interventions and programs so that we as career counselors may develop more precise linkages between the resources invested in our services and the resulting products. In this way, we can increase the effectiveness and efficiency of the services we provide in a more rational way.

DEFINING CAREER DEVELOPMENT

Accountability in career development has been an elusive and troubling issue. The mere defining of what is meant by career development seems to be confusing. For example, Pietrofesa and Splete (1975) defined career development as "an on-going process that occurs over the life span and includes home, school, and community experiences related to an individual's self-concept and its implementation in life styles as one lives life and makes a living" (p. 4). Gysbers and Moore (1975) defined career development as "self-development over the life span through the integration of the roles, settings, and events of a person's life" (p. 648). McDaniels and Gysbers (1992) further refined this definition by adding factors of gender, ethnic origin, religion, and race to the original definition of career development. Such nonlimiting definitions of career development suggest that career programs provide services that facilitate whatever Pietrofesa and Splete, Gysbers and Moore, or McDaniels and Gysbers refer to as "career development." With such global definitions, how does a counselor establish accountability for services rendered with any degree of precision?

Reardon, Lenz, Sampson, and Peterson (2000, p. 6) took a slightly different perspective in providing a definition of career development that is more closely tied to academic disciplines. Drawing on the definitions provided by Sears (1982) in *The Vocational Guidance Quarterly,* they viewed career development as "the total constellation of economic, sociological, psychological, educational, physical, and chance factors that combine to shape one's career." Career development can also be understood as the implementing of a series of integrated career decisions over the life span (Peterson, Sampson, Lenz, & Reardon, 2002). This multifaceted view of career development is so complex that it almost defies measurement in practice.

Another approach toward understanding the phenomenon of career development may be an analysis of the activities counselors typically perform when career development services are offered. According to Drier (1977), Splete (1978), and Hoyt and Evans (1974), career development activities include (a) developing and clarifying self-concepts, (b) relating occupational information to self-information, (c) teaching decision-making skills, (d) providing opportunities for occupational reality-testing, and (e) assisting individuals in educational and occupational placement. However, at this point, the question still remains, "For what are the counselors who perform such activities held accountable?"

A fourth avenue for pursuing the meaning of career development may be the analysis of statements pertaining to the outcomes of career development services. Campbell, Walz, Miller, and Kriger (1973) asked, "Does a career development program meet the needs of students at a manageable cost?" (p. 194). The National Vocational Guidance Association (1979) enunciated one evaluation standard relevant to the intent of this chapter: "Students demonstrate increased competencies in self-understanding of the world of work and leisure, career planning, decision making, and the ability to take action" (p. 108). Drier (1977) suggested the following outcome criteria: (a) increased use of community resources, (b) decreased dropout and absenteeism from school, (c) increased involvement of parents and teachers in guidance delivery, (d) increased work-related experiences, and (e) increased use of counseling services.

Such outcome criteria may be helpful for the formulation of the intended effects of career development interventions, but one important dimension of intended outcomes consistently appears to be omitted—namely, those changes in perceptual and cognitive thought processes that enable individuals to make satisfying and informed career choices. In other words, although much attention has been devoted to describing counselor interventions and the ensuing general effects, the cognitive capacities that clients acquire as a direct result of career development interventions have yet to be clearly conceptualized and articulated. The central point of this chapter is that the development of occupational knowledge and self-knowledge, career problem-solving and decision-making skills (sometimes referred to as competencies; Peterson & Burck, 1982), and metacognitions should lie at the core of the intended outcomes of any career development intervention and should form the nucleus of an accountability system.

The National Career Development Guidelines (Kobylarz, 1996) provide another method for defining career development outputs (see Appendix C for a list of career competencies by area of skill and age level). Additional information about this guidelines initiative is available at http://icdl.uncg.edu/ncdg.html. The three areas of skill include self-knowledge, educational and occupational exploration, and career planning. Work on the development of these guidelines began in 1986 through the initiative of the National Occupational Information Coordinating Committee and professional associations and groups interested in standardizing practices in the career area. The list of competencies, along with performance indicators identified by the program developer, provides a common set of career outputs that have consensus support from a wide variety of interest groups, including parents, educators, employers, career professionals, political leaders, and other citizens. It might be noted that these are not called *standards* because the sponsoring agencies and organizations did not seek to impose national accountability; therefore, the term *guidelines* was substituted.

One other national initiative that seeks to specify career development outcomes was undertaken by the National Career Development Association with the adoption on March 16, 1993, of *A Policy Statement of the National Career Development Association Board of Directors*. This document is available at http://ncda.org/about/polcdps.html#conclude. This policy statement includes definitions of terms in the career area; a philosophical statement regarding work in the United States; policy directives regarding career interventions related to the family and pre-school-age youth, children in grades K–6, and those in grades 7–9 and 10–12; and career development for adults and retired persons. Such statements by the leading national organization working in the career development field help to standardize and clarify the nature and purposes of career programs.

In a CIP approach to accountability in career development, client changes are assessed first in terms of the cognitive skills, knowledge, and attitudes (SKAs) acquired as a direct result of career interventions. These are the *primary* effects. Criteria such as job satisfaction, satisfaction with services, job acquisition rates, employment tenure, ventures in career exploration, or successful placement in schools or jobs are viewed as the consequential or *secondary* effects of intervention. A CIP approach is therefore based on the assessment of two levels of effects: primary client changes, which concern the development of new cognitive capabilities; and secondary changes, which relate to the manner in which these newly acquired capacities are applied to making effective career and lifestyle decisions. This two-stage approach to defining the results of career services programs permits stronger, more precise linkages between the resources invested in an intervention and the results. In economic terms, the primary programmatic effects may be considered outputs, and the secondary effects may be considered outcomes (Kaufman & English, 1979).

EFFECTS OF CAREER INTERVENTIONS

In an effort to learn more about the impact of career interventions, including individual counseling, group counseling, workshops, self-help approaches, and career courses, several meta-analyses have been undertaken. These studies provide insight into the effects of career interventions. Spokane and Oliver (1983) reported that group or class interventions were more effective than individual counseling or other interventions. Later, Oliver and Spokane (1988) reported an analysis of 240 treatment-control comparisons in 58 studies comparing 11 different types of career interventions. They found that career guidance classes produced the largest effect size with regard to client gains resulting from the assortment of career interventions considered. Classes were followed by workshops, individual counseling, group counseling, computer-assisted guidance programs, and self-directed interventions. Classes also involved the greatest number of hours and sessions but were the most expensive intervention according to Oliver and Spokane (1988). They concluded that although career interventions are generally effective, individual and structured group interventions are most cost-effective. Furthermore, they noted that group interventions have a cost advantage because of the numbers of clients that can be helped at a single time.

Hardesty (1991) also conducted a meta-analysis consisting of 12 studies that evaluated career development courses offered for credit. Results of this meta-analysis confirmed previous research findings concerning overall positive effects of undergraduate career courses on increasing both career decidedness (48% more certain) and career maturity (40% more capable of making a realistic decision) of college students. However, Hardesty noted that the long-term effects of career courses—within a year or two or longer after completion of the courses—had not been established. More recently, Folsom and Reardon (in press) examined career course interventions from the perspective of both outputs and outcomes.

Another recent meta-analysis by Whiston, Sexton, and Lasoff (1998) examined 47 studies conducted between 1983 and 1995, including 9 studies of career classes. They found that career classes were the third most effective career intervention out of eight different categories of interventions examined. Career classes followed individual and group counseling in effectiveness but were ahead of group test interpretation, workshops, computer interventions, counselor-free interventions, and other nonclassified interventions. The researchers found that classes followed counselor-free interventions and computer interventions as least costly. Individual and group counseling showed strong, positive effects on career outcomes; however, self-directed interventions again appeared least potent.

Brown and Krane (2000) summarized these meta-analytic studies and noted that career interventions are effective because the average client outscores the average nonclient by about one-half a standard deviation. How, why, and for whom the interventions work were inconclusive. In conducting a series of meta-analyses on 62 studies, Ryan (1999) and Brown and Krane (2000) concluded that demonstrably effective career interventions have five common elements:

1. Allow clients to clarify career and life goals in writing
2. Provide clients with individualized interpretations and feedback (e.g., test results)

3. Provide current information on the risks and rewards of selected occupations and career fields
4. Include study of models and mentors who demonstrate effective career behavior
5. Assist in developing support networks for pursuing career aspirations

Brown and Krane suggested that career counselors and others designing and evaluating the impact of career interventions should assess the extent to which at least three of the five listed elements are included in the intervention. We would add that these five elements have been a continuing theme in the presentation of a CIP-based approach to career services. These elements are also included in the CIP accountability model described later in this chapter.

ASSUMPTIONS AND PROPOSITIONS

Ultimately, the aim of career development interventions should be to foster changes in the ways clients perceive themselves and the world of work and in the ways clients incorporate such perceptions in the service of generalized career problem-solving skills (Weitz, 1964). In order to demonstrate the linkage among resources invested in human service interventions, cognitive development, and results, the following assumptions are made:

1. There is a set of fundamental cognitive abilities (namely, generic problem-solving and decision-making skills) and knowledge that undergirds effective career problem solving and decision making. These abilities include such subordinate skills as Communication, Analysis, Synthesis, Valuing, and Execution (CASVE), as described in Chapter 2.
2. A career development intervention is defined as a learning event in which knowledge and cognitive skills are prescribed, mastered, and applied to solving career problems, making career decisions, executing them, and achieving satisfaction with jobs and life in general. The basic elements of a learning event are (a) an objective stated in performance terms, (b) learning activities designed to foster the attainment of the objective, and (c) a measure to ascertain whether the objective has been attained.
3. There is a causal linkage between the acquisition of career problem-solving and decision-making skills in a career development intervention and subsequent career and life adjustment.
4. The cost for the delivery of a career service intervention is determined by accounting in monetary terms for all the resources required to administer an intervention that enables a cohort of clients with common career problems to achieve a desired level of proficiency in self-knowledge and occupational knowledge, CASVE skills, and metacognitions. Cohorts can either be intact groups, as in group counseling, or an identified set of individuals with common problems who use the career service within a certain time frame.
5. A career services program is composed of an integrated set of career service interventions. Administratively, it is an organization unit with a mission, goals, and a budget.

In order to establish an accountability system, one must be able to document the results of career service interventions in measurable terms and to account for the resources invested in them (Niles & Harris-Bowlsbey, 2002). Therefore, one side of our accountability model concerns documentation of the activities and results of a career service intervention; the other side addresses the accounting of resources to deliver the intervention (see Figure 14.1). Thus, the proposed accountability model is a value-added model in which clients acquire a new capability (or set of capabilities) that they did not possess prior to participation in a career service intervention.

THE FIVE COMPONENTS OF EFFECTIVENESS

In the CIP accountability model, the effectiveness of an intervention depends on (a) a diagnosis of client needs, (b) a prescription of activities to help the client address such needs, (c) the documentation of plans and activities that describe the process of intervention, (d) the outputs or primary effects of the intervention, and (e) the outcomes or effects of the primary changes. This model—diagnosis, prescription, process, outputs, and outcomes (DPPOO)—is elaborated in the following sections of this chapter. Basically, the proposed approach involves identifying the skills and knowledge to be acquired in an intervention, the prescribing and documenting of learning activities to help clients achieve them, the measuring of changes in perceptions and cognitions, and finally, the determining of whether these changes are manifested in subsequent life-adjustment outcomes.

Diagnosis

In a CIP approach, client problems are defined in terms of needs (Kaufman, 1972) that are the discrepancies or gaps between existing levels and desired levels of knowledge and skill development. The objectives of a career service intervention are derived from the common needs of a group of individuals (Burck & Peterson, 1975). Accountability at the diagnostic stage, therefore, requires an analysis of client problems to identify the knowledge and skills needed to solve those problems, a description of the assessment techniques used to ascertain entry-level knowledge and skill performances, documentation of the entry-level performance by the group, and a statement of the desired level of attainment by the group (i.e., the objectives for the intervention). Table 14.1 presents diagnostic information for a six-week workshop for a group of 20 unemployed adults seeking career guidance. The differences between the entry levels of development and the desired levels of development of cognitive skills and knowledge constitute the needs of this cohort of clients. A cohort is a group of clients with common career problems who experience the same career service intervention.

Prescription

The prescription stage involves the development of a plan for counselor and client activities to meet the diagnosed needs—that is, the knowledge and skill gaps. The development of specified skills, knowledge, and attitudes (SKAs) is the objective of

Figure 14.1 The Components of an Accountability Model Based on CIP

From *Career Development and Services: A Cognitive Approach* (p. 396), by G. W. Peterson, J. P. Sampson, Jr., and R. C. Reardon, 1991, Pacific Grove, CA: Brooks/Cole.

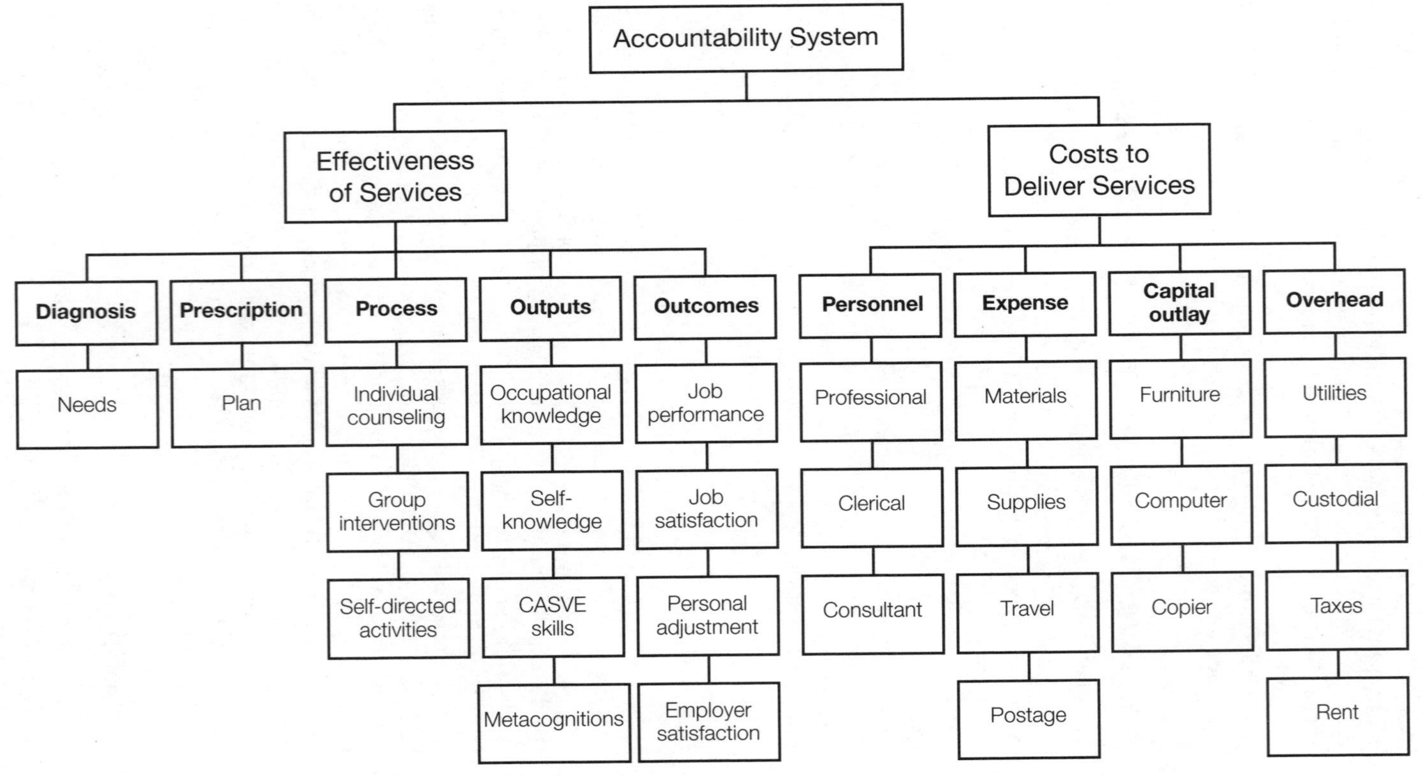

Table 14.1 Diagnostic and Output Data for a Six-Week Career Course for 20 Unemployed Adults

Skill	Assessment Technique	Entry Level of Development	Desired Level of Development	Achieved Level of Development
Metacognition: problem-solving heuristic	Success and failure incidents; career choice scenarios	70% described a trial-and-error strategy for securing a job.	80% can apply the five-step CASVE problem-solving model to job search and selection.	90% could apply the five-step problem-solving model to job search and selection.
Communication skills	Written response to simulated job interview questions; job interview role-play	25% gave effective responses to written employer challenges; 35% gave effective responses in a simulated job interview.	80% give assertive responses to written employer challenges; 80% give assertive responses to simulated job interview questions.	95% could write assertive responses to interview questions; 80% demonstrated assertive responses in a role-play.
Analytical skills	Open-ended question asking clients to list and rank reasons why they have difficulty securing a job	75% listed the first reason as a factor outside their control (e.g., prejudice of employers or no work available).	90% list the first reason as lack of job competence skills, lack of information about new jobs, inadequate educational experience, etc.	85% gave the first reason as a factor over which they have control.
Synthesis skills	OAQ[a]; list of educational or training opportunities for chosen jobs	60% listed no more than two suitable occupations; 50% listed one; 50% could not list appropriate training opportunities.	80% can list at least five suitable occupations; 80% can list at least one training or educational facility in the community for each occupation.	85% could list at least five suitable occupations; 95% could list appropriate training opportunities in the community for each alternative.

[a] Occupational Alternatives Question (Slaney, 1978).

career service interventions; a task analysis can be used to develop a series of learning activities that lead clients from simple to complex skills (Gagne, 1985). The mastery of a content domain, which precedes cognitive skill development, may be structured through content analyses in which clients master certain sets of facts, concepts, rules, or operations on which to base higher-order problem-solving skills. For example, career development concepts for the intervention presented in Table 14.1 might include a knowledge of communication response modes (such as defensiveness, assertiveness, and aggressiveness); the factors affecting the supply of applicants and demand for workers for a given occupation in the community; and the relationships among education, training, and job requirements. For children and adolescents, learning activities may be structured along the cognitive and moral developmental lines proposed by Inhelder and Piaget (1958).

Process

Therapeutic and educational processes are the series of activities, both planned and unplanned, performed by the client and the counselor to bring about change in the diagnosed skill and knowledge gaps. For accountability purposes, it is important to record accurate and detailed descriptions of counselor and client activities, the attainment of milestones leading to the acquisition of desired skills and knowledge, the accomplishment of prescribed tasks or experiences, or scores on progress tests or inventories. The most important data to collect are those that indicate progress made toward the development of skills or the mastery of new knowledge. In the six-week workshop for unemployed adults, the documentation of the process could consist of recording the attendance at the following activities: three hours of listening-skill training; a 30-minute videotape on employability skills plus one hour of discussion; a one-hour presentation of child-care opportunities in the community; three hours of assertiveness skill training with a short written assignment; and an interview rehearsal.

Outputs

The outputs of a successful career development intervention are the new skills and knowledge that are acquired, such as the development of communication skills, the capacity to analyze career problems, the ability to formulate feasible courses of action, a clearer understanding of one's own values and the values operating in a social or work environment, and increased planning skills that lead to the successful attainment of self-determined goals. These primary client changes are the direct result of career service interventions. Earlier, we discussed the National Career Development Guidelines (Kobylarz, 1996; Appendix C) as one initiative designed to standardize the specification of career program outputs. Accountability for output requires documenting the gains made in self-knowledge and occupational knowledge, CASVE skills, and metacognitions from entry to exit performance levels for a cohort treatment group. These are sometimes referred to as performance indicators. Sampson, Peterson, Reardon, and Lenz (2000) identified about 40 instruments that might be used to assess changes in outputs as the result of career intervention programs, and Kapes and Whitfield (2001) provided additional information about other measures of career outputs. The output data for the six-week career course are presented in the last column of Table 14.1, "Achieved Level of Development."

Outcomes

The outcomes of a career development intervention are the effects that result from new cognitive or perceptual capacities (i.e., the outputs). These new cognitive and perceptual capacities may include the following:

1. A more focused and organized plan for career exploration
2. Reduced fear of success or failure
3. Greater toleration and understanding of temporary career indecision
4. Successful job placement
5. Greater satisfaction with a chosen college major
6. Greater job satisfaction and/or life satisfaction
7. Greater harmony among work, family, and leisure responsibilities
8. Reduced absenteeism from school or work
9. Increased performance in school or work

Although there are published measures related to these outcomes—for example, the Satisfaction with Life Scale (Diener, Emmons, Larsen, & Griffin, 1985)—for most purposes, a homemade instrument that is more directly related to the objectives of a given intervention may provide more valid information than a published instrument. The inclusion of open-ended questions may provide the counselor with valuable qualitative information about the intervention as well. Critical incident methods (Flanagan, 1954), in which clients report successes and failures following a career service intervention, may also be extremely helpful. In order to assess the enduring effects of an intervention, one-month, six-month, and one-year follow-up studies are recommended. The NACE (1995) provides additional examples of outcomes that indicate a career services program effectiveness.

DETERMINATION OF COSTS

Determining the costs of conducting a career service intervention can be a complex endeavor, especially if one uses a full-cost accounting model. It may be difficult to determine the causal linkage between resources and results in a career development intervention (Peterson & Burck, 1982). Nevertheless, with the projected long-term trend of steady or diminishing resources for human service programs, the determination of cost-effectiveness becomes important for program survival. Niles and Harris-Bowlsbey (2002) noted that "evaluation is sometimes done in order to determine whether the outcomes of delivering services are worth the money and other resources being invested" (p. 394).

Cost accounting involves a complex set of procedures; we wish only to introduce a method for determining the costs of career services programs. An approximation of the cost to manage a career service intervention can be determined by summing the cost components for personnel, materials and supplies, and overhead (i.e., administrative, security, and custodial expenses, phone, and utilities) for each component (Haller, 1974). The costs of diagnostic procedures for a career development program include counselor time for intake interviews and for record keeping, purchase of assessment materials, counselor time for proctoring and scoring tests, and overhead. The costs of prescription activities include counselor time for interviews, for developing plans for activities, and for reviewing plans with colleagues and supervisors; purchase of materials and supplies; and overhead. Process costs include the counselor's time to prepare materials and to organize, schedule, and administer activities, as well as expenses related to supplies, duplication, room rent, and phones. Output costs include counselor time to develop and administer assessments, conduct interviews, record data, analyze data, and report results. Outcome costs may entail counselor time to develop and mail questionnaires, conduct follow-up interviews, and write reports, in addition to expenses related to the production, duplication, and dissemination of reports.

Cost-Effectiveness

Once the costs for a career service intervention are determined, they can be related to the gain in knowledge and skill—that is, to the outputs. The ratio of client gain to dollars invested in the service can be calculated. This output/cost ratio may be compared with those of other career service interventions with similar goals, objectives, and client characteristics to ascertain which are most effective (most client gain) or most efficient (most gain per dollar) (Knezevich, 1973). A career services program is the aggregate of all the career service interventions taking place during an interval of time, such as a month, a semester, or a year. The cost of running a career services program is the sum of the costs of the separate career service interventions.

Table 14.2 presents an example of the determination of costs to implement a career intervention. The intervention is a six-week course for 20 unemployed adults. It is housed in a career center in a local library and is staffed by one counselor with a master's degree who earns $25,000 per year and one secretary who earns $12,000 per year.

For computation purposes, these salaries are reduced to $12.00 per hour for the counselor and $5.75 per hour for the secretary. The counselor and secretary put in equal amounts of time for all components. There are no capital expenditures such as purchase of equipment or furniture, or renovations. Overhead or indirect cost (utilities, custodial, and so on) is set at 8% of the direct cost (personnel plus expenses). The cost to administer and evaluate the adult education intervention for the 20 clients who achieved the results portrayed in Table 14.1 was $2,403. Note that $1,775 (73.9%) of the cost was for personnel; this proportion is characteristic of labor-intensive interventions. Note also that the costs of documentation of outputs ($245.70) and outcomes ($299.70) together accounted for 22.7% of the total cost of the intervention. Thus, an accountability system that requires documentation of results may necessitate additional expenditures. This fact is often overlooked by politicians or administrators, who demand more accountability for the same cost of services.

Table 14.2 Cost Data for a Six-Week, Three-Hours-per-Week Career Course for 20 Unemployed Adults

Component	Counselor Hours	Direct Cost: Personnel	Direct Cost: Expense	Overhead	Total
Diagnosis (intake interview, testing, scoring, preparation)	30	$ 532.50	$ 50.00	$ 46.60	$ 629.10
Prescription (complete and discuss career exploration plan with each client)	10	177.50	50.00	18.20	245.70
Process (delivery of activities plus promotion and preparation)	40	710.00	200.00	72.80	982.80
Output (documentation of learning through tests, questionnaires, interviews)	10	177.50	50.00	18.20	245.70
Outcome (documentation of implementation of learning through tests, questionnaires, interviews)	10	177.50	100.00	22.20	299.70
Total	100	$1,775.00	$450.00	$178.00	$2,403.00

Unit Cost

The unit cost for these 20 adult learners was $120.15 ($2,403.00 ÷ 20) per client. If there were fewer clients, the unit cost would increase. If there were more clients, the unit cost would decrease. The effectiveness of an intervention also tends to decrease when there are more clients, but this decrease is not linear. Figure 14.2 shows examples of curves relating unit cost and effectiveness for different types of interventions. The nature of each curve may be related to the skills, knowledge, and attitudes to be mastered and to the entry characteristics of the clients. Generally, the imparting of knowledge has a lower unit cost than the imparting of skills. Remedial treatments requiring intensive emotional support for persons with substantial mental health problems typically have high unit costs. For an additional example of a career program cost analysis, see Reardon (1996).

REQUIREMENTS TO IMPLEMENT A CIP APPROACH

There are four fundamental requirements to implement an information processing approach to accountability in career service interventions and programs:

1. A knowledge of the skills and content domains that underlie rational career decision-making processes in certain contexts

Figure 14.2 The Relationship Between Effectiveness and Unit Cost (Resources per Client) in Human Service Programs

From *Career Development and Services: A Cognitive Approach* (p. 402), by G. W. Peterson, J. P. Sampson, Jr., and R. C. Reardon, 1991, Pacific Grove, CA: Brooks/Cole.

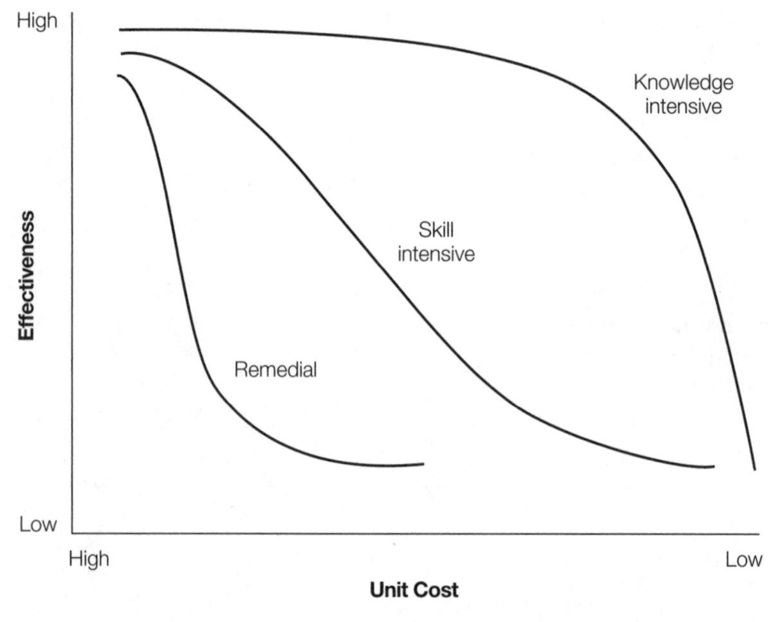

2. A knowledge of the conditions that bring about the development of knowledge and skills in clients
3. Valid and sensitive measures to detect subtle changes resulting from career service interventions
4. A basic knowledge of program planning and budgeting to document the resources invested in career service interventions

These four requirements demand that counselors become familiar with new research findings in cognitive and developmental psychology, with methods of measuring changes in cognition and perception, and with human service program management. Unfortunately, these areas of study are typically given very little emphasis in the training of career counselors. However, if we view career counseling as fostering skills and knowledge that can be used throughout life, instead of merely helping an individual with a single occupational choice in time, then becoming familiar with these domains of knowledge becomes imperative.

IMPLICATIONS

The proposed accountability model described in this chapter provides a paradigm for defining the results of career development services by drawing a distinction between outputs (the direct changes in individuals as a result of service) and outcomes (the ways in which such client gains are actualized in daily living). This distinction provides a more precise perspective about what counselors can be held accountable for. Counselors can reasonably be held more accountable for the knowledge and skills that clients acquire in career service interventions than for the ways in which changes are implemented in the course of daily living; such changes may be influenced by a host of capricious environmental factors, such as a change in the economic base of a community due to a plant closing or the elimination of a military base. Paradoxically, at the programmatic level, a cohort of clients with similar career development problems should demonstrate worthwhile effects for both the individual and society at the outcome level if the intervention is to be considered effective. More specific, a counselor can be held accountable for helping clients evaluate their abilities and interests, for clarifying career goals, or for acquiring employability skills. However, counselors can be held accountable only in a limited way for whether any individual secures a job in a specified length of time. At the aggregate level, over an extended period of time, counselors can be held accountable for whether a cohort of clients acquires jobs or chooses major fields of study that are satisfying.

Perhaps more important, the model compels a rethinking of the aims of career services. In addition to focusing career service interventions on such issues as the acquisition of career information, job search strategies, and interviewing skills (which are some of the important fundamental skills in career development), career counselors should also view their interventions in relation to a more comprehensive perspective that enhances career problem-solving and decision-making skills. If counselors can help individuals surmount and transcend their immediate career problems or crises so that they may acquire enduring capabilities that will enable them to manage their own career development over a lifetime, perhaps then a truly valuable service will have been provided. By demonstrating that clients have acquired new problem-solving capabilities (outputs) and can apply them to their daily lives (outcomes), accountability requirements will be met as well.

SUMMARY

This chapter focused on the problems of defining accountability and career development in operational form so that resources could be tied to results. In order to accomplish this, it is useful to distinguish between the outputs of career service interventions and their outcomes. A five-component effectiveness model and a basic cost model were introduced, with examples of data for each. The effectiveness of career service interventions is a function of the degree to which individuals acquire self-knowledge and occupational knowledge and develop thinking (CASVE) skills. A method for determining costs to administer a career service intervention based on a CIP approach was also introduced. The requirements to implement the accountability approach and the possible implications of the approach were discussed.

GETTING THE MOST BENEFIT FROM READING THIS CHAPTER

To effectively learn the material in this chapter, complete one or more of the following activities:

- Locate a career development service, and ask the director to see the budget of the service. Have the director describe and explain the budget.
- Locate a career service, and identify an intact group. This group could be intact in a statistical sense—that is, an aggregate of individuals with common career problems; they need not actually meet as a group. Describe the outputs for the group. Describe the intended outcomes. Ascertain the direct and indirect costs of conducting the group. Where might cost savings be realized without reducing the effectiveness? How might effectiveness be increased without increasing the costs?
- Develop an evaluation strategy to document the effectiveness and the costs for the group you studied in the previous activity.
- Locate an established career services program, and ask for a copy of any recent internal program evaluation report. Determine the extent to which it includes the various components outlined in this chapter.

REFERENCES

Brown, S. D., & Krane, N. E. R. (2000). Four (or five) sessions and a cloud of dust: Old assumptions and new observations about career counseling. In S. B. Brown & R. W. Lent (Eds.), *Handbook of counseling psychology* (3rd ed.) (pp. 740–766). New York: John Wiley.

Burck, H., & Peterson, G. W. (1975). Needed: More evaluation, not research. *The Personnel and Guidance Journal, 53,* 563–569.

Campbell, R., Walz, G., Miller, J., & Kriger, S. (1973). *Career guidance: A handbook of methods.* Columbus, OH: Charles Merrill.

Crabbs, S. K., & Crabbs, M. A. (1977). Accountability: Who does what to whom, when, where, and how? *School Counselor, 25,* 104–109.

Diener, E., Emmons, R. A., Larsen, R. J., & Griffin, S. (1985). The satisfaction with life scale. *Journal of Personality Assessment, 49,* 71–75.

Drier, H. N. (1977). *Programs of career guidance, counseling, placement, follow-up, and follow through: A future perspective.* Columbus: Ohio State University, National Center for Research in Vocational Education.

Flanagan, J. C. (1954). The critical incident technique. *Psychological Bulletin, 51* (4), 327–358.

Folsom, B., & Reardon, R. (in press). College career courses: Design and accountability. *Journal of Career Assessment.*

Gagne, R. M. (1985). *The conditions of learning and theory of instruction* (4th ed.). New York: Holt, Rinehart & Winston.

Gysbers, N. C., & Moore, E. J. (1975). Beyond career development: Life career development. *The Personnel and Guidance Journal, 53,* 647–652.

Haller, E. J. (1974). Cost analysis for education program evaluation. In W. J. Popham (Ed.), *Evaluation in education: Current applications* (pp. 399–450). Berkeley, CA: McCutchan.

Hardesty, P. H. (1991). Undergraduate career courses for credit: A review and meta-analysis. *Journal of College Student Development, 32,* 184–185.

Henderson, R., & Shore, B. (1974). Accountability for what to whom? *Social Work, 19,* 387–388, 507.

Hoyt, K. B., & Evans, R. N. (1974). *Career education: What it is and how to do it* (2nd ed.). Salt Lake City, UT: Olympus.

Inhelder, B., & Piaget, J. (1958). *The growth of logical thinking from childhood to adolescence.* New York: Basic Books.

Kapes, J., & Whitfield, E. (Eds.) (2001). *A counselor's guide to career assessment instruments* (4th ed.). Tulsa, OK: National Career Development Association.

Kaufman, R. (1972). *Educational system planning.* Englewood Cliffs, NJ: Prentice Hall.
Kaufman, R., & English, E. (1979). *Needs assessment: Concept and application.* Englewood Cliffs, NJ: Educational Technology Publications.
Knapper, E. Q. (1978). Counselor accountability. *The Personnel and Guidance Journal, 57,* 27–30.
Knezevich, S. J. (1973). *Program budgeting (PPBS).* Berkeley, CA: McCutchan.
Kobylarz, L. (1996). *National Career Development Guidelines: K–adult handbook* [On-line]. Available: http://icdl.uncg.edu/ncdg.html.
McDaniels, C., & Gysbers, N. C. (1992). *Counseling for career development: Theories, resources, and practice.* San Francisco: Jossey-Bass.
National Association of Colleges and Employers. (1995). *Sourcebook for conducting evaluations and measurements of career services.* Bethlehem, PA: Author.
National Vocational Guidance Association, Commission on Criteria for Guidance Programs. (1979). Guidelines for a quality career guidance program. *The Vocational Guidance Quarterly, 28,* 99–110.
Niles, S. G., & Harris-Bowlsbey, J. (2002). *Career development interventions in the 21st century.* Upper Saddle River, NJ: Merrill/Prentice Hall.
Oliver, L. W., & Spokane, A. R. (1988). Career-intervention outcome: What contributes to client gain. *Journal of Counseling Psychology, 35,* 447–462.
Peterson, G. W., & Burck, H. (1982). A competency approach to accountability in human service programs. *The Personnel and Guidance Journal, 60,* 491–495.
Peterson, G. W., Sampson, J. P., Jr., Lenz, J. G., & Reardon, R. C. (2002). A cognitive information processing approach to career problem solving and decision making. In D. Brown (Ed.), *Career choice and development* (4th ed.) (pp. 312–369). San Francisco: Jossey-Bass.
Pietrofesa, J., & Splete, H. (1975). *Career development theory and research.* New York: Grune & Stratton.
Reardon, R. C. (1996). A program and cost analysis of a self-directed career decision-making program in a university career center. *Journal of Counseling and Development, 74,* 280–285.
Reardon, R. C., Lenz, J. G., Sampson, J. P., Jr., & Peterson, G. W. (2000). *Career development and planning: A comprehensive approach.* Pacific Grove, CA: Wadsworth–Brooks/Cole.
Ryan, N. E. (1999). Career counseling and career choice goal attainment: A meta-analytically derived model for career counseling practice (Doctoral dissertation, Loyola University of Chicago, 1999). *Dissertation Abstracts International, 05A,* 1464.
Sampson, J. P., Jr., Peterson, G. W., Reardon, R. C., & Lenz, J. G. (2000). Using readiness assessment to improve career services: A cognitive information processing approach. *The Career Development Quarterly, 49,* 146–174.
Sears, S. (1982). A definition of career guidance terms: A National Vocational Guidance Association Perspective. *The Vocational Guidance Quarterly, 31,* 137–143.
Splete, H. (1978). *Career development counseling* (Colorado Career Information System Monograph). Boulder: University of Colorado.
Spokane, A. R., & Oliver, L. W. (1983). The outcomes of vocational intervention. In S. H. Osipow & W. B. Walsh (Eds.), *Handbook of vocational psychology* (pp. 99–136). Hillsdale, NJ: Lawrence Erlbaum Associates.
Weitz, H. (1964). *Behavior change through guidance.* New York: John Wiley.
Whiston, S. C., Sexton, T. L., & Lasoff, D. L. (1998). Career-intervention outcome: A replication and extension of Oliver and Spokane (1988). *Journal of Counseling Psychology, 45,* 150–165.

15 CHAPTER Strategic Planning for Career Services

This chapter explores strategic thinking, operations planning, and strategic planning as ways to help us anticipate important social and organizational changes so that we may continue to offer timely and responsive career services. After reviewing this chapter, the reader should be able to (a) define strategic thinking and strategic planning, (b) contrast strategic planning with operations planning, (c) describe the six steps in strategic planning, (d) relate strategic planning to the Cognitive Information Processing paradigm and to accountability, and (e) describe the four principal roles of the modern career counselor. This chapter is organized as follows:

- Strategic Planning and the Aims of Career Services
- Social Trends
- Strategic Planning
- Why Strategic Planning Is Necessary
- Guidelines for Strategic Planning
- Strategic Planning, Cognitive Information Processing, and Accountability
- Roles of the Career Services Practitioner
- Summary
- Getting the Most Benefit from Reading This Chapter

STRATEGIC PLANNING AND THE AIMS OF CAREER SERVICES

At the beginning of the 20th century, Frank Parsons and other leaders of the progressive movement in the United States engaged in "strategic planning," which led to the development of the vocational guidance movement and the beginnings of the counseling profession. Although there is no documentation of their work that is actually labeled strategic planning, the evidence suggests that is exactly what they did. The counseling profession, indeed the nation, is still called on to engage in strategic planning regarding social policies and institutions that will enable citizens to work effectively, both at the individual level and the societal level. Camille DeBell (2001) provided a thoughtful analysis of the social conditions in the United States 100 years ago that led to the development of career guidance and counseling. She pointed out that "although the world of work is still responding to some trends initiated a century ago (such as globalization, immigration, equity concerns, technological advance), there are also exponential changes, and the world of work is not the same as it was even a decade ago. It is essential that career practitioners in all their varied work environments help clients understand this and prepare for the unpredictable—the twenty-first century of work" (p. 87).

This chapter relates the principles of accountability introduced in Chapter 14 to the principles of strategic planning and demonstrates how strategic planning can be used to offer relevant and effective career development services in a rapidly changing world. From a strategic planning perspective, the two principal aims of modern career services are to (a) provide learning opportunities to help individuals acquire new knowledge and capabilities that will enable them to become better career problem solvers and decision makers and (b) be responsive to the needs of the clients, organizations, or communities that receive these services. These aims require a continual assessment of both the internal and the external environment of the career services program. Through strategic planning, career services programs will be better prepared to compete for resources, as well as to attain their goals and objectives.

SOCIAL TRENDS

We believe there are four social trends that will have an impact on the career development of individuals and the offering of career services to assist them. These four social trends include the global economy, the growth of technology, new ways of working, and changing family and work roles. These trends will compel career services providers to be mindful of strategic questions such as the following:

- What is our business?
- Who are our primary clients?
- What are their needs?
- How can we as career counselors foster decision-making skills in clients that will enable them to make informed choices in their quest to improve the quality of their lives?

The Global Economy

Peter Drucker is a management consultant who has written almost 30 books about trends in the world of work. His views are widely read and often controversial. In his work *Post-Capitalist Society,* Drucker (1993) argued that the world is once again in a period of enormous transformation. The earlier transformations included the Reformation, the Renaissance, and the American Revolution. "This time it is not, however, confined to Western society and Western history. Indeed, it is one of the fundamental changes that there is no longer a 'Western' history or, in fact a 'Western' civilization. There is only world history and world civilization—but both are 'Westernized.' It is moot whether this present transformation began with the emergence of the first non-Western country, Japan, as a great economic power . . . or with the computer—that is, with information becoming central" (p. 3).

Indeed, Drucker believes that by 2010 or 2020, the world will be a very different kind of place—it will be nonsocialist and postcapitalist. Its primary resource will be knowledge (i.e., useful information); nation-states will be replaced by megastates; and it will be a society of organizations, each devoted to a specific task. One of the leading groups in this new world society will be the "knowledge workers," who know how to allocate knowledge and information to productive use. Drucker continued: "The knowledge society [where knowledge workers will be employed] must have at its core the concept of the educated person. It will have to be a universal concept, precisely because the knowledge society is a society of knowledges and because it is global—in its money, its economics, its careers, its technology, its central issues, and above all, in its information" (p. 212).

In summary, Drucker believes that future careers will occur in a global context where persons having management and information processing skills will work in an information society. Moreover, these knowledge workers will find themselves at work as members of organizations and teams, each seeking to accomplish its own limited objectives. This vision is complex and requires some thoughtful reflection for more complete comprehension.

The Growth of Technology

Judy and D'Amico (1997) asserted that the pace of technological change in today's economy has never been greater. Moreover, it will increase in an exponential manner. They indicated that the "creative destruction" brought by technology to national economies, organizations, and individual workers will be even more powerful in the 21st century than in the past. It is virtually impossible to overestimate the impact of technology on careers and the provision of career services. Indeed, the growth of the Internet has the potential to radically change the way in which career services programs are provided to various constituencies.

New Ways of Working

Many persons have grown up with the idea of working 8 to 5 and 40 hours a week in a professional job—that just seemed to be the natural order of things. Of course, physicians, nurses, plumbers, and police officers work odd schedules, but most of us have regular weekday jobs. Perhaps nothing in the career and work areas has changed as much as the "way we work." The new work patterns include options such as flextime, part-time, job sharing, temporary, and home-based work/telecommuting patterns. There are abundant implications for career services inherent in this area of social change.

Changing Family and Work Roles

Sociologists have noted that the patterns of work for men and women so common in the United States now are only about 100 years old. Before the industrial revolution, men and women both worked on the farm or in the shop and shared child-care and housekeeping duties. With the rise of manufacturing and industry in the late 1800s, men increasingly left the farm to pursue higher-paying jobs in factories in the cities. Women were left at home to care for children and manage the domestic responsibilities. In the past 50 years, beginning during World War II in the 1940s, women have increasingly also begun to work outside the home (Gilbert & Eldridge, 1994). The dual-career family, or in some cases the dual-earner family, where both the man and woman are working outside the home, has had a huge impact on the way most of us work today and will work in the future. The implications for career services are readily apparent.

Elizabeth McKenna (1997), writing in *When Work Doesn't Work Anymore*, suggested that men and women (especially the latter) "have to figure out who they are and what their own definitions of success are (apart from business achievements) in order to negotiate the emotional contract they have made with their careers. And no matter what the decision, there are trade-offs" (p. 38). She noted that success on the job often comes at the price of success in family and personal life. Later, McKenna noted that future generations will "have a different definition of success than we have" (p. 251) and a very different way of working.

For a summary interpretation of all these social changes, we can turn to Jerry Hage (1995), an industrial/organizational psychologist who has studied issues associated with modern work for many years and has important ideas on this topic. He argued that we must develop more complex ways of thinking about life in this modern world. "[P]eople must learn to live in complex role-sets, each with a large number of role-relationships in which negotiations about role expectations or behavior become one of the major capacities for successful role performance. Furthermore, to adjust to the constant changes in society that provide the context for both the family and the workplace, people in post-industrial society need to have complex and creative minds, be adaptive and flexible, and know how to understand symbolic communications" (p. 487). If Hage is correct, we have no choice but to think in more complex ways about our careers, to develop new schemata for solving career problems and making career decisions.

Reardon, Sampson, and Lenz (2000) suggested that these kinds of social trends will have an impact on the nature of career services. They noted that career services customers, clients, patrons, patients, advisees, individuals, students, or whatever label is used, will probably have the characteristics of a "career shopper," a person considering the use of resources and services for assistance in career problem solving and decision making. Career shoppers represent a new variation on these traditional roles of helper and person helped in the career service delivery process. Shoppers are sometimes described as browsers, clientele, potential purchasers or buyers, or lookers. Career shoppers often preview, examine, or try out career-related resources or services before they access them or commit themselves. This could include previewing career resources such as books, Web sites, and computer-based guidance systems, or career services such as counseling, workshops, or courses. In the language of Cognitive Information Processing theory, career shoppers are, to varying degrees, aware of a gap between where they are and where they would like to be—for example, clearer educational goals, a new job, a more prestigious occupation, or more life satisfaction—in their career development.

Depending on the nature of their career shopping experience and their evaluation of the career resources and services they preview, career shoppers then commit themselves to using a resource or seeking assistance from a provider, or they continue shopping. In effect, career shoppers screen themselves into or out of career services. For example, they decide to buy a career book at the bookstore, to take a career test on the Internet, or become the client of a professional career counselor after considering the perceived costs and potential benefits of the options they have previewed.

In a comprehensive career center, which provides services in a physical location and in a virtual setting using the World Wide Web, counselors can expect to increasingly encounter career shoppers. These could include parents, students, advisees, community members, alumni, and persons from other nations. Career shoppers, such as those in a retail clothing store, are often looking for bargains and value and are very conscious of time. Frequently, they want information that will enable them to become more informed career shoppers.

We now turn to ways in which career service providers can prepare to respond to these trends and issues.

STRATEGIC PLANNING

Strategic thinking and planning are capabilities that enable us as career counselors to anticipate important social and organizational changes so that we may continue to offer timely and responsive career services. Bill Banis (1997), the director of University Career Services at Northwestern University, noted: "Assuming that every organization is headed somewhere, if we do not intentionally set strategy, we run the risk of having our program's direction shaped haphazardly or by others" (p. 22).

Strategic Thinking

Strategic thinking involves the integration of planning, leadership, and management (Cope, 1987; Omahe, 1982). Strategic thinking asks such questions as, Where does the organization or community in which this career service program is located want to go? and Are we in the right business relative to other businesses in our environment? Cope defined strategic thinking as "the process of developing a vision of where the institution wants to go, and then developing strategies (plans) on how to get there" (quoted in Hoadly & Zimmer, 1982, p. 16).

Strategic thinking may be further illuminated by contrasting it with the concept of operational planning. Strategic thinking may be thought of as doing the right things (effectiveness) (Ballantine & Watts, 1989), whereas operational planning may be thought of as doing things right (efficiency). Following are other contrasts between these two concepts (Cope, 1987, p. 8):

STRATEGIC THINKING	OPERATIONAL PLANNING
Formulation	Implementation
What	How
Where	How
Ends	Means
Vision	Plans
Effectiveness	Efficiency
Strategizing	Planning
Risk	Control

Strategic thinking demands that career services personnel continually monitor services relative to the core functions of the organization they serve. For example, from a CIP perspective, career services in schools should be perceived as sharing in the development of the intellect; that is, the development of problem-solving skills in career decision making should exist on the same plane as the development of problem-solving skills in mathematics, the natural sciences, the social sciences, or the humanities. They all are concerned with human development and the individual's adaptation to a complex and changing world. Thus, career services in schools should be envisioned as a vital aspect of the total curriculum of the school and should be part of the required curriculum for all levels of public education.

Strategic thinking involves integrating three components:

1. Formulating a vision of the *right things* to do (strategic planning)
2. Achieving *consensus* and acquiring the *resources* to do the right things (leadership)
3. Implementing a plan to do *things right* (management)

Maintaining effective career services programs demands that career counselors, in addition to providing facilitative conditions for human growth and knowing how to help individuals develop career problem-solving skills, must also possess the capacity for thinking strategically about the nature of services they are presently providing and about those to be provided in the future.

Strategic Planning

From its inception in business (Ansoff, 1985), to its application in higher education (Cope, 1987), to its adoption in career service delivery (Watts & Sampson, 1989), strategic planning has been defined as the formulation and attainment of organizational goals through the securing and distribution of resources in competitive environments. The ultimate purpose of strategic planning is to maintain and enhance the viability of a program in a broader organizational and environmental context—that is, to maintain a piece of the action within the organization. Strategic planning involves determining a direction of growth and development internal to the organization in relation to the forces and direction of change in the external environment. Ideally, this will enhance the position of the organization in the relentless competition for resources in the environment. Cope offered the following comprehensive definition:

- Strategic planning is an open-systems approach to steering an enterprise over time through uncertain environmental waters. It is a proactive problem-solving behavior directed externally at conditions in the environment and a means to find a favorable competitive position in the continual competition for resources. Its primary purpose is to achieve success with its mission while linking the institution's future to anticipated changes in the environment in such a way that the acquisition of resources (e.g., money, personnel, staff, students, goodwill) is faster than the depletion of resources (p. 3).
- Strategic planning requires a vision of the future, a vision that is more often developed from intuition, opinions, and qualitative information than from the kinds of empirical data used in operational planning. Strategic thinking and planning involve a forward-thinking and proactive approach to the offering of career services.

In the provision of career services, the vision is derived from the answer to these questions: What services will our clients require to help them make career decisions 5 or 10 years from now (internal environment), and how will this career decision-making activity complement the core functions of the organization (external environment)? It is important for counselors to be familiar with future possibilities in the offering of career services (e.g., self-directed, interactive technological delivery systems). Even more important, career counselors must be able to anticipate the future directions of the organization in which the career service is located (e.g., a university may wish to place greater emphasis on community involvement and on partnerships with private industry to generate more revenue).

Before exploring issues and methods in strategic planning, it is important to focus on two related topics: (a) boundary spanning and (b) structure and function. Banis (1997) noted that career services have boundary-spanning roles within and outside organizations. External forces, such as lowering admissions requirements or losing an academic program's accreditation, can affect career services. Moreover, the state of the regional or national economy can affect student and employer relations with career services programs. The boundary-spanning networks in which career services are provided need to be clarified and understood before undertaking strategic planning activities.

In addition, the organizational structure of a career center will have bearing on functions and operations. These structural relationships include geographic realities and the placement of career services operations in contiguous space or scattered in several buildings across a campus. New functions will require new administrative structures and management relationships. Creating flowcharts can help track the flow of client services, budget resources, and staff relationships as a precursor to strategic planning activities. The structure of the organization should be supported by a logical rationale that can be readily grasped by staff and constituents.

WHY STRATEGIC PLANNING IS NECESSARY

Strategic planning is a method by which career services programs may maintain and enhance their position relative to other service providers in an organization; it is also a way to keep abreast of the evolution of the organizational mission in order to maintain the alignment of the programs with the core functions of the parent organization. In an educational institution, a career services program can become an integral part of the curriculum through offering courses for credit. In a corporation, a career services program may be involved in selecting personnel, allocating and distributing human resources, handling promotions, developing career ladders, enhancing productivity, and facilitating outplacement. In the community, a career services program may be aligned with the broad area of adult and community education through service delivery organizations such as libraries, community service centers, churches, fraternal organizations, and the like. We have learned from our own experience that unless career services are perceived as integral to the organizational mission, they are likely to be at a severe disadvantage in the competition for resources within the organization.

Strategic planning also relates to problems that are seemingly internal to the career services program. For example, the career services staff may not have a clear sense of purpose other than to provide assistance to drop-in clients; budgets may be cut, even though things seem to be going well; the determination of whether to invest in a new technological delivery capability may be problematic; or members of the counseling staff may feel alienated and isolated from other professionals in the organization. Such problems can often be traced to the lack of an integrating vision of success and sense of mission. According to Bryson (1988), the very process of strategic planning "can facilitate communication and participation, accommodate divergent interests and values, and foster orderly decision making and successful implementation" (p. 5).

GUIDELINES FOR STRATEGIC PLANNING

The strategic planning process may be thought of as an organizational metacognitive activity that begins with the question, Are we doing the right things? and moves toward the question, Are we doing things right? The first question concerns *what* issues—for example, What will the future be? What will be different? What business are we in?; the second question involves *how* issues—for example, How will we implement our mission? How will we obtain the resources to achieve and maintain our mission? The process of moving from *what* to *how* may be described in terms of six steps, as presented in Figure 15.1.

The following steps may be used by a strategic planning committee as a guideline to structure a sequence of activities. We recommend that the committee include not only representatives internal to the program but also representatives external to

Figure 15.1 A Six-Step Strategic Planning Process

From *Career Development and Services: A Cognitive Approach* (p. 414), by G. W. Peterson, J. P. Sampson, Jr., and R. C. Reardon, 1991, Pacific Grove, CA: Brooks/Cole.

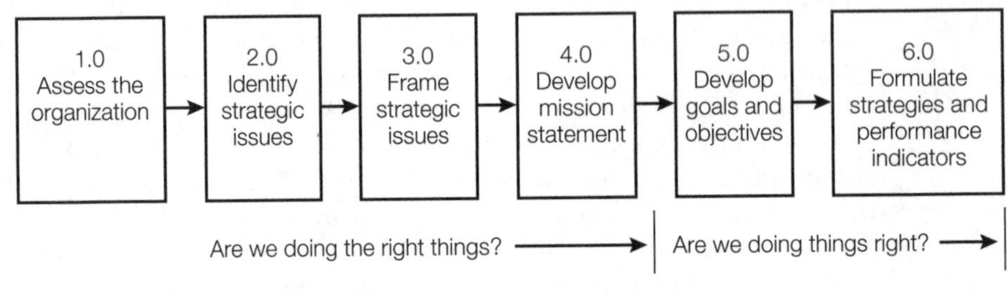

the program—such as senior administrators, persons known for unusual, forward-thinking ideas, clients of the program, and a neutral process leader who does not have a vested interest in the outcome of the process.

Step 1: Assess the Organization

The first step involves undertaking an audit of the organization's present mandates, mission, goals, and visions from both an internal perspective (that of the career services program itself) and an external perspective (that of the organization and the community in which the service is located). The assessment phase is analogous to the Communication phase in the CASVE problem-solving cycle. In this step in strategic planning, the career counseling staff and related personnel critically reexamine the organizational context of the career services program.

From a strategic perspective, an organizational assessment involves an examination of the organization's *strengths, weaknesses, opportunities,* and *threats* (SWOTs). Applying the principle of triangulation in naturalistic inquiry (Guba, 1978; Guba & Lincoln, 1981; Patton, 1980), the investigation of SWOTs for a career services program should include gathering data from representatives of three groups: (a) career services program staff, (b) clients of the program, and (c) the leaders and managers of the organization in which the career services program is located who are responsible for the allocation of human and nonhuman resources. Each of these groups will have its own views on the functioning of a career services program. In an interview format using open-ended questions, the strategic planning committee should ask the representatives of each group the following questions.

- *Strengths* (what the career services program is doing right): What are the principal functions and purposes of the career service center? How well does it perform each function? Can you give examples of successful performance?

- *Weaknesses* (what the career services program is doing wrong): Of the functions the career service provides, which might be improved? Can you cite instances in which the service could have been performed better? From your perspective, how might each of these functions be improved?
- *Opportunities* (whether the career services program is in the right business): Are there functions that are not being provided by the career services program and that ought to be considered for adoption? If so, what are some of the reasons you believe each of these functions should be considered? Are there any functions the career services program ought to consider curtailing or eliminating? If so, what are some of the reasons?
- *Threats* (what the prospects are for the continuing growth and health of the organization and what the competition will be for resources within the parent organization): What are the future goals of the parent organization? How might the human services, including the career services program, respond to the future needs of the organization?

From the data gathered from the interviews, a synthesis should emerge about how the career services program is perceived by the constituencies that directly influence its operation and maintenance. In some cases, the planning committee may wish to secure the assistance of an independent team of evaluators to conduct the assessment.

Step 2: Identify Strategic Issues

In the second step, the strategic planning committee identifies strategic issues, as opposed to operations issues. The committee may use the direct approach, the goals approach, or the vision-of-success approach (Barry, 1986).

The *direct approach* progresses in a straightforward, linear fashion from a review of mandates, mission, and SWOTS to the identification of strategic issues. The direct approach works well in the pluralistic, partisan, and relatively fragmented world of public nonprofit organizations—as long as there is a "dominant coalition" committed to seeing the strategic planning process through to fruition (Bryson, 1988). For example, a career center in a large public college or university, which has maintained a consistent track record, may wish to conduct an evaluation and planning exercise to ensure the continued vitality of the service.

The *goals approach* entails establishing goals and objectives for the program and then identifying the strategies to achieve them. The National Career Development Guidelines (Kobylarz, 1996) discussed earlier could be relevant here. This approach requires a broad and deep agreement as to what the goals should be, a strong authority structure, a narrowly defined mission, and few potential stakeholders. An example where this approach might be appropriate is a private secondary school with a small career service center whose principal function is to facilitate college choice.

An organization may use the *vision-of-success approach* when it must develop a picture of itself in the future that maximizes the successful fulfillment of its mission. Strategic issues arise as the gap between where the organization is and where it should be becomes clear. This approach should receive strong consideration when the organization in which the career services program is housed faces a strong need for drastic change. This approach is useful when the leaders of the organization realize that it is probably in the wrong business and must find the right business. In this case, short scenarios become working documents. For example, a public college or university may be compelled to reexamine and reduce its student services when funds are cut as a result of a major economic recession (as occurred in 1974); the university may no longer be able to afford intensive, long-term, one-on-one career counseling. In such a case, new and creative thinking is obviously called for (refer to Chapter 12 for a case history of how one university counseling service coped with such a crisis).

Step 3: Frame Strategic Issues

In the third step, framing issues, the planning committee should give each issue a litmus test to determine the extent to which that issue is strategic. Strategic issues are hallmarked by the following characteristics:

- The challenge or opportunity is long-range (two or more years from now rather than this year or the next).
- The impact will extend beyond the program to several departments and have an impact on the entire organization.
- There will be considerable budgetary risks.
- The resolution of the issue will involve new goals, resources, policies, facilities, and staff changes.
- It is unclear what the best approach would be to resolve the issue.
- The lowest level of management to deal with the issue is a corporation's or agency's department head, a school principal, a university dean, or a college department head.
- The consequence of not addressing the issue is major, long-term service disruption.
- The issue is emotionally charged.

Thus, an issue such as "Should we redesign our office Web page to enhance the provision of career services?" is more strategic than an issue such as "Should we adopt a computer-assisted career guidance system to facilitate the exploration of career alternatives?"

Issues should be framed in ways that make the choices clear. Bryson (1988) outlined some useful questions to examine issues:

> What is the issue, conflict, or dilemma? Why is it an issue? What is it about the program's mission, mandates, or SWOTs that makes it an issue? Who says it is an issue? What are the consequences of not doing something about it? Can we do something about it? Is there a way to combine or eliminate issues? Should issues be broken down into two or more issues? (pp. 159–160)

The focus of the planning committee at this stage should be on issues, not answers or solutions. There should be agreement among key decision makers outside the planning committee that the issues are important and worthy of inclusion in the process.

Step 4: Develop Mission Statement

The fourth step is the development of a statement of the mission of the program. The planning committee may develop a working draft of the mission statement, which can then be reviewed by the stakeholders in the program. The mission statement may go through several rounds or passes among the stakeholders before the final draft is established. Earlier, we presented the mission statement for the Career Center at Florida State University, and we reprint it here:

> The mission of the FSU Career Center is to provide comprehensive career services, train career service practitioners, conduct life/career development research, and disseminate information about life/career services and issues to the university community, the nation, and the world. (Florida State University, 2000)

A mission statement reflects the philosophy, theory, purpose, and assumptions underlying a career services program. It is the final step addressing the question, Are we doing the right things?

Step 5: Develop Goals and Objectives

The next question is, Are we doing things right? The mission statement now becomes an organizing principle for the development of goal statements that relate to the broad intents of the program. Objectives are more specific and less abstract than goals. A goal usually takes three to five years to attain, whereas an objective can be accomplished in one year. There are often several subordinate objectives to each goal. An example of a goal might be to establish an interactive computer network to facilitate academic advising. An example of an objective could be to develop a computer software program that gives students independent access to an up-to-date transcript after giving a password and their social security number.

Step 6: Formulate Strategies and Performance Indicators

The sixth step in strategic planning involves formulating strategies and performance indicators. A strategy is the sequence of events required to achieve an objective. Examples of strategies are the identification of milestones or progress steps, the naming of those persons responsible for attaining the objectives, and the naming of those persons in charge of the financial resources necessary to accomplish the objectives. Performance indicators for outputs and outcomes can be used to measure the degree to which goals and objectives are accomplished and to satisfy accountability requirements, as discussed in Chapter 14.

STRATEGIC PLANNING, COGNITIVE INFORMATION PROCESSING, AND ACCOUNTABILITY

The question explored in this section is, How can principles of strategic planning be linked to the offering of effective career services that enhance career problem-solving and decision-making skills? We view strategic planning as defining the limits of authorized organizational activity within which the fostering of career development can occur. Strategic planning determines the organizational boundary as well as the budget allocated to sponsor the activities within that boundary.

The following are some examples of strategic issues related to the boundaries of the service within a postsecondary setting: Should career service activities, now embedded within the activities of a general counseling center, be removed and offered within a separate organization entity? Should career services include self-directed options, one-on-one assistance, or group counseling approaches? Should a career service include freshman orientation or academic advising? Should it include job placement or cooperative educational opportunities? Are career services integrally involved with the general education program through the offering of career development courses for academic credit? Should the career services be involved in alumni career development activities? Should career services be offered on-line, or should students have to come in to the office for services?

Examples of strategic issues in a corporate setting might include the following: Should career services be offered in-house or contracted out to independent service providers? Should managers or supervisors be involved in an in-house career service? How are the career services integrated with personnel recruitment, selection, training, promotion, termination, and outplacement? Should a career service incorporate employee assistance programs that treat alcoholism and drug abuse? Should the career service be integrally involved in the organization's own planning and organizational development?

In both educational and industrial settings, strategic planning should determine a map for the offering of services in relation to the support services offered by other programs and departments within the organization. Once the boundary conditions are established through strategic planning, several issues arise.

The Client Population

The boundary conditions define who is eligible to receive services and who is not. Clients are those persons who meet the eligibility criteria and choose to avail themselves of the career services offered by a program. We find it helpful to distinguish between primary clients and secondary clients. In CIP terms, *primary clients* are those who are eligible to receive career services that facilitate the development of career problem-solving and decision-making skills—for example, students, and also persons who are not regular members of the organization and who may pay for its services, such as alumni, faculty, or individuals from the community. *Secondary clients* are those who are affected by the primary clients' changed capacity for career problem solving—for example, prospective employers, faculty advisers, spouses, and parents. In corporate settings, the primary client may be the employee, and the secondary clients may be the company's customers and stockholders, the members of the employee's family, and the community businesses and societies that benefit from a high-performing organization.

Although operations planning affects the allocation of funds for services to primary clients, strategic planning typically affects the funds allocated from the institutional budget for secondary as well as primary clients. Thus, the goals of a career services program must be consistent with institutional goals if adequate funds are to be obtained for career services (Watts & Sampson, 1989).

The Domain of Client Decisions

Once the boundary conditions have been delineated, the next task is to identify the kinds of career decisions that are made by the client population. Are they choosing majors? Selecting elective courses? Identifying plausible career paths? Locating part-time work? Seeking job training? A survey, in the form of a checklist of decisions with open-ended responses, can be sent to a sample of the client population; this is an inexpensive and effective way of identifying the kinds and frequencies of decisions made by the clients. An additional means for gathering data might involve the use of focus groups (National Association of Colleges and Employers, 1995; Stewart & Shamdasani, 1990).

Having tabulated data from surveys, focus groups, or other means used to assess the domain of client decisions, the career counselor should decide which decisions will be the main focus of the career service; for example, is the career service in the academic advising business, the financial aid business, the placement business, or the general student adjustment business? Circumscribing the domain of client decisions to be addressed requires an examination of the mission of the career service center in relation to the missions of the other services available to the client population within the organization.

Information and Services Required

Having established parameters for determining the kinds of decisions that are of principal concern to the service, the question now becomes, What resources will clients require to help them acquire self-knowledge, occupational knowledge, decision-making skills (the CASVE cycle), and metacognitions to enhance their capabilities for making sound decisions? The career counselor should review each decision (or category of decisions) in the domain in terms of (a) the kinds of component knowledges (self and occupational) and cognitive skills required to make the decisions; (b) the client's general learning capabilities, such as verbal aptitude; and (c) the availability of alternative means of delivering the information and providing learning events. This examination requires that the counselor envision how a variety of clients who use the center may be helped to make decisions. From this procedure a complete "shopping list" is developed for information resources, for media delivery options, and for the kinds of human interventions to be offered by the center.

Once the shopping list is complete, the members of the career counseling staff should develop a budget to allocate financial resources to the purchase of materials and supplies and to hire staff. Clearly delineating the domain of client decisions that the career center addresses minimizes the risks of either under- or overpurchasing materials, of hiring either too many or too few individuals, or of hiring individuals with either too many or too few credentials. The career center should now be in a position not only to do the right things but also to do things right.

Effectiveness of the Services

Strategic planning is linked to accountability through the cognitive information paradigm. As discussed in Chapter 14, the career center may gauge its effectiveness by the degree to which clients are acquiring the component knowledges and skills (outputs) required to make the decisions that are consistent with the mission of the center. By taking cohort samples of individuals with similar entry-level characteristics and common decisions to make, a career services program can demonstrate gains in self-knowledge, occupational knowledge, problem-solving and decision-making skills, and metacognitions. These gains may be measured by one or more of the 40 instruments identified by Sampson, Peterson, Reardon, and Lenz (2000) in a pretest-posttest, quasi-experimental design. The gain scores can be related to data acquired through follow-up surveys that assess how the knowledge and skills were used to make real-life decisions (outcomes).

In a complete evaluation strategy, output and outcome data are secured for each decision included within the mission of the center. Such information can be used not only for making programmatic decisions related to the allocation of financial resources but also for communicating the effectiveness of the services to stakeholders external to the program, such as parents, central administrators, or the personnel of complementary student support services (Niles & Harris-Bowlsbey, 2002).

ROLES OF THE CAREER SERVICES PRACTITIONER

One of the intents of this book is to present a way of thinking about career development and career counseling that relates theory and practice. We believe that the traditional scenario of career counseling—that of listening attentively, one-on-one, to a client's career and life problems, administering a battery of inventories, and interpreting the results—will play a decreasing part in the professional life of career counselors. New and more complex roles will overlay this traditional career counseling role. Figure 15.2 shows a hierarchy of concentric, overlapping roles. The traditional role of career counselor continues to be at the core, but it is included within (a) a teacher-educator role, (b) a designer-developer-evaluator role, and (c) a strategic planner role, the most abstract level of professional functioning. Each role is subsumed by a more complex role, and each requires a unique subset of knowledge and skills.

Counselor

In the counselor role, the professional is able to provide the core facilitative conditions to foster growth and change, as described by Rogers (1951, 1957, 1962) and Carkhuff and Berenson (1967). We believe it is vital for clients to know that someone in a career service center understands the nature of their problems and feelings and to receive assurance that they will be provided with competent assistance. Career counseling may be viewed as a therapeutic event in the broadest sense; that is, the counselor provides an intervention according to the directions of growth determined by the client (Weitz, 1964).

Figure 15.2 | Hierarchy of Career Counseling Roles

From *Career Development and Services: A Cognitive Approach* (p. 421), by G. W. Peterson, J. P. Sampson, Jr., and R. C. Reardon, 1991, Pacific Grove, CA: Brooks/Cole.

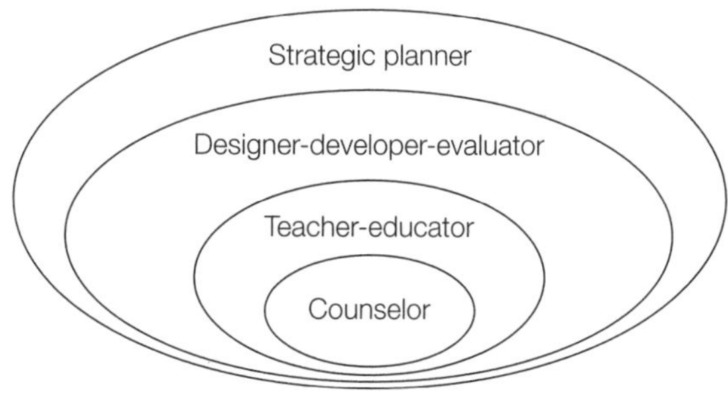

Teacher-Educator

From a CIP perspective, it is not enough to provide only the facilitative conditions for change in career counseling. If clients are to acquire new decision-making capabilities, the career counseling enterprise must also be viewed as a learning event. Following Carl Rogers's articulation of the necessary and sufficient conditions of therapy, Robert Gagne (1985) formulated a set of necessary conditions for learning. Helping clients acquire knowledge and cognitive skills takes career counseling to a completely different realm of professional activity. To function in the teacher-educator role, career counselors must draw on the fields of educational and cognitive psychology. Viewing counseling as a learning event requires that the client and the counselor agree on a set of intended learning outcomes and ways to attain them.

Designer-Developer-Evaluator

In addition to providing conditions for individual growth and learning, career counselors must also think in terms of offering services and programs to a population of potential clients. At this level, counselors must be prepared to design, develop, and deliver effective and efficient interventions using a variety of means to help individuals enhance their decision-making skills. A career counselor must be able to design an instructional system in which the environment is structured to foster certain kinds of learning. Thus, client learning outcomes become the focal point for determining the effectiveness of the service. Counselors and media are viewed as learning resources that are available to the client to foster the attainment of knowledge, skills, and attitudes. The role of designer-developer-evaluator requires a cognitive refraining from the traditional counselor-client relationship—a change from viewing the relationship as an end in its own right to viewing it as a means to attain certain ends (that is, new knowledge and skills).

Strategic Planner

The career counselor, as a strategic planner, focuses on the contribution of career counseling services to the good of the organization and the community. Functioning in this role requires perhaps the highest level of conceptualization of one's role as counselor. It draws on the visions and ideals of both the profession and the organization. As a strategic planner, the counselor becomes proactive in promoting the career service by constantly entertaining the possibility for extending the services made available by the organization, rather than being reactive, as is typically the case when the counselor serves individual clients. The strategic planning role also requires that career counselors possess a strong belief in the worth of their profession for enhancing the quality of life. The strategic planner says, "I have something of value to offer individuals that deserves an important place in the functioning of the organization." Members of the staff, and especially the director of a career services program, should concentrate on how well the program is serving the organization and the community and should be always exploring the possibility for extending the range of career service offerings that are an integral part of the core functions of the organization.

In order to prepare counselors to play the strategic planner role, the profession must reconceptualize counselor training programs (Vacc & Bardon, 1989). Career development can no longer be relegated to a single course in a generic counseling and guidance program. Effective training programs must include the mastering of knowledge from the fields of educational psychology; cognitive psychology; instructional media and systems; family systems; organizational dynamics; and program planning, budgeting, and evaluation. We do not see the introduction of such course content as merely add-ons to existing curricula; we recommend the redesign of counselor education and counseling psychology curricula. Such redesign can be accomplished by engaging in the very strategic planning processes just advocated. Let us make sure we are doing the right things in addition to doing things right.

SUMMARY

This chapter introduced the concepts of strategic thinking, operations planning, and strategic planning as ways of thinking about the formulation of the intents of career services. A six-stage process was described that can be used as a guideline for the strategic planning process, in which a planning committee begins with the question, Are we doing the right things? and progresses to the question, Are we doing things right? The activity of strategic planning was linked to Cognitive Information Processing theory and to accountability through the delineation of the client population to be served and the types of decisions the service is designed to help the clients to make. Primary clients, those who acquire new knowledge and skills, were contrasted with secondary clients, those who are the benefactors of changes in the primary clients. The effectiveness of a career service is ultimately determined by the degree to which clients acquire new capabilities and the relevance of these capabilities to the core functions of the organization in which the career service is located. The chapter closed with a description of the emerging roles of the career practitioner: counselor, teacher-educator, designer-developer-evaluator, and strategic planner.

GETTING THE MOST BENEFIT FROM READING THIS CHAPTER

To effectively learn the material in this chapter, complete one or more of the following activities:

- Form a strategic planning group of five or six persons. Locate a career service in the community, and design a strategic planning process that service could employ.
- Approach the redesign of your present counseling curriculum from (a) an operations planning mode and (b) a strategic planning perspective. Describe the differences in the inputs, processes, and outputs of these two planning processes. Share your findings with the faculty.
- Locate a career services program in your community, and conduct an investigation of how its mission, goals, and objectives were derived. To what degree were strategic planning principles used?
- Locate a career services program in your community, and describe the characteristics of its clientele. Discuss with the staff counselors how the trends toward a global economy, technological innovation, new ways of working, and new work/family roles in the labor force will likely influence (a) the nature of the career services offered and (b) the client's consideration of career alternatives.

REFERENCES

Ansoff, I. H. (1985). *Corporate strategy: An analytical approach to business policy for growth and expansion.* New York: McGraw-Hill.

Ballantine, M., & Watts, A. G. (1989). Computers and careers guidance services: Integrating the technology into the organisation. In A. G. Watts (Ed.), *Computers in careers guidance: Report of the second European conference on computers in careers guidance and of its teleconference with the USA* (pp. 18–22). Cambridge, England: Careers Research and Advisory Centre.

Banis, W. (1997). A strategic management model for career services. *Journal of Career Planning and Employment, 58* (1), 21–24, 57–60.

Barry, B. W. (1986). *Strategic planning workbook for non-profit organizations.* St. Paul, MN: Amherst H. Wilder Foundation.

Bryson, J. M. (1988). *Strategic planning for public and non-profit organizations: A guide to strengthening-sustaining organizational achievement.* San Francisco: Jossey-Bass.

Carkhuff, R. R., & Berenson, B. G. (1967). *Beyond counseling and therapy.* New York: Holt, Rinehart & Winston.

Cope, R. G. (1987). *Opportunity for strength: Strategic planning clarified with case examples* (ASHE-ERIC Higher Education Report No. 8). Washington, DC: George Washington University Clearinghouse on Higher Education.

DeBell, C. (2001). Ninety years in the world of work in America. *The Career Development Quarterly, 50,* 77–88.

Drucker, P. F. (1993). *Post-capitalist society.* New York: HarperBusiness.

Florida State University. (2000). *Career center manual* [On-line]. Available: www.career.fsu.edu/techcenter/designing_career_services/practical_strategies/.

Gagne, R. M. (1985). *The conditions of learning and theory of instruction* (4th ed.). New York: Holt, Rinehart & Winston.

Gilbert, L. A., & Eldridge, N. S. (1994). Gender and dual-career families: Implications and applications for the career counseling of women. In W. B. Walsh & S. H. Osipow (Eds.), *Career counseling for women* (pp. 135–164). Hillsdale, NJ: Lawrence Erlbaum Associates.

Guba, E. (1978). *Toward a method of naturalistic inquiry in educational evaluation.* Los Angeles: University of California, Center for the Study of Evaluation.

Guba, E., & Lincoln, Y. S. (1981). *Effective evaluation.* San Francisco: Jossey-Bass.

Hage, J. (1995). Post-industrial lives: New demands, new prescriptions. In A. Howard (Ed.), *The changing nature of work* (pp. 485–512). San Francisco: Jossey-Bass.

Hoadly, J. A., & Zimmer, B. E. (1982). A corporate planning approach to institutional management: A preliminary report on the RMIT experience. *Journal of Tertiary Education Administration, 9,* 15–26.

Judy, R. W., & D'Amico, C. (1997). *Workforce 2020: Work and workers in the 21st century.* Indianapolis, IN: Hudson Institute.

Kobylarz, L. (1996). *National Career Development Guidelines: K–adult handbook.* Stillwater, OK: National Occupational Information Coordinating Committee Training and Support Center.

McKenna, E. P. (1997). *When work doesn't work anymore: Women, work, and identity.* New York: Delacorte Press.

National Association of Colleges and Employers. (1995). *Sourcebook for conducting evaluations and measurements of career services.* Bethlehem, PA: Author.

Niles, S. G., & Harris-Bowlsbey, J. (2002). *Career development interventions in the 21st century.* Upper Saddle River, NJ: Merrill/Prentice Hall.

Omahe, K. (1982). *The mind of the strategist: The art of Japanese business.* New York: McGraw-Hill.

Patton, M. C. (1980). *Qualitative evaluation methods.* Beverly Hills, CA: Sage.

Reardon, R. C., Sampson, J. P., Jr., & Lenz, J. G. (2000). Career assessment in a time of changing roles, relationships, and contexts. *Journal of Career Assessment, 8,* 351–359.

Rogers, C. R. (1951). *Client-centered therapy.* Boston: Houghton Mifflin.

Rogers, C. R. (1957). The necessary and sufficient conditions of therapeutic personality change. *Journal of Consulting and Clinical Psychology, 22,* 95–103.

Rogers, C. R. (1962). The interpersonal relationship: The core of guidance. *Harvard Educational Review, 32,* 416–429.

Sampson, J. P., Jr., Peterson, G. W., Reardon, R. C., & Lenz, J. L. (2000). The viability of readiness assessment in contributing to improved career services: A response to Jepsen. *The Career Development Quarterly, 49,* 179–185.

Stewart, D. W., & Shamdasani, P. N. (1990). *Focus groups: Theory and practice* (Applied Social Research Methods Series, Vol. 20). Newbury Park, CA: Sage.

Vacc, N. A., & Bardon, J. I. (1989). *The reconceptualization of counselor education: A context for influencing human service.* Unpublished manuscript, University of North Carolina at Greensboro.

Watts, A. G., & Sampson, J. P., Jr. (1989). Strategic planning and performance measurement: Impressions for career services in higher education. *British Journal of Guidance & Counselling, 17* (1), 34–48.

Weitz, H. (1964). *Behavior change through guidance.* New York: John Wiley.

Florida State University Career Center Module Sheets

CURRICULAR-CAREER INFORMATION SERVICE (CCIS) • THE CAREER CENTER • THE FLORIDA STATE UNIVERSITY

MODULE I

CCIS INTRODUCTION

Everything You've Always Wanted To Know About CCIS

The purpose of CCIS is to assist you in solving current career problems and making appropriate career and academic decisions, as well as helping to improve your skills in solving future career problems.

Objectives

1. To introduce you to CCIS.
2. To help you select the activities that will assist you in solving your career problems.

Below Are Activities To Help You Achieve These Objectives

a. Examine a Career Center brochure located on the rack near the Career Center entrance to learn more about CCIS services and programs.

b. Ask a Career Advisor to explain CCIS and the career advising process to you.

c. Attend a Career Center tour. Ask for a current schedule of Career Center events or view them at: www.career.fsu.edu/calendar.html

d. Browse through the remaining module sheets on the yellow rack to learn more about some of the common concerns addressed through the career advising process.

Revised 4/02

If you need assistance please consult with the Career Advisor at the help desk.
This module is available in an alternative format upon request.

CURRICULAR-CAREER INFORMATION SERVICE (CCIS) • THE CAREER CENTER • THE FLORIDA STATE UNIVERSITY

MODULE II

GUIDELINES FOR CAREER DECISION-MAKING

What's Involved In Making A Career Decision?

Objectives

1. To help you identify areas that are important to consider in making career choices.
2. To help you learn and apply the skills involved in career problem-solving and decision making.

Below are Activities to Help You Achieve These Objectives

a. Review the "What's Involved in Career Choice" sheet to gain a greater awareness of the career decision-making process.

b. Review "A Guide to Good Decision Making" sheet to explore more effective ways to make career decisions.

c. Review the "Career Choice Resources" handout and/or books catalogued IA in The Career Center Library.

d. Review materials in the Module II folder in the Mobile File (file #1).

e. Attend a Career Center workshop on "Choosing a Major."

f. With the assistance of a Career Advisor, complete the "Guide to Good Decision-Making Exercise."

g. Register for Unit I and II of the Introduction to Career Development Class - SDS 3340. A course syllabus is available for your review in the back of the Mobile File (file #1) or at the following Web address: www.career.fsu.edu/student/current/choose_a_major/sds_3340/syllabus.html

Revised 4/02

If you need assistance please consult with the Career Advisor at the help desk.
This module is available in an alternative format upon request.

CURRICULAR-CAREER INFORMATION SERVICE (CCIS) • THE CAREER CENTER • THE FLORIDA STATE UNIVERSITY

MODULE III

SELF-ASSESSMENT

Looking At You

Objectives

1. To help you examine some of your interests, values, and skills.
2. To help you relate your self-knowledge to occupations, fields of study, or jobs for further exploration.

Below Are Activities To Help You Achieve These Objectives

Read the Rationale Statement on the back page.

See a Career Advisor to discuss your situation, select appropriate activities for your career concerns, and complete the Individual Career Learning Plan.

Interests

1. Complete the Self-Directed Search (SDS), computer or paper version.
2. Complete the "Interest Profiles" in the CHOICES computer system to explore occupational and search for the occupations feature in the occupations database which allows you to search for occupations and programs of study based on the Holland interest assessment.
3. Complete the Uniact Interest Inventory in the "Learning About Self and Career" component in Hall 1 of the DISCOVER computer program.
4. Complete the "Interests" portion of "Self-Assessment" on the SIGI PLUS computer program.

Values

1. Complete the "Values" portion of Self-Assessment on the SIGI PLUS computer program.
2. Complete the Values Card Sort.
3. Complete the Values Inventory in the "Learning About Self and Career" component in Hall 1 of the DISCOVER computer program.
4. Complete the Work Importance Locator in the CHOICES system to learn more about your work values and what is important to you in a job or use the search for occupations to identify options based on your General Workplace skills or transferable work skills.

Over

Skills

1. Complete the Skills Checklist on the CHOICES computer program.
2. Complete the Motivated Skills Card Sort.
3. Complete the Abilities Assessment in the "Learning About Self and Career" component in Hall 1 of the DISCOVER computer program.
4. Complete the "Activities" portion of Self-Assessment on the SIGI PLUS computer program.
5. Use the Skills section of SIGI PLUS.
6. Interact with the MicroSkills computer program.

Rationale

A critical part of learning how to make career decisions involves looking at oneself and answering the following questions:

1. What kind of activities am I interested in?
2. What sort of values do I have that might be an important part of exploring possible occupations, fields of study, or jobs?
3. What kinds of skills and abilities do I possess or need to develop?

The answers to these "I stated" questions are important ones because they provide useful information for making career decisions and solving career problems throughout one's life. This self-knowledge helps us both expand and narrow the options that we are considering at any given point in life.

This Module identifies self-assessment activities available to you that will prove to be interesting, fun, and informative. In consultation with a Career Advisor, you may complete any of these activities with respect to your individual needs.

When you have completed the selected activities, you are encouraged to meet with a Career Advisor again to discuss the results of your self-assessment and the implications for your career development.

Other Activities Available to You

a. Complete the Occupational Card Sort.

b. Complete the College or FSU Majors Card Sort. Discuss with a career advisor how the majors you are considering reflect your interest, values and skills.

c. Register for Units I and II of SDS 3340 - Introduction to Career Development. A course syllabus is located in the back of the Mobile File (file #1) or at the following web address: www.career.fsu.edu/ccis/sds3340.html

d. Attend one of The Career Center's "Choosing a Major" workshops.

e. Review the handout "Career Choice Resources" and any books catalogued IA in the Career Center Library.

Revised 4/02

If you need assistance please consult with the Career Advisor at the help desk.
This module is available in an alternative format upon request.

CURRICULAR-CAREER INFORMATION SERVICE (CCIS) • THE CAREER CENTER • THE FLORIDA STATE UNIVERSITY

MODULE IV

INFORMATION SOURCES

Information: What's Available Out There And Where To Find It

Objective

1. To help you identify and locate Career Center resources and other information related to your educational and career planning needs.

Below Are Activities To Help You Achieve This Objective

a. Visit the Career Library in A4101 UC and perform a search using Career Key for the topic of interest to you. Career information resources are available to you in the following formats: Print: Books, Periodicals, Files, Multi-media: CD-Roms, Computer Systems, Internet Resources, Videotapes

b. Review a diagram (see back) of the Career Center's Library in A4101 UC, to see the locations of various career library print and multi-media resources.

c. Talk with the Librarian, a library assistant, or a Career Advisor about Internet information resources that might be helpful for your career planning needs.

d. Perform a search using the Web LUIS system (www.fsu.edu/~library/luis.html) to locate resources on career planning that are available on campus through inter-library loan.

e. Perform a search using the State Archives and library catalog (http://dlis.dos.state.fl.us/barm/fsa.html) system to locate resources on career planning that are available at the State Library of Florida.

(over for map)

Revised 4/02

If you need assistance please consult with the Career Advisor at the help desk.
This module is available in an alternative format upon request.

CURRICULAR-CAREER INFORMATION SERVICE (CCIS) • THE CAREER CENTER • THE FLORIDA STATE UNIVERSITY

MODULE V

LINKING EDUCATION AND WORK

Matching Majors And Jobs

Objective

To help you learn how specific job titles relate to college majors or fields of study.

Below Are Activities To Help You Achieve This Objective

a. Review printed materials in the Module V "Matching Majors and Jobs" folders in the Mobile File (file #1), specifically the "Match Majors" sheets; visit the Career Center Web site: www.career.fsu.edu/ccis/matchmajor/matchmenu.html

b. Read sections in these books or others found in Area IIC of the Career Center Library.

IIC AA C7	The College Board Guide to 150 Popular College Majors
IIC AA P4	College Majors & Careers
IIC AA R61	The Career Connection
IIC AA R62	The Career Connection II

c. Perform a search on Career Key under the topic "Occupation by Major" to get a list of relevant Career Center Library resources. Ask a Career Advisor for assistance.

d. Use the College Majors Card Sort to find majors and occupational opportunities. Ask a Career Advisor for assistance.

e. Review employment information in the FSU *Undergraduate Academic Program Guide* www.academic-guide.fsu.edu for various programs of study at FSU.

f. Use the *Dictionary of Holland Occupational Codes* (DHOC) (IIA G6), available on the Career Center Library Ready Reference shelves. Part 3 links Instructional Program Titles to three-letter Holland Codes. These Holland Codes can then be used to find occupations in the DHOC or the SDS Occupations Finder.

g. Use the "Search by Major" feature in SIGI PLUS, www.facts.org; click on the Career Resources link to access SIGI PLUS on-line.

Over

h. Review selected Employer Directories that list organizations by major, career, or geographical areas located in section VI of the Career Center Library. Ask a Career Advisor for assistance.

i. Consult with Career Center staff members in Placement Services 4119 UCA and Career Experience Opportunities (CEO), 4131 UCA.

j. With the assistance of a Career Advisor, use the Seminole Connection database www.career-recruit.fsu.edu/acfsu/welcome.htm to see what types of positions individuals have entered with their majors.

k. Review job notice files, organized by career areas, government agencies, overseas employment, and educational settings, to see the types of majors required by employers for specific positions.

l. Use the "Major to Career Converter" available on MonsterTrak, www.monstertrak.com

Revised 4/02

If you need assistance, please consult with the Career Advisor at the help desk.
This module is available in an alternative format upon request.

CURRICULAR-CAREER INFORMATION SERVICE (CCIS) • THE CAREER CENTER • THE FLORIDA STATE UNIVERSITY

MODULE VI

EMPLOYMENT OUTLOOK

Job Forecasts And Your Career Plans

Objectives

1. To describe the present distribution of workers in different job areas, e.g., gender, race.
2. To describe the projected employment trends in various occupations.
3. To understand the complexity and accuracy of employment forecasting.
4. To identify the lowest and highest employment demand areas.

Below Are Activities To Help You Achieve These Objectives

a. Perform a search on Career Key under the topics National Outlook and Florida Outlook.

b. Read materials in the Career Library Module VI folders in the Mobile File. "Occupational Outlook" contains information regarding forecasts nationwide, while "Florida Outlook" contains projections for the various geographic sections of Florida. For additional information on the Florida Labor Market, visit the following web site: http://lmi.floridajobs.org. For information on the general outlook for the U.S. job market visit the following Web site: http://www.acinet.org

c. Scan resources such as:
IIA O25 Occupational Outlook Handbook (web address: http://stats.bls.gov/oco/home.htm)
IC W7 American Almanac of Jobs and Salaries
IIA E6 Vol 2-Vol 4 Encyclopedia of Careers and Vocational Guidance
IIA CIC-13 Career Info. Center: Employment Trends
ID F5 Florida Occupational Employment Statistics Wage Report
IC I5 U.S. Industry & Trade Outlook

d. Review occupational information materials located in the vertical files for outlook information on specific occupations (file #2) and get print-outs on specific occupations from computer-assisted career guidance systems.

Revised 4/02

If you need assistance please consult with the Career Advisor at the help desk.
This module is available in an alternative format upon request.

CURRICULAR-CAREER INFORMATION SERVICE (CCIS) • THE CAREER CENTER • THE FLORIDA STATE UNIVERSITY

MODULE VII

LEISURE PLANNING

Your Lifestyle

Objective 1

To understand the need for balancing one's work role with non-work roles.

Below Are Activities To Help You Achieve This Objective

a. Perform a computer search on Career Key to locate specific resources in The FSU Career Center Library on lifestyle and leisure time. Topics are listed under "Career and Life Planning."

b. Review information on the Career Rainbow in Life Roles of Hall 1 on the DISCOVER computer program. Develop your own life/career rainbow to illustrate the importance of various liferoles.

c. Review the section of "The Three Boxes of Life" (IA B62) pertaining to "Lifelong Leisure or Playing."

Objective 2

To understand one's personal characteristics in relation to leisure planning.

Below Are Activities To Help You Achieve These Objectives

a. Review "The Leisure Activities Finder" for activities related to Holland codes.

b. Complete the "Values" section of Self-Assessment on the SIGI PLUS computer program to explore the importance of leisure in your life in relation to other values.

c. Use the "Activities Card Sort" to assist you in identifying activities for leisure time.

Objective 3

To become aware of leisure activities in your local area.

Below Are Activities To Help You Achieve This Objective

a. Visit or call the FSU Campus Recreation, Room 136 Tully Gym (644-2430) http://fsu.campusrec.com/index.shtml or the Leach Student Recreation Center, Leach Center Room 210E (644-0548), http://fsu.campusrec.com/leach/

b. Check the FSU Student Handbook for recreational activities available to students. Available online at: www.fsu.edu/Books/Student-Handbook/

c. Check the local newspaper (see Friday's Limelight" section of the *Tallahassee Democrat*) for listings of recreational opportunities and club activities (e.g., Tallahassee Parks & Recreation Dept., YMCA/YWCA, Apalachee Canoe Club, Capitol City Cyclists, Florida Trail Association, Sierra Club, Gulf Winds Track Club, etc.); also see the on-line edition of The Tallahassee Democrat's Entertainment weekly, www.tdo.com/break/index.htm

d. Review selected sections of the Tallahassee phone book, e.g., Calendar of Events, Attractions, Arts & Entertainment, Spectator Sports, and Recreation & Conservation.

e. Review Module 7 (Mobile File #1) materials on leisure planning.

Revised 4/02

If you need assistance please consult with the Career Advisor at the help desk.
This module is available in an alternative format upon request.

CURRICULAR-CAREER INFORMATION SERVICE (CCIS) • THE CAREER CENTER • THE FLORIDA STATE UNIVERSITY

MODULE VIII

CAREER PLANNING FOR ETHNIC AND OTHER MINORITIES

For Diverse Populations

This module has been prepared for individuals who may want to explore how ethnicity, age, sexual orientation or other topics may relate to their career planning. Its purpose is to spotlight Career Center resources that might be especially useful in this exploration.

Objective
To assist you in identifying career planning resources and information of interest to diverse populations.

Below Are Activities To Help You Achieve This Objective

a. Perform a search on Career Key in the Diverse Populations menus under Career and Life Planning or Education and Training to locate any Career Center Library material for ethnic and other minorities.

b. Review materials on African-Americans, Hispanics, Gays/Lesbians/Bisexuals/Transgendered and Older Workers in the Module VIII "Diverse Populations" files located in the Mobile File (file #1).

c. Read occupational files for information on opportunities in various fields for diverse populations (file #2).

d. Skim through minority student magazines in the library which feature career planning articles.

e. Check out various Web sites with career resources for diverse populations:
   http://www.aarp.org/working_options/home.html
   http://www.black-collegian.com/
   http://www.eop.com/
   http://www.gaywork.com
   http://www.nshp.org/jobs.htm

f. See a CEO staff member (Room A4128 UC) for information regarding Sigma Chi Iota, a career development honorary for minority students.

g. Review information in the following books:
   Best Careers for Bilingual Latinos: IG1 K4
   The Colorblind Career: IGI S7
   Gay and Lesbian Professionals in the Closet: IG1 D4
   Native American Connections: IG1 R51

h. Consult with Career Center staff for special concerns.

Revised 4/02

If you need assistance please consult with the Career Advisor at the help desk.
This module is available in an alternative format upon request.

CURRICULAR-CAREER INFORMATION SERVICE (CCIS) • THE CAREER CENTER • THE FLORIDA STATE UNIVERSITY

MODULE IX

CAREER DECISION MAKING FOR THE ADULT WOMAN

Especially For Her

The module assumes that (1) you are a woman ready to make a career change; (2) you probably have some family responsibilities; (3) you would like to enter or reenter the work force, but are not sure what field would be right for you or who would hire you; (4) you are prepared to undertake further education, but are not sure it will get you where you want to go; and/or (5) you would like help in stepping back to take a clear, objective look at yourself and your options.

Objectives

1. To provide you with the opportunity for self-assessment: to examine your skills, interests, accomplishments, experiences, and motivations.
2. To assist you in locating sources of information which will help you shape a tentative educational and/or career plan for yourself.

Below Are Activities To Help You Achieve This Objective

a. Discuss your situation with a Career Advisor.

b. Review Module III, "Looking At You," to identify self-assessment activities which may be beneficial to you.

c. Pick up a copy of "Career Resources for Women" in The Career Center Library (kept on top of the occupational files) to see what resources are available.

d. Perform a Career Key search using one of the following menu topics: 1) "Career & Life Planning": "Lifestyles"--Dual Career Couples; 2) "Special groups"--Women; and 3) Education & Training to locate available resources in the Career Center Library.

e. Read materials in Module 9-"Opportunities for Women" in the Mobile File (file #1).

f. Review or read books in the Career Center library relating to women & work - Section IG4.

g. Visit the following Websites for more information on women and work:
http://www.dol.gov/dol/wb/
http://careerplanning.about.com/cs/forwomenonly/
http://www.ivillage.com/work

h. Use Seminole Connection (http://www.career.fsu.edu/acfsu/welcome.cfm) to network with alumni and friends of Florida State University who may be in career areas in which you have an interest.

i. Learn about women's organizations for specific professions that interest you using the National Trade & Professional Associations directory VIE N3 (Page 700).

Revised 4/02

If you need assistance please consult with the Career Advisor at the help desk.
This module is available in an alternative format upon request.

CURRICULAR-CAREER INFORMATION SERVICE (CCIS) • THE CAREER CENTER • THE FLORIDA STATE UNIVERSITY

MODULE X
CAREER PLANNING FOR STUDENTS WITH DISABILITIES

Objective

1. To assist you in locating sources of career planning information of special interest to persons with disabilities including information on the Americans with Disabilities Act.

Below Are Activities To Help You Achieve This Objective

a. Review articles and pamphlets in the Module X folder in the Mobile File.

b. Perform a search on Career Key under "Career & Life Planning-Special Groups" to locate Career Center Library materials on career and educational planning for persons with disabilities.

c. Read sections in the following books:
IG3 A4 Successful Job Search Strategies for the Disabled
IG3 D6 College and Career Success For Students With Learning Disabilities
IG3 K5 Career Success for People with Physical Disabilities
IG3 R7 Job Search Handbook for People with Disabilities
IG3 U5 Americans with Disabilities Act Handbook
IG3 W4 Job Strategies for People with Disabilities
IIIE3 L4 A World of Options for the 90's: A Guide to International Educational Exchange, Community Service and Travel for Persons With Disabilities

d. Read the amended version of The Americans With Disabilities Act of 1990 located in the Module X folder in the Mobile File or read a summary online at www.dol.gov/odep/pubs/misc/summada.htm.

e. Consult with staff in the Student Disability Resource Center, Kellum Hall (644-9566-voice or 644-8504-TDD) Room 08 (http://www.fsu.edu/~staffair/dean/StudentDisability/index.html), or Division of Blind Services, Kellum Hall (488-5133) Room 12.

f. Consider participation in Advocates for Disability Awareness, an FSU student organization (644-9566).

g. Visit the Job Accommodation Network on-line at www.jan.wvu.edu.

h. Explore disability resources from the government and other organizations at www.dol.gov/dol/audience/aud-disability.htm or www.disabilityinfo.gov.

i. Consult with Career Center staff members for special concerns.

Revised 11/02

If you need assistance please consult with the Career Advisor at the help desk.
This module is available in an alternative format upon request.

CURRICULAR-CAREER INFORMATION SERVICE (CCIS) • THE CAREER CENTER • THE FLORIDA STATE UNIVERSITY

MODULE XI

EXPLORING AND ADJUSTING TO NEW WORK SITUATIONS

Career Transitions

Objective 1

To explore the issues involved in job and career transitions.

Below Are Activities To Help You Achieve This Objective

a. Discuss your situation with a Career Advisor and evaluate options; individual counseling appointments on selected days or drop-in career advising during normal hours are both possible.

b. Perform a search using Career Key to locate the Career Center Library resources which address "Career and Life Planning/Career Transitions" or review "Career Center Resources for Mid-Life Change" located on the Occupational Files (File #2) cabinet near the Career Key computer.

c. Review materials in the Module XI "First Job Issues" folder in the Mobile file (file #1).

d. Review materials in the Module XI "Career Changers" folder in the Mobile file (file #1).

Objective 2

To identify the kind of change desired or adjustments needed.

Below Are Activities To Help You Achieve This Objective

a. Interact with the MICRO SKILLS computer-assisted career guidance program to review skills from previous work roles, rate level of satisfaction, and relate them to future possibilities. (Provides Holland Codes and a list of occupations compatible with skills).

b. Complete the Skills Checklist in the CHOICES computer system to select transferable skills you might wish to use in searching for new or alternative occupations.

c. Complete the Values Card Sort in the SIGI PLUS computer system to clarify what is important or desirable to you in your career change.

d. Review CCIS Module II, "What's Involved in Making a Career Decision?" for possible activities.

Objective 3

To begin changing or adjusting your situation.

Below Are Activities To Help You Achieve This Objective

a. For career changes, review Module III, "Looking At You," for additional self-assessment activities.

b. For lifestyle changes, review Module VII, "Your Lifestyle."

c. For job changes, review Module XIII, "Your Job Campaign."

d. Interact with the DISCOVER and SIGI PLUS computer-assisted career guidance programs.

Revised 1/02

If you need assistance please consult with the Career Advisor at the help desk.
This module is available in an alternative format upon request.

CURRICULAR-CAREER INFORMATION SERVICE (CCIS) • THE CAREER CENTER • THE FLORIDA STATE UNIVERSITY

MODULE XII

EXPLORING CAREER INTERESTS THROUGH WORK

Get Experience!

Objective

1. To assist you in identifying resources which will help you obtain experience relevant to your career interest areas.

a. Read selected resources in the Career Center Library:

Volunteer

Volunteer USA IVD C2
Volunteer! IVD C6
Alternatives to the Peace Corps IVD L61
Volunteer Opportunities IVD T2
Good Works: A Guide to Social Change Career VIB2 C4
Response 2001: Directory of Volunteer Opportunities IVD C3

Summer/Holidays

How to Get a Job on a Cruise Ship IVC K3
Summer Jobs for Students IVC S8
Overseas Summer Jobs 2000 IVC S81

Co-op/Internship

Washington D.C. Internships in Law and Policy IVB C3
National Directory of Arts Internships IVB C4
The Student Guide to Mass Media Internships (1197) IVB C55 Vols. I & II
Internships: A Directory for Career Finders IVB G5
Peterson's Internships 2000 IVB I5
The Back Door Guidebook IVB L3
National Directory of Internships IVB N3
The Internship Bible IVB 04
International Internships IVB P5
The Access Guide to International Affairs Internships: Washington, D.C. IVB S4
Yale Daily News Guide to Internships IVB S65

b. Perform a search using Career Key under topics in "Work Experience" to locate other Career Center resources.

c. Attend a CEO orientation session and review the resources at the CEO Office, Suite 4128, Building A, University Center or on the web at: http://www.career.fsu.edu/student/current/internships_and_co-ops/index.html. Paid and non-paid placements are available with employers in Florida, the Southeast, & nationwide along with information on federal and state co-ops, internships, summer jobs & volunteer experiences.

d. Refer to the Job Choices series to find out about employers currently seeking candidates in the areas of Business and Science and Engineering.

e. Review articles in Module XII in the Mobile File (file #1).

f. Refer to "Volunteer Opportunities (IVD T2)" for contacts & information related to volunteering in Tallahassee and beyond.

g. Check the Florida State University General Bulletin for internship information in selected majors.

h. Visit the Student Employment Services Office, located in the Office of Financial Aid, Suite A4400 of the University Center, for information on the College Work-Study Program and the College Career Work Experience Program. View the listings online at: http://www.finaid.fsu.edu/jlad.html

i. Visit the Center for Civic Education and Service to learn about volunteer and service opportunities that will allow you to gain experience or visit their Web site at www.fsu.edu/~service/. The Center is located at 930 West Park Avenue at the corner of West Park Avenue and Wildwood Drive near the Leach Center.

Revised 4/02

If you need assistance please consult with the Career Advisor at the help desk.
This module is available in an alternative format upon request.

CURRICULAR-CAREER INFORMATION SERVICE (CCIS) • THE CAREER CENTER • THE FLORIDA STATE UNIVERSITY

MODULE XIII

EMPLOYABILITY SKILLS

Your Job Campaign

Objective 1
To help you start your job search.

a. View "The Very Quick Job Search" video (Room, A4108)

b. Attend a Career Center "Job Search Strategies" workshop.

c. Pick up a copy of "Job Search Resources in CCIS," located on top of File 2. Review selected resources catalogued in Section V of the Career Center library.

d. Review current articles in the "Job Hunting" file located in the Module XIII section of the Mobile File (file #1).

e. Pick up a copy of the Career Objective Guide on the cabinet near Career Key or view the guide on-line: http://www.career.fsu.edu/ccis/guides/developing.html

f. Look through the Career Library's job files and employment subscription notebooks for current openings.

g. Ask a Career Advisor for a copy of the guide "Internet Job Search" guide to learn about using the Internet and the world wide web (WWW) in your job search.

Objective 2
To write a resume appropriate for your job objective.

a. Pick up a copy of the Resume Writing Guide located on top of the cabinet next to Career Key or view the guide on-line at http://www.career.fsu.edu/ccis/guides/resume_prep.html; examine sample resumes available in The Career Center Library on the Ready Reference shelf.

b. Attend The Career Center's "Resume Writing" and/or "Resume Critiquing" workshops. Ask a Career Advisor for a current schedule or view the schedule on-line at: http://www.career.fsu.edu/calendar_of_events.cfm.

c. Review articles on Resume Writing in the "Job Hunting" file located in the Module XIII section of the Mobile File (file #1).

d. Use Career Key to obtain a list of Career Center Library resources on resume writing. Choose "Job Hunting" from the main menu. Then choose "Resume Writing" from the next menu.

e. Go into Hall 4 of DISCOVER and use the resume section of "Prepare for Job Search" to learn about sections of a resume, view samples, and create your own resume.

Objective 3
To write letters for your job campaign.

a. Pick up a copy of the Letter Writing Guide, located on top of the cabinet near Career Key or view the guide on-line: http://www.career.fsu.edu/ccis/guides/write_eff.html. Review sample letters in the notebooks on the Ready Reference shelf.

b. Review current articles in the "Job Hunting" file, Module XIII section of the Mobile File (file #1).

c. Use "Career Key" to obtain a list of Career Library resources on writing letters. Choose "Job Hunting" from the main menu & then "Letter Writing" from the next menu.

d. Go into Hall 4 of DISCOVER; use the cover letter section of "Prepare for Job Search" to learn about letters used in the job search, view samples, and create your own.

Objective 4
To become informed about services available to you from Career Placement Services.

a. Review the Career Placement Services (CPS) orientation on-line at http://www.career.fsu.edu/cps/orientation-fa01/sld001.htm to learn about on-campus interviewing and other services available to you through CPS.

b. Obtain a copy of the Career Guide, a booklet describing job hunting assistance available through The Career Center.

c. Register with Career Placement Services for any on-campus interviews appropriate to your career objectives, and to make your resume available for referral to prospective employers.

d. Attend any of the Career Center Expos to meet prospective employers, check on-line for dates and times at http://www.career.fsu.edu/expos/expos-students.html; check in the Career Center library or on the Internet for lists of additional career expos around the region and country.

Objective 5
To prepare yourself for your job interview.

a. Pick up a copy of the Interview Preparation Guide located on top of the cabinet next to Career Key or view the guide on-line: http://www.career.fsu.edu/ccis/guides/inter_skills.html.

b. Participate in a mock interview through the FSU Career Center.

c. View selected Career Center videotapes or CD-Roms on Interviewing (Room A4108).

d. Attend a Career Center Interviewing workshop. Ask a Career Advisor for a workshop schedule or look on-line at: http://www.career.fsu.edu/calendar_of_events.cfm.

e. Review current articles in the "Job Hunting" file located in the Module XIII section of the Mobile File (file #1).

f. Use "Career Key" to obtain a list of resources on interviewing. Choose "Job Hunting" from the main menu. Then choose "Interviewing" from the next menu.

Revised 10/02

If you need assistance please consult with the Career Advisor at the help desk.
This module is available in an alternative format upon request.

CURRICULAR-CAREER INFORMATION SERVICE (CCIS) • THE CAREER CENTER • THE FLORIDA STATE UNIVERSITY

MODULE XIV

OPPORTUNITIES FOR EDUCATION AND EMPLOYMENT

Going Abroad

Objective 1

To help you explore issues and locate opportunities for study abroad.

a. Perform a search on Career Key under the topic of "Education and Training," "Alternative Education," "Overseas Study Programs" to get a list of relevant resources in the Career Center Library.

b. Review the "Study Abroad" guide located in the Career Center Library.

c. Review materials in the "Study Abroad" and "Internships Abroad" folder in the Mobile File #1 Module XIV.

d. Review materials in the "Overseas Study Programs" files located in The Career Center Library (File #7).

e. Visit the study abroad Web site at www.studyabroad.com

f. Contact the FSU International Programs Office, on the 5th level, University Center, Suite A5500 or visit their Web site: http://www.international.fsu.edu/.

Objective 2

To help you explore issues and locate opportunities for work abroad.

a. Perform a search on Career Key under the topic of "Employment Information," "Overseas Employers" to get a list of relevant resources in The Career Center Library.

b. Review the "Work Abroad" guide located in the Career Center Library .

c. Review materials in the "Going Abroad" folders in Mobile File #1 Module XIV.

d. Review Module XIII, "Your Job Campaign," for resources that may assist you with other components of your job search.

e. Review "Overseas Non-Teaching" and the "Overseas Teaching" job notices files for job opportunities (located on the tables in the Career Library below the clock).

f. Check out Internet sites related to overseas jobs, e.g., http://international.monster.com/, http://www.overseasjobs.com

Revised 4/02

If you need assistance please consult with the Career Advisor at the help desk.
This module is available in an alternative format upon request.

CURRICULAR-CAREER INFORMATION SERVICE (CCIS) • THE CAREER CENTER • THE FLORIDA STATE UNIVERSITY

MODULE XV

EXPLORING GRADUATE EDUCATION

Going to Graduate School

Objective 1

To explore issues and activities which are important to you in pursuing graduate/professional education.

Below Are Activities To Help You Achieve This Objective

a. Look at The Career Center Library "Going to Graduate School Guide" located in the folder labeled Module 15 "Exploring Graduate Education" in the Mobile File (file #1),

b. Review additional materials in the mobile file folder for Module 15 "Exploring Graduate Education,"

c. Attend a "Going to Graduate School" workshop.

Objective 2

To identify graduate/professional education programs in your chosen field of study.

a. Review selected general resource books:**

The Best Business Schools IIB 10 G5
The Best Law Schools IIB 211 P68
The Best Medical Schools IIB 261 P7
Medical School Admissions Adviser IIB 261 K3
Peterson's Guides to Graduate & Professional Programs Ready Reference Shelf
Peterson's Guide to MBA Programs IIB 10 P4

** For additional information on graduate programs and advanced degrees, get a complete Career Key printout.

b. Use the Discover and Choices computer programs to search for graduate programs matching selected criteria.

Objective 3
To investigate selected graduate/professional education programs.

a. Review the appropriate sections of the general resource books listed on the previous page.

b. Review graduate program materials in file #4; see FSU information in file #3.

c. Visit http://gradschools.com to access information about graduate programs, fellowships, and admissions tests. Also, visit any world wide web sites for institutions in which you have an interest.

d. Obtain program & university materials for your own use by writing/telephoning both the program office and graduate admissions office of those programs you wish to consider further (this information can easily be found in the Peterson's Guide).

e. Arrange for a personal interview with appropriate faculty/ staff in programs you are seriously considering. If this is not possible, write, telephone, or e-mail.

f. Talk to FSU faculty or students that might be familiar with the programs you are considering. Ask to see the FSU Faculty Resource Directory located at the Career Advisor desk.

g. For rankings of graduate and professional programs, review The Gourman Report, IIIC G42 or look on-line at http://www.usnews.com/usnews/edu/beyond/bcrank.htm

h. Attend the Career Center's Graduate & Professional School Expo held during the fall semester.

Objective 4
To develop an application strategy for gaining admission to your graduate/professional programs of choice.

a. Read the chapter "Applying to Graduate and Professionals Schools" located in Peterson's Graduate and Professional Programs: An Overview. Also visit www.petersons.com for additional information on applying to graduate school.

b. Read articles related to graduate/professional school admissions located in Module 15 - "Exploring Graduate Education" of the Mobile File (file #1).

c. Review resources on personal statements and admission essays in section IIIC of the Career Center Library. See the sample personal statement notebook on the ready reference shelf.

d. Find out about, register for, prepare for, and take the appropriate admission test(s).
Visit Evaluation Services in 106 William Johnston building for information on the various tests.
See information materials in the mobile file for Module 15.
See specific resources in the Career Center Library:
Getting Into Law School IIB 211 M2
Medical School Admission Advisor IIB 261 K3

e. Investigate financing options for graduate/professional education.
Review financial aid resource materials in Section IIIF & the Fellowship/Grad Asst folder.
Visit the STAR Center in the FSU Office of Financial Aid.
Write to your program(s) of choice to ask about financial aid.
Read the chapter "Financial Aid for Graduate & Professional Education" located in Peterson's.
Use the financial aid awards database in the Choices computer program. Available online at: www.florida.echoices.com

Revised 4/02

If you need assistance please consult with the Career Advisor at the help desk.
This module is available in an alternative format upon request.

CURRICULAR-CAREER INFORMATION SERVICE (CCIS) • THE CAREER CENTER • THE FLORIDA STATE UNIVERSITY

MODULE XVI

ACADEMIC PROGRAM SELECTION

Choosing a Major

Objective 1

1. To identify what factors are important to you in selecting a major.
2. To discover fields of study that you might find interesting.

a. Attend a "Choosing a Major" workshop. See the schedule at the Career Advisor desk for date, time, and location or check out the Events Calendar on the Career Center web site: www.career.fsu.edu/calendar_of_events.cfm

b. Complete the "Major Expectations" section of the Career Center booklet "Choosing a Major or a Career." Ask a Career Advisor to get it for you.

c. Complete appropriate self-assessment activities; review Module III "Looking at You" and discuss your situation with a Career Advisor.

d. Review the "FSU Undergraduate Programs by Holland/SDS Categories" sheet to identify FSU programs consistent with your self-assessment.

Objective 2

1. To broaden your general awareness of majors available at Florida State and elsewhere.
2. To find detailed information about specific majors.

A. Acquaint yourself with the variety of college majors available at institutions around the country:

1. Examine various directories located on top of the file cabinets next to the Career Library reference desk.
   a. Peterson's Guide to Four-Year Institutions
   b. Chronicle Four-Year College Databook

2. Review:
   College Majors and Careers: A Resource Guide for Effective Life Planning IIC AA P4
   The College Board Guide to 150 Popular College Majors IIC AA C7
   The Career Connection: A Guide to College Majors and Their Related Careers IIC AA R61
   The Career Connection: A Guide to Technical Majors and Their Related Careers IIC AA R62.

3. Use the College or FSU Majors Card Sort to help identify majors that would be of interest to you.

B. Learn more about specific majors available at FSU:

1. See the *Florida State University General Bulletin* for a list of degree and certificate programs. Visit the FSU Registrar's web site to review the General Bulletin: http://registrar.fsu.edu/.

2. Get specific information about majors that interest you in *the Undergraduate Academic Program Guide* http://www.academic-guide.fsu.edu/ and the *FSU General Bulletin*.

3. Perform a computer search using Career Key to locate Career Center Library resources which address majors of interest to you.

4. Review printed materials in File #3 on FSU Academic Programs.

5. Refer to the Faculty Resource Directory, at the Career Advisor desk, to find faculty and advisor names and phone numbers, or use the Advisor Search Function on the FSU Web Page (www.fsu.edu/current/undergraduate/academics.shtml). Make an appointment with a faculty member, advisor or another departmental staff member to acquire more information about a particular major.

C. Learn more about majors available at other colleges/ universities.

1. Use the directories on top of the file cabinets next to the Career Library Reference Desk to identify institutions with programs in which you have an interest.

2. Perform a search on the CHOICES or DISCOVER computer programs to identify institutions which may offer programs in your field(s) of interest. CHOICES is offered online at www.florida.echoices.com.

3. Obtain further information about programs at other institutions.

   a. Write or call institutions and/or specific departments for catalogs and academic program information. See the FSU Undergraduate Academic Program Guide for specific contact information, available online at http://www.academic-guide.fsu.edu/.

   b. Conduct a search on the Internet for information sites on institutions in which you have an interes

   c. Search out catalogs available on the FSU campus:
      i. Strozier Library, (basement) Documents Department - Micro-Materials section.
      ii. Undergraduate Studies, 3rd Level, UC Bldg. A, Room 3400-selected schools only.

Objective 3

1. To enhance your ability to make an informed decision.

A. Review Module II, "What's Involved In Making A Career Decision?"

B. Review the sheet, "A Guide To Good Decision Making."

C. Complete the "Guide to Good Decision-Making Exercise."

D. Talk to a Career Advisor about special problems getting in the way of your "major decision."

Revised 10/02

If you need assistance please consult with the Career Advisor at the help desk.
This module is available in an alternative format upon request.

Career Counseling Competencies and Performance Indicators, Revised Version, 1997

APPENDIX B

CAREER DEVELOPMENT THEORY

Theory base and knowledge considered essential for professionals engaging in career counseling and development. Demonstration of knowledge of:

1. Counseling theories and associated techniques.
2. Theories and models of career development.
3. Individual differences related to gender, sexual orientation, race, ethnicity, and physical and mental capacities.
4. Theoretical models for career development and associated counseling and information-delivery techniques and resources.
5. Human growth and development throughout the life span.
6. Role relationships that facilitate life-work planning.
7. Information, techniques, and models related to career planning and placement.

INDIVIDUAL AND GROUP COUNSELING SKILLS

Individual and group counseling competencies considered essential to effective career counseling. Demonstration of ability to:

1. Establish and maintain productive personal relationships with individuals.
2. Establish and maintain a productive group climate.
3. Collaborate with clients in identifying personal goals.

4. Identify and select techniques appropriate to client or group goals and client needs, psychological states, and developmental tasks.
5. Identify and understand clients' personal characteristics related to career.
6. Identify and understand social contextual conditions affecting clients' careers.
7. Identify and understand familial, subcultural and cultural structures and functions as they are related to clients' careers.
8. Identify and understand clients' career decision-making processes.
9. Identify and understand clients' attitudes toward work and workers.
10. Identify and understand clients' biases toward work and workers based on gender, race, and cultural stereotypes.
11. Challenge and encourage clients to take action to prepare for and initiate role transitions by:
    - locating sources of relevant information and experience,
    - obtaining and interpreting information and experiences, and acquiring skills needed to make role transitions.
12. Assist the client to acquire a set of employability and job search skills.
13. Support and challenge clients to examine life-work roles, including the balance of work, leisure, family, and community in their careers.

INDIVIDUAL/GROUP ASSESSMENT

Individual/group assessment skills considered essential for professionals engaging in career counseling. Demonstration of ability to:

1. Assess personal characteristics such as aptitude, achievement, interests, values, and personality traits.
2. Assess leisure interests, learning style, life roles, self-concept, career maturity, vocational identity, career indecision, work environment preference (e.g., work satisfaction), and other related lifestyle/development issues.
3. Assess conditions of the work environment (such as tasks, expectations, norms, and qualities of the physical and social settings).
4. Evaluate and select valid and reliable instruments appropriate to the client's gender, sexual orientation, race, ethnicity, and physical and mental capacities.
5. Use computer-delivered assessment measures effectively and appropriately.
6. Select assessment techniques appropriate for group administration and those appropriate for individual administration.
7. Administer, score, and report findings from career assessment instruments appropriately.
8. Interpret data from assessment instruments and present the results to clients and to others.
9. Assist the client and others designated by the client to interpret data from assessment instruments.
10. Write an accurate report of assessment results.

INFORMATION/RESOURCES

Information/resource base and knowledge essential for professionals engaging in career counseling. Demonstration of knowledge of:

1. Education, training, and employment trends; labor market information and resources that provide information about job tasks, functions, salaries, requirements and future outlooks related to broad occupational fields and individual occupations.
2. Resources and skills that clients utilize in life-work planning and management.
3. Community/professional resources available to assist clients in career planning, including job search.
4. Changing roles of women and men and the implications that this has for education, family, and leisure.
5. Methods of good use of computer-based career information delivery systems (CIDS) and computer-assisted career guidance systems (CACGS) to assist with career planning.

PROGRAM PROMOTION, MANAGEMENT, AND IMPLEMENTATION

Knowledge and skills necessary to develop, plan, implement, and manage comprehensive career development programs in a variety of settings. Demonstration of knowledge of:

1. Designs that can be used in the organization of career development programs.
2. Needs assessment and evaluation techniques and practices.
3. Organizational theories, including diagnosis, behavior, planning, organizational communication, and management useful in implementing and administering career development programs.
4. Methods of forecasting, budgeting, planning, costing, policy analysis, resource allocation, and quality control.
5. Leadership theories and approaches for evaluation and feedback, organizational change, decision making, and conflict resolution.
6. Professional standards and criteria for career development programs.
7. Societal trends and state and federal legislation that influence the development and implementation of career development programs.

Demonstration of ability to:

8. Implement individual and group programs in career development for specified populations.
9. Train others about the appropriate use of computer-based systems for career information and planning.
10. Plan, organize, and manage a comprehensive career resource center.
11. Implement career development programs in collaboration with others.
12. Identify and evaluate staff competencies.

13. Mount a marketing and public relations campaign in behalf of career development activities and services.

COACHING, CONSULTATION, AND PERFORMANCE IMPROVEMENT

Knowledge and skills considered essential in relating to individuals and organizations that impact the career counseling and development process. Demonstration of ability to:

1. Use consultation theories, strategies, and models.
2. Establish and maintain a productive consultative relationship with people who can influence a client's career.
3. Help the general public and legislators to understand the importance of career counseling, career development, and life-work planning.
4. Impact public policy as it relates to career development and workforce planning.
5. Analyze future organizational needs and current level of employee skills and develop performance improvement training.
6. Mentor and coach employees.

DIVERSE POPULATIONS

Knowledge and skills considered essential in relating to diverse populations that impact career counseling and development processes. Demonstration of ability to:

1. Identify development models and multicultural counseling competencies.
2. Identify developmental needs unique to various diverse populations, including those of different gender, sexual orientation, ethnic group, race, and physical or mental capacity.
3. Define career development programs to accommodate needs unique to various diverse populations.
4. Find appropriate methods or resources to communicate with limited-English-proficient individuals.
5. Identify alternative approaches to meet career planning needs for individuals of various diverse populations.
6. Identify community resources and establish linkages to assist clients with specific needs.
7. Assist other staff members, professionals, and community members in understanding the unique needs/characteristics of diverse populations with regard to career exploration, employment expectations, and economic/social issues.
8. Advocate for the career development and employment of diverse populations.
9. Design and deliver career development programs and materials to hard-to-reach populations.

SUPERVISION

Knowledge and skills considered essential in critically evaluating counselor or career development facilitator performance, maintaining and improving professional skills. Demonstration of:

1. Ability to recognize own limitations as a career counselor and to seek supervision or refer clients when appropriate.
2. Ability to utilize supervision on a regular basis to maintain and improve counselor skills.
3. Ability to consult with supervisors and colleagues regarding client and counseling issues and issues related to one's own professional development as a career counselor.
4. Knowledge of supervision models and theories.
5. Ability to provide effective supervision to career counselors and career development facilitators at different levels of experience.
6. Ability to provide effective supervision to career development facilitators at different levels of experience by:
   - knowledge of their roles, competencies, and ethical standards,
   - determining their competence in each of the areas included in their certification,
   - further training them in competencies, including interpretation of assessment instruments,
   - monitoring and mentoring their activities in support of the professional career counselor; and scheduling regular consultations for the purpose of reviewing their activities.

ETHICAL/LEGAL ISSUES

Information base and knowledge essential for the ethical and legal practice of career counseling. Demonstration of knowledge of:

1. Adherence to ethical codes and standards relevant to the profession of career counseling (e.g., NBCC, NCDA, and ACA).
2. Current ethical and legal issues that affect the practice of career counseling with all populations.
3. Current ethical/legal issues with regard to the use of computer-assisted career guidance systems.
4. Ethical standards relating to consultation issues.
5. State and federal statutes relating to client confidentiality.

RESEARCH/EVALUATION

Knowledge and skills considered essential in understanding and conducting research and evaluation in career counseling and development. Demonstration of ability to:

1. Write a research proposal.

2. Use types of research and research designs appropriate to career counseling and development research.
3. Convey research findings related to the effectiveness of career counseling programs.
4. Design, conduct, and use the results of evaluation programs.
5. Design evaluation programs that take into account the need of various diverse populations, including persons of both genders, differing sexual orientations, different ethnic and racial backgrounds, and differing physical and mental capacities.
6. Apply appropriate statistical procedures to career development research.

TECHNOLOGY

Knowledge and skills considered essential in using technology to assist individuals with career planning. Demonstration of knowledge of:

1. Various computer-based guidance and information systems as well as services available on the Internet.
2. Standards by which such systems and services are evaluated (e.g., NCDA and ACSCI).
3. Ways in which to use computer-based systems and Internet services to assist individuals with career planning that are consistent with ethical standards.
4. Characteristics of clients that make them profit more or less from use of technology-driven systems.
5. Methods to evaluate and select a system to meet local needs.

Career Development Competencies by Area and Level

APPENDIX **C**

Career Development Competencies by Area and Level				
	Elementary	Middle/ Junior High School	High School	Adult
Self-Knowledge	Knowledge of the importance of self-concept.	Knowledge of the influence of a positive self-concept.	Understanding the influence of a positive self-concept.	Skills to maintain a positive self-concept.
	Skills to interact with others.	Skills to interact with others.	Skills to interact positively with others.	Skills to maintain effective behaviors.
	Awareness of the importance of growth and change.	Knowledge of the importance of growth and change.	Understanding the impact of growth and development.	Understanding developmental changes and transitions.
Educational and Occupational Exploration	Awareness of the benefits of educational achievement.	Knowledge of the benefits of educational achievement to career opportunities.	Understanding the relationship between educational achievement and career planning.	Skills to enter and participate in education and training.
	Awareness of the relationship between work and learning.	Understanding the relationship between work and learning.	Understanding the need for positive attitudes toward work and learning.	Skills to participate in work and lifelong learning.
	Skills to understand and use career information.	Skills to locate, understand, and use career information.	Skills to locate, evaluate, and interpret career information.	Skills to locate, evaluate, and interpret career information.
	Awareness of the importance of personal responsibility and good work habits.	Knowledge of skills necessary to seek and obtain jobs.	Skills to prepare to seek, obtain, maintain, and change jobs.	Skills to prepare to seek, obtain, maintain, and change jobs.
	Awareness of how work relates to the needs and functions of society.	Understanding how work relates to the needs and functions of the economy and society.	Understanding how societal needs and functions influence the nature and structure of work.	Understanding how the needs and functions of society influence the nature and structure of work.

Career Planning	Understanding how to make decisions.	Skills to make decisions.	Skills to make decisions.	Skills to make decisions.
	Awareness of the interrelationship of life roles.	Knowledge of the interrelationship of life roles.	Understanding the interrelationship of life roles.	Understanding the impact of work on individual and family life.
	Awareness of different occupations and changing male/female roles.	Knowledge of different occupations and changing male/female roles.	Understanding the continuous changes in male/female roles.	Understanding the continuing changes in male/female roles.
	Awareness of the career planning process.	Understanding the process of career planning.	Skills in career planning.	Skills to make career transitions.

Available: http://icdl.uncg.edu/ft/120899-04.html (International Career Development Library).

The National Career Development Guidelines: Competencies and Indicators

APPENDIX D

ELEMENTARY SCHOOL STUDENT

Self-Knowledge

COMPETENCY I: **Knowledge of the importance of self-concept.**

Describe positive characteristics about self as seen by self and others.

Identify how behaviors affect school and family situations.

Describe how behavior influences the feelings and actions of others.

Demonstrate a positive attitude about self.

Identify personal interests, abilities, strengths, and weaknesses.

Describe ways to meet personal needs through work.

COMPETENCY II: **Skills to interact with others.**

Identify how people are unique.

Demonstrate effective skills for interacting with others.

Demonstrate skills in resolving conflicts with peers and adults.

Demonstrate group membership skills.

Identify sources and effects of peer pressure.

Demonstrate appropriate behaviors when peer pressures are contrary to one's beliefs.

Demonstrate awareness of different cultures, lifestyles, attitudes, and abilities.

COMPETENCY III: **Awareness of the importance of growth and change.**

Identify personal feelings.

Identify ways to express feelings.

Describe causes of stress.

Identify and select appropriate behaviors to deal with specific emotional situations.

Demonstrate healthy ways of dealing with conflicts, stress, and emotions in self and others.

Demonstrate knowledge of good health habits.

Educational and Occupational Exploration

COMPETENCY IV: **Awareness of the benefits of educational achievement.**

Describe how academic skills can be used in the home and community.

Identify personal strengths and weaknesses in subject areas.

Identify academic skills needed in several occupational groups.

Describe relationships among ability, effort, and achievement.

Implement a plan of action for improving academic skills.

Describe school tasks that are similar to skills essential for job success.

Describe how the amount of education needed for different occupational levels varies.

COMPETENCY V: **Awareness of the relationship between work and learning.**

Identify different types of work, both paid and unpaid.

Describe the importance of preparing for occupations.

Demonstrate effective study and information-seeking habits.

Demonstrate an understanding of the importance of practice, effort, and learning.

Describe how current learning relates to work.

Describe how one's role as a student is like that of an adult worker.

COMPETENCY VI: **Skills to understand and use career information.**

Describe work of family members, school personnel, and community workers.

Identify occupations according to data, people, and things.

Identify work activities of interest to the student.

Describe the relationship of beliefs, attitudes, interests, and abilities to occupations.

Describe jobs that are present in the local community.

Identify the working conditions of occupations (e.g., inside/outside, hazardous).

Describe way in which self-employment differs from working for others.

Describe how parents, relatives, adult friends, and neighbors can provide career information.

COMPETENCY VII: **Awareness of the importance of personal responsibility and good work habits.**

Describe the importance of personal qualities (e.g., dependability, promptness, getting along with others) to getting and keeping jobs.

Demonstrate positive ways of performing working activities.

Describe the importance of cooperation among workers to accomplish a task.

Demonstrate the ability to work with people who are different from oneself (e.g., race, age, gender).

COMPETENCY VIII: **Awareness of how work relates to the needs and functions of society.**

Describe how work can satisfy personal needs.

Describe the products and services of local employers.

Describe ways in which work can help overcome social and economic problems.

Career Planning

COMPETENCY IX: **Understanding how to make decisions.**

Describe how choices are made.

Describe what can be learned from making mistakes.

Identify and assess problems that interfere with attaining goals.

Identify strategies used in solving problems.

Identify alternatives in decision-making situations.

Describe how personal beliefs and attitudes affect decision making.

Describe how decisions affect self and others.

COMPETENCY X: **Awareness of the interrelationship of life roles.**

Describe the various roles an individual may have (e.g., friend, student, worker, family member).

Describe work-related activities in the home, community, and school.

Describe how family members depend on one another, work together, and share responsibilities.

Describe how work roles complement family roles.

COMPETENCY XI: **Awareness of different occupations and changing male/female roles.**

Describe how work is important to all people.

Describe the changing life roles of men and women in work and family.

Describe how contributions of individuals both inside and outside the home are important.

COMPETENCY XII: **Awareness of the career planning process.**

Describe the importance of planning.

Describe skills needed in a variety of occupational groups.

Develop an individual career plan for the elementary school level.

MIDDLE/JUNIOR HIGH SCHOOL STUDENT

Self-Knowledge

COMPETENCY I: **Knowledge of the influence of a positive self-concept.**

Describe personal likes and dislikes.

Describe individual skills required to fulfill different life roles.

Describe how one's behavior influences the feelings and actions of others.

Identify environmental influences on attitudes, behaviors, and aptitudes.

COMPETENCY II: **Skills to interact with others.**

Demonstrate respect for the feelings and beliefs of others.

Demonstrate an appreciation for the similarities and differences among people.

Demonstrate tolerance and flexibility in interpersonal and group situations.

Demonstrate skills in responding to criticism.

Demonstrate effective group membership skills.

Demonstrate effective social skills.

Demonstrate understanding of different cultures, lifestyles, attitudes, and abilities.

COMPETENCY III: **Knowledge of the importance of growth and change.**

Identify feelings associated with significant experiences.

Identify internal and external sources of stress.

Demonstrate ways of responding to others when under stress.

Describe changes that occur in the physical, psychological, social, and emotional development of an individual.

Describe physiological and psychological factors as they relate to career development.

Describe the importance of career, family, leisure activities to mental, emotional, physical, and economic well-being.

Educational and Occupational Exploration

COMPETENCY IV: **Knowledge of the benefits of educational achievement to career opportunities.**

Describe the importance of academic and occupational skills in the work world.

Identify how the skills taught in school subjects are used in various occupations.

Describe individual strengths and weaknesses in school subjects.

Describe a plan of action for increasing basic educational skills.

Describe the skills needed to adjust to changing occupational requirements.

Describe how continued learning enhances the ability to achieve goals.

Describe how skills relate to the selection of high school courses of study.

Describe how aptitudes and abilities relate to broad occupational groups.

COMPETENCY V: **Understanding the relationship between work and learning.**

Demonstrate effective learning habits and skills.

Demonstrate an understanding of the importance of personal skills and attitudes to job success.

Describe the relationship of personal attitudes, beliefs, abilities, and skills to occupations.

COMPETENCY VI: **Skills to locate, understand, and use career information.**

Identify various ways that occupations can be classified.

Identify a number of occupational groups for exploration.

Demonstrate skills in using school and community resources to learn about occupational groups.

Identify sources to obtain information about occupational groups, including self-employment.

Identify skills that are transferable from one occupation to another.

Identify sources of employment in the community.

COMPETENCY VII: **Knowledge of skills necessary to seek and obtain jobs.**

Demonstrate personal qualities (e.g., dependability, punctuality, getting along with others) that are needed to get and keep jobs.

Describe terms and concepts used in describing employment opportunities and conditions.

Demonstrate skills to complete a job application.

Demonstrate skills and attitudes essential for a job interview.

COMPETENCY VIII: **Understanding how work relates to the needs and functions of the economy and society.**

Describe the importance of work to society.

Describe the relationship between work and economic and societal needs.

Describe the economic contributions workers make to society.

Describe the effects that societal, economic, and technological change have on occupations.

Career Planning

COMPETENCY IX: Skills to make decisions.

Describe personal beliefs and attitudes.

Describe how career development is a continuous process with a series of choices.

Identify possible outcomes of decisions.

Describe school courses related to personal, educational, and occupational interests.

Describe how the expectations of others affect career planning.

Identify ways in which decisions about education and work relate to other major life decisions.

Identify advantages and disadvantages of various secondary and postsecondary programs for the attainment of career goals.

Identify the requirements for secondary and postsecondary programs.

COMPETENCY X: Knowledge of the interrelationship of life roles.

Identify how different work and family patterns require varying kinds and amounts of energy, participation, motivation, and talent.

Identify how work roles at home satisfy needs of the family.

Identify personal goals that may be satisfied through a combination of work, community, social, and family roles.

Identify personal leisure choices in relation to lifestyle and the attainment of future goals.

Describe advantages and disadvantages of various life role options.

Describe the interrelationships between family, occupational, and leisure decisions.

COMPETENCY XI: Knowledge of different occupations and changing male/female roles.

Describe advantages and problems of entering nontraditional occupations.

Describe the advantages of taking courses related to personal interest, even if they are most often taken by members of the opposite gender.

Describe stereotypes, biases, and discriminatory behaviors that may limit opportunities for women and men in certain occupations.

COMPETENCY XII: Understanding the process of career planning.

Demonstrate knowledge of exploratory processes and programs.

Identify school courses that meet tentative career goals.

Demonstrate knowledge of academic and vocational programs offered at the high school level.

Describe skills needed in a variety of occupations, including self-employment.

Identify strategies for managing personal resources (e.g., talents, time, money) to achieve tentative career goals.

Develop an individual career plan, updating information from the elementary-level plan and including tentative decisions to be implemented in high school.

HIGH SCHOOL STUDENT

Self-Knowledge

COMPETENCY I: **Understanding the influence of a positive self-concept.**

Identify and appreciate personal interests, abilities, and skills.

Demonstrate the ability to use peer feedback.

Demonstrate an understanding of how individual characteristics relate to achieving personal, social, educational, and career goals.

Demonstrate an understanding of environmental influences on one's behaviors.

Demonstrate an understanding of the relationship between personal behavior and self-concept.

COMPETENCY II: **Skills to interact positively with others.**

Demonstrate effective interpersonal skills.

Demonstrate interpersonal skills required for working with and for others.

Describe appropriate employer and employee interactions in various situations.

Demonstrate how to express feelings, reactions, and ideas in an appropriate manner.

COMPETENCY III: **Understanding the impact of growth and development.**

Describe how developmental changes affect physical and mental health.

Describe the effect of emotional and physical health on career decisions.

Describe healthy ways of dealing with stress.

Demonstrate behaviors that maintain physical and mental health.

Educational and Occupational Exploration

COMPETENCY IV: **Understanding the relationship between educational achievement and career planning.**

Demonstrate how to apply academic and vocational skills to achieve personal goals.

Describe the relationship of academic and vocational skills to personal interests.

Describe how skills developed in academic and vocational programs relate to career goals.

Describe how education relates to the selection of college majors, further training, and/or entry into the job market.

Demonstrate transferable skills that can apply to a variety of occupations and changing occupational requirements.

Describe how learning skills are required in the workplace.

COMPETENCY V: Understanding the need for positive attitudes toward work and learning.

Identify the positive contributions workers make to society.

Demonstrate knowledge of the social significance of various occupations.

Demonstrate a positive attitude toward work.

Demonstrate learning habits and skills that can be used in various educational situations.

Demonstrate positive work attitudes and behaviors.

COMPETENCY VI: Skills to locate, evaluate, and interpret career information.

Describe the educational requirements of various occupations.

Demonstrate use of a range of resources (e.g., handbooks, career materials, labor market information, and computerized career information delivery systems).

Demonstrate knowledge of various classification systems that categorize occupations and industries (e.g., *Dictionary of Occupational Titles*).

Describe the concept of career ladders.

Describe the advantages and disadvantages of self-employment as a career option.

Identify individuals in selected occupations as possible information resources, role models, or mentors.

Describe the influence of change in supply and demand for workers in different occupations.

Identify how employment trends relate to education and training.

Describe the impact of factors such as population, climate, and geographic location on occupational opportunities.

COMPETENCY VII: Skills to prepare to seek, obtain, maintain, and change jobs.

Demonstrate skills to locate, interpret, and use information about job openings and opportunities.

Demonstrate academic or vocational skills required for a full- or part-time job.

Demonstrate skills and behaviors necessary for a successful job interview.

Demonstrate skills in preparing a resume and completing job applications.

Identify specific job openings.

Demonstrate employability skills necessary to obtain and maintain jobs.

Demonstrate skills to assess occupational opportunities (e.g., working conditions, benefits, opportunities for change).

Describe placement services available to make the transition from high school to civilian employment, the armed services, or postsecondary education/training.

Demonstrate an understanding that job opportunities often require relocation.

Demonstrate skills necessary to function as a consumer and manage financial resources.

COMPETENCY VIII: **Understanding how societal needs and functions influence the nature and structure of work.**

Describe the effect of work on lifestyles.

Describe how society's needs and functions affect the supply of goods and services.

Describe how occupational and industrial trends relate to training and employment.

Demonstrate an understanding of the global economy and how it affects each individual.

Career Planning

COMPETENCY IX: **Skills to make decisions.**

Demonstrate responsibility for making tentative educational and occupational choices.

Identify alternatives in given decision-making situations.

Describe personal strengths and weaknesses in relationship to postsecondary education/training requirements.

Identify appropriate choices during high school that will lead to marketable skills for entry-level employment or advanced training.

Identify and complete required steps toward transition from high school to entry into postsecondary education/training programs or work.

Identify steps to apply for and secure financial assistance for postsecondary education and training.

COMPETENCY X: **Understanding the interrelationship of life roles.**

Demonstrate knowledge of life stages.

Describe factors that determine lifestyles (e.g., socioeconomic status, culture, values, occupational choices, work habits).

Describe ways in which occupational choices may affect lifestyle.

Describe the contribution of work to a balanced and productive life.

Describe ways in which work, family, and leisure roles are interrelated.

Describe different career patterns and their potential effect on family patterns and lifestyle.

Describe the importance of leisure activities.

Demonstrate ways that occupational skills and knowledge can be acquired through leisure.

COMPETENCY XI: **Understanding the continuous changes in male/female roles.**

Identify factors that have influenced the changing career patterns of women and men.

Identify evidence of gender stereotyping and bias in educational programs and occupational settings.

Demonstrate attitudes, behaviors, and skills that contribute to eliminating gender bias and stereotyping.

Identify courses appropriate to tentative occupational choices.

Describe the advantages and problems of nontraditional occupations.

COMPETENCY XII: **Skills in career planning.**

Describe career plans that reflect the importance of lifelong learning.

Demonstrate knowledge of postsecondary vocational and academic programs.

Demonstrate knowledge that changes may require retraining and upgrading of employees' skills.

Describe school and community resources to explore educational and occupational choices.

Describe the costs and benefits of self-employment.

Demonstrate occupational skills developed through volunteer experiences, part-time employment, or cooperative education programs.

Demonstrate skills necessary to compare education and job opportunities.

Develop an individual career plan, updating information from earlier plans and including tentative decisions to be implemented after high school.

ADULT

Self-Knowledge

COMPETENCY I: **Skills to maintain a positive self-concept.**

Demonstrate a positive self-concept.

Identify skills, abilities, interests, experiences, values, and personality traits and their influence on career decisions.

Identify achievements related to work, learning, and leisure and their influence on self-perception.

Demonstrate a realistic understanding of self.

COMPETENCY II: **Skills to maintain effective behaviors.**

Demonstrate appropriate interpersonal skills in expressing feelings and ideas.

Identify symptoms of stress.

Demonstrate skills to overcome self-defeating behaviors.

Demonstrate skills in identifying support and networking arrangements (including role models).

Demonstrate skills to manage financial resources.

COMPETENCY III: **Understanding developmental changes and transitions.**

Describe how personal motivations and aspirations may change over time.

Describe physical changes that occur with age and adapt work performance to accommodate these.

Identify external events (e.g., job loss, job transfer) that require life changes.

Educational and Occupational Exploration

COMPETENCY IV: **Skills to enter and participate in education and training.**

Describe short- and long-range plans to achieve career goals through appropriate educational paths.

Identify information that describes educational opportunities (e.g., job training programs, employer-sponsored training, graduate and professional study).

Describe community resources to support education and training (e.g., child care, public transportation, public health services, mental health services, welfare benefits).

Identify strategies to overcome personal barriers to education and training.

COMPETENCY V: **Skills to participate in work and lifelong learning.**

Demonstrate confidence in the ability to achieve learning activities (e.g., studying, taking tests).

Describe how educational achievements and life experiences relate to occupational opportunities.

Describe organizational resources to support education and training (e.g., remedial classes, counseling, tuition support).

COMPETENCY VI: **Skills to locate, evaluate, and interpret information.**

Identify and use current career information resources (e.g., computerized career information systems, print and media materials, mentors).

Describe information related to self-assessment, career planning, occupations, prospective employers, organizational structures, and employer expectations.

Describe the uses and limitations of occupational outlook information.

Identify the diverse job opportunities available to an individual with a given set of occupational skills.

Identify opportunities available through self-employment.

Identify factors that contribute to misinformation about occupations.

Describe information about specific employers and hiring practices.

COMPETENCY VII: Skills to prepare to seek, obtain, maintain, and change jobs.

Identify specific employment situations that match desired career objectives.

Demonstrate skills to identify job openings.

Demonstrate skills to establish a job search network through colleagues, friends, and family.

Demonstrate skills in preparing a resume and completing job applications.

Demonstrate skills and attitudes essential to prepare for and participate in a successful job interview.

Demonstrate effective work attitudes and behaviors.

Describe changes (e.g., personal growth, technological developments, changes in demand for products or services) that influence the knowledge, skills, and attitudes required for job success.

Demonstrate strategies to support occupational change (e.g., on-the-job training, career ladders, mentors, performance ratings, networking, continuing education).

Describe career planning and placement services available through organizations (e.g., educational institutions, business/industry, labor, community agencies).

Identify skills that are transferable from one job to another.

COMPETENCY VIII: Understanding how the needs and functions of society influence the nature and structure of work.

Describe the importance of work as it affects values and lifestyle.

Describe how society's needs and functions affect occupational supply and demand.

Describe occupational, industrial, and technological trends as they relate to training programs and employment opportunities.

Demonstrate an understanding of the global economy and how it affects the individual.

Career Planning

COMPETENCY IX: Skills to make decisions.

Describe personal criteria for making decisions about education, training, and career goals.

Demonstrate skills to assess occupational opportunities in terms of advancement, management styles, work environment, benefits, and other conditions of employment.

Describe the effects of education, work, and family decisions on individual career decisions.

Identify personal and environmental conditions that affect decision making.

Demonstrate effective career decision-making skills.

Describe potential consequences of decisions.

COMPETENCY X: Understanding the impact of work on individual and family life.

Describe how family and leisure functions affect occupational roles and decisions.

Determine effects of individual and family developmental stages on one's career.

Describe how work, family, and leisure activities interrelate.

Describe strategies for negotiating work, family, and leisure demands with family members (e.g., assertiveness and time management skills).

COMPETENCY XI: Understanding the continuing changes in male/female roles.

Describe recent changes in gender norms and attitudes.

Describe trends in the gender composition of the labor force and assess implications for one's own career plans.

Identify disadvantages of stereotyping occupations.

Demonstrate behaviors, attitudes, and skills that work to eliminate stereotyping in education, family, and occupational environments.

COMPETENCY XII: Skills to make career transitions.

Identify transition activities (e.g., reassessment of current position, occupational changes) as a normal aspect of career development.

Describe strategies to use during transitions (e.g., networks, stress management).

Describe skills needed for self-employment (e.g., developing a business plan, determining marketing strategies, developing sources of capital).

Describe the skills and knowledge needed for preretirement planning.

Develop an individual career plan, updating information from earlier plans and including short- and long-range career decisions.

From *National Career Development Guidelines: K–Adult Handbook*, by L. Kobylarz, 1996, Stillwater, OK: National Occupational Information Coordinating Committee Training and Support Center.

Subject Index

Name Index

TO THE OWNER OF THIS BOOK:

I hope that you have found *Career Counseling and Services* useful. So that this book can be improved in a future edition, would you take the time to complete this sheet and return it? Thank you.

School and address: ______________________________

____

Department: ______________________________

Instructor's name: ______________________________

1. What I like most about this book is: ______________________________

____

____

2. What I like least about this book is: ______________________________

____

____

3. My general reaction to this book is: ______________________________

____

____

4. The name of the course in which I used this book is: ______________________________

____

5. Were all of the chapters of the book assigned for you to read? ______________

   If not, which ones weren't? ______________________________

6. In the space below, or on a separate sheet of paper, please write specific suggestions for improving this book and anything else you'd care to share about your experience in using this book.

____

____

____

____

OPTIONAL:

Your name: ____ Date:__________

May we quote you, either in promotion for *Career Counseling and Services*, or in future publishing ventures?

Yes: __________ No: __________

Sincerely yours,

James P. Sampson, Jr., Robert C. Reardon,
Gary W. Peterson, and Janet G. Lenz

FOLD HERE

NO POSTAGE
NECESSARY
IF MAILED
IN THE
UNITED STATES

BUSINESS REPLY MAIL

FIRST CLASS PERMIT NO. 358 PACIFIC GROVE, CA

POSTAGE WILL BE PAID BY ADDRESSEE

ATTN: Lisa Gebo / Helping Professions Editor

BROOKS/COLE/THOMSON LEARNING
511 FOREST LODGE ROAD
PACIFIC GROVE, CA 93950-9968

FOLD HERE